Cornerstone on Social Housing Fraud

This book is again dedicated to my beautiful wife Yasmin and sadly now departed but wonderful and much-loved parents.

Cornerstone on Social Housing Fraud

Third Edition

Andrew Lane LLB (Hons)
Barrister, Cornerstone Barristers

cornerstone barristers

Bloomsbury Professional

LONDON • DUBLIN • EDINBURGH • NEW YORK • NEW DELHI • SYDNEY

BLOOMSBURY PROFESSIONAL

Bloomsbury Publishing Plc
50 Bedford Square, London, WC1B 3DP, UK
1385 Broadway, New York, 10018, USA

Bloomsbury Publishing Ireland Ltd
29 Earlsfort Terrace, Dublin 2, D02 AY28, Ireland

First published in Great Britain 2026

1

British Library Cataloguing-in-Publication Data

A catalogue record for this book is available from the British Library.

ISBN: print 978 1 52653 193 3
ePub 978 1 52653 194 0
ePDF 978 1 52653 195 7

Typeset by Evolution Design and Digital Ltd (Kent)
Printed and bound by TJ Books, Padstow

FSC www.fsc.org MIX Paper | Supporting responsible forestry FSC® C013056

For product safety related questions contact productsafety@bloomsbury.com.

To find out more about our authors and books, visit www.bloomsburyprofessional.com. Here you will find extracts, author information, details of forthcoming events and the option to sign up for our newsletters.

Foreword

It is difficult, if not impossible, to watch the news or pick up a newspaper without seeing another story about the housing crisis. At the heart of that crisis is the chronic shortage of social housing. Hundreds of thousands of people sit on waiting lists with little realistic prospect of an offer, while hundreds of thousands more, including many families with children, are living in temporary accommodation.

There is no single solution to the housing crisis. We need more homes, of course, but we also need to make better use of the homes we already have. For every 100 new social homes built, it is estimated that around 10 properties are lost to one form of tenancy fraud or another. With around 4.8 million social homes in England and Wales, that could mean that as many as 480,000 homes are being denied to those who genuinely need them. To put that into perspective, that's roughly equivalent to housing a city the size of Bristol.

So why is this seemingly so tolerated? Why is there still a 'nothing to see here' position from many social landlords when it comes to tenancy fraud? What can social landlords do to have almost half a million homes to ease their burgeoning waiting lists? They can start by listening to the absolute expert on social housing fraud in the social housing and legal sectors, and that is Andrew Lane.

For those looking for answers, there are few people better placed to provide them than Andrew Lane. Over many years, Andrew has established himself as one of the leading authorities on social housing fraud. His knowledge, experience and practical understanding of the subject are reflected throughout this book.

This 3rd edition of *Cornerstone on Social Housing Fraud* deserves a place on the desk of every housing professional and legal practitioner involved in protecting the integrity of social housing, from CEOs, to Housing Officers, to Lettings Officers and their legal teams. Whether the issue is application fraud, false representations, unlawful subletting or any of the many other forms of tenancy fraud encountered by landlords, Andrew explains not only the law but also the practical steps needed to identify, investigate and address the problem.

The book covers every stage of the process, from evidence gathering and investigation through to civil remedies, criminal proceedings and unlawful profit orders. It also incorporates the latest legislative and case law developments, ensuring that readers have access to an up-to-date and authoritative guide. Importantly, Andrew's accessible style makes complex areas of law understandable and usable for both housing professionals and lawyers alike.

If we are serious about tackling the housing crisis, then tackling tenancy fraud must be part of the conversation. Recovering homes that have been misused or obtained dishonestly will not solve the crisis on its own, but it can make a real difference to the lives of those waiting for a place to call home.

This book provides the knowledge and tools to help make that difference.

Katrina Robinson MBE
Solicitor and Chair of the Tenancy Fraud Forum

Current titles in the 'Cornerstone on …' series

Cornerstone on Anti-social Behaviour (2nd edn, 2019)
– ISBN 978 1 52650 864 5

Cornerstone on Councillors' Conduct and Standards in Public Life (2nd edn, 2024)
– ISBN 978 1 52652 511 6

Cornerstone on Information Law (2019)
– ISBN 978 1 78451 411 2

Cornerstone on the Planning Court (2nd edn, 2021)
– ISBN 978 1 52651 672 5

For further information, visit www.bloomsburyprofessional.com.

Preface

The 2nd edition of this book was published in the first half of 2021 and, some five years on, it has been, in some senses, surprising how much I have revised and updated.

We have, of course, seen significant housing reforms brought in since that time, not least in the form of the Renters' Rights Act 2025. However, a lot of the fundamentals remain the same and much of my emphasis this time has been on the practicalities of considering, formulating and pursuing, in particular, possession claims.

We have also seen a change in government (and plenty of changes of prime minister), although a continuing housing crisis and lack of social housing.

Whilst social housing fraud has been a particular interest for me, I would never claim to be THE expert and have been so privileged during my work in this area to come across so many wonderful and lovely investigators, social housing staff, lawyers and academics who have informed and inspired me and continue to do so.

This may well be my last involvement in this work before passing on the mantle to a younger and more energetic colleague. I have, as always, received wonderful support and guidance from Bloomsbury Professional, not least from Peter Smith, Ellie Coull and Abby Smart.

On a personal level, my mum and dad have both unfortunately passed away since the last edition. I could not have wished for more supportive and precious parents, and they remain an inspiration to me. The same is true of my wife Yasmin and two sons, Aatif and Zain, about whom I could not be prouder (or more grateful!).
I hope readers find this book of some assistance in their work, and thank you for reading.

Andy Lane
May 2026

About the author

Andy was called to the Bar in 1999 and has practised since that time in the social housing and public law fields. He is a member of Cornerstone Barristers and has his own (occasional) blog, Cornerstone on Social Housing Fraud. Before coming to the Bar he worked in advice work in both the statutory and voluntary sector and was for four years, in the early 1990s, a local councillor on Oxford City Council, including a period as Chair of the Housing Committee. He is married to Yasmin and they have two children (now adults!), Aatif and Zain, and maintains an unhealthy obsession with Manchester United.

Contents

Table of cases

[*All references are to paragraph numbers*]

S

T

Table of statutes

[All references are to paragraph numbers]

Table of Statutory Instruments

[*All references are to paragraph numbers*]

CHAPTER 1

Fraud in the Social Housing Sector

> 'It is, of course, a fundamental and reasonable principle of law that a person cannot take advantage of his own fraud and profit from his own wrong.'[1]

INTRODUCTION

1.1 Social housing fraud has long been a concern of local authorities, housing associations, central government and those individuals in housing need. It takes many forms. While the focus is often on the actions of tenants and would-be tenants, regrettably there are occasions when someone working for or on behalf of the landlord is also involved.

1.2 This is, of course, a serious matter, not least at a time when social housing is still an increasingly scarce resource and demand for it far exceeds supply.[2] A Commons Library Research Briefing explained in March 2024:[3]

> 'Research for the National Housing Federation (NHF), an industry body representing housing associations, has estimated there are around 4.2 million households in England with some form of unmet housing need. The research also estimates that for 1.6 million households, "social renting would be the most appropriate tenure to meet that need".'

1.3 On 12 December 2024 the (now former) Deputy Prime Minister and Secretary of State for Housing, Communities and Local Government, Angela Rayner MP, said:[4]

> 'I will not hesitate to do what it takes to build 1.5 million new homes over five years and deliver the biggest boost in social and affordable housebuilding in a generation.'

1 Lord Justice Mummery in *Islington LBC v Uckac & another* [2006] EWCA Civ 340, [2006] 1 WLR 1303 at [47].

2 The earlier House of Commons Library briefing 'Tackling the under-supply of housing in England' (January 2021) reported: 'Estimates have put the number of new homes needed in England at up to 345,000 per year, accounting for new household formation and a backlog of existing need for suitable housing'.

3 'Social rented housing in England: Past trends and prospects' by Hannah Cromarty and Cassie Barton.

4 In a joint press release with the Prime Minister announcing various planning reforms.

1.4 Right to buy and right to acquire rights in England for many social housing tenants (even with reduced discounts in the case of the former introduced in November 2024), along with continued below-market rents and the perennially high-cost private rented sector, mean that the attraction of and need for the social housing sector have never been greater. Consequently, it is more susceptible to and a target for fraud, whether that means:

- obtaining a social housing unit to which one is not entitled;
- making a profit by sub-letting the whole or part of the demised premises;
- using it to make money through short-term lets through sites such as Airbnb and Booking.com in breach of the tenancy agreement;
- claiming a right to statutory succession or to be made a discretionary offer of a tenancy on false facts;
- obtaining significant benefits by exercising a right to buy or acquire when, in fact, there is no such entitlement; or
- allowing others to stay in premises no longer required or used by the tenant, whether for payment or not, without the knowledge or approval of the landlord.

1.5 The need for effective and focused action on social housing fraud is, therefore, of crucial importance, now more than ever.

THE BOOK

1.6 The purpose of this book remains, in its third edition, to set out clearly the options available to local housing authorities and housing associations, primarily by reference to England (unless otherwise stated), in seeking to detect and act upon housing fraud as referred to at **1.4**. That is all the more the case in Wales since the implementation of the Renting Homes (Wales) Act 2016, as referred to at **1.34** and **1.35** below.

1.7 It has always been written with four particular questions in mind:

(1) What are the options available to a social landlord seeking to obtain the evidence to detect fraud?

(2) How can they, in practical terms and employing best practice, recover the premises which have been 'misused' by the tenant?

(3) Can they receive financial 'compensation' from the fraudsters?

(4) What are the criminal repercussions of the fraud?

1.8 There are inevitably gaps, not least because there is so much overlap with matters of general housing law better covered elsewhere. For example, Chapter 2, in dealing with the discretionary ground for possession pertaining to a tenant who has obtained their tenancy by reason of a false statement, addresses, in an admittedly but necessarily cursory fashion, questions of public law and discrimination when looking at potential defences.

1.9 Some ancillary matters, such as universal credit housing costs, housing benefit, council tax reduction or council tax fraud are also left to other reference materials, though these will frequently be considered and dealt with alongside the question of possession of premises, prosecution and recovery of monies from the errant tenant. For example, if someone is found to have been sub-letting their flat whilst living elsewhere, and is still claiming housing benefit or the housing element of universal credit, then there will inevitably be an issue of overpayment and possible criminal prosecution for the same. Similarly, evidence of, say, council tax fraud may well lead to, or be connected with, the misuse of premises, enabling a landlord to ultimately seek its recovery.

1.10 The focus is on good and pragmatic practice. However, such corollary issues are, it is hoped, sufficiently 'flagged up' to demonstrate that, in certain situations, considerations outside the purview of this book must also be addressed.

THE FIGURES

1.11 Housing Associations and other private registered providers that own 1,000 or more social housing units must provide an annual report to the Regulator of Social Housing[5] on fraud losses.[6]

1.12 Yet by definition it is next to impossible to gain a completely accurate picture of the extent of the fraud impacting upon the social housing sector, although there are good indicators. In November 2012 the (now defunct) Audit Commission published its annual report *Protecting the Public Purse* (PPP). This estimated that social landlords had lost control of the allocation of nearly 98,000 properties in England.[7] The report provided the main evidential base for the Prevention of Social Housing Fraud Act 2013 (PSHF) referred to below.

1.13 The Audit Commission's final PPP Report in 2014 showed that 3,030 local authority properties had been recovered from tenancy fraudsters (an increase of 15% on the previous year). The loss to local government of housing fraud was estimated then at £845 million,[8] with a further £919 million loss to housing associations.

1.14 However, it was not all doom and gloom. Between 2009/10 and 2013/14, the total number of cases of housing tenancy fraud detection increased by 92%.

5 Smaller associations have the option of so doing.
6 'NROSH + Fraud reporting – Guidance for Registered Providers' (March 2024). See also the Regulator's Guidance 'Our role and approach to regulating landlords' (February 2024) and the 'Governance and Financial Viability Standard' (2015) at para 2.7.
7 They had estimated 50,000 units in 2011.
8 National Fraud Office, Annual Fraud Indicator 2013.

1.15 In 2015 the PPP Report, produced by the European Institute for Combating Corruption and Fraud, warned about the implications of any extension of the 'right to buy' scheme to housing associations:

> '97. We draw to the government's attention the significant levels of fraud that councils have detected within the current RTB scheme for council housing stock. Housing associations, with a few notable exceptions, do not have either an equivalent capacity or capability to tackle RTB fraud.
>
> 98. We encourage the government to incorporate within the proposed legislative extension sufficient measures to protect housing associations against RTB fraud.'

1.16 The 2015 report identified an estimated 6.89% fall in tenancy fraud investigations and, in keeping with the previous year's report, a 448.26% rise in right to buy investigations with a total savings valuation of the two areas of £96.6 million. The report also identified the most common types of social housing fraud:[9]

Fraud type	*Percentage*
Abandonment	34%
Subletting	32%
Succession/Assignment	19%
Other	15%

1.17 Four years later, the Chartered Institute of Public Finance and Accountancy's (CIPFA) annual Fraud and Corruption Tracker, published on 19 November 2019, found that an estimated 3,632 instances of council housing fraud took place in 2018/19, down from 4,733 the year before. This included right to buy frauds reducing from 1,518 in 2017/18 to 652 in 2018/19 (during the same period, sales fell 21%).

1.18 CIPFA explained the downward trend by identifying a number of factors, including:

- the successful efforts of local authorities in tackling housing fraud;
- improvements in reviews of housing allocations; and
- low rates of tenancy turnover.

1.19 Throughout this period, from 1996, there has also been the work and evidence of the National Fraud Initiative (NFI).[10] This operates a biennial data-matching exercise involving 1,100 public and private bodies and is run by the Cabinet Office. Its most recently published report, at the time of this book's preparation, was in 2022 and demonstrated that the NFI's work assisted in the

9 See p 21 of the Report.
10 Operating under statutory powers to be found in the Local Audit and Accountability Act 2014.

removal of 6,736 false applications from the waiting lists of 102 local housing authorities (LHAs) and the recovery of 25 properties.[11]

1.20 Bringing matters more up to date and by way of example:

(a) In April 2023 the Tenancy Fraud Forum (TFF) and the Fraud Advisory Panel ('the Panel') published 'Lost homes, lost hope: social housing fraud in England – recovering social homes for those in need', which found that at least 148,000 social homes in England 'were subject to some sort of tenancy fraud', a rising figure and one that constituted a fifth of social homes in London, and 1 in 30 elsewhere in England. The average cost of 'lost properties' was assessed at £42,000 each.

(b) In 2025 an 'exclusive analysis' for the 'Local Government Chronicle' found that:[12]

> 'Almost 5,200 social homes could be recovered from fraudsters each year if councils recovered as many homes as the best-performer in their region. Such a scale of recoveries would save them £300m annually, putting a big dent in temporary accommodation bills which hit record levels of £2.3bn in 2023–24.'

DETECTION OF FRAUD

1.21 In many instances, social housing landlords are alerted to potential tenancy fraud by matters such as:

- neighbour 'suspicion';
- activity at the premises and a high number of complaints;
- persons other than tenant/household being seen at the premises whilst tenancy audit, repair, annual gas safety inspection etc visits are being carried out;
- lack of response to letters and calling cards;
- no contact from tenant/household (eg about repairs);
- credit on rent account or, conversely, high arrears;
- partner agencies reporting concerns; and
- investigations carried out upon receipt of a right to buy application.

1.22 Tenet Law's updated report, 'Fraud NOT on the agenda' (2024), felt able to conclude:

> 'All housing associations state that they take fraud seriously. That being said, low positioning on risk registers and limited investment in counter-

11 These somewhat underwhelming figures are said to have been largely as a result of the Covid-19 pandemic.

12 20 May 2025, by Keith Cooper.

fraud activity – in part driven by a severe lack of statistical evidence reinforced by nil returns – contributes to confirmation bias and the sector-wide underestimation of risk especially when compared with other sectors.'

1.23 The Panel's 'Tackling Fraud in the Social Housing Sector'[13] may now be over ten years old but still bears consideration on the question of detection, encouraging as it does, amongst other measures:

- regular tenancy audits;
- use of appropriate application forms, however the property was allocated;
- requirement for colour photographs of tenant at sign-up;
- making the reporting of tenancy fraud suspicions as easy as possible; and
- use of due diligence of tenants – credit reports, shared databases, etc.

1.24 The issue of fraud detection is relevant across the whole social landlord organisation and care needs to be taken to ensure that data and other systems and individuals encourage a free-flow of information, and that use is made of external agencies such as the NFI. What is clear is that those bodies who have bespoke fraud roles/teams achieve better returns.[14]

LEGISLATION

1.25 Recovery of social housing units obtained either by fraud and/or subject to misuse by means of abandonment, sub-letting or parting with possession is, evidence permitting, comparatively straightforward, for periodic tenancies at least. Housing legislation, in particular the Housing Acts of 1985, 1988 and 1996, provides for such eventualities and the basis upon which to take action.

1.26 In the criminal arena, the Proceeds of Crime Act 2002 and Sentencing Act 2020 (and its predecessor legislation) have long provided a potential avenue to the recovery of monies lost by fraud, both in criminal and civil proceedings, whilst the Fraud Act 2006 sets out a comparatively simple and comprehensive range of offences to allow for successful prosecutions against those involved in any fraud, housing-related or otherwise.

1.27 Additionally, the PSHF provides a comprehensive and focused route to criminal prosecution of those sub-letting or parting with possession of their premises, recovery of any profit gained by reason of such activities, clarity as to the impact of sub-letting and parting with possession on (non-shared ownership)

13 'Tackling Fraud in the Social Housing Sector: A Short Guide for Directors and Senior Managers of Housing Associations' (London: Fraud Advisory Panel, December 2015).

14 See, for example, the response to a freedom of information request to the Regulator of Social Housing, reported in the April 2024 edition of Housing Quality Magazine in an article entitled 'The unreported world of tenancy fraud'.

assured tenancies and investigation powers supplemented by regulations made under the Act.

1.28 All this is in addition to allocation and homelessness fraud offences under sections 171 and 214 of the Housing Act 1996, and benefit fraud offences such as can be found, for example, in the Council Tax Reduction Schemes (Detection of Fraud and Enforcement Regulations) (England) Regulations 2013[15] and sections 111A and 112 of the Social Security Administration Act 1992 (offences of dishonest representations for obtaining benefit and false representation for obtaining benefit respectively).

1.29 However, the PSHF is most obviously and deliberately focused on the social housing sector alone. The Explanatory Notes to the Act explain the purpose of the legislation:

> '4. The policy rationale for the new provisions is to ensure that social housing is being occupied by those to whom it was allocated, and that local authorities have access to more information in order to be able to detect fraud in the social housing stock. Whilst the current law provides that a secure tenant who has sub-let or parted with possession of the whole dwelling-house ceases to be a secure tenant and that a tenant who is not in occupation of the dwelling-house cannot be an assured tenant (which enables the landlord to gain possession of the dwelling-house more easily), this has not proved to be an adequate deterrent to sub-letting and parting with possession, as tenants only risk losing the tenancy of a property in which they do not live.'

1.30 The next two sections in this chapter deal with two pieces of legislation coming into effect since the second edition of this book was produced. Before briefly addressing those Acts, it should be stressed that there are, as one might imagine, other legislative changes such as the Public Authorities (Fraud, Error and Recovery) Act 2025,[16] the Data (Use and Access) Act 2025 and the impending Commonhold and Leasehold Reform Bill (published in draft form at the time of writing). These will be considered, along with other legislative, regulatory and case-law developments, as and where appropriate in later chapters.

RENTERS' RIGHTS ACT 2025

1.31 There are frequently changes in law around the time of working on and completing the final draft for any legal text. The Renters' Rights Act 2025, which

15 SI 2013/501: summary offences of false representations for the purpose of obtaining a council tax reduction (reg 7) and failure to notify of changes of circumstances (reg 8).

16 The Act's preamble explains it as: 'An Act to make provision about the prevention of fraud against public authorities and the making of erroneous payments by public authorities; about the recovery of money paid by public authorities as a result of fraud or error; and for connected purposes'.

received royal assent on 27 October 2025, is a particularly significant reform to highlight here, despite its primary focus on the private rented sector, for three primary reasons.

1.32 Firstly, it will bring an end to fixed-term tenancies in the private sector, including housing associations. Secondly, shared ownership agreements will no longer be assured tenancies (save for some existing arrangements described elsewhere).[17] Finally, the extra oversight imposed on local authorities in respect of the private rented sector will, if not properly funded, make it even more difficult than many authorities already find it to establish and maintain bespoke 'fraud teams'.

1.33 The precise changes will be advised as and where necessary in the following chapters.

RENTING HOMES (WALES) ACT 2016

1.34 The previous editions of this book have generally applied to Wales, even though the primary focus has always been on the law as it applies to England (see **1.6** above). That has changed since the introduction of significant reforms to the housing system in Wales by reason of the Renting Homes (Wales) Act 2016 brought into effect from 1 December 2022.[18]

1.35 That legislation has led to the replacement of tenancies with occupation contracts, and the introduction of obligatory terms and changes to certain issues such as sub-letting.

CONCLUSION

1.36 The main priority of many housing practitioners is to identify the means they have at their disposal to properly investigate a potential fraud, along with enjoying a clear understanding of the point at which proceedings for the recovery of money and/or premises, can and should be instituted.

1.37 That this represents a more focused look at housing fraud is clear; indeed, the TFF was established in April 2012 to bring social landlords together to combat tenancy fraud. The HQN January 2025 report on 'Tackling tenancy fraud – taking a proactive approach' was able to summarise:

> 'All registered providers must take action to prevent and tackle tenancy fraud. It is clearly stated in the Tenancy Standard and was highlighted in

17 Renters' Rights Act 2025, s 31.

18 The Renting Homes (Wales) Act 2016 (Consequential Amendments) Regulations 2022 (SI 2022/1166) have, for example, introduced certain amendments to the PSHF to reflect these reforms.

> the sector risk profile, published in the autumn of 2024. It is a significant cost to the public purse and a waste of valuable resources. Social housing organisations can take much more action to tackle this abuse and free up homes for people in need of social housing.'

1.38 This chapter begins, as before, with a quotation from a Court of Appeal judgment and will end with one too, although this time it is the Criminal Division of the Court of Appeal dealing with a renewed permission application against sentence. In *R v Gerald Kenyon*[19] the court was faced with a case where the local authority tenant had moved out of his premises and started sub-letting his flat. He later submitted a right to buy application but was prevented from going through with that process when the true position came to light. In the Crown Court at Woolwich, he was convicted of five offences of fraud by failing to disclose information and was sentenced to a total of 18 months' imprisonment. This case is further dealt with in Chapter 7 but, in dismissing the 'wholly unmeritorious' renewed application for permission to appeal, Mrs Justice Yip (as she then was) gave some idea of the 'cost' of the defendant's behaviour then applicable at paragraph 7 of her judgment:

> 'The evidence suggested that the applicant made around £10,000 in profit. The cost to the council was greater. They were not able to provide the property to someone who needed it and instead had to pay around £26,000 for that person to be in free accommodation. Further, the applicant had attempted to unjustly purchase the property at a discount of over £100,000. The judge found that the offending had taken place for at least six years and was driven by pure greed. The applicant was living elsewhere and was denying someone else in need of council accommodation in order to gain for himself. He stood to gain a huge amount had his plan to buy the property succeeded.'

19 [2021] EWCA Crim 68.

CHAPTER 2

Tenancy Procured by False Statement

- Ground 5 (Housing Act 1985)
- Ground 17 (Housing Act 1988)
- [Rescission]

Key points

- The Housing Acts of 1985 (secure tenancies) and 1988 (assured tenancies) provide identical, discretionary grounds for possession in Schedule 2 – Grounds 5 and 17 respectively (hereafter referred to as 'the Ground' in this chapter) – to deal with tenants who obtain their tenancies because of a false statement.
- The Ground permits the landlord to rely on omissions as well as a false statement (eg a failure to inform the prospective landlord of a relevant change of circumstance).
- The statement can come from a third party but will only be relevant in such a case if it was made at the tenant's instigation.
- If the landlord does not, in fact, rely on the false statement or omission, then the Ground is not made out.
- If the Ground is available, the landlord cannot then usually (see **2.16**) seek the remedy of rescission.
- Flexible tenancies have their own particular process, as explained at **2.63–2.76**.
- For introductory tenancies, a landlord will simply seek (mandatory) possession in the usual way provided for at Part 5 of the Housing Act 1996 – service of a section 128 notice, section 129 review (if requested) and claim.

INTRODUCTION

2.1 In most instances in which fraudulent activity has led to someone obtaining social housing, the social landlord's primary concern is to recover possession of the premises so that it can be re-allocated to another household in accordance with its allocation scheme[1] or any nomination agreement.

1 Housing Act 1996, s 166A(14) imposes a statutory obligation on local housing authorities: 'A local housing authority in England shall not allocate housing accommodation except in accordance with their allocation scheme'.

2.2 This is most obviously the case when the original reason for the allocation proves to be flawed because of a misrepresentation either by or at the instigation of the tenant.

2.3 For example, if a person has only been allocated housing because they *falsely* represented in their application form that their family were living in overcrowded accommodation, can the landlord seek possession in reliance on such a misrepresentation?

2.4 In broad terms, and in the circumstances explored below, the answer to this question is 'yes' and by 'ordinary' possession proceedings (though note below the additional requirements for flexible tenancies).[2] Schedule 2 to the Housing Acts of both 1985 (secure tenancies)[3] and 1988 (assured tenancies)[4] provides the *discretionary* Ground for possession for this very purpose.

2.5 Of course, if a mandatory ground for possession is also available at the time the misrepresentation is discovered,[5] which may be many years after the tenancy commenced, or the landlord is otherwise entitled to possession in domestic law,[6] it may prefer to rely on that ground or entitlement, either in addition to or instead of the (discretionary) Ground.

2.6 This chapter focuses, however, on how a social landlord can recover premises occupied by a tenant under a secure or assured tenancy on the basis that it was procured by way of a false statement or relevant omission.

2.7 Before addressing the Ground, however, an analysis is first provided of what may have been thought of as the more obvious and appropriate common law remedy of rescission. This would have the effect of voiding any tenancy agreement *ab initio*.[7]

RESCISSION

2.8 Chapter 1 begins with the words of Lord Justice Mummery:[8]

2 See, eg, *North Hertfordshire DC v Carthy* [2003] EWCA Civ 20. In that case the Carthys had legitimately applied to the local authority as homeless but had failed to advise them prior to the allocation of social housing that in fact their home in the Philippines had since been completed, was habitable and was available to them. See **2.28** below.

3 Ground 5.

4 Ground 17.

5 For example, an absolute ground for possession (Housing Act 1985, s 84A, or Housing Act 1988, Ground 7A) or Ground 8 in Schedule 2 to the 1988 Act, which provides a mandatory ground in respect of rent arrears or there is a sub-letting question which might encourage use of the notice to quit 'route' in a periodic tenancy scenario.

6 For example, following the service and expiry of a notice of proceedings for possession under s 128 of the Housing Act 1996 where the tenant has an introductory tenancy.

7 Ie treating the tenancy agreement as if it never existed (see **2.10–2.11** below).

8 *Islington LBC v Uckac & another* [2006] EWCA Civ 340, [2006] 1 WLR 1303 at [47].

'It is, of course, a fundamental and reasonable principle of law that a person cannot take advantage of his own fraud and profit from his own wrong.'

2.9 His judgment, though, went on immediately after this citation to demonstrate that such an obvious and reasonable principle is neither absolute nor guaranteed:

> '47 … *The provisions of the Housing Act 1985 have produced a situation in which it is possible for a person in the assumed position of the first defendant to violate that principle.* The fact that she was a party to the fraudulent representation and was not, when she stepped into her husband's shoes, a bona fide purchaser for value without notice does not prevent her from resisting an application for an order for possession of the flat under the 1985 Act. The unpalatable result is that, as a result of the assignment, she is in a stronger legal position than her husband was and that she is occupying a flat which should be available for the occupation of a homeless person making an honest application to the council for accommodation.' (emphasis added)

2.10 As referred to at **2.7**, it might be thought that, if a tenant has procured their tenancy by means of a false representation, the landlord would have a clear remedy at common law – namely rescission – which would avoid the need to rely on any discretionary ground for possession or to address the ancillary issues raised in such cases such as the reasonableness of making any such order and whether it should be outright or suspended/postponed on terms (let alone the more 'fraught' process required for flexible tenancies, explained further below). Etherton LJ said in *Brian James Potter v Stephen Gerard Crispin Dyer*:[9]

> 'It is trite law that a person to whom a fraudulent misrepresentation has been made, which has induced that person to enter into a contract or other transaction, is entitled on discovery of the fraud to elect either to affirm or to rescind what was so induced. An election will only take place if it is communicated to the other party in clear and unequivocal terms.'

2.11 Indeed, rescission is an equitable, and therefore discretionary, remedy, which would seem ideal in cases of tenancies obtained by false statement (it is also available, for example, in right-to-buy frauds – see **5.33–5.38**). In essence, it 'undoes' the fraud and takes the parties back to the position they were in *before* they entered into the tenancy agreement. That is not, of course, always possible; there may, for example, be instances where an agreement has been affirmed by the landlord.[10] Yet for the reasons set out in the following paragraphs, there are more fundamental bars to the use of this remedy in a false statement case.

9 [2011] EWCA Civ 1417 at [56].

10 *Long v Lloyd* [1958] 1 WLR 753 – an innocent misrepresentation case concerning the purchase of a lorry where serious faults were discovered two days after purchase. The Court of Appeal held that the place of delivery was the proper place for examination and acceptance, and any right the purchaser may have had to rescind the contract was barred by his acceptance of the lorry once delivery had taken place.

2.12 Put bluntly, rescission is not available in respect of secure or assured tenancies procured by fraudulent misrepresentation (as indicated in the Key points section, with introductory tenancies the better route to recovery of possession is by the mandatory process provided for in Part 5 of the Housing Act 1996).[11] Instead, Parliament has provided an alternative means of recovering possession – the Ground.[12] This has effectively *ousted* the common law jurisdiction.[13]

2.13 In *Islington LBC v Uckac & another*,[14] the facts of which are referred to at **2.23–2.25** below, Lord Justice Dyson explained why that should be the case as follows:

> 'In my judgment, the express wording of section 82, when read with section 84, is a negative enactment in Coke's sense. It clearly shows that *Parliament intended to take away from landlords the right to bring secure tenancies to an end by rescission, whether for misrepresentation or on any other ground. Schedule 2 provides a detailed and exhaustive code of the grounds on which a landlord may bring a secure tenancy to an end and obtain an order for possession.* It is to be assumed that Parliament decided on policy grounds that a landlord should be able to bring a secure tenancy to an end and obtain an order for possession where it has been induced to grant a tenancy by a fraudulent misrepresentation, but not where it has been so induced by an innocent or negligent misrepresentation.' (emphasis added)

2.14 In the later judgment of *Birmingham City Council v Qasim*[15] the local authority claimed seven secure tenancies were void as they had been wrongly granted by an officer of the authority *outside* the statutory allocation scheme. There was no evidence that the tenants who had been granted these tenancies had made any payments for them or, unlike in *Uckac*, otherwise induced the officer to grant them a tenancy.

2.15 The Court of Appeal dismissed the local authority's appeal against the dismissal of their possession claim and held that the allocation of housing accommodation did not extend to the actual grant of a tenancy. The failure of the authority was one of allocation, which was a public law obligation.[16] There was nothing in the Housing Act 1996, which covered the allocation scheme requirements at Part 6, to suggest that the secure tenancies made as a result of an 'improper' allocation were themselves legally defective.

11 See **2.63–2.76** below concerning flexible tenancies.

12 That is, Housing Act 1985, Sch 2, Ground 5 (secure tenancies) and Housing Act 1988, Sch 2, Ground 17 (assured tenancies).

13 *Islington LBC v Uckac & another* [2006] EWCA Civ 340, [2006] 1 WLR 1303 at [27]–[30] *per* Dyson LJ. See **2.16**, however, where dishonesty is shown on the part of *both* parties.

14 Ibid, para 29 *per* Dyson LJ.

15 [2009] EWCA Civ 1080, [2010] PTSR 471.

16 In the earlier authority of *R v Port Talbot BC ex parte Jones* [1988] 2 All ER 207, the respondent authority had granted a secure tenancy of a property to a member of the council. The tenancy was not allocated in accordance with the authority's waiting list and in a public law challenge the leader of the council successfully applied for judicial review, with the court quashing the decision to grant the tenancy and declaring the grant of the tenancy to be void.

2.16 Lord Neuberger, however, went on to consider *Uckac* and left open the remedy of rescission where dishonesty was shown on *both* parties' part:

> '*42 Neither the decision in Islington [2006] 1 W.L.R. 1303 nor our conclusion on this appeal by any means necessarily imply that, in a case where both the applicant and an officer of the authority are involved in dishonestly enabling the applicant to obtain a tenancy, the authority would be precluded from setting aside the tenancy or treating it as void.* It may be arguable that ground 5 could be interpreted to cover such a case (in which case the reasoning in Islington [2006] 1 W.L.R. 1303 would appear to apply), or it may very well be that the reasoning in this judgment could be distinguished where the tenant is dishonestly involved in the inappropriate allocation. These are issues which would have to be considered as and when such a case arises.' (emphasis added)

2.17 That would therefore seem to leave open the argument that, where a tenancy has been procured by the fraud of *both* the landlord officer *and* the tenant, rescission *is* available, whereas:

(a) if the fraud is just on the part of the tenant, then the Ground is the appropriate (and indeed only) means, if security of tenure persists, of seeking possession and rescission is not available;[17]

(b) if the fraud is conversely just on the part of the officer of the landlord, then subject to any ultra vires argument (ie it was clear that the officer did not have the ostensible authority to allocate the premises),[18] the tenancy agreement is good and valid.

2.18 Of course, in those cases raised at **2.16** where it is believed that the 'rogue' officer and tenant were *jointly* complicit in the fraud, the landlord may decide to plead, in the alternative:

- rescission (see **2.16**);
- trespass (cf the ultra vires reference at **2.17**(b)); or
- reliance on the Ground (see **2.59** onwards).

2.19 Conversely, as indicated at **2.5**, where security of tenure has been lost, permanently or otherwise – for example, because of sub-letting or the tenant's failure to occupy the premises as their only or principal home – then rescission arguably remains an option because the Ground is not then available. In practical terms where this happens, however, proceeding in reliance on a notice to quit in respect of periodic tenancies or section 146 notice in flexible tenancy, private registered provider of social housing fixed-term assured tenancy and shared ownership cases,[19] as further described at Chapters 3 and 4, may be the better –

17 See, eg, paras 32 and 35 of Lord Neuberger's judgment.

18 See **2.100–2.102**.

19 Ie assuming a breach of tenancy can be identified (not normally an issue where the issue is sub-letting or the tenant living elsewhere).

and legally and evidentially easier – route to recover possession of the premises in issue. Suffice to say, in conclusion, that rescission remains an extremely uncommon final remedy in housing cases.

THE GROUND

2.20 Turning then to the statutory route for possession of the premises, as noted in **2.4** above, the Housing Acts of 1985 and 1988 provide for the Ground, a discretionary and identically worded (ie between Grounds 5 and 17) ground for possession, which is demonstrated where:

> 'The tenant is either the person or one of the persons to whom the tenancy was granted and the landlord was induced to grant the tenancy by a false statement made knowingly or recklessly by:
>
> (a) the tenant, or
>
> (b) a person acting at the tenant's instigation.'

MATTERS TO PROVE

2.21 The Ground has six primary elements:

(1) There must be a material statement: see **2.38–2.40**.

(2) The statement must be false and the definition encompasses omissions: see **2.27–2.37**.

(3) It must be made before the tenancy is granted: see **2.35**.

(4) It may be made by either the tenant (or one of joint tenants), or someone acting at their instigation: see **2.41–2.45**.

(5) It must be made in the knowledge that it is false, or the maker must be reckless as to the statement's accuracy: see **2.46–2.48**.

(6) The statement must induce the landlord to grant the tenancy: see **2.49–2.58**.

2.22 The language of the Ground also signifies that the tenancy to which it refers is *the* tenancy granted immediately following the misrepresentation. It follows, therefore, that if, for example, a tenant obtains an assured tenancy in reliance on a false statement, but later assigns the tenancy to another, then the opportunity to seek possession on this Ground is lost.

2.23 We see this in *Uckac*[20] where a couple applied to the local authority as being homeless. The authority granted the husband a secure tenancy of a two-bedroom flat which, a year later, he (otherwise validly) assigned to his wife.

20 See para 12 *per* Dyson LJ.

2.24 The authority later discovered that the information contained in the couple's original homelessness application concerning their previous addresses was false and issued a claim either to repossess the premises based on the Ground or, alternatively, to rescind the tenancy agreement for misrepresentation.

2.25 The trial judge rejected the claims, finding, as a preliminary issue, that there was no right to rescind the tenancy and that the Ground was only available in respect of the person to whom the tenancy had been granted (ie the husband). The Court of Appeal agreed (see Mummery LJ's explanation at paragraph 47 of the judgment, set out at **2.9** above).

2.26 As a 'postscript' to this *Uckac* ruling, however,[21] the Court of Appeal did allow the local authority's application to re-amend their particulars of claim to plead, in the alternative, that the original grant of the tenancy to the second respondent (the husband) had been null and void, as it depended on the local authority's decision to accept a full duty to make accommodation available to the defendants under the homelessness provisions of Part 7 of the Housing Act 1996. That decision was, it was argued, itself void as it had been induced by fraud and/or was based on a fundamental mistake of fact.

FALSE STATEMENT

2.27 Turning back to the substance of the Ground (see **2.20**), and the six elements that must be demonstrated (see **2.21**), although it refers exclusively to a 'statement', a material omission may also give the landlord a ground for possession. An obvious example would be an applicant's failure to notify either their would-be landlord or the person charged with nominating/allocating its accommodation of a relevant change of circumstances.

2.28 In *North Hertfordshire DC v Carthy*,[22] for example, the defendant family was placed in temporary accommodation by the local housing authority, having returned to the country after running out of money while building a property in the Philippines. The following year they were allocated accommodation.[23] By that time, however, they had obtained the funds to make the Philippines property habitable again and had done so.

2.29 At trial, the Recorder had dismissed the authority's possession claim on the premise that the omission had not induced the authority to grant the tenancy. The Court of Appeal allowed the authority's appeal and remitted the case to

21 Ibid, paras 36–41 *per* Dyson LJ.

22 [2003] EWCA Civ 20 – see fn 2 above.

23 Had the change been noted prior to the grant of the tenancy, the authority would have been entitled to revisit and rescind the decision that it had an obligation to house the applicant under Housing Act 1996, s 193, if that decision had resulted from a fundamental mistake of fact: *Porteous v West Dorset DC* [2004] EWCA Civ 244, [2004] HLR 30.

a different judge in order that they could consider the issue of whether it was reasonable to make a possession order.[24]

2.30 The court considered the relevance of the tenant's failure to update the landlord and the nature of any continuing representation by *omission*. Mr and Mrs Carthy did not dispute the fact that the Recorder was wrong on the question of inducement even though he had found in their favour on that issue. Lord Justice Sedley indicated that he also was likely to have found the same had he been required to do so.

2.31 When the omission is the result of a failure to update a local housing authority or housing association about information that was accurate at the time it was first included in a housing application or similar form, the situation is usually straightforward. Most forms of this type will require the applicant to sign not only a declaration attesting to the accuracy of the content at the time of its production, but also an agreement contained therein that the applicant will inform the would-be landlord/nominator of any changes in the information provided.

2.32 Not all allocations of social housing, however, rely on application forms and even those that do may not have clarity in requiring the applicant to update. Is there a general requirement to advise the authority or association of material information, absent any such agreement? Sedley LJ, again, suggested there might be when he said in *Carthy*:

> '8. The recorder accepted that Mr Carthy was in breach of these obligations. Indeed it is arguable that even if he had not signed the material forms, he would have been guilty of making a false statement by not correcting a *continuing* representation. *It may well be that not every relationship or situation carries such an obligation, but it is clear in my view that the information which is needed by a housing authority to process claims for temporary accommodation for the homeless, and equally that is needed to decide whether to offer secure accommodation to people on the housing list, constitutes a continuing representation by an applicant*. One has only to refer to section 196 of the Housing Act 1996[25] to see why this is so. If so, it brings with it a duty to tell the council of any change in circumstances which is capable of affecting the council's actions in response to the application.' (emphasis added)

2.33 Indeed, section 214 of the Housing Act 1996, considered in more detail in Chapter 7, makes criminal offences of the following representations and omissions:

24 The Recorder had not gone on to consider whether it was reasonable to make a possession order given his finding that the information should not have made any difference to the allocation of a secure tenancy.

25 This provision, now repealed by s 4(5) of the Homelessness Reduction Act 2017, dealt with those becoming threatened with homelessness intentionally. It expressly referred to the applicant doing or failing to do something the likely result of which was that they would be forced to leave their existing accommodation.

(a) making a false statement;

(b) withholding information; and

(c) failing to notify changes,

committed when false information is provided with a view to inducing the local housing authority to provide Part 7 homelessness accommodation or assistance. The section states in terms:

> '(2) If before an applicant receives notification of the local housing authority's decision on his application there is any change of facts material to his case, he shall notify the authority as soon as possible.'

2.34 Section 171 of the Housing Act 1996 provides for a similar criminal offence in the context of social housing allocation under Part 6 of the 1996 Act:

> '(1) A person commits an offence if, in connection with the exercise by a local housing authority of their functions under this Part–
>
> (a) he knowingly or recklessly makes a statement which is false in a material particular, or
>
> (b) he knowingly withholds information which the authority have reasonably required him to give in connection with the exercise of those functions.'

Unlike section 214(2), however, it does not expressly provide for any extended criminal offence for failing to inform the authority of a change of circumstances in the same manner (though note sub-section (b)).

2.35 As noted in *Carthy* (and referred to in **2.31** above), most allocation forms will include a requirement for the applicant to inform the would-be landlord or nominator of any such changes. It would certainly be good practice, it is suggested, to include such a requirement in all application forms, in case the landlord later wishes to seek possession because of an alleged omission at the time of the application or at any stage before the actual allocation of social housing.

2.36 It follows from the above that, in most instances, applicants must inform the local housing authority or nominator of any changes in circumstance in cases of Part 6 allocation and homelessness applications, as well as other social housing allocation cases in which the applicant is informed of such a requirement. Any failure to do so can satisfy the first two steps in this Ground – a material false statement by omission.

2.37 Whether, more generally, a failure to disclose a material change of circumstances amounts, in the words of Sedley LJ in *Carthy*, to a 'continuing representation' is a moot point and is, as yet, undecided, though in *Akinbolu v Hackney LBC*,[26] a case in which the tenant had not advised the authority of his immigration status and was not asked about it either, the court held at [270]:

26 (1997) 29 HLR 259. The tenant was not asked by the local authority and did not provide any information about his immigration status. The Court of Appeal allowed his appeal against a refusal to grant him an injunction to re-enter the premises and found that he was a secure tenant.

> 'The circumstances in which the tenant took possession prima facie created a tenancy and any argument to the contrary is fanciful. A process through the courts is required even in the case of a tenancy the grant of which was induced by a false statement under Ground 5. *This appellant was not guilty of any misrepresentation to or deception of the housing authority.* Even if the tenant condition is not satisfied so that a tenancy is not a secure tenancy, an application to the court for possession is required.' (emphasis added)

MATERIALITY

2.38 If a false statement has been made, it is necessary to consider whether the statement:

(a) is material and made knowingly or recklessly;

(b) is made by the tenant, or somebody acting at the tenant's instigation; and

(c) impacts upon the decision to grant a tenancy of the premises concerned.

2.39 To establish that the statement was material, the landlord will need to adduce evidence about the impact that it had on the decision to grant a tenancy, and where the tenant would have been placed in its allocation scheme or that of the nominating authority had the correct information been provided.

2.40 If, for example, the tenant gives their year of birth as 1962 rather than the real year of 1963, this is unlikely to have been material in most instances or induced any grant of a tenancy. Conversely, if they have failed to record that they owned or had an interest in accommodation elsewhere, this is likely to have been extremely material to the grant of the particular tenancy.

INSTIGATION

2.41 Grounds 5 and 17 were both extended by the Housing Act 1996[27] to include statements made by a third party at the tenant's instigation, in addition to those made by the tenant.

2.42 In *Merton LBC v Richards*, Pill LJ explained the meaning of 'instigate':[28]

> '32 … On any view "instigate" means more than tolerate. It means to bring about or initiate. The Latin source of the word, as mentioned in the *Concise Oxford Dictionary*, is instigare: to urge or incite. The ground refers to instigation and not merely to someone "acting on behalf of the tenant". On the judge's findings of fact, there was no instigation by the respondent in this case.'

27 Housing Act 1996, ss 102 and 146 – with effect from 12 February 1997 (Ground 5) and 28 February 1997 (Ground 17).

28 [2005] EWCA Civ 639, [2005] HLR 44.

2.43 In *Richards*, the tenant was greatly assisted by her mother, a housing officer, in arranging an exchange with an elderly tenant, Mrs Mahon. In fact, Mrs Mahon had made it clear to the tenant's mother that she had no intention of moving to the daughter's flat and was rather going to live with her family in Lowestoft.

2.44 At trial the Recorder found that the tenant had been unaware of Mrs Mahon's true intentions. Chadwick LJ said:

> '39 The judge found that the respondent did not, herself, know that the statement as to Mrs Mahon's intentions was false at the time when the tenancy was granted. Nor was she reckless in that regard. Other tribunals might have reached a different conclusion on that issue. If a different conclusion had been reached, it would have been difficult, if not impossible, to attack that conclusion in this court. But the question in this court is whether there was material on which the judge could reach the conclusion which he did reach. For the reasons which Pill L.J. has set out—and with which I agree—there was sufficient material for the judge to reach the conclusion on that issue which he did.'

2.45 Simply acting on the tenant's behalf, therefore, is not necessarily the same as acting at the tenant's instigation: the latter requires the tenant actively to incite a third party to make a false statement, which then leads to the grant of the tenancy.[29]

KNOWLEDGE AND RECKLESSNESS

2.46 It follows, from the plain language of the Ground, that the tenant must not only make or instigate the statement but must also know that it is false, or be reckless about its accuracy.[30] For example, this may be the case where they claim not to own or have an interest in any other premises but:

(a) they are still aware that they are registered as a joint owner of residential accommodation with their former partner following a right-to-buy purchase some years before; or

(b) they thought they might be so registered but 'couldn't be bothered' to find out;

though not arguably where:

(c) they had been advised by their former partner that the previous premises were now in the former partner's sole name as previously agreed by both parties.

29 Ibid, para 33 per Pill LJ.
30 Ibid, para 51 per May LJ.

2.47 This is, in any event, potentially an important distinction, not because the Ground itself distinguishes between knowledge and recklessness, but because the degree of culpability on the tenant's part could be relevant when the court considers whether it is reasonable to make a possession order, once the Ground is satisfied.[31]

2.48 The issue of reasonableness, in the context of possession claims brought on this Ground, is dealt with at **2.81–2.99** below.

INDUCEMENT

2.49 The last element of this Ground requires the landlord to demonstrate that the false statement played '... a real and substantial part, though not by itself a decisive part, in inducing [it] to act'.[32]

2.50 For example, if the tenant had completed an application form for housing and failed to refer to an existing tenancy but the landlord had paid no regard to the form (or that part of it) when granting the tenancy, then the Ground may not be satisfied (though note **2.51** onwards).

2.51 It has been suggested that there is a presumption[33] that. if the false statement is sufficiently material,[34] it is a fair inference of fact that the landlord has been induced by it to grant the tenancy.[35]

2.52 In *Windsor and District Housing Association v Hewitt*,[36] Ms Hewitt applied to transfer from her one-bedroom flat in part, she said, because she needed a second bedroom for her son, who was also her carer. Over two years later, she was offered and accepted a tenancy of a two-bedroom, ground-floor flat. Around this time, she also spoke to somebody at the Association and said that she was likely to live at the property on her own.

2.53 The landlord brought a claim to repossess the property pursuant to the Ground but did not succeed at first instance because:

(a) it could not show that the false statement had been made knowingly or recklessly; and

(b) it could not prove that it had been induced to grant the tenancy by reason of the false statement, not least because of the tenant's clear representation at the time of the letting that she would be living there alone.

31 *Rushcliffe BC v Watson* (1991) 24 HLR 124, CA at [127] *per* Nourse LJ. In that case it was not disputed that Ground 5 was satisfied, the trial turning solely on the question of whether it was reasonable to make a possession order.

32 *JEB Fasteners Ltd v Marks Bloom & Co* [1983] 1 All ER 583 *per* Stephenson LJ at [589 A–B].

33 *Waltham Forest LBC v Roberts* [2004] EWCA Civ 940, [2005] HLR 2, paras 42–43.

34 *Downs v Chappell* [1997] 1 WLR 426 *per* Hobhouse LJ at [433].

35 *Smith v Chadwick* (1884) 9 App Cas 187 *per* Lord Blackburn at [1961].

36 [2011] EWCA Civ 735, [2011] HLR 39.

2.54 The Court of Appeal allowed the Association's appeal. It found that the first reason for the trial judge's decision was unsustainable, given that it was Ms Hewitt's own case (though not accepted by the trial judge) that her son did live with her after all.

2.55 As for the seemingly honest information given by her at the time of the letting, this had been given for data purposes only and was not a document relied upon when letting the premises. It was not, therefore, sufficient to rebut the presumption that the false statement had induced the Association to grant her a tenancy.

2.56 It follows that false statements pertaining to material matters are likely to lead to a finding of inducement, unless it can be shown as a matter of fact that the statement either did not form part of the landlord's reason for granting the tenancy or was not considered by the landlord in any event.

2.57 In *Oshin v Greenwich RBC*[37] the Court of Appeal held that the trial judge had been entitled to find that an applicant's false statement on her social housing application form as to her immigration status – she said she had not lived outside the UK in the last five years when she had – had induced Greenwich Council to grant her a secure tenancy.

2.58 One of the arguments she pursued on appeal was to the effect that, right or wrong, the answer to the question in issue was not in any event determinative of her eligibility for social housing. It would though have led to further, more specific inquiries being made and Floyd LJ, in delivering the main judgment of the court and dismissing Ms Oshin's appeal, concluded:

> '31. I accept that, in order to be material, the false statement must be relevant to whether the applicant is eligible for social housing. That, however, is not the same thing as requiring that the statement be directly determinative of that question. The appellant's false statements did not mean that she was entitled to social housing, but they still had sufficient materiality to be capable of inducing the local authority to grant her a tenancy when she was not entitled to one ….'

NOTICE PROCEDURE: DISCRETIONARY GROUND FOR POSSESSION: PERIODIC TENANCY

2.59 If a social landlord is satisfied that it has a credible case pursuant to the Ground then, before taking such possession action, it will not only need to serve[38] a notice seeking possession in reliance on the Ground but should also pay

37 [2020] EWCA Civ 388, [2020] PTSR 1351.

38 Unless the Court considers it just and equitable to dispense with the requirement for such a notice: Housing Act 1985, s 83(1)(b) (secure tenancies)/Housing Act 1988, s 8(1)(b) (assured tenancies).

particular regard to any relevant pre-action protocol and internal policies that may be relevant to the proposed action.

2.60 What may be thought as the most obvious pre-action protocol – 'The Pre-Action Protocol for Possession Claims by Social Landlords' – in fact has no application to a claim relying on the Ground, rather focusing as it does on rent arrears and mandatory possession claims. However, regard does need to be had to the Practice Direction on Pre-action Conduct and Protocols, in particular paragraphs 3 and 6:[39]

> '3. Before commencing proceedings, the court will expect the parties to have exchanged sufficient information to–
>
> (a) understand each other's position;
>
> (b) make decisions about how to proceed;
>
> (c) try to settle the issues without proceedings;
>
> (d) consider a form of Alternative Dispute Resolution (ADR) to assist with settlement;
>
> (e) support the efficient management of those proceedings; and
>
> (f) reduce the costs of resolving the dispute.'
>
> '6. Where there is a relevant pre-action protocol, the parties should comply with that protocol before commencing proceedings. Where there is no relevant pre-action protocol, the parties should exchange correspondence and information to comply with the objectives in paragraph 3, bearing in mind that compliance should be proportionate. The steps will usually include–
>
> (a) the claimant writing to the defendant with concise details of the claim. The letter should include the basis on which the claim is made, a summary of the facts, what the claimant wants from the defendant, and if money, how the amount is calculated;
>
> (b) the defendant responding within a reasonable time – 14 days in a straightforward case and no more than 3 months in a very complex one. The reply should include confirmation as to whether the claim is accepted and, if it is not accepted, the reasons why, together with an explanation as to which facts and parts of the claim are disputed and whether the defendant is making a counterclaim as well as providing details of any counterclaim; and
>
> (c) the parties disclosing key documents relevant to the issues in dispute.'

39 Failure to comply with the Practice Direction could impact upon any costs order made or may lead to a sanction or a stay being applied to allow for compliance: see paras 13 to 16 of the Practice Direction.

2.61 It follows that a pre-action letter is advisable setting out the social landlord's case and evidential basis for it. Whilst it may not elicit any, or any significant, response, experience has shown that, in some cases, it is sufficient to encourage the tenant to give up their tenancy.

2.62 As for the notice seeking possession,[40] this will be valid for 12 months from the date provided for in the notice after which proceedings may be issued.[41] The minimum period of time between service of the notice and the date specified in the notice after which proceedings can be instituted is 14 days for assured tenancies, and 28 days for secure tenancies.[42]

NOTICE PROCEDURE: DISCRETIONARY GROUND FOR POSSESSION: FLEXIBLE TENANCY[43]

2.63 As indicated above, matters are not so straightforward regarding *flexible tenancies*[44] (and remaining fixed-term assured tenancies pending full implementation of the Renters' Rights Act 2025 reform).[45] The Ground remains available for such cases and the pre-action conduct is as set out at **2.60–2.61**. However, there are a number of factors that require special consideration:

(a) because of the statutory provisions impacting upon flexible tenancies as explained at **2.64**; and

40 Remembering that the Court does have the power to dispense with the requirement for any notice (though this should not be seen as a 'usual' order) – s 83(1)(b) Housing Act 1985 (secure tenancies), s 8(1)(b) Housing Act 1988 (assured tenancies).

41 Housing Act 1985, s 83(4) (secure tenancies)/Housing Act 1988, s 8(3)(c) (assured tenancies).

42 Housing Act 1985, s 83(5) (secure tenancies)/Housing Act 1988, s 8(4B) (assured tenancies). Changes to be introduced to assured tenancy notices by Renters' Rights Act 2025, s 3(3)(f) have, at the time of writing, still to be brought into force and will not impact in any event upon the notice period for Ground 17.

43 The second edition dealt with assured fixed-term tenancies as well; but, as these will become a thing of the past because of the Renters' Rights Act 2025 (s 1 which introduces Housing Act 1988, s 4A – see n 45), this has not been included in the body of this chapter. Suffice to say that, at present, Housing Act 1988, s 7(6) requires there to be a forfeiture/re-entry clause in order that a notice seeking possession can then be served citing Ground 17 (and possession proceedings can be pursued thereafter as with periodic tenancies). See **2.63**(b).

44 Introduced by the Localism Act 2011 (creating secure flexible tenancies, a form of secure fixed-term tenancies).

45 As the MHCLG policy paper 'Implementing the Renters' Rights Act: Social Housing' (10 April 2026) explained:
'All new, and most existing, assured tenancies will become assured periodic (rolling) tenancies. Section 21 so-called "no-fault" evictions will also be abolished alongside updates to the grounds for possession.
While the Act is being commenced for private landlords from 1 May 2026, it will only apply in relation to assured tenancies of social housing provided by PRPs from October 2027.
For the purposes of the Renters' Rights Act, a "social housing assured tenancy" means an assured tenancy of social housing (within the meaning of Part 2 of the Housing and Regeneration Act 2008) where the landlord is a private registered provider of social housing. Most affected social housing will be low-cost rental accommodation as defined in section 69 (which includes being let at a rent below market rate).'

(b) given that, unlike the residual arrangements for pre-Renters' Rights Act 2025, fixed-term assured tenancies (ie certain shared ownership agreements) where:

(i) forfeiture is not applicable by reason of section 45 of the Housing Act 1988;[46]

(ii) there is a re-entry/forfeiture clause and provision in the agreement for the Ground to be used;[47] and

(iii) the Ground can thereby be relied upon following service of a notice seeking possession,

do not apply, of course, to flexible tenancies which are rather expressly legislated for in Part 4 (sections 107A–107E) of the Housing Act 1985.

2.64 The difficulty arises for *flexible tenancies* by reason of the distinct security of tenure provision to be found in section 82(1)–(2) of the Housing Act 1985:

> '(1) A secure tenancy which is either–
>
> (a) a weekly or other periodic tenancy, or
>
> (b) a tenancy for a term certain but subject to termination by the landlord,
>
> cannot be brought to an end by the landlord except as mentioned in subsection (1A).
>
> (1A) The tenancy may be brought to an end by the landlord–
>
> (a) obtaining—
>
> (i) an order of the court for the possession of the dwelling-house, and
>
> (ii) the execution of the order,
>
> (b) obtaining an order under subsection (3), or
>
> (c) obtaining a demotion order under section 82A.
>
> (2) In the case mentioned in subsection (1A)(a), the tenancy ends when the order is executed.'

2.65 This confirms that a fixed-term secure tenancy, where 'subject to termination by the landlord'[48] (eg by means of a break clause, though see **2.75**(3)), will only end where a possession order has been executed or where there has been a demotion order *or section 82(3) order*[49] *terminating the fixed-term tenancy* in reliance on the forfeiture provision as referred to at **2.67–2.69**.[50]

46 *Artesian Developments Ltd v Beck* [2000] QB 541 at [549].
47 See Housing Act 1988, s 7(6).
48 Housing Act 1985, s 82(1)(b).
49 See **2.67**.
50 Ibid, s 82(1A).

2.66 If it were not for the section 82(3) provision, set out in the next paragraph, then as was previously the case pre-Renters' Rights Act 2025 with fixed-term assured tenancies (including shared ownership agreements) highlighted at **2.63**, the landlord would simply need to serve a notice seeking possession relying on the Ground in reliance on the forfeiture clause (that should have been) set down in the agreement.

2.67 *However*, section 82(3) of the Housing Act 1985 effectively provides that a local authority landlord is rather required to adopt a two-stage process. *First*, they must terminate the tenancy in reliance on the usual provision for re-entry or forfeiture (ie by service of a section 146 notice in non-rent arrears cases) *before* or at the same time as serving a notice seeking possession (see **2.74**). They cannot get possession by only adopting the first part of this process as this would only allow for an order terminating the tenancy:

> '(3) Where a secure tenancy is a tenancy for a term certain but with a provision for re-entry or forfeiture, the court shall not order possession of the dwelling-house in pursuance of that provision, but in a case where the court would have made such an order it shall instead make an order terminating the tenancy on a date specified in the order and section 86 (periodic tenancy arising on termination of fixed term) shall apply.'

2.68 The above analysis was initially the subject of some discussion and dispute. However, in March 2022 the Supreme Court settled any debate.[51] In *Croydon LBC v Kalonga*, it was held that a flexible tenancy could not be determined before the expiry of the fixed term unless the tenancy agreement contained an 'early termination' provision such as a break clause or a forfeiture clause.[52] When, in an earlier and different, though related, context, complaint was made that, in the absence of rescission, fixed-term secure tenancies could not be terminated by the landlord, Lord Neuberger had responded:[53]

> '… there is no reason why a fixed-term tenancy should not contain a provision for re-entry or forfeiture for misrepresentation. Secondly, even if the 1985 Act does not permit a landlord, before the expiry of a fixed-term secure tenancy, to obtain possession on the grounds that the tenancy was induced by a tenant's fraudulent misrepresentation, this is an insufficient reason for failing to give effect to the plain meaning of section 82(3)(4). For the reasons already given, the statutory scheme clearly excludes the common law right of rescission.'

2.69 Returning to *Kalonga*, Lord Briggs JSC explained:

> '42. This does not mean, as the Court of Appeal thought, that the landlord can never seek possession on the statutory grounds in relation to a fixed-

51 [2022] UKSC 7, [2023] AC 1.
52 Lord Briggs JSC at [30]–[40].
53 *Uckac*, para 35.

term tenancy, and is invariably confined to seeking termination in lieu of forfeiture. Thus, if the tenancy agreement contains a landlord's break clause exercisable at any time after (say) two years, then the landlord can seek possession thereafter under any of the statutory grounds, but not before. Before then the tenancy will not be "subject to termination by the landlord" otherwise than perhaps by forfeiture. After then, it will be. Once two years have passed, the landlord can terminate the tenancy under its terms (by complying with any specified break-notice requirement) but only if one of the statutory grounds is also available.

43. The same analysis applies in relation to termination by forfeiture, although it operates by a different method. If the tenancy agreement contains no forfeiture clause, then the 1985 Act and its predecessor create no statutory equivalent. *Thus a fixed-term tenancy without a forfeiture clause or a break clause cannot be terminated under the Acts until it expires by effluxion of time.* It simply lacks any provision for earlier termination which satisfies section 82(1)(b). But if the tenancy agreement does have a forfeiture clause (but no break clause), then the tenancy cannot be terminated otherwise than by termination in lieu of forfeiture, under section 82(3). This is because, if it has not been, the tenant is able to say, in defence to a purely statutory claim for possession, "my tenancy is not yet subject to termination by the landlord under section 82(1)(b) because the only provision in my tenancy agreement for early termination (forfeiture) is not yet exercisable or (as in this case) has not been exercised". *The exercise of the landlord's right to forfeit must comply with section 82(3) and (4) with the result that (if relief is not obtained by the tenant) a follow-on periodic tenancy ensues under section 86, which qualifies under section 82(1A)(a) for termination by a statutory possession order.*' (emphasis added)

2.70 No determination as to the breach will be required from the First-tier Tribunal (Property Chamber), as would normally be the case for long leases, because the flexible tenancy would, in all probability, not be for a period exceeding 21 years and therefore not defined as a 'long lease'.[54]

2.71 For flexible tenancies, therefore, a section 146 notice[55] *is* required as a Ground case is a non-rent arrears breach. Section 146 provides:

'(1) A right of re-entry or forfeiture under any proviso or stipulation in a lease for a breach of any covenant or condition in the lease shall not be enforceable, by action or otherwise, unless and until the lessor serves on the lessee a notice–

54 Commonhold and Leasehold Reform Act 2002, ss 76–77, 168(4) and 169(5). It is different for shared ownership agreements, of course, since the introduction of the Renters' Rights Act 2025, where they are clearly long leases and possession is by way of forfeiture. At the time of writing, the government has published the (draft) Commonhold and Leasehold Reform Bill which will, amongst other matters, abolish the existing forfeiture process and replace it with a lease enforcement regime.

55 Law of Property Act 1925.

(a) specifying the particular breach complained of; and

(b) if the breach is capable of remedy, requiring the lessee to remedy the breach; and

(c) in any case, requiring the lessee to make compensation in money for the breach;

and the lessee fails, within a reasonable time thereafter, to remedy the breach, if it is capable of remedy, and to make reasonable compensation in money, to the satisfaction of the lessor, for the breach.'

2.72 It will be immediately apparent from the above analysis that there therefore *does* need to be a term or condition of the tenancy which has been said to have been breached (or, in the alternative, an operable break clause).

2.73 It also follows, and section 82(4) of the 1985 Act makes this clear, that the usual forfeiture issues, such as waiver (such as by acceptance of rent) and the availability to the defendant tenant of relief applications,[56] etc, very much apply:

'(4) Section 146 of the Law of Property Act 1925 (restriction on and relief against forfeiture), except subsection (4) (vesting in under-lessee), and any other enactment or rule of law relating to forfeiture, shall apply in relation to proceedings for an order under subsection (3) of this section as if they were proceedings to enforce a right of re-entry or forfeiture.'

2.74 As for process and as accepted by Arnold LJ in the Court of Appeal in *Kalonga*,[57] there is no apparent reason why a post-termination possession claim reliant on a notice seeking possession could not also then be pleaded *alongside* the termination claim (seeking thereby both remedies).[58] This would be a sensible approach given a periodic tenancy arises automatically at the termination of the flexible tenancy.[59] Section 83 of the 1985 Act, which deals with service of a notice seeking possession, allows for such a service and process, providing:

'(6) Where a notice under this section is served with respect to a secure tenancy for a term certain, it has effect also with respect to any periodic tenancy arising on the termination of that tenancy by virtue of section 86; and subsections (3) to (5)[60] of this section do not apply to the notice.'

2.75 In summary, therefore, where seeking to take possession action because of relevant incorrect information having been given or omitted prior to the grant of tenancy:

56 Ibid, s 146(2).
57 [2021] EWCA Civ 77, [2021] QB 962 at [63].
58 As prescribed by Part II of the Schedule to the Secure Tenancies (Notices) Regulations 1987 (SI 1987/755).
59 Housing Act 1985, s 86(1).
60 These provisions include the requirement to provide a date in the notice after which any possession proceedings may be begun.

(1) In periodic tenancy cases – secure or assured – this simply requires (assuming the tenant or at least one of the joint tenants continues to live at the premises as their only or principal home, or their spouse or civil partner does) the service of a notice seeking possession relying on the Ground followed by the issuing of proceedings for possession. If there is no such occupation, then security of tenure will have been lost and a notice to quit can be served to end the remaining common law tenancy at its expiry (see **3.3**).

(2) The notice seeking possession route remains open, despite the Renters' Rights Act 2025 reforms, for fixed-term assured tenancies where the landlord is a private registered provider of social housing until October 2027 (see fn 45), assuming that there is a 'provision for re-entry, for forfeiture, for determination by notice or otherwise' (section 7(6)(b) of the Housing Act 1988).

(3) For flexible tenancies, there must be provision for early termination in the tenancy agreement, whether that be an operable break clause or a forfeiture provision (which would require reliance on a breach of tenancy claim such that a term should be included 'mirroring' the Ground). In the latter instance the landlord must proceed by way of service of a section 146 notice and proceedings to terminate the tenancy in lieu of forfeiture under section 82(3).

(4) However, this can be done *at the same time* as service of a notice seeking possession relying on the Ground, and only one set of possession proceedings is required including the relief of terminating the flexible tenancy and seeking possession 'against the periodic tenancy that will then arise'.

(5) If security tenure is lost in fixed-term tenancy cases (which includes flexible tenancies) then the options for the social landlord include forfeiture proceedings or, less obviously, rescission.

2.76 Finally under this part, section 119 of the Housing and Planning Act 2016, which is still not yet in force at the time of writing, seeks, somewhat unsuccessfully, to clarify and simplify matters for flexible tenancies by amending section 82 of the Housing Act 1985 for new fixed-term secure tenancies by inserting a new sub-section (amongst other amendments set out in the Act):

> '(A1) A fixed-term secure tenancy of a dwelling-house in England that is granted on or after the day on which paragraph 4 of Schedule 7 to the Housing and Planning Act 2016 comes fully into force cannot be brought to an end by the landlord except by—
>
> (a) obtaining–
>
> (i) an order of the court for the possession of the dwelling-house, and
>
> (ii) the execution of the order, or
>
> (b) obtaining a demotion order under section 82A.
>
> (A2) A secure tenancy can be brought to an end by the landlord as mentioned in subsection (A1)(a) whether or not the tenancy contains terms for it to be brought to an end' (emphasis added).

STANDARD OF PROOF

2.77 The ensuing possession claim will be a civil matter and decided accordingly on the balance of probabilities standard. This is best explained by:

(a) Lord Nicholls' statement in *In re H (Minors) (Sexual Abuse: Standard of Proof)* [1996] AC 563 at [586C–H]:

> 'The balance of probability standard means that a court is satisfied an event occurred if the court considers that, on the evidence, the occurrence of the event was more likely than not. When assessing the probabilities the court will have in mind as a factor, to whatever extent is appropriate in the particular case, that the more serious the allegation the less likely it is that the event occurred and, hence, the stronger should be the evidence before the court concludes that the allegation is established on the balance of probability … [T]his does not mean that where a serious allegation is in issue the standard of proof required is higher. It only means that the inherent probability or improbability of an event is itself a matter to be taken into account when weighing the probabilities and deciding whether, on balance, the event occurred.'

(b) Lord Hoffmann's statement in *Re B (Children)*:[61]

> 'the more serious an allegation is, the less likely it is that the event occurred and, hence, the stronger should be the evidence before the court concludes that the allegation is established on the balance of probability.'

2.78 This approach has to be applied carefully, however, and must be properly understood. HHJ Richard Williams (sitting as a Judge of the High Court) said in *Singh v Jhutti and another*:[62]

> '… I consider that the correct position in relation to the standard of proof is that, while it is right to consider the inherent probability of an allegation in light of the particular circumstances of the case in determining whether it has been proved on the balance of probabilities, there is no legal requirement that the more serious the allegation, the more cogent the evidence needed to prove it. The civil standard of proof (balance of probabilities) does not vary with the gravity of the alleged misconduct.'

2.79 It is often not possible to call the person who decided to grant the tenancy to give evidence that they were induced to do so by the tenant's representation, but this is, though to be avoided if at all possible, not necessarily fatal to the possession claim.

2.80 In *Waltham Forest LBC v Roberts*,[63] Newman J considered the concept of the 'presumption of inducement' and absence of the local authority's actual decision-maker:

61 [2009] 1 AC 11 at [14]–[15].
62 [2021] EWHC 2272 (Ch) at [117].
63 [2004] EWCA Civ 940, [2005] HLR 2 at para 37.

> '37 … The judge was strongly influenced by the absence of evidence from the actual decision maker and rejected the evidence which was before him about the Authority's policy in responding to housing applications. *In so far as he is to be taken to have concluded that without evidence from the actual decision maker, the burden of proof could not be discharged, he was plainly wrong.* No basis for the existence of such a strict evidential requirement has been made out. Nor could it be, for there are none save that it is to be noted that in certain circumstances, to which I shall refer later, a presumption of inducement can arise. The Authority called its rehousing manager, Mr Bourne. His evidence, which was uncontradicted, was that in accordance with its policy, the Authority would have wanted to investigate the true position. As a result, he stated it was unlikely that Mrs Roberts would have been granted a tenancy of this particular accommodation, at the date it was granted, had the Authority known of her joint ownership of 143 Westdown Road. Her ownership would have generated inquiries into who was living at the property, the type of security the owners had and the amount of equity in the property.' (emphasis added)

REASONABLENESS

2.81 The Ground is, as noted above, a discretionary one and so, even if made out and there are no issues with the landlord's notice, the court must go on to consider whether:

(a) it is reasonable to make a possession order;[64] and

(b) if so, whether that order should be outright or its enforcement suspended on terms.[65]

2.82 The leading authority on the court's role in assessing reasonableness remains *Cumming v Danson*,[66] in which Lord Greene MR held that:

> 'In considering reasonableness under section 3(1), it is, in my opinion, perfectly clear that the duty of the judge is to take into account all relevant circumstances as they exist at the date of the hearing, that he must do in what I venture to call a broad, common-sense way as a man of the world, and come to his conclusion giving such weight as he thinks right to the various factors in the situation. Some factors may have little or no weight, others may be decisive, but it is quite wrong for him to exclude from his consideration matters which he ought to take into account.'

2.83 It necessarily follows that some circumstances will militate against the making of an outright order for possession, or indeed the making of any possession order.

64 Housing Act 1985, s 84(2)(a); Housing Act 1988, s 7(4).
65 Housing Act 1985, s 85(2); Housing Act 1988, s 9(2).
66 [1942] 2 All ER 663.

2.84 Factors such as:

- delay on the part of the landlord;
- laxity of procedures; and
- hardship for the defendant if evicted,

are just three issues that, it has been suggested, are potentially relevant when considering the question of reasonableness.[67] The court should conversely also take into account the nature and degree of the false statements which have been made and the surrounding circumstances (though see **2.90**).[68] In *Shrewsbury & Atcham BC v Evans*,[69] Beldam LJ said at [132]:

> 'The effect of the decisions, in my view, is that in a case such as this, where there has been a deliberate lying to obtain public housing that only in exceptional cases would the court consider the effect of the homelessness legislation. It is not the function of the court to decide whether or not a person is intentionally homeless. That is the function of the local authority and has been entrusted to the local authority by Parliament.'

2.85 A Convention right defence (usually under Article 8 of the ECHR) is unlikely to provide a defendant with much comfort, though,[70] any more than a defence based on a wider public law challenge. Having said that, in 2020 the Court of Appeal had cause to consider a Ground 17 possession claim where the public sector equality duty (PSED) was found to have been breached.

2.86 In *Luton Community Housing Trust v Durdana*[71] the Court of Appeal found that, whilst the trial judge was right to find that there had been a breach of the PSED, it was highly likely that, had the Trust carried out a proper assessment, it would have come to the same conclusion in respect of the claim. As it was thereafter not in a position to consider whether it was reasonable to make a possession order, the Court of Appeal allowed the Trust's appeal and remitted the claim to the county court to consider whether it was reasonable to make an order in the current circumstances:[72]

> 'Although for the reasons which I have given the judge was wrong to have dismissed the claim for a breach of the PSED, had she rejected that defence, she would still have needed to consider whether it was reasonable in all the circumstances to make the order. The judge in [58] of her judgment expressed the view that it would not have been reasonable to make the order because the claimant had not complied with the PSED but she declined to carry out any appraisal of her own as to whether it would be reasonable to make the order. The consideration of reasonableness which

67 *Lewisham LBC v Akinsola* (2000) 32 HLR 414 at 417 *per* Sedley LJ.
68 *Shrewsbury & Atcham BC v Evans* (1998) 30 HLR 123, CA.
69 Ibid.
70 *Thurrock BC v West* [2012] EWCA Civ 1435, [2013] HLR 5 at paras 22–31.
71 [2020] EWCA Civ 445; [2020] HLR 27.
72 Patten LJ at [37].

the court is required to carry out under s.7(4) HA 1988 will undoubtedly bring into account many of the factors I have already referred to but it will be a consideration of matters as they stand now rather than in 2018 and the scope of the enquiry may be wider. In any event, it is not something which this court is equipped to carry out on the material available for the purposes of this appeal.'

2.87 It could be said that such defences are better dealt with in any event under the umbrella of 'reasonableness'. In handing down the judgment of the court in *Manchester City Council v Romano; Manchester City Council v Samari*,[73] Lord Justice Brooke remarked, with reference to discrimination arguments in discretionary possession claims:

> '64 In our judgment, it would be preferable, in a case involving a secure tenancy or an assured tenancy, for the tenant to assert the matter on which he relies as part of his case that it would be unreasonable for the court to make a possession order, rather than to complicate the proceedings by adding a formalistic counterclaim for a declaration or an injunction.'

2.88 It is, though, worth noting, when considering some of the common examples of public law or discrimination defences:

- Section 11(2) of the Children Act 2004 applies to local authorities and other designated public bodies and concerns the safeguarding and promotion of the welfare of children, but as Sharp LJ said in *Mohamoud v Kensington & Chelsea RLBC*:[74]

  > '67 Further, as in *Collins*, it is difficult to see how the s11(2) duty adds anything material to the art.8 analysis. If it does so, it seems to me, more as a matter of form, rather than substance.
  >
  > …
  >
  > 70 If however, contrary to my view, there was a duty to conduct an assessment as the appellants assert, I do not think these facts show any basis for interfering with the possession orders that were made, as there is no link between the making of those orders and a failure to conduct such an assessment. It would follow that a failure to comply with such a duty did not give rise to a defence to the claims in any event: see *Wandsworth LBC v Winder* [1985] A.C. 461 HL at 509E–F and *London Borough of Hackney v Lambourne* (1993) 25 H.L.R. 172 at 181.'

- Equally, the PSED[75] is unlikely to add significant weight to the tenant's defence: as reasonableness is in issue, the factors to which section 149 of the Equality Act 2010 refers would, in all probability, be considered by the court in any event (and see **2.86–2.87**).

73 [2004] EWCA Civ 834, [2005] 1 WLR 2775 – the Disability Rights Commission intervening in both cases.

74 [2015] EWCA Civ 780, [2015] HLR 38.

75 Equality Act 2010, s 149.

- As for discrimination,[76] the likely form would be indirect discrimination (section 19 of the Equality Act 2010) and the tenant would need to identify the provision, criterion or practice complained of and why its application puts them at a 'particular disadvantage'. As Beldam LJ said in *Evans* at [132]:[77]

  > 'In my view, the court could take into account, as was said, the current position in which the appellant found herself, but at the same time it would have to have in mind, as I have previously indicated, the great importance to be attached to honesty in making application for public housing accommodation.'

2.89 Whilst the detail of discrimination and public law defences is beyond the scope of this book, if a landlord believes it has sufficient evidence to justify a possession claim under the Ground, then when making a decision to issue such a claim, and keeping its prosecution under review, it would be prudent to not only be satisfied of the evidence but also:

(a) consider the tenant's present circumstances in full and any culpability that could be laid at the door of the landlord or any third party;

(b) address, in particular, any issues surrounding any relevant, protected characteristic,[78] such as disability, as well as any wider public law issue;

(c) consider the impact on and integrity of the allocation scheme in operation, including the interests of those awaiting allocation of social housing; and

(d) comply with any necessary pre-action protocol (see **2.60**).

2.90 It has been said by the Court of Appeal that the nature and degree of the tenant's untrue statements could only be considered relevant to the question of reasonableness in exceptional circumstances; the attitude and response of the defendant when the fraud was exposed being a more reasonable factor to consider.[79]

2.91 That approach stands in marked contrast to the treatment of reasonableness claims brought on other grounds for possession. In *City West Housing Trust Ltd v Massey*,[80] conjoined anti-social behaviour possession cases,[81] Arden LJ observed, when considering the required cogency of evidence necessary to allow suspension of the enforcement of a possession order:

> '53 However, because each case must be considered on its own facts, the judge has to decide whether there is a sound basis for saying that the

76 Under the Equality Act 2010.

77 Though see *Lewisham LBC v Malcolm* [2007] EWCA Civ 763, [2008] Ch 129 (overturned on appeal: [2008] UKHL 43, [2008] 1 AC 1399).

78 Equality Act 2010, s 4 – the protected characteristics are age; disability; gender reassignment; marriage and civil partnership; pregnancy and maternity; race; religion or belief; sex; and sexual orientation.

79 *Shrewsbury & Atcham BC v Evans* (1998) 30 HLR 123 *per* Beldam LJ at 132.

80 [2016] EWCA Civ 704, [2017] 1 WLR 129.

81 Housing Act 1988, Sch 2, Grounds 12 and 14.

tenant changed his or her ways. There is no absolute rule that a tenant who has lied in his evidence cannot ever succeed in having a SPO made in his favour. Even though lies have been told, it may be appropriate for a district judge none the less to make the assessment that cogent evidence exists which provides a real hope that the terms of the tenancy agreement will be respected in future. That will require careful consideration and appropriate explanation when the district judge gives his reasons for making an SPO.'

2.92 The courts have, significantly, held in possession claims based on the Ground that when considering whether it is reasonable to make a possession order the judge is entitled to take into account the *public interest* in discouraging deceitful applications for housing, which result in the unjust relegation of honest applicants. Nourse LJ said in *Rushcliffe BC v Watson* in reference to the relevance of considering the 'public interest':[82]

> 'I think it desirable to emphasise that what the judge was doing was considering whether it was reasonable to make an order for possession. Mr. Westgate accepts that, in doing that, the judge was entitled, and indeed bound, to take account of the public interest. But he says that he took too narrow a view of it, in particular by not recognising the public interest in keeping a family together as a unit. The judge's view of the public interest was wrongly confined to a policy of discouraging deceitful applications which result in the unjust relegation on the housing list of applicants who are honest.
>
> Again I cannot accept this submission. I am quite certain that the judge recognised the public interest in keeping a family together as a unit. But since he thought that there was no real likelihood that this family would be split up, that was not something which affected his consideration of the public interest in this case. On the broader aspect of the public interest the judge was fully entitled to attach the importance which he evidently did to the policy to which I have referred. The statistics which he recounted demonstrate the acute shortages in the plaintiff's housing stock.'

2.93 *Rushcliffe* also serves as a helpful reminder to landlords that, if they wish to rely on the Ground it makes sense to provide evidence of those affected by such deceitful applications, along with other information, such as:

(a) the number of people on the landlord's allocation list, or that of the nominating authorities;

(b) the average wait time for accommodation; and

(c) the likely outcome of the tenant's application if they had not misrepresented their position.

82 (1991) 24 HLR 124, CA at [130]–[131].

2.94 Further, in claims brought on the Ground, the court will only consider the effect on the tenant of making a possession order *in exceptional circumstances*. In *Evans*,[83] the Court of Appeal dismissed the tenant's argument that the trial judge had failed to give proper weight to the fact that she might be found intentionally homeless if evicted (see **2.103** below) and that the family might not be able to stay together if the possession order was made.

2.95 Indeed, in *Lewisham LBC v Akinsola*,[84] the Court of Appeal expressly rejected an argument that a possession order would be futile as it would – it was said – simply require the authority to secure accommodation for the errant defendant, who had lied about being homeless to obtain the accommodation in the first place. There were, in effect, still issues for the authority to decide upon any homelessness application, such as intentionality.[85]

2.96 The court did, however, caution that, if a homelessness application would manifestly succeed or fail, this may be a relevant factor when considering the reasonableness of a possession order.[86]

2.97 Some 27 years on, however, with greater reliance by local housing authorities on the private rented sector to discharge their homelessness duties, it may properly be argued that, even if the household were likely to be owed the full housing duty, it did not necessarily follow that they would be offered social housing such that possession from such stock would still be warranted.

2.98 In *Evans*, Beldam LJ in any event cautioned against 'overplaying' the potential re-housing card when he said at [132]:

> 'Those who are on the housing list who have an equal or even greater claim to public housing would, in my view, justly be indignant to find that the court did not think it reasonable in circumstances where someone has obtained accommodation by a deliberate and flagrant lie, to make an order for possession merely because the effect of the order would result in the occupant having to be considered by the local authority as homeless or intentionally homeless.'

83 (1998) 30 HLR 123, CA at [132] *per* Beldam LJ, though see *Southwark LBC v Erekin* [2003] EWHC 1765, [2003] JHL D96, in which the High Court refused to overturn a county court decision that it would not be reasonable to make a possession order under this Ground, even though the defendant had been sent to prison for fraud for obtaining the tenancy, because the defendant's children had been enjoying a stable home life in the property with the defendant's mother.

84 (2000) 32 HLR 414.

85 Note *R v Exeter City Council, ex p Glidden and Draper* [1985] 1 All ER 493 in this respect, in which it was held that it would not be reasonable to permit the tenant to continue to occupy accommodation which the landlord wishes to recover because of discovered fraud.

86 In *Shrewsbury and Atcham BC v Evans* (1998) 30 HLR 123 at [132], Beldam LJ had previously said: '... only in exceptional cases would the court consider the effect of the homelessness legislation. It is not the function of the court to decide whether or not a person is intentionally homeless. That is the function of the local authority and has been entrusted to the local authority by Parliament'.

and, in the context of fraudulent sub-letting, Turner J remarked in *Poplar HARCA v Begum & Rohim*:[87]

> '... it is not compassionate to allow profiteering fraudsters indefinitely to continue to occupy premises and thereby exclude from such accommodation more needy and deserving families.'

2.99 Finally, though discretionary, the Ground is in some respects 'all or nothing'. There is, it is suggested, little merit in the landlord securing a possession order, the enforcement of which is suspended on terms, in the absence of any credible conditions of suspension (unless there are other discretionary grounds being relied on, such as regards rent arrears or anti-social conduct). In these cases, the mischief has already happened; and of necessity it cannot happen again for that particular tenancy.

INTERNAL FRAUD

2.100 There are, regrettably, occasions where tenancies are procured by means of internal fraud. In such cases the key question is whether the tenant was aware, or should have been aware, that the sign-up process was irregular and that the internal staff member involved did not have the requisite authority to grant the tenancy (and, as such, no tenancy was in fact created). In legal terms, the issue is one of 'ostensible authority'.

2.101 In *London & Quadrant Housing Trust v Stokes*,[88] Martin Spencer J cited with approval from the judgment below:

> 'So far as the doctrine of ostensible authority is concerned, the judge dealt with this briefly at paragraphs 39 and 40 of his judgment, where he said:
>
> "39 In relation to the law, I accept Mr Lane's submission that Rennie and Miller did not have sufficient authority. They were acting outside their responsibilities; from their very nature, as they were not involved in allocations. The officers did, however, have ostensible authority in my view to bind the Trust pursuant to the test set out by Toulson J in Ing Re (UK) Ltd v R&V Versicherung AG [2006] EWHC 1544 at [99].
>
> 40. The reasons for this are they satisfy the two requirements in ostensible authority, namely:
>
> (a) by indication of all the circumstances of the case, that is by being presented with documentation by legitimately appointed housing officers, the claimant represented to the defendant that they had authority to act as their agent in the circumstances; and

87 [2017] EWHC 2040 (QB), [2017] HLR 42 at para 40.
88 [2022] EWHC 1120 (QB) at para 24.

(b) the first defendant has clearly relied upon that representation by entering into the tenancy agreement which she signed.

In my view, that is satisfied as a test.'"

2.102 He went on to find that the trial judge had been entitled to find that two employees of the appellant, whilst acting fraudulently, had had ostensible authority to sign the respondent up to a tenancy agreement – the agreement had been on a genuine document produced by the appellant, and the individual respondent had been an honest witness who had had no reason to believe that her tenancy was anything other than a regular transaction.

HOMELESSNESS

2.103 We have focused in this chapter on the recovery of premises obtained by reason of a false representation. For reasons of general interest and completeness, it is interesting to see how the courts may deal with subsequent homelessness appeals brought by the errant (now former) tenant in challenging an intentionality finding. This is briefly referenced at **2.94–2.97** above in the context of the reasonableness assessment.

2.104 What happens to a tenant who has been repossessed from their home because of the Ground? One might have thought they would almost certainly be found to be intentionally homeless, and therefore not owed the full housing duty[89] (for the local housing authority to secure suitable accommodation), because they were in effect the 'authors of their own misfortune'.

2.105 On 31 January 2025, HHJ Grimshaw gave judgment in the County Court at Wolverhampton in the section 204 (homelessness) appeal of *Emilia Munemo v The City of Wolverhampton Council*.[90] He allowed the appeal against the review decision's finding of intentionality and found that:[91]

> 'The Appellant was not intentionally homeless as it was not her conduct that caused her to cease to occupy the property (it was her ineligibility as it was in *Chishimba*) and it would not be reasonable for her to continue to occupy the Property where she had no entitlement to it and where the Respondent sought possession of the Property on that basis.'
>
> 'I therefore find that the Property was not reasonable for the Appellant to continue to occupy on the basis that she was not entitled to a tenancy of the Property in the first place and was only granted a tenancy by the Respondent as a result of her deception.'

89 Housing Act 1996, s 193(2).
90 (2025) EWCC 4.
91 Ibid, paras 107 and 111.

2.106 There was a definite logic to this first-instance decision, and it purported to follow earlier Court of Appeal authorities such as *Chishimba v Kensington and Chelsea RLBC*,[92] but it was not without its inconsistencies and flaws. In particular, the appellant had a lawful tenancy, however it had been secured, and the possession order was not made on a mandatory basis but rather because the court had determined that it was reasonable to make a possession order and that such an order should be made outright.

2.107 On 20 March 2026 the Court of Appeal brought what may be seen as a profound dose of common sense to this issue when giving judgment in the *Munemo* appeal. In allowing the authority's appeal, Stuart-Smith LJ explained:[93]

> '36. … When considering the question whether the accommodation that the applicant has ceased to occupy in consequence of the applicant's deliberate act or omission, is available for his occupation and/or whether it would be reasonable for him to continue to occupy the accommodation, the applicant may not rely upon that deliberate act or omission to support a conclusion that the accommodation is not available and/or that it would not be reasonable for him to occupy it.'
>
> '46. Applying *Denton* to the facts of the present case, if one ignores the misrepresentation that was the relevant deliberate act (which the applicant may not rely on (as per [36] above)), there was no basis for an assertion that the property was not available or that it would not have been reasonable for Ms Munemo to continue to occupy it. All of the evidence provided to the Council initially and available to the reviewing officer and the Courts has been to the effect that Thompson Avenue was satisfactory for Ms Munemo to occupy and that it would have been reasonable for her to continue to occupy had she not, in consequence of her deliberate act, had to cease occupation …'
>
> '47. I do not consider that there is any justification for extending the principles adopted in *Chishimba* to the facts of the present appeal. It would have the consequence that any person who induces the grant of a tenancy of suitable and satisfactory accommodation by deception will not be intentionally homeless if that deception subsequently causes them to cease to occupy their accommodation. Such an outcome would, in my judgment emasculate section 191 and prevent it from achieving its statutory purpose, which I take to include discouraging the obtaining of accommodation by deception.'

CONCLUSION

2.108 If a secure tenancy or assured tenancy has been procured by a false representation or omission, then possession proceedings may be available on the

92 [2013] EWCA Civ 786, [2014] PTSR 49.
93 [2026] EWCA Civ 329 at paras 36 and 46–47.

discretionary Ground – Ground 5 (secure tenancies) or 17 (assured tenancies). This is the usual route in seeking to repossess the premises and, generally, the remedy of rescission will not be available.

2.109 Once there has been an assignment or ending of the wrongly allocated tenancy, then the Ground will not be available.

2.110 Where security of tenure has been lost – for example, where the tenant no longer lives at the premises as their only or principal home – rescission may be a possible remedy though there may be more practical sense in acknowledging the tenancy and seeking to terminate it by the usual 'notice to quit' or forfeiture route, depending upon the evidence of the sub-letting, parting with possession or only or principal home scenario.

2.111 If the fraud is committed by *both* an officer of the social landlord and the recipient tenant, then again rescission *may* be available if a tenancy is found to be in existence (see **2.100–2.102**). This pleading would usually be by way of alternative remedy, depending upon the relevant factual make-up.

2.112 Finally, the particular and distinct hurdles that may impinge upon a flexible tenancy, as explained at **2.63–2.76**, need to be appreciated and care taken both in how the original tenancy agreement is drafted and in how the tenancy is sought to be terminated (and possession taken).

CHAPTER 3

Misuse of Property

- Sub-letting
- Parting with possession
- Short-term lets
- Possession claims

Key points

- Sub-letting or parting with possession of the whole of the demised premises will lead to an automatic and permanent loss of security of tenure for secure and assured tenancies (though *not* if a 'protected' pre-Renters' Rights Act 2025 ('RRA25') shared ownership lease which retains assured tenancy status in certain circumstances).[1]
- Secure or assured status cannot be regained in such circumstances, even if the tenant resumes occupation of the premises, save by the grant of a fresh tenancy.
- Lack of direct evidence of such activity may not be fatal to a landlord's claim for possession, if proper inferences can be drawn from the proven facts.
- For periodic tenancies, the service of a notice to quit will bring the remaining common law tenancy to an end, with effect from its expiry.
- The RRA25 will ultimately end the option of fixed-term tenancies in cases of assured tenancies (see fn 45 in Chapter 2), but local housing authorities can still opt to adopt the equivalent model, namely flexible

1 From 27 December 2025, any new shared ownership agreement is a long lease excluded from assured status following amendments to Housing Act 1988, Sch 1. Section 31(5) of the RRA25 provides, 'Where, immediately before the day on which this section comes into force, proceedings for an order for possession under section 8 of the 1988 Act in reliance on a valid notice given under that section of that Act have been commenced in relation to a tenancy and have not been concluded, or have not been commenced but have not become time-barred— (a) the tenancy remains an assured tenancy, and the notice remains valid, until any time when such proceedings in reliance on the notice become time-barred or are concluded, and (b) until that time the amendments made by subsections (1) and (4) do not apply in relation to the tenancy".

tenancies.[2] Along with shared ownership leases, which the RRA25 has in all but a small number of cases moved out of Housing Act 1988 jurisdiction (see fn 1), these fixed-term arrangements cannot be ended by means of a notice to quit. In such cases, possession in reliance on an appropriately worded 'forfeiture provision' will be needed.[3]

- A secure tenant has the right to take in lodgers and sub-letting or parting with possession of part of the premises is available to such tenants with the written permission of their landlord. Failure to get such authority can lead to a ground for possession – breach of tenancy – provided for in Schedule 2 to the Housing Acts 1985 (secure tenancies – Ground 1) and 1988 (assured tenancies – Ground 12).
- It is an implied term of most assured tenancies[4] that in order to sub-let or part with possession of the whole or part of the subject premises (or, indeed, assign the same) the landlord's consent is required.[5]
- Introductory tenancies can be ended in the same way as for secure tenancies upon sub-letting or parting with possession of the whole – see **3.27**. Any such activity in respect of part of the premises may simply lead to a notice being served under section 128 of the Housing Act 1996, and mandatory possession proceedings thereafter being issued (subject to review).

INTRODUCTION

3.1 Chapter 2 concerns instances where the tenant should never have been allocated the social housing unit in the first place. This chapter, conversely, considers the situation where they acquired the tenancy in a proper fashion[6] but have not dealt with the premises appropriately thereafter. In short, they have allowed others to 'take over' the premises, either in whole or in part.

2 Housing Act 1985, s 107A states in terms that 'a flexible tenancy is a secure tenancy' and refers to fixed terms of two years or more. Fixed-term tenancies will no longer be a feature of private registered provider stock (ie assured tenancies) following the implementation of the RRA25 provisions covering this element. The Ministry of Housing, Communities and Local Government Policy Paper of 13 November 2025, 'Implementing the Renters' Rights Act 2025: Our roadmap for reforming the Private Rented Sector', advises that the assured periodic tenancy regime will begin in the private rented sector from 1 May 2026.

3 Nearly Legal identified an interesting question with regard to 'anti-sub-letting' provisions in right-to-buy leases whilst looking at Airbnb issues on 28 March 2017 given the provision of Housing Act 1985, Sch 6, para 17(1) (which concerns right to buy) – 'A provision of the lease, or of an agreement collateral to it, is void insofar as it purports to prohibit or restrict the assignment of the lease or the subletting, wholly or in part, of the dwelling-house.'

4 Housing Act 1988, s 15(3) explains those tenancies where there is no such implied term: see **3.36**.

5 Housing Act 1988, s 15(1).

6 Although it will also apply to tenants who improperly obtained the tenancy because they are still tenants and the landlord may choose to deal with it accordingly, instead of or in addition to forms of recovery discussed in Chapter 2.

3.2 The question of sub-letting or parting with possession of premises by a tenant is, to varying degrees and in all practical senses, an issue of evidence, though it is important to understand some basic factors underpinning security of tenure and the impact on this caused by such activity, as well as the proper and appropriate court processes to undertake in order to secure possession of the subject premises.

3.3 As will be explained further below, it is the mere fact of statutory protection provided for by the Housing Acts of 1985 (secure tenancies) and 1988 (assured tenancies) that prevents a secure or assured periodic tenancy from being brought to an end on a mandatory ground by means of an otherwise properly served and valid notice to quit.[7] In short:

Security of Tenure

- A secure, introductory or assured tenancy retains its status for as long as the tenant or, in a joint tenancy situation, at least one of the tenants occupies the demised premises as their only or principal home.[8]
- In fact, this basic premise is further extended[9] by the fact that a spouse or civil partner can occupy the said property in the absence of the tenant and security is retained for as long as the marriage or civil partnership persists (assuming the departing tenant does not serve a notice to quit).[10] This may, however, be a breach of tenancy (see bullet point below).
- If security of tenure is lost because the whole of the premises has been sub-let or the tenant has parted with possession of the same, then it cannot be 'regained',[11] save by the parties entering into a fresh tenancy.
- Conversely, if it is lost because the tenant(s) simply no longer live there as their only or principal home then this has 'merely' an ambulatory effect, such that security of tenure can be regained if the tenant (or at least one of them in joint tenancy cases, or their spouse/civil partner) returns to live at the premises before, in the case of a periodic tenancy, the expiry of any valid notice to quit properly served.[12] See Chapter 4 for further details.
- The tenant(s) in that situation will, however, have undoubtedly breached either an express or implied term of their tenancy – which requires them

7 Housing Act 1985, s 82 (secure tenancies)/Housing Act 1988, s 5 (assured tenancies).

8 Housing Act 1985, ss 79(1) and 81 (secure tenancies)/Housing Act 1988, s 1(1)(b) (assured tenancies)/Housing Act 1996, s 125(5)(a) (introductory tenancies).

9 Family Law Act 1996, s 30(4)(b) (as amended by the Civil Partnership Act 2004).

10 See *Derwent Housing Association v Taylor* [2016] EWCA Civ 508, [2016] HLR 25, para 4 where the Court of Appeal confirmed that Family Law Act 1996, s 30 only conferred rights of occupation on the tenant's spouse/civil partner whilst the tenant remains entitled to occupy the dwelling house; once the tenancy had been terminated by notice to quit, s 30 did not apply.

11 Housing Act 1985, s 93(2) (secure tenancies)/Housing Act 1988, s 15A(2) (assured tenancies).

12 See *Hussey v Camden LBC* (1995) 27 HLR 5 at [7]–[8] *per* Leggatt LJ.

or at least one of the joint tenants to live at the premises as their only or principal home – by not living there, such that it provides the landlord with the option and in many instances an addition or alternative to the notice to quit approach where the facts are unclear, of serving a notice seeking possession in reliance on the said breach.

- A notice to quit, and possession claim in reliance on the same, is only available, therefore, where the tenancy is periodic and security of tenure is lost, which will be where:
  - the tenant has sub-let or parted with possession of the *entirety* of the premises, or
  - the tenant has moved away and did not live there any longer as their only or principal home *at the time the notice to quit expires*.

3.4 This chapter is, therefore, primarily concerned with the question of sub-letting and parting with possession (with particular focus on periodic tenancies) and not the concept of 'only or principal home', which is dealt with more fully in Chapter 4. Of course, it is true to say that if the tenant has sub-let or otherwise parted with possession of their premises then they are by definition not living there themselves. The phrase 'primarily concerned' is also deliberately phrased in acknowledgment of the fact that it must be addressed *to a degree* where such activity relates to only part of the premises and action. In such a situation, the tenant's residence will make a difference to questions of criminal sanction and the exact nature of any possession claim.

3.5 As seen from the above, it is a topic which may present both a mandatory and discretionary possession ground for the social landlord. As such and in relation to a mandatory claim (ie in reliance on a notice to quit), they ought to be alive to the Pre-action Protocol for Possession Claims by Social Landlords:

> 'PART 3 MANDATORY GROUNDS FOR POSSESSION
>
> **3.1** This Part applies in cases where, if a social landlord proves its case, the court must, in principle, grant possession and where s.89(1) Housing Act 1980 applies
>
> **3.2** Before issuing any such possession claim a social landlord—
>
> (a) should write to the occupants explaining why it currently intends to seek possession and requiring the occupants, within a specified time, to notify the landlord in writing of any personal circumstances or other matters which they wish to have taken into account. In appropriate cases, such a letter could accompany any notice to quit or notice seeking possession and so would not necessarily delay the issue of proceedings; and
>
> (b) should consider any representations received and, if they decide to proceed with a claim for possession, give brief written reasons for doing so.

3.3 The social landlord should include with its claim form, or in any witness statement filed under CPR 55.8(3), a schedule stating—

(a) whether it has (by a statutory review procedure or otherwise) invited the defendant to make representations of any personal circumstances or other matters which they wished to be taken into account before the social landlord issued the proceedings;

(b) if representations were made, whether and how they were considered and with what outcome; and

(c) brief reasons for bringing proceedings.

Copies of any relevant documents which the social landlord wishes the court to consider in relation to the proportionality of the landlord's decision to bring the proceedings should be attached to the schedule.'

3.6 If a discretionary Ground is pursued, **2.60** in the previous chapter explains the Practice Direction to follow. First, however, the definitions of 'sub-letting' and 'parting with possession' must be explained.

WHAT IS SUB-LETTING?

3.7 'Sub-letting' requires the whole premises or part of the premises to be let out to a third party or parties:[13]

- with exclusive possession (see **3.17**, **3.75**);
- for a term at a rent; and
- with an intention to create legal relations between the parties.[14]

Normally it will be noticeably clear whether a particular living situation is properly characterised as a sub-letting.

3.8 In *Brent LBC v Cronin*,[15] the defendant, a secure tenant of the local authority, suffered from epilepsy and wished to stay with his sister-in-law away from his home for a short time. A friend of his suggested that a couple live in his one-bedroom flat in his absence. The defendant thereupon entered into an oral agreement with this couple under which they were to pay a deposit to him of £20, in addition to a weekly payment of £40 per week for the flat. The couple were given the keys to the flat and duly moved in. As for the defendant, he went, as planned, to stay with his sister-in-law.

3.9 The local authority landlord learned of this arrangement and began possession proceedings based on alleged sub-letting of the whole of the let

13 *Street v Mountford* [1985] AC 809 at [818C–F] *per* Lord Templeman.

14 To be judged by the parties' conduct and not by their professed intentions: ibid at [821C–D] and [822B–C] *per* Lord Templeman.

15 (1998) 30 HLR 43.

premises, having first served a notice to quit. At trial, the defendant was able to successfully argue that he had not, in fact, sub-let or parted with possession of his flat at all and that this was never his intention.

3.10 The trial judge did accept that the couple had:

- exclusive possession of the premises,
- for a term at a rent,

but also found that the tenant's plans were confused and uncertain, and that he had only intended to be away for a short time and further had not intended to part with possession of the flat.

3.11 There was certainly a superficial attractiveness to such arguments because the defendant may well have fully and genuinely intended to return to the premises at some time in the future. The Court of Appeal, however, rejected such an approach and took a clear view that, as all the elements for a tenancy had been created between the defendant and the couple, as set out at **3.7** above, a tenancy had, in fact, been formed.

3.12 The court therefore accepted the authority's appeal, Sir Ralph Gibson summarising the rejection of the trial judge's approach as follows:[16]

> 'The judge was not, in law, in my judgment, entitled to decide the nature of the transaction by reference to the uncommunicated intention or uncertainty of Mr Cronin. This is a clear, longstanding principle of law (see *Chitty on Contract* 7th edn, para 12–040 and cases there cited). We were referred to those passages by Miss McAllister.
>
> The appellants were entitled to have their claim for possession determined according to law. The special needs and vulnerability of Mr Cronin are matters to be dealt with by a different agency.'[17]

3.13 The Court of Appeal rejected the relevance of any subjective intention to return. To adopt the phrase of Lord Justice Waite, a tenancy is a tenancy, whether for a long or short period.

WHAT IS PARTING WITH POSSESSION?

3.14 'Parting with possession' is not as easily defined as 'sub-letting'.

16 Ibid at [47].

17 It is fair to say that the relevance of subjective intentions was left open by the Court of Appeal in *Dreamgate Properties Ltd v Arnot* (1998) 76 P&CR 25 because it was able to decide the question on objective considerations alone. In *London Baggage Company v Railtrack plc* [2000] L&TR 439, Mr Justice Pumfrey said at [445] 'It is not settled whether the intention of the parties, to which regard must be had, includes their subjective and uncommunicated intentions.'

3.15 Whilst sub-letting of the whole will encompass the 'parting with possession' definition, the latter also covers much wider forms of arrangement. For example, if a tenant purports to assign their tenancy to a third party and allows the latter into exclusive occupation in anticipation of the same, then this may constitute parting with possession, the elements for a tenancy being entirely absent to allow a finding of sub-letting. Similarly, an unauthorised tenants' 'swap' of properties would not be sub-letting, but would, in all probability, constitute a parting with possession.

3.16 Conversely, a 'caretaker' arrangement, where the tenant asks someone to look after the premises during their (prolonged) absence (eg during a period of imprisonment, hospitalisation or employment away from the area) does not, if properly constituted, fall within the parting with possession definition, nor do (usually) other forms of occupation under a licence. Why?

3.17 The key to this distinction is the question of *exclusive possession*, the first of the elements referred to at **3.7** above. In *Stenning v Abrahams*,[18] Farwell J explained the importance of this definition:

> 'A lessee cannot be said to part with the possession of any part of the premises unless his agreement with his licensee wholly ousts him from the legal possession of that part. If there is anything in the nature of a right to concurrent user there is no parting with possession. Retention of a key may be a negative indicium, and the authorities on the whole show that nothing short of a complete exclusion of the grantor or licensor from the legal possession for all purposes amounts to a parting with possession. The fact that the agreement is in form a licence is immaterial, as the licence may give the licensee so exclusive a right to the legal possession as to amount to a parting with possession.'

3.18 The courts have therefore settled on the 'test' of whether those in physical occupation have the right to exclude all others from the premises, including the tenant.[19]

SECURITY OF TENURE

Introduction

3.19 Now that the definitions of sub-letting and parting with possession are, hopefully, understood, the question of how these impact upon the tenant's security of tenure comes to the fore. The underlying factors are summarised at 3.3, which also deals with the inevitable 'nuances', such as the role and effect of having a spouse or civil partner.

18 [1931] 1 Ch 470 at 473.
19 *Lam Kee Ying v Lam Shes Tong* [1975] AC 247 at 256C *per* Sir Harry Gibbs.

Secure tenancies

3.20 A secure tenancy only remains as such, and security of tenure is therefore only retained:[20]

> '... at any time when the conditions described in sections 80 and 81 as the landlord condition and the tenant condition are satisfied'.

3.21 The landlord condition has no relevance to this issue, but rather it is section 81 of the Housing Act 1985 that requires attention. This sets out the tenant condition simply as:

> '... the tenant is an individual and occupies the dwelling-house as his *only or principal home*; or, where the tenancy is a joint tenancy, that each of the joint tenants is an individual and at least one of them occupies the dwelling-house as his only or principal home.' (emphasis added)

Assured tenancies

3.22 As with secure tenancies, section 1(1) of the Housing Act 1988 provides that an assured tenancy only remains as such if and for so long as:

> '(b) the tenant or, as the case may be, at least one of the joint tenants occupies the dwelling-house as his only or principal home.'

Only or principal home

3.23 It follows from these statutory provisions that security of tenure cannot be retained for secure, assured or introductory tenants if they do not remain in occupation as their only or principal home.

3.24 The only or principal home concept and the repercussion of its loss is dealt with, as previously noted, in appropriate detail in Chapter 4 and **3.3** above.

3.25 Paragraphs **3.31–3.42** look at when sub-letting or parting with possession is only in respect of *part* of the premises. Where it concerns the whole premises, statutory provisions make the issue more straightforward.

Sub-letting or parting with possession of whole

3.26 Section 93 of the Housing Act 1985[21] confirms the permanent loss of security of tenure for secure tenants in such circumstances:

20 Housing Act 1985, s 79(1).

21 This section is not applicable to a secure tenancy from a co-operative housing association by reason of s 109.

'(2) If the tenant under a secure tenancy parts with the possession of the dwelling-house[22] or sublets the whole of it (or sublets first part of it and then the remainder), the tenancy ceases to be a secure tenancy and cannot subsequently become a secure tenancy.'

3.27 If an introductory tenant sub-lets the whole, then they similarly lose that status if there has been sub-letting or parting with possession of the whole (or indeed if they no longer live at the premises as their only or principal home). Section 125 of the Housing Act 1996 provides:

'(5) A tenancy ceases to be an introductory tenancy if, before the end of the trial period–

(a) *the circumstances are such that the tenancy would not otherwise be a secure tenancy,*

(b) a person or body other than a local housing authority or housing action trust becomes the landlord under the tenancy,

(c) the election in force when the tenancy was entered into or adopted is revoked, or

(d) the tenancy ceases to be an introductory tenancy by virtue of section 133(3) (succession).' (emphasis added)

3.28 As with **3.26** above, section 15A of the Housing Act 1988 has provided, with effect from 5 November 2013,[23] for assured tenants to also permanently lose security of tenure in such circumstances:

'(1) Subsection (2) applies if, in breach of an express or implied term of the tenancy, a tenant of a dwelling-house let under an assured tenancy to which this section applies–

(a) parts with possession of the dwelling-house, or

(b) sub-lets the whole of the dwelling-house (or sub-lets first part of it and then the remainder).

(2) The tenancy ceases to be an assured tenancy and cannot subsequently become an assured tenancy.'

3.29 Section 15A of the 1988 Act has never applied to shared ownership leases and, as such, loss of security of tenure for those pre-RRA25 arrangements retaining assured status,[24] through not living at the premises as the tenant's only or principal home, is ambulatory.[25]

22 Defined at s112 as 'a house or a part of a house'.

23 Prior to this time an assured tenant was able to argue that even if they had sub-let or parted with possession of the whole of their premises then as long as they had a genuine intention to return there was no loss of security of tenure: *Ujima Housing Association v Ansah* (1997) 30 HLR 831 and *Waltham Forest Community Based Housing Association v Fanning* [2001] L&TR 41.

24 Not all shared ownership agreements entered into prior to the commencement of the RRA25 were assured in status, but the vast majority were.

25 See Housing Act 1988, s 15(3), (5).

3.30 It follows that for periodic secure and assured tenancies, and introductory tenancies, a notice to quit should be served to bring the remaining common law tenancy to an end:[26]

- prior to taking possession action; and
- prior to following the necessary protocol (see **3.5**).

And for shared ownership arrangements (less than 100% share) a notice seeking possession is the appropriate notice if the tenant has moved back in and it retains assured status despite the RRA25 amendments, otherwise a section 146 notice (as with flexible tenancies – see **3.64–3.70**) should be used.

Notice to Quit

To: Edward Hazard, 2 Stamford Bridge, London, SW18 1DD

From: Ferguson Housing Association, Andrew Herrera Way, Pocket, Manchester, M20 1LV

We give you NOTICE TO QUIT and you are to deliver up possession of 2 Stamford Bridge, London, SW18 1DD on 30 November 20XX or the day on which a complete period of your tenancy expires next after the end of four weeks from the date of service of this notice

Dated: 16 October 20XX

Signed: ....

Position:

Important information for tenants[27]

1 If the tenant or licensee does not leave the dwelling, the landlord or licensor must get an order for possession from the court before the tenant or licensee can lawfully be evicted. The landlord or licensor cannot apply for such an order before the notice to quit or notice to determine has run out.

2 A tenant or licensee who does not know if he has any right to remain in possession after a notice to quit or a notice to determine runs out can obtain advice from a solicitor. Help with all or part of the cost of legal advice and assistance may be available under the Legal Aid Scheme. He should also be able to obtain information from a Citizens' Advice Bureau, a Housing Aid Centre or a rent officer.

---

26 Housing Act 1996, s 125(6).

27 Notices to Quit etc (Prescribed Information) Regulations 1988/2201, Sch 1.

WHAT IF THE SUB-LETTING/PARTING WITH POSSESSION ONLY RELATES TO *PART* OF THE PREMISES?

3.31 We know the following from the Key Points section above:

(a) A secure or periodic assured tenant[28] is entitled to sub-let or part with possession of part of the premises as long as:[29]

- they have the (written[30]) consent of the landlord; and
- *they themselves, or at least one of joint tenants or their spouse/civil partner, continues to live at the premises as their only or principal home.*

(b) Consent of the landlord in a secure tenancy case should not be unreasonably withheld and will be treated as given if it is so.[31]

(c) A secure tenant is also entitled to have lodgers (as opposed to sub-tenants) in the premises and does not need the consent of the landlord to do so[32] (see **3.35**).

(d) Despite the more restrictive nature of periodic assured tenancies, an assured tenant will be able to take in lodgers to the extent that, in those cases, no possession in fact passes[33] (see **3.36**).

3.32 If, therefore, a sole tenant lets out a room, for example, in their three-bedroom premises and moves out to live elsewhere then, as indicated at **3.3** and **3.31** above:

(a) they may well have lost security of tenure *not* because of the sub-letting/parting with possession – because they have not done this in respect of the *whole* of the premises – but due to the fact that they no longer live at the premises as their only or principal home (see Chapter 4); and

(b) this activity is almost certainly also a breach of tenancy both in respect of the letting of the room, if without consent of the landlord, and the failure of the tenant to live at the premises as their only or principal home (and probably also a failure to advise their landlord of absence from the home for longer than the specified period, usually 21 or 28 days, if that is such an express term).

3.33 It necessarily follows that, if the sub-letting or parting with possession of part of the demised premises represents a breach of tenancy – whether of an express or implied term – and the tenant continues to live there, then the

28 A periodic assured tenancy can have a condition prohibiting or allowing any such sub-letting or parting with possession unless it is a statutory periodic tenancy or one arising under Local Government and Housing Act 1989, Sch 10 (see Housing Act 1988, s 15(3)).

29 Housing Act 1985, s 93(1)(a) (secure tenancies)/Housing Act 1988, s 15(1) (assured tenancies).

30 Housing Act 1988, s 15(1), dealing with assured tenancies, does not specify that the consent must be in writing.

31 Housing Act 1985, s 94(2) – there is no such restriction in periodic assured tenancy cases.

32 Ibid, s 93(1)(b).

33 *Edwards v Barrington* [1901] 85 LT 650 HL; *Segal Securities Ltd v Thoseby* [1963] 1 QB 887.

proper notice to serve prior to any possession proceedings is a notice seeking possession and *not* a notice to quit (which would not be available anyway for a shared ownership agreement, remaining fixed-term assured tenancy or flexible tenancy, as is clear from **3.61–3.70** which also cautions about the use of the section 146 notice for the reasons raised at **2.69–2.73**).

3.34 To put it another way, the tenancy would continue in its secure/assured/ introductory tenancy form despite the breach of tenancy *unless* the tenant(s) have also themselves moved out such that they can be properly said to no longer live there as their only or principal home (in which case the Housing Acts are of no application in determining the tenancy, and a notice to quit is required in periodic tenancy cases, a section 146 notice and forfeiture otherwise).

3.35 Sub-letting or parting with possession of *part* of the relevant premises is not without some statutory restriction. For secure tenants, section 93 of the Housing Act 1985 provides:

> '(1) It is a term of every secure tenancy that the tenant–
>
> (a) may allow any persons to reside as lodgers in the dwelling-house, but
>
> (b) will not, without the written consent of the landlord, sublet or part with possession of part of the dwelling-house.'

3.36 As for assured *periodic* tenants, section 15 of the Housing Act 1988 provides:

> '(1) Subject to subsection (3) below, it shall be an implied term of every assured tenancy which is a periodic tenancy that, except with the consent of the landlord, the tenant shall not–
>
> (a) assign the tenancy (in whole or in part); or
>
> (b) sub-let or part with possession of the whole or any part of the dwelling-house let on the tenancy.
>
> …
>
> (3) In the case of a periodic tenancy which is not a statutory periodic tenancy or an assured periodic tenancy arising under Schedule 10 to the Local Government and Housing Act 1989 subsection (1) above does not apply if–
>
> (a) there is a provision (whether contained in the tenancy or not) under which the tenant is prohibited (whether absolutely or conditionally) from assigning or sub-letting or parting with possession or is permitted (whether absolutely or conditionally) to assign, sub-let or part with possession; or
>
> (b) a premium is required to be paid on the grant or renewal of the tenancy.'[34]

34 The words 'a statutory periodic tenancy' in sub-section (3) are to be omitted (on a date still to be fixed at the time of writing) by reason of RRA25, Sch 2, para 27.

3.37 It follows that the primary issues, where only part of the premises is subject to investigation and inquiry, are:

(1) Does the tenant(s) still live at the premises as their only or principal home?

(2) If not, security of tenure has been lost whilst that remains the case (as with any only or principal home case) and a notice to quit is required to end the remaining common law tenancy in a periodic tenancy case (see **3.30**) and a section 146 notice otherwise.

(3) If the tenant remains living at the premises, have they the permission of the landlord for any sub-letting or parting with possession *of part*?

(4) If not, this will be a breach of tenancy and a notice seeking possession (periodic secure tenancy/assured tenancy) or section 146 notice (flexible tenancy) could be served as well as a notice seeking possession in reliance on:

- Ground 1 (secure tenancies), 'Rent lawfully due from the tenant has not been paid *or an obligation of the tenancy has been broken or not performed*' (emphasis added); or
- Ground 12 (assured tenancies), 'Any obligation of the tenancy (other than one related to the payment of rent) has been broken or not performed',

to Schedule 2 to the Housing Acts of 1985 and 1988 respectively.

(5) Is it sensible to serve in a periodic tenancy case both a notice to quit and, in the alternative, a notice seeking possession (breach of tenancy), and rely on and plead both in any subsequent possession claim?

(6) This could be especially helpful and appropriate where the evidence for the landlord of misuse of the whole premises is not necessarily compelling, or where the tenant may resume occupation of the premises, in an only or principal home case, prior to the expiry of the notice to quit, thereby coming back under the auspices and protection of the relevant Housing Act, and requiring a notice seeking possession as the first step in any possession claim.

3.38 The concern of landlords with sub-letting or parting with possession of part of the demised premises without consent is primarily the potential to cause problems elsewhere (eg anti-social behaviour of the new occupiers, housing benefit fraud, etc). In any event, as seen above:

- this may be a breach of tenancy warranting the service of a notice seeking possession and/or section 146 notice (and possession proceedings);
- the tenant may not be living at the premises (another breach of tenancy and if security of tenure has been lost – see 'only or principal home' section at **3.23** – may justify the service of a notice to quit section 146 notice);
- this may be a criminal offence pursuant to section 1 or 2 of the Prevention of Social Housing Fraud Act 2013 (see Chapter 7); and
- the arrangement may attract and warrant an unlawful profit order application, whether that be as part of a possession claim, criminal proceedings (see Chapter 7) or by means of separate Part 7 claim (see Chapter 5).

3.39 One of the most striking and stark examples of sub-letting of part was seen in August 2017 in the case of *Poplar HARCA v Begum and anor*.[35] In *Begum*, the tenants had moved away from the demised premises – a two-bedroom flat – and had let it out to a family, save for one of the bedrooms which they kept locked. The Recorder found at trial that the tenants had:

> '… deliberately kept the locked second bedroom at the flat containing toys and a cot as camouflage to deceive the appellant into believing, in the event of an inspection, that they and their children were still living at the flat.'

3.40 Because of the treatment of the second bedroom, the claim for possession based on the notice to quit was not accepted because there had been no parting with possession *of the whole*.

3.41 On appeal, Mr Justice Turner overturned the suspended possession order made by the Recorder on discretionary grounds and instead substituted it with a 21-day outright possession order. He remarked:

> '39. Putting it bluntly, I am entirely satisfied that the Recorder was taken in by the respondents. I make the following observations:
>
> (i) The respondents' case was so clouded by a miasma of lies that there was no evidence to support the Recorder's conclusion that they, with their children, had decided to move in with the first respondent's mother for wholly altruistic reasons. Indeed, on their case, they had never moved in at all.
>
> (ii) If the real reason for moving in were to look after the first respondent's brother, they could have done this without, at the same time, renting out their flat for profit to Ms Rehana and Mr Ahmed.
>
> (iii) It was but a short walk from the flat to the first respondent's home, a fact which further undermines the conclusion that it was necessary for the whole family to decamp completely to allow the first defendant access to attend to her brother when needed.
>
> 40. The fact that the Recorder exercised his discretion on a demonstrably flawed basis means that this Court must exercise that discretion afresh. In doing so, notwithstanding the passage of time since the hearing before the Recorder, I am entirely satisfied that it would be wrong to exercise my discretion to suspend the possession order in this case. In particular, the sheer scale and persistence of the respondent's initial fraudulent deceit aggravated by further and subsequent drug-related offending wholly justifies the condign consequences of an outright order. I would stress that it is not compassionate to allow profiteering fraudsters indefinitely to continue to occupy premises and thereby exclude from such accommodation more needy and deserving families. In particular, in this case, there was a

35 [2017] EWHC 240 (QB), [2017] HLR 42.

complete dearth of material which could amount to cogent evidence that the respondents would mend their ways in future. Accordingly, possession will be granted to take effect in 21 days from the date of this judgment.'

3.42 Whilst not precisely on all fours with the public policy approach towards Grounds 5 and 17 as described in Chapter 2, and there were other (drug) issues present, this authority does stress the high hurdle an errant tenant may have to overcome to avoid an outright possession order, especially if caught breaching their tenancy by moving out and sub-letting or parting with possession of part of the demise.

SHORT-TERM LETS

3.43 How does the above analysis of the law relating to sub-letting and parting with possession apply to short-term letting arrangements, such as are made through companies such as Airbnb and Booking.com? Do they satisfy either definition?

3.44 In *Bermondsey Exchange Freeholders Ltd v Ninos Koumetto (as Trustee in Bankruptcy of Kevin Geoghehan Conway*,[36] HHJ Luba QC, sitting in the County Court at Central London, was faced with an appeal from a long leaseholder in respect of an injunction granted by the court below and which prevented him from letting out his flat on short-term lets. One of the relevant tenant covenants of his agreement relied upon by the freehold owner, the claimant, read as follows:

> 'Not to part with or share possession of the whole of the Demised Premises or permit any company or person to occupy the same save by way of an assignment or underlease of the whole of the Demised Premises.'

3.45 The appeal was substantively dismissed, though there was a probable agreed variation of the injunction, and on the application of the clause referred to above the judge concluded as far as the question of letting was concerned:

> '56. Despite Mr Hanham's attractive submissions that a decision that there had been an 'underletting' was not open to her, I am not satisfied that there were the necessary features here to displace the presumption from Street v Mountford that the provision of exclusive possession of premises to another for a period and for payment for that period constitutes a letting.
>
> 57. *Neither the short duration of the arrangement, nor any notional provision for 'services' (such as leaving the flat stocked with material from which to assemble a breakfast or other meal), nor reservation of a right of entry, nor any combination of those features, displace that presumption from applying to an Airbnb-style arrangement.*' (emphasis added)

36 (2018) EW Misc B10 (CC).

3.46 That conclusion in part relied upon dicta in the Australian case of *Swan v Uecker*[37] at [80] where Croft J was considering whether an Airbnb-type arrangement was properly seen as a licence or letting:

> '… the context provided by the terms of the particular apartment lease are important. Although this apartment lease is a residential lease, many commercial leases restrict the tenant from sub-leasing, assigning the lease, granting any licence to occupy all or part of the leased premises or otherwise parting with possession without the landlord's prior consent. *Broad terms such as this would prevent, for example, sub-letting or licensing without the landlord's consent and would avoid the need – as in the present case – to characterise the nature of the same arrangement like the AirBnB arrangement for occupation of the whole of the leased premises as a sub-lease or a licence.*' (emphasis added)

3.47 Use of demised premises for short-term lets may also represent a (further) breach of tenancy in any event. Two Upper Tribunal (Lands Chamber) cases demonstrate this. First, *Newcova v Fairfield Rents Ltd*[38] concerned a tenant covenant to use the premises as a private residence. HHJ Bridge, whilst warning that each case was fact-specific and depended 'upon the construction of the particular covenant in its own factual context',[39] determined that the First-tier Tribunal (FTT) had been right to find a breach and *crucially* that use as a private residence required occupation 'as a home':[40]

> '53. I have reached the view, consistent with the decision of the Ft T, that the duration of the occupier's occupation is material. It does seem to me that in order for a property to be used as the occupier's private residence, there must be a degree of permanence going beyond being there for a weekend or a few nights in the week. In my judgment, I do not consider that where a person occupies for a matter of days and then leaves it can be said that during the period of occupation he or she is using the property as his or her private residence. The problem in such circumstances is that the occupation is transient, so transient that the occupier would not consider the property he or she is staying in as being his or her private residence even for the time being.'

3.48 The second case was *Triplerose Ltd v Beattie & Beattie*[41] which followed *Nemcova* (the FTT having distinguished it). The Deputy Chamber President, Martin Rodger QC, was faced with a similar covenant and the question:

> 'whether the use of a residential flat for short-term lets breached the covenant not to use or permit the flat to be used "for any purpose other than as a private dwellinghouse for occupation by one family at any one time".'

37 [2016] VSC 313.

38 [2016] UKUT 303 (LC), [2017] 1 P & CR 4.

39 At para 55.

40 Relying in particular on *Caradon District Council v Paton* [2000] 3 EGLR 57, *Tendler v Sproule* [1947] 1 All ER 193 and *Falgor Commercial SA v Alsabahia Inc* [1986] 1 EGLR 41.

41 [2020] UKUT 180 (LC), [2020] HLR 37.

3.49 He rejected the argument that the FTT 'had been wrong to disregard the decision of the Court of Appeal in *Tendler v Sproule*[42] that the taking in of paying guests was a breach of a covenant not to use premises for a business',[43] there in fact being no challenge to the FTT's finding that no trade was being carried on at the premises, but allowed the appeal against the FTT's finding that the short-term lets were not in breach of the covenant whereby there was to be no use other than 'as a private dwellinghouse':

> '32. Whether looked at individually or in combination, the five factors identified by the FTT as distinguishing paragraph 18 from any other prohibition on use other than as a private dwellinghouse or residence, do not justify its conclusion. It is not a case of conferring a right to short term letting or licensing, then taking it away; properly understood, the lease permits only such short term letting as is consistent with use as a private dwellinghouse.
>
> 33. On the facts found by the FTT the individuals who occupied the flat for weekends or other short periods after responding to internet advertisements were not using the flat as a private dwellinghouse for occupation by one family at any one time. By permitting that use Mr and Mrs Beattie were in breach of paragraph 18 of Schedule 4 of their lease. The first ground of appeal is therefore allowed.'

3.50 The conclusion to be drawn from the above paragraphs can be summarised as follows:

(a) Short-term lets *can* be seen as, in law, a sub-letting (as opposed to a lodger arrangement) for the purposes of the Housing Acts 1985 and 1988.

(b) This will be a particular issue where the let is of the whole premises, given that sub-letting and parting with possession of *part* of the premises *will* be allowed with the landlord's consent (not to be unreasonably withheld in secure tenancy cases) either by express provision or sections 93 and 94 of the Housing Act 1985 and section 15 of the Housing Act 1988.

(c) They may also represent other breaches of tenancy, such as any requirement to use the premises as a private residence.

(d) The latter may have particular relevance to shared ownership agreements which frequently contain such covenants.

3.51 Social landlords would be well-advised to make it clear what their position is on short-term lets in their tenancy agreement. This needs to acknowledge, for secure tenancies, that sub-letting or parting with possession of the premises is allowed *with the consent of the landlord* but that sub-letting/ parting with possession of the whole is not and that this latter scenario would

42 [1947] 1 All ER 193.
43 At para 34.

also encompass short-term let arrangements.[44] For assured tenancies, section 15(1) of the Housing Act 1988 is to similar effect save that there is no express provision about consent not being unreasonably withheld.

POSSESSION CLAIMS (PERIODIC TENANCIES)

3.52 The possession claim will usually be issued in the county court[45] and will follow the usual format:

- N5 Claim form;
- N119 Particulars of claim; and
- Annex to particulars of claim.[46]

3.53 There is no reason why claims cannot be pleaded in the alternative (as suggested in **3.37**(5)), and it is the practice of some landlords not to use the N119 Particulars of claim, but to simply draft their own.[47] Whichever approach they adopt – N119 plus annex or separate particulars of claim – this must be served with the N5 Claim form.[48]

3.54 Paragraph 2.1 of Practice Direction 55A states:[49]

> '**2.1** In a possession claim the particulars of claim must:
>
> (1) identify the land to which the claim relates;

44 Housing Act 1985, s 93(1)(b) – note that consent is not to be unreasonably withheld by reason of s 94.

45 PD55A, para 1.1(1) – although para 1.3 goes on to say, '1.3 Circumstances which may, in an appropriate case, justify starting a claim in the High Court are if – (1) there are complicated disputes of fact; (2) there are points of law of general importance; or (3) the claim is against trespassers and there is a substantial risk of public disturbance or of serious harm to persons or property which properly require immediate determination'.

46 PD55A, para 1.5 states: 'The claimant must use the appropriate claim form and particulars of claim form'. This includes the N5 and N119.

47 Though see fn 46 above.

48 CPR 55.4.

49 Also note that CPR 16.4 provides: '16.4 (1) Particulars of claim must include – (a) a concise statement of the facts on which the claimant relies; (b) if the claimant is seeking interest, a statement to that effect and the details set out in paragraph (2); (c) if the claimant is seeking aggravated damages or exemplary damages, a statement to that effect and his grounds for claiming them; (d) if the claimant is seeking provisional damages, a statement to that effect and his grounds for claiming them; and (e) such other matters as may be set out in a practice direction.

(2) If the claimant is seeking interest he must – (a) state whether he is doing so – (i) under the terms of a contract; (ii) under an enactment and if so which; or (iii) on some other basis and if so what that basis is; and (b) if the claim is for a specified amount of money, state – (i) the percentage rate at which interest is claimed; (ii) the date from which it is claimed; (iii) the date to which it is calculated, which must not be later than the date on which the claim form is issued; (iv) the total amount of interest claimed to the date of calculation; and (v) the daily rate at which interest accrues after that date. (Part 22 requires particulars of claim to be verified by a statement of truth.)'.

(2) state whether the claim relates to residential property;

(3) state the ground on which possession is claimed;

(4) give full details about any mortgage or tenancy agreement; and

(5) give details of every person who, to the best of the claimant's knowledge, is in possession of the property.

Residential property let on a tenancy

2.2 Paragraphs 2.3 to 2.4B apply if the claim relates to residential property let on a tenancy.

2.3 If the claim includes a claim for non-payment of rent the particulars of claim must set out:

(1) the amount due at the start of the proceedings;

(2) in schedule form, the dates and amounts of all payments due and payments made under the tenancy agreement for a period of two years immediately preceding the date of issue, or if the first date of default occurred less than two years before the date of issue from the first date of default and a running total of the arrears;

(3) the daily rate of any rent and interest;

(4) any previous steps taken to recover the arrears of rent with full details of any court proceedings; and

(5) any relevant information about the defendant's circumstances, in particular:

 (a) whether the defendant is in receipt of social security benefits; and

 (b) whether any payments are made on his behalf directly to the claimant under the Social Security Contributions and Benefits Act 1992.

2.3A If the claimant wishes to rely on a history of arrears which is longer than two years, he should state this in his particulars and exhibit a full (or longer) schedule to a witness statement.

2.4 If the claimant knows of any person (including a mortgagee) entitled to claim relief against forfeiture as underlessee under section 146(4) of the Law of Property Act 1925 (or in accordance with section 38 of the Senior Courts Act 1981, or section 138(9C) of the County Courts Act 1984):

(1) the particulars of claim must state the name and address of that person; and

(2) the claimant must file a copy of the particulars of claim for service on him.

> **2.4A** If the claim for possession relates to the conduct of the tenant, the particulars of claim must state details of the conduct alleged.
>
> **2.4B** If the possession claim relies on a statutory ground or grounds for possession, the particulars of claim must specify the ground or grounds relied on.'

3.55 It is also worth noting the 'warning' frequently given by the courts, as seen recently in *Paul Byrne & anor v William George James Arthur & anor*,[50] where HHJ Richard Williams (sitting as a Judge of the High Court) cited from *Civil Fraud* (1st edn):

> '*The second aspect is that any allegation of fraud must be made clearly, unequivocally and with sufficient particularity so that the defendant understands the case he is required to meet. As we note below, the representation which is said to have been made fraudulently will need to be identified with precision (something that is particularly important where the representation is said to be implicit or derived from conduct).* As to the mental element of the tort, these requirements do not necessarily mean that the word "fraud" or "dishonesty" has to be used, since the facts alleged may be consistent only with an allegation of fraud; but if those facts are also consistent with innocence, then the pleader must make it plain that fraud is alleged. *It bears note that the common formula "the Defendant knew or ought to have known" is not sufficient for these purposes, since it is treated as being a composite allegation of constructive knowledge with an allegation of actual knowledge with an allegation of constructive knowledge in the alternative.*' (emphasis added)

3.56 As for the pleading of any claim, an example is set out below:

Example Annex to Particulars of Claim (N119 should be used as well and reference the Annex)

Introduction

1. The claimant is a private registered provider of social housing and the freehold owner of 7 Best Avenue, Charlton, BC9 7GG ('the premises'), a three-bedroom house. On 1 May 2015 they entered into an assured non-shorthold periodic tenancy agreement ('the Agreement') with the defendant in respect of the (residential) premises, to commence on 4 May 2015. A copy of the said agreement and current conditions is attached at Exhibit A.

50 [2025] EWHC 1136 (Ch) at para 144. It is long established that the primary facts relied upon to justify the inference of dishonesty/fraud must be pleaded along with the allegation itself: see, for example, *Crypto Open Patent Alliance v Wright* [2023] EWHC 2642 (Ch), [2024] 1 All ER 1104 (Comm) at paras 39–41.

2. The defendant was born on 20 June 1982 and at the commencement of his tenancy stated, as contained in the Agreement, that he would reside there with his partner and two children, then aged four and two years.

3. The weekly rent at the premises was £83.15 at the tenancy's commencement and would now be £92.10 per week if the tenancy had persisted. Use and occupation charges in respect of the same are currently £13.16 per day.

4. As at the date this claim is being prepared, 5 October 2025, the rent/use and occupation account is in arrears in the sum of £3,412.55. A Schedule of Account detailing the said arrears is attached at Exhibit B.

Grounds for possession

5. Possession of the premises is being sought on the primary basis that:
   (a) The defendant sub-let the whole of the premises to Ms Tyra Moss.
   (b) This arrangement commenced on or around 6 November 2023 to on or around 20 September 2024.

6. The defendant thereby permanently lost security of tenure pursuant to section 15A(1) and (2) of the Housing Act 1988 (and in any event security of tenure was lost pursuant to section 1(1)(b) of the Housing Act 1988).

7. A notice to quit served on the premises in accordance with clause 6.1 of the agreement on 19 July 2024 brought the remaining common law tenancy to an end at its expiry. A copy of the said notice is attached at Exhibit C with a certificate of service.

8. In the alternative, the claimant relies on Ground 12 of Schedule 2 to the Housing Act 1988:

   'Any obligation of the tenancy (other than one related to the payment of rent) has been broken or not performed.'

9. A notice seeking possession was served on the premises – a copy of the said notice is attached at Exhibit D with a certificate of service – in accordance with clause 6.1 of the agreement on 19 July 2024 and the breaches of tenancy alleged are clause 3.1 and clause 3.3 of the Agreement:

   '3.1 The tenant shall live at the premises as their only or principal home.'

   '3.3 The tenant shall not sub-let or part with possession of the premises at any time save that so long as they comply with clause 3.1:

   (a) They may have a lodger if the premises are a two-bedroom property or above, or

   (b) They may sub-let or part with possession of part of the premises only with the express and prior written agreement of the landlord.'

10. Insofar as paragraphs 5 to 7 above are not made out, the claimant maintains:
    (a) The tenant has at times during the tenancy not lived at the premises as his only or principal home. This is a breach of clause 3.1 of the agreement.
    (b) Further, or in the alternative, he has at times sub-let part of the premises, in particular to Ms Tyra Moss, without obtaining the prior consent of the claimant. This is in breach of clause 3.3(b) of the agreement.

11. For the avoidance of doubt, paragraphs 5 to 7 above represent the claimant's primary position, with paragraphs 8 to 10 being their case in the alternative.

Relevant matters

12. The defendant was interviewed under caution by Charlton District Council on 2 September 2024. He admitted that he and his family had been living in alternative accommodation since early November 2023. He denied that he had sub-let or was sub-letting the Premises to Ms Tyra Moss but admitted that she lived there. He said she was a family friend who did not pay rent and that he had moved out of the premises temporarily because of his partner's employment.

13. The claimant believes the defendant returned to live at the premises with his family on or around 20 September 2024 and required Ms Moss to leave forthwith (which she did).

14. Insofar as the claimant is required to rely on Ground 12, it is averred that it would be reasonable to make a possession order, and that such an order should be outright, because:
    (a) Social housing is a scarce resource, especially in the borough in which the premises are located.
    (b) Even if only part of the premises was sub-let, then this may be an offence pursuant to section 2 of the Prevention of Social Housing Fraud Act 2013.
    (c) There are currently 1,232 households on the waiting list of the local authority who nominate to the claimant's properties for three-bedroom accommodation.
    (d) The defendant has not been open or forthcoming with the claimant or the local authority investigating this matter.

15. There is no underlessee or mortgagee entitled to claim relief from forfeiture.

Unlawful profit order

16. The claimant also seeks an unlawful profit order pursuant to section 5 of the Prevention of Social Housing Fraud Act 2013. In particular, the claimant satisfies the requirements for such an order provided for at section 5(4) of the said Act:

(a) the claimant is a private registered provider of social housing;
(b) the tenancy between the parties is not a shared ownership lease;
(c) in breach of an express or implied term of the tenancy, the defendant has sub-let or parted with possession of the whole or part of the premises;
(d) the defendant ceased to occupy the premises as their only or principal home; and
(e) the defendant received money because of the conduct described in paragraph (c).

17. Attached to this annex, at Exhibit E, is a schedule detailing the unlawful profit order sought by the claimant. It confirms:
    (a) The relevant sub-letting period is from 6 November 2023 to 20 September 2024.
    (b) During that period, the defendant received £7,000 from Ms Moss.
    (c) During the same period, the claimant received £2,300 from the defendant, purporting to be rent.

18. The appropriate sum therefore sought by the claimant is £4,700.00.

19. The claimant also seeks interest on such sum pursuant to section 69 of the County Courts Act 1984 for such period and at such a rate as the court shall deem fit.

AND the claimant claims:

1. Possession of the premises.
2. A judgment for arrears of rent and/or use and occupation.
3. An unlawful profit order.
4. An order that the defendant pay use and occupation charges until possession of the premises is given up.
5. Interest pursuant to section 69 of the County Courts Act 1984.
6. Costs.

Statement of truth

[I believe] [the (claimant or as may be) believes] that the facts stated in this [name document being verified] are true. [I understand] [The (claimant or as may be) understands] that proceedings for contempt of court may be brought against anyone who makes, or causes to be made, a false statement in a document verified by a statement of truth without an honest belief in its truth.

3.57 If the mandatory claim succeeds (eg sub-letting of the whole is found) then the court's powers are limited in the order it can make. Section 89 of the Housing Act 1980 allows a 14-day maximum for any order unless exceptional hardship can be shown by the defendant, in which case that period can be extended for up to six weeks:

'89. Restriction on discretion of court in making orders for possession of land.

(1) Where a court makes an order for the possession of any land in a case not falling within the exceptions mentioned in subsection (2) below, the giving up of possession shall not be postponed (whether by the order or any variation, suspension or stay of execution) to a date later than fourteen days after the making of the order, unless it appears to the court that exceptional hardship would be caused by requiring possession to be given up by that date; and shall not in any event be postponed to a date later than six weeks after the making of the order.

(2) The restrictions in subsection (1) above do not apply if–

(a) the order is made in an action by a mortgagee for possession; or

(b) the order is made in an action for forfeiture of a lease; or

(c) the court had power to make the order only if it considered it reasonable to make it; or

(d) the order relates to a dwelling-house which is the subject of a restricted contract (within the meaning of section 19 of the 1977 Act); or

(e) the order is made in proceedings brought as mentioned in section 88(1) above.'

3.58 An order for possession in such a case would normally read along the following lines:

Example Possession Order (based on a notice to quit)

1. The defendant do give the claimant possession of [the premises] on or before [date] *or* forthwith. This is a mandatory ground.
2. There be judgment for the claimant against the defendant in the sum of £x in respect of rent/use and occupation arrears, and the defendant do pay the claimant use and occupation charges at the daily rate of £x from [date of order] until possession is given up.
3. There be an unlawful profit order against the defendant in the sum of £x, including interest.
4. The defendant do pay the claimant's costs summarily assessed at £x (assuming a fast-track/one-day trial[51] – otherwise, they are likely to go off for detailed assessment, if not agreed). If the defendant is legally aided, then the following will be added:

   '... to be subject to a determination of the defendant's ability to pay such costs pursuant to section 26 of the Legal Aid, Sentencing

51 PD44, para 9.2.

and Punishment of Offenders Act 2012, such determination to be adjourned generally with permission to restore.

5. There be a detailed assessment of the defendant's legal aid costs *(if the defendant is legally aided).*

3.59 As can be seen from the example Particulars of Claim, one argument that is sometimes used in possession claims by a landlord in cases where the tenant retains security of tenure, and as such questions of reasonableness arise, is that misuse of social housing stock is an especially serious matter. It may even represent an offence, such as under the Prevention of Social Housing Fraud Act 2013.[52]

3.60 Here, the more 'hard-line' approach, such as can be seen from the Grounds 5 and 17 cases described at Chapter 2 and at **3.39–3.42**, is *prima facie* appropriate.

SHARED OWNERSHIP

3.61 Shared ownership arrangements have always looked to Schedule 1 to either the Housing Act of 1985 or 1988 (ie depending upon the landlord, local authority or, as is more commonly the case, a housing association) to determine whether they are excluded or not from the relevant statutory protection and oversight. Most shared ownership arrangements have as a result, prior to the RRA25 reforms, been assured shorthold tenancies.

3.62 Despite recent argument[53] as to the extent of application of long lease legislation to these tenancies, such as the Commonhold and Leasehold Reform Act 2002, the RRA25 has ended much of this debate by the amendment of Schedule 1 to the Housing Act 1988 so as to have the effect of excluding shared ownership agreements from assured tenancy status (excepting some cases where a notice seeking possession or possession proceedings/order were present at the time of the legislation's commencement – see fn 1 above) – they are, in effect, long leases.

3.63 This means that recovery of premises subject to shared ownership agreements, because of breaches of lease concerning sub-letting/parting with possession activity, is by the usual forfeiture route described below, with the additional requirement that a section 168(4) declaration, as referenced in **3.65**, is first required. It also means that the common preference to seek enforcement by way of injunction rather than possession is likely to be even more worth considering.

52 Section 1 or 2 – see Chapter 7.

53 See, for example, *Avon Ground Rents Ltd v Canary Gateway (Block A) RTM Co Ltd* [2023] EWCA Civ 616, [2023] 1 WLR 3516.

FORFEITURE: FLEXIBLE TENANCIES

3.64 If one is considering a flexible tenancy, and noting that, as referenced in the previous paragraph, an injunction application is a possible option to ensure compliance with a term of the agreement, then if security of tenure has been lost, the remedy for the landlord is usually by way of forfeiture proceedings (that remains the case for remaining private registered providers of social housing fixed-term assured tenancies pending the RRA25 reform implementation – see fn 45 in Chapter 2). Some of the issues concerning these forms of tenancy are set out in Chapter 2 at **2.63–2.75**. *This also includes the approach in discretionary ground cases (which will apply in breach of tenancy cases where security of tenure is maintained, such as where the sub-letting or parting with possession is of part only of the premises) where a notice seeking possession will be served along with a section 146 notice.*

3.65 Turning back to no security of tenure cases, possession action is necessarily by way of forfeiture (as is the case for shared ownership matters pre- and post-RRA25 where there is no security of tenure), following service of a section 146 notice (and not following service of a notice to quit). The usual requirements for a landlord to obtain a determination from the First-tier Tribunal (Property Chamber) as to the breach of agreement, pursuant to section 168(4) of the Commonhold and Leasehold Reform Act 2002, before they can issue the required section 146 notice, is not required in flexible tenancy cases as this provision only applies to long leases.

3.66 Turning briefly again to shared ownership cases, the RRA25 has meant that, save for a small number of agreements made prior to this Act's commencement (see fn 1 and **3.61–3.63** above), these are all to be treated as long leases, whether or not the tenant has staircased to 100%.[54]

3.67 What is clear, from *Scala House & District Property Company Ltd v Forbes and others*,[55] is that a breach of covenant not to assign underlet or part with possession is *not* a breach capable of remedy within the meaning of section 146(1) of the Law of Property Act 1925. Lord Justice Russell said in this regard:[56]

> 'After this review of the cases I come to the conclusion that *breach by an unlawful subletting is not capable of remedy at all*. In my judgment the introduction of such breaches into the relevant section for the first time by section 146 of the Act of 1925 operates only to confer a statutory ability to relieve the lessee from forfeiture on that ground. The subterm has been effectively created subject only to risks of forfeiture: *it is a complete breach*

54 In any event, in 2023 the Court of Appeal in *Avon Ground Rents Ltd v Canary Gateway (Block A) RTM Co Ltd* [2023] EWCA Civ 616, [2023] 1 WLR 3516, a right to manage case, held that a tenant with a shared ownership lease 'granted for a term of years certain exceeding 21 years' had a 'long lease' within the meaning of Commonhold and Leasehold Reform Act 2002, s 76, regardless of whether they had acquired a 100% interest in the property.

55 [1973] 3 WLR 14.

56 Ibid at [588]–[589].

> *once and for all: it is not in any sense a continuing breach.* If the law were otherwise a lessee, when a subtenancy is current at the time of the section 146 notice, would have a chance of remedying the situation without having to apply for relief. *But if the unlawful subletting had been determined before the notice, the lessee could only seek relief from forfeiture.* The only escape from that wholly unsatisfactory difference would be to hold that in the second example by some analogy the lessor was disabled from issuing a writ for possession. But I can find nothing in the section to justify that limitation on the common law right of re-entry, bearing especially in mind that a lessor might discover a whole series of past expired unlawful sublettings which might well justify a refusal to grant relief in forfeiture proceedings.
>
> I stress again that where there has been an unlawful subletting which has determined (and which has not been waived) there has been a breach which at common law entitles the lessor to re-enter: nothing can be done to remedy that breach: the expiry of the subterm has not annulled or remedied the breach: in such case the lessor plainly need not, in his section 146 notice, call upon the lessee to remedy the breach which is not capable of remedy, and is free to issue his writ for possession, the possibility of relief remaining. Can it possibly be that, while that is the situation in such case, it is otherwise if the lessee has failed to get rid of the subterm until after a notice served? Is the lessee then in a stronger position and the lessor in a weaker position? In my judgment not so. These problems and questions arise only if such a breach is capable of remedy, which in my judgment it is not. I consider that *Capital & Counties Property Co. Ltd. v. Mills* [1966] E.G.D. 96, if correctly reported, was wrongly decided. I should add that I find some support for my opinion in the comments of Fraser J. in *Abrahams v. Mac Fisheries Ltd.* [1925] 2 K.B. 18, *35, who expressed the view that the exceptions in section 14 (6) of the Act of 1881 (as to, inter alia,* subletting) were made to cover cases where the breach cannot be remedied specifically.' (emphasis added)

3.68 The usual forfeiture issues such as waiver, as noted by Russell LJ, may therefore be relevant in preventing a landlord from relying on any sub-letting/parting with possession breach (not least, of course, where the complained of activity has ceased), though the irredeemable nature of the breach means that this is less likely to happen 'by accident'.

3.69 If relief from forfeiture is granted this may be conditional, and is in any event difficult to achieve (though in no consent cases for partial sub-letting/parting with possession cases, the question of whether the landlord *would* have granted permission if asked, or could not reasonably have withheld consent, may well be relevant).[57]

57 *West Layton Ltd v Ford (Executrix of the Estate of Louis Joseph, deceased) and another* [1979] QB 593.

3.70 For the sake of accuracy, it should also be noted that, in *Scala House*, relief from forfeiture was given. Part of the rationale for this was:[58]

> 'Third: as I have indicated, the defendants did unscramble the situation in June by an agreement which involved surrender of the subtenancy and a discontinuance of any parting with possession. The agreement envisages the possibility of a future assignment of the lease by the first defendant to the second and third defendants, and erroneously provided that if that should happen the second and third defendants, in addition to continuing to pay the £25 to £35 weekly to the first defendant, should also bear the rent under the lease which hitherto has, of course, been borne by the first defendant. This was admittedly an error in drafting: it was intended that the first defendant in effect should continue to bear the lease rent by equivalent reduction of the weekly payments. This error, which remains in the documents, I record.'

EVIDENCE

3.71 It is frequently the case that evidence in support of any sub-letting or parting with possession case is, initially at least, perceived as being limited and inconclusive. Where a sole tenant of a one-bedroom flat has been found to be sub-letting and evidence is available of the tenancy agreement they entered into with the sub-tenant, which contains an address for the tenant other than the demised premises, this makes for an easy case that is not the norm.

3.72 More usually, there are suggestions and indications of such activity – neighbour reports of other persons living at the premises (or, conversely, a lack of any sighting of the tenant and/or other expected household members), contractors and repair operatives finding persons other than the tenant answering the door when they visit the premises, etc. Chapter 6 gives further details as to measures that may be taken by a landlord to improve their chances of evidential success in any legal action they take.

3.73 To give one well-known example, in *Hussey v London Borough of Camden*,[59] the local authority argued that their tenant had sub-let his local authority flat to the second defendant whilst he lived elsewhere. Indeed, the trial judge found:

(a) That the tenant *had* occupied other premises as his only or principal home in the latter part of 1986 and 1987.

(b) The only person shown on the electoral register for the relevant premises in 1987 was the second defendant.

(c) From 1989 to 1990 the tenant occupied yet another flat as his principal residence.

58 *Scala House* at [590] *per* Russell LJ.
59 (1995) 27 HLR 5.

(d) The tenant had thereby lost security of tenure, and therefore the judge made a possession order.

3.74 There was, however, no evidence of any tenancy agreement between the first and second defendants or that rent was paid, and also there was no evidence that the first defendant did not occupy the flat as his only or principal home on the expiry of the notice to quit, which had not been served by the plaintiffs until January 1991.

3.75 In allowing the tenant's appeal, Lord Justice Leggatt was compelled to remark:[60]

> 'It is obvious that from time to time others were in sole occupation of it, but it does not follow that they enjoyed exclusive possession. Mr Hussey's right to enter and use the premises if and when he chose was not negatived. There might have been proof that he gave up his key, or of the manner in which rent was paid either to him by another or by another in his stead. There was no such evidence.
>
> In my judgment the vital ingredient necessary to prove that Mr Hussey had ceased to be a secure tenant, that he had for some period or periods parted with possession of 10 Brockham House, was simply not proved either by direct evidence or by way of inference from the proven facts. Even though, for some periods, he did cease to occupy 10 Brockham House as his principal home, he was not shown to have parted with possession of it. Since there was no evidence that Mr Hussey was not occupying the flat as his only or principal home upon expiry of the notice to quit, despite his absence in Greece, the tenant condition was satisfied and the possession order ought not to have been made.'

3.76 In short, the trial judge had asked himself the wrong question and did not apply his mind to the right one – whether for any period before January 1991 (the time of the notice to quit) the first defendant had sub-let or parted with possession of his flat; this defect could not on the findings as presented be corrected by way of direct or 'inference evidence'.

3.77 Some 10 years later, Lord Justice Mummery addressed the issue of a lack of direct evidence again, in *Lambeth LBC v Vandra*:[61]

> '8. In my judgment, the fact that there is another possible explanation for the state of affairs found by the housing officer does not mean that there was no evidence or insufficient evidence for the inferences made by the district judge as to subletting of the whole. The absence of direct evidence is not fatal. Judges are entitled, when finding facts, to make inferences as a matter of probability from the primary facts which are established.'

60 Ibid at [11].
61 [2005] EWCA Civ 1801, [2006] HLR 19.

3.78 In *Vandra,* the so-called primary facts were:

(a) The tenant was not in occupation of the premises on either of the authority's two visits.

(b) Conversely, five other people were seen at the premises at these two visits.

(c) There was no evidence or signs of occupation by Miss Vandra and her four children.

(d) There were Yale locks on all rooms (and an additional padlock on one).

(e) There were no signs of any room being used as a living room.

(f) Four of the occupants said they paid rent to Kim (the name of Miss Vandra's caretaker).

3.79 The Court of Appeal found that the authority was entitled to claim that an explanation was called for from Miss Vandra as to why she was not at the premises, and why others were paying to be there. The district judge, in turn, at the trial had been entitled to reject her explanations. The authority's appeal was allowed and the district judge's possession order restored.

3.80 These two authorities illustrate that the court must direct itself to the right questions. For example:

(a) Has the tenant sub-let or parted with possession of the whole? If so and a valid notice to quit has been properly served, then a possession order should be made. It is irrelevant in such circumstances if the 'tenant' has returned to live at the premises.

(b) If not, have they sub-let or parted with possession of *part* of the demised premises?

(c) If so, was this in breach of tenancy (ie without consent)? Would it be reasonable – in reliance on a notice seeking possession[62] – to make a possession order (and should that order be suspended on terms or made outright)?

(d) If there was any sub-letting or parting with possession of part *and* the tenant(s) were not themselves living at the premises as their only or principal home at the time of the expiry date in any valid notice to quit properly served then security of tenure is lost and a possession order should be made.

(e) Lack of direct evidence (eg tenancy agreement between the tenant and sub-tenant) is not necessarily fatal to any possession claim.

(d) The stronger the evidence, the more likely it is that the '*tenant*' is going to be required by the court to explain away the seemingly compelling evidence.

62 Although the court has the power to dispense with the requirement for such a notice if they consider it just and equitable to do so – Housing Act 1985, s 83(1)(b) (secure tenancies)/ Housing Act 1988, s 8(1)(b) (assured tenancies).

3.81 Chapter 6 deals with the question of investigation and evidence in more focused detail, while Chapter 7 covers criminal sanctions including those flowing from sub-letting or parting with possession activities.

SUB-TENANTS' RIGHTS

3.82 It is well-established that a possession action is one *in rem* not *in personam*. That simply means that if an outright order is made then all persons in occupation of the subject premises at the time of enforcement – tenants, household members, sub-tenants, etc – will be required to leave. If a social landlord therefore secures a possession order against their tenant(s) because of sub-letting, then it impacts upon the sub-tenant every bit as much as, if not more than in practice, on the tenant. So, what can the sub-tenant do?

3.83 They will not be able to move back into the premises (unless the claimant landlord allows them to, which would, to say the least, be highly unlikely). Can they take action against their landlord, the (now former) tenant? The obvious cause of action would be a damages claim for a breach of the covenant for quiet enjoyment (and/or in certain cases, a claim under sections 27 and 28 of the Housing Act 1988).

3.84 In *Brem v Murray*[63] *a* tenant who had 'stood by' while his sub-tenant was evicted from her home by his landlord was found to be not liable in damages to the sub-tenant for breach of the covenant of quiet enjoyment. The reasoning was that the covenant did not protect against intrusion and disturbance by persons other than an immediate landlord, and it did not impose upon the immediate landlord any positive obligation to stop intrusions or disturbances by anybody else.[64]

3.85 However, that case would only be relevant if the superior landlord had unlawfully entered the premises (thereby potentially incurring a tortious liability towards the displaced sub-tenant). In the possession order scenario, that would not, of course, be the case, and the breach of the covenant for quiet enjoyment damages claim against the tenant landlord would resume its place as the obvious remedy to the displaced former sub-tenant.

CONCLUSION

3.86 If sub-letting or parting with possession is properly evidenced then there are obvious remedies available to the landlord, both in terms of possession of the premises and, at times, recovery of compensation and other monies (as addressed further in Chapters 5 and 7).

63 [2022] EWHC 1479 (QB), [2023] 2 P & CR 13.
64 See *Westlaw* Case Digest.

3.87 When it is obvious that someone other than the tenant(s) has been living at the premises then there are often questions as to the nature of the third-party occupation – family friend 'loose' arrangement, legitimate 'caretaker' scenario in the enforced absence of the tenant abroad, in prison, etc, temporary 'let', unpaid scenario or, of course, a true and actionable sub-let.

3.88 Evidence is, of course, key as to the true nature of the occupation, but it may in any event be such as to, if not shift the burden of proof to the tenant, at least require an explanation as to the apparent improper use of the premises.

3.89 Possession claims pleaded in the alternative (eg by way of notice to quit *and* notice seeking possession in an assured tenancy case) are not uncommon as the true facts may remain unclear pre-trial. As if to highlight the inherent problems of accuracy and consistency in many cases (not least between tenant and sub-tenant), Mr Justice Turner remarked somewhat witheringly in a non-housing case, *McClelland v Elvin*:[65]

> '31 … The murky absence of documentary formality formed a background against which both the claimant and defendant appeared for much of the time to have assumed the roles of determined competitors in an implausibility contest.'

3.90 Finally, as with many of the civil scenarios dealt with in this book, criminal sanctions may also apply alongside the civil remedies sought for sub-letting or parting with possession. See Chapter 7 for further details.

65 [2017] EWHC 2795 (QB).

CHAPTER 4

Only or Principal Home/Succession

- Not using premises as main home
- Succession to tenancy
- Late appeal/set aside

Key points

- To retain security of tenure, a tenant – or at least one of the joint tenants – must live at the demised premises as their only or principal home.
- However, occupation by a spouse or civil partner is to be treated as occupation by the tenant for these purposes.
- A tenant can go in and out of security of tenure (although this may constitute a breach of tenancy), as long as they do not sub-let or part with possession of the whole of the premises; if the premises in a periodic tenancy scenario are not their only or principal home upon the expiration date specified in a properly served and valid notice to quit, then security is lost permanently from that date.
- Conversely, if the tenant has not sub-let or parted with possession of the whole and returns to live at the premises *prior* to the expiry of any notice to quit then they will have acted in breach of their tenancy by living away, and possession action can be taken on discretionary grounds for breach of tenancy in reliance on a notice seeking possession (periodic tenancy or any remaining assured fixed term) or forfeiture and notice seeking possession (flexible tenancy) – see **2.63–2.75** and **3.64–3.70**.
- In addition, any remaining assured fixed-term tenancies may have a break clause that can be operated to end the tenancy.
- A social landlord can extend the statutory rights of succession beyond the basic statutory provision for spouses and civil partners (and those living together as such) – see **4.24–4.32** below.
- A set aside or late appeal may be available to a landlord where the fraud is discovered *after* initial court determination.
- See **3.3** for a 'round-up' of security of tenure issues.

INTRODUCTION

4.1 The previous chapters have dealt with the most obvious social housing fraud topics: obtaining the property by misrepresentation (including omission) and sub-letting or parting with possession of the whole or part of the premises. Here we address the issues of:

(a) the tenant not living in the allocated property as their only or principal home;

(b) 'fraudulent' succession to a social tenancy; and

(c) late appeals/set aside of orders.

4.2 Whilst the only or principal home topic does not necessarily indicate fraud in the strict sense, it is certainly 'misuse' of premises (not simply as an undoubted breach of tenancy but also by way of preventing its use by some other person or family in housing need) and relevant as a concept elsewhere in any event (eg when dealing with unlawful profit orders).[1]

4.3 As was made clear in Chapter 3, sub-letting the whole of premises – or parting with possession of the same – is an obvious example of the tenant not living there as their only or principal home. This chapter goes on to address situations which are, perhaps, not so straightforward and sets out the important principles in issue, including by way of decided court authorities. Any possession claim alleging no succession or a loss of security of tenure by an existing tenant will, in broad terms and as discussed in Chapters 2 and 3, be by way of primary reliance on a properly served notice to quit (periodic tenancies), or notice seeking possession in reliance on a statutory ground for possession, such as the mandatory Ground 7 for assured tenancies,[2] or use of the forfeiture or section 90 procedure (devolution of term certain) in flexible tenancy cases (see examples at **3.64** and **4.36**).

ONLY OR PRINCIPAL HOME

Overview

4.4 It is invariably an express, but in any event an implied,[3] term of secure and assured tenancies that the tenant(s) must live in the demised premises as their only or principal home. Chapter 3 explains this, in particular at **3.3** and **3.23–3.25**. To re-cap:

1 See Chapter 5.

2 At the time of writing, Ground 7 reads: 'The tenancy is a periodic tenancy (including a statutory periodic tenancy), or a fixed term tenancy of a dwelling-house in England, which has devolved under the will or intestacy of the former tenant and the proceedings for the recovery of possession are begun not later than twelve months after the death of the former tenant or, if the court so directs, after the date on which, in the opinion of the court, the landlord or, in the case of joint landlords, any one of them became aware of the former tenant's death'. See **4.36**(c). The ground is subject to revisions to be brought in by Renters' Rights Act 2025, Sch 1, para 23.

3 Housing Act 1985, s 81 (secure tenancies)/Housing Act 1988, s1(1)(b) (assured tenancies).

(a) The requirement for the tenant to live at the demised premises as their only or principal home is ambulatory[4] such that, whilst security of tenure may be lost during periods of absence, it is capable of being regained as long as:

- the tenant has not sub-let or parted with possession of the whole of the premises (in which case, security of tenure is, as shown in Chapter 3, permanently lost); and

- the tenant, in a periodic tenancy case, returns to live at the said premises prior to the expiry of any valid notice to quit properly served.[5]

(b) If it is a joint tenancy, as long as one of the joint tenants lives at the premises then it is irrelevant and of no effect, for security of tenure purposes, if the others do not. The importance of this principle can be seen in *Haringey LBC v Ahmed & Anor*[6] where the local authority sought possession following the service of a notice to quit.

The husband had signed a first tenancy agreement, a second tenancy agreement was then signed by him and his mother (the mother later serving a notice of termination), and a third just by the mother. Ultimately both the husband and then the mother left the premises and the local authority served a notice to quit re the third tenancy.

When the authority sought possession the trial judge held that the husband had been acting as his wife's agent when he entered into the first agreement and that they were therefore still joint tenants, such that the possession claim failed.

The Court of Appeal rejected this conclusion and allowed the local authority's appeal, and held that there was no conduct from which it could reasonably be inferred that the husband had acted as his wife's agent in relation to the first tenancy agreement; the first tenancy was a sole tenancy in the husband's name.

This is all in the context of appeals against findings of fact being treated with caution by the appellate courts, Hamblen LJ acknowledging:

> '31. In summary, such interference will only be justified where a critical finding of fact is unsupported by the evidence or where the decision is one which no reasonable judge could have reached.'

(c) If the tenant's spouse or civil partner lives at the premises rather than the tenant themselves then that is treated as occupation by the tenant until the formal ending of those arrangements (eg divorce). Section 30(4) of the Family Law Act 1996[7] provides (with A as the tenant and B as the spouse/ civil partner):

4 *Crawley Borough Council v Sawyer* (1987) 20 HLR 98, CA.
5 See *Hussey v Camden LBC* (1995) 27 HLR 5 at [7]–[8] *per* Leggatt LJ.
6 [2017] EWCA Civ 1861, [2018] HLR 9.
7 Amended by the Civil Partnership Act 2004, Sch 9 and the Renting Homes (Wales) Act 2016 (Consequential Amendments) Regulations 2022, SI 2022/1166.

'(4) B's occupation by virtue of this section–

...

(b) if B occupies the dwelling-house as B's only or principal home, is to be treated, for the purposes of the Housing Act 1985, Part I of the Housing Act 1988, Chapter 1 of Part 5 of the Housing Act 1996, the Prevention of Social Housing Fraud Act 2013 and the Renting Homes (Wales) Act 2016, as occupation by A as A's only or principal home.'

4.5 In relation to the last point, it followed that in *Derwent Housing Association v Taylor*,[8] where the tenant wife left the demised premises whilst her non-tenant husband remained, she still had to serve a notice to quit to bring the tenancy to an end:[9]

> '11 It follows, in my judgement, that as a matter of interpretation of the Family Law Act, 1996, B has no home rights once A has validly terminated the tenancy. I do not consider that this conclusion is called in question by the Human Rights Act 1988 . B has, of course, the right under art.8 of the European Convention on Human Rights and Fundamental Freedoms to respect for his home. In *Sims v Dacorum Borough Council* [2015] UKSC 63; [2015] AC 133 the Supreme Court decided that the common law rule which enabled one of two joint tenants to terminate a periodic tenancy by notice to quit without the consent of the other was not incompatible with art. 8 or with art. 1 of the First Protocol. The ability of the sole tenant to terminate the tenancy without the consent of her spouse is, in my judgment, an even stronger case. However, as the Supreme Court held in *Simms*, B would, at least in principle, be entitled to raise the proportionality of his eviction, thus giving effect to art. 8. That has not thus far been raised in this case, and whether such an argument would succeed is, of course, a different matter. For these reasons, I would dismiss the appeal.'

4.6 In that case the husband had unsuccessfully argued that once his wife had left the marital home he had, in effect, become the tenant such that her notice to quit was of no effect. This submission was given short shrift by the Court of Appeal who reminded the parties that the Family Law Act 1996 was merely regulating the rights of spouses *as between themselves*.[10]

4.7 As an aside, it is open to a landlord and tenant to agree to waive the requirements of section 5(1)(b) of the Protection from Eviction Act 1977[11] (four weeks' notice to quit):[12]

8 [2016] EWCA Civ 508, [2016] HLR 25.

9 For there to be a surrender of a joint tenancy, all tenants must agree to the surrender: see **4.7**, *Greenwich LBC v McGready* (1983) 6 HLR 36 at [40] and the *Sanctuary* case at fn 10.

10 See *Sanctuary Housing Association v Campbell* [1999] 1 WLR 1279 concerning the 1996 Act's predecessor, the Matrimonial Homes Act 1983.

11 Section 5 is to be amended in respect of assured tenancies at the time of writing by reason of Renters' Rights Act 2025, s 20 with particular reference to a tenant's notice to quit being 'extended' to two months in the absence of any agreement.

12 *Hackney LBC v Snowden* (2001) 33 HLR 49, para 22 *per* Peter Gibson LJ.

> 'It is open to the landlord and the tenant, for whose sole benefit section 5 of the 1977 Act was enacted, to waive its requirements. Mr Alomo contended that, as a matter of public policy or public interest, the court should be slow to infer an intention or agreement to waive a requirement such as that imposed by section 5 of the 1977 Act, particularly in the absence of any evidence that the parties had specifically addressed their minds to that requirement.'

If there are joint tenants, though (and as recorded at fn 9), *all* must agree.[13]

Defining the term

4.8 Turning to the substantive issue of how 'only or principal home' is properly defined, it should first be noted that it is a *question of fact* for the court to decide,[14] though a simple 'day count' comparison for times spent at the premises and time spent away is unlikely to be sufficient or determinative on its own.[15]

4.9 Indeed, the day count issue was most obviously disregarded in *Hammersmith & Fulham LBC v Clarke*[16] where Lord Justice Keene remarked, in rejecting the authority's appeal against a trial judge's finding that the tenant had an objective and enduring intention to return to her home despite being a permanent resident in a nursing home:[17]

> '28 Was there then no evidence on which he could have come to the conclusion which he did? Certainly there was evidence pointing towards an intention to remain in the nursing home. Mrs Clarke had a permanent placement there. She did sign the note of 14 January and she did spend the vast majority of her time between then and the trial at the nursing home. On the other hand, her grandson and his wife continued occupying the premises as they had previously done with her. They would undoubtedly have allowed her back, as indeed they did from time to time, so there was no impediment to her return. It does seem probable, as Mr Wragg conceded at one point, that her furniture remained there. Certainly there was no evidence that it had been moved elsewhere. She was, after all, back living there at the date of the trial, so it seems that her furniture was probably there. That is not only relevant to occupation generally but it may also assist on the issue of intention.'

13 *Hounslow LBC v Pilling* (1993) 25 HLR 305.

14 *Ujima Housing Association v Ansah* (1998) 30 HLR 31 and *Peabody Donation Fund Governors v Grant* (1982) 6 HLR 41 (the latter being a succession case).

15 *Dove v Havering LBC* [2017] EWCA Civ 156, [2017] HLR 19, para 34 *per* Lewison LJ.

16 (2001) 33 HLR 77.

17 It is worth noting that the Court of Appeal decided in *Dudley Metropolitan Council v Mailley* [2023] EWCA Civ 124, [2023] 1 WLR 1837 that the statutory requirement for the family member to have been residing with the tenant at the time of the latter's death did not discriminate against the daughter of a secure tenant by preventing her succeeding to the tenancy after the tenant died while permanently residing in a care home.

4.10 A person may be in occupation of premises as a home even though they are not currently living there. The *length of the tenant's absence* from the premises of which possession is sought, or other circumstances relevant to that absence, may however raise the presumption that the premises have ceased to be the tenant's principal home.[18]

4.11 Where the tenant's absence is *sufficiently prolonged* to raise the inference that they have ceased to occupy the dwelling, the burden then falls on the tenant to demonstrate that their only or principal residence continues.[19]

4.12 In *Islington LBC v Boyle*,[20] Lord Justice Etherton helpfully summarised the relevant principles at paragraphs 55 and 65 of his judgment:

(a) The length or other circumstances of the tenant's absence may raise the inference that the premises ceased to be their principal home, and the burden of proving the contrary then falls on the tenant.

(b) To rebut that presumption, it is not sufficient for the tenant to simply prove that at the material time it was their *subjective* intention to return and belief that the dwelling remained their principal home. The *objective* facts must bear out the reality of that belief and intention both in the sense that:

- the intention and belief are or were genuinely held;
- the intention and belief themselves reflect reality (though a date or time period of return is not necessarily required); and
- there must be some 'formal, outward and visible sign of the intention to return'.

The reason for the absence, the length and other circumstances of the absence and (where relevant) the anticipated future duration of the absence, as well as statements and conduct of the tenant, will all be relevant to that objective assessment.

(c) The court's focus is on the enduring intention of the tenant, which, depending on the circumstances, may not be displaced by fleeting changes of mind.

(d) 'Second home' cases must be looked at with particular care.

(e) The issue is *one of fact* to be determined in the light of the evidence as a whole, and in respect of which the trial judge's findings of primary fact can only be overturned on appeal if they were perverse (the Appeal Court may, in an appropriate case, substitute its own inferences drawn from those primary facts).

18 *Brown v Brash* [1948] 2 KB 247, CA and *Islington LBC v Boyle* [2011] EWCA Civ 1450, [2012] PTSR 1093.

19 *Brown v Brash* [1948] 2 KB 247, CA at 254.

20 [2011] EWCA Civ 1450, [2012] PTSR 1093.

4.13 It follows that, for example, a visit to see family abroad for six months may be perfectly in order, especially where the family live some way off and/or face-to-face contact is otherwise rare. Similarly, a temporary placement abroad for work purposes may be equally as explicable and will not fall foul of the only or principal home condition.

4.14 Looking at an 'extreme' example of the approach – and one which may not be decided the same way today, though the principles it established remain good law – in the Rent Act[21] authority of *Tickner v Hearn*,[22] the Court of Appeal upheld the decision of the trial judge that the tenant was still protected *despite* the fact that she had been in a mental hospital for six years, was 73 years of age and was unlikely ever to return to her home. It was found that she always considered the premises as her home and hoped to return, a hope for which there was *some* chance.

4.15 A note of caution was though given by Lord Justice Ormerod:[23]

> 'For my part, however, I am of the opinion that to establish an intention to return by itself is not necessarily sufficient to obtain the protection of the Acts. The ultimate fact to be established is the fact of occupation, for it is only those in occupation whom the Act protects. If a tenant is out of occupation for some time he must at least prove an intention to return; but if the circumstances of the case are such that by reason of mental or physical illness or for some other reason the intention, even if clearly and bona fide held, seems most unlikely to be achieved within a reasonable time, it must surely be open to the judge in a proper case to find as a fact that the tenant is not in occupation. It seems to me that some of the reported cases have gone very far in the protection of the tenant.'

4.16 In the more recent authority of *Crawley BC v Sawyer*,[24] the tenant went to live with his partner in 1985 and in the following year both his electricity and gas at his local authority flat were disconnected. His landlord became aware of the situation the following year; when they spoke to the tenant he admitted that he was living with his partner and that they intended to purchase her home.

4.17 A notice to quit was served soon after and, although the tenant broke up with his partner shortly afterwards, he did not return to the premises until after the expiry date in the notice to quit.

21 In contrast to the position under the Rent Acts, a secure or assured tenant must not only show that the premises remain their home, but that they are their only or principal home: *Ujima Housing Association v Ansah* (1998) 30 HLR 31. The Court of Appeal in *Crawley BC v Sawyer* (1988) 20 HLR 98 held that there was no material difference between occupation as a 'home' under the Housing Act 1985 (and, by extension, the Housing Act 1988) and a 'residence' required to sustain a statutory tenancy under the Rent Acts (see Rent Act 1977, s 2).

22 [1960] 1 WLR 1406.

23 Ibid at [1416].

24 (1988) 20 HLR 98.

4.18 The Court of Appeal dismissed the local authority's appeal from their failed possession claim and found that, following on from the Rent Act approach, the temporary absence of a tenant who intended to return to live in the premises did not deprive them of statutory protection. Lord Justice Parker explained at [102]:

> 'The position as at the time the notice to quit was served was that the girlfriend had already told him that he had to get out. He did not, in fact, move back into Cobnor Close until after the expiry of the notice to quit, but in my view it was well open to the learned judge to have come to the conclusion that, both when the notice to quit was served and when it expired and indeed throughout the whole period, Cobnor Close remained his principal home. That the matter was a matter for the learned judge to conclude on the facts appears clearly from the decision of this court in *Peabody Donation Fund Governors v. Grant* (1982) 6 H.L.R. 41. The learned judge reached his conclusion here on evidence on which he was, in my view, entitled to reach that conclusion. I am unable to accept that in reaching it he misdirected himself in any way as to the law.'

4.19 The Court of Appeal had cause to look at this question again in late 2024 in the factually unusual case of *Hackney LBC v Weintraub*.[25] Rabbi Weintraub had been a tenant of the council since 2002, initially as a joint tenant with his now deceased spouse. From approximately 2017 he stopped sleeping at the premises because he did not feel comfortable there and rather spent extended periods at the synagogue and his daughter's address.

4.20 That same year he sought to exercise the right to buy as part of a plan to convert the basement into a flat so that he could return to the premises and not be alone. His application was rejected and he tried again in 2018. This was also refused and the authority served a notice to quit in 2019. In response the Rabbi sought a declaration that he had a right to buy and, though this was refused at first instance, he succeeded on appeal before Zacaroli J (as he then was).

4.21 The Court of Appeal dismissed the authority's appeal. In giving the main judgment, Asplin LJ explained:[26]

> 'As Zacaroli J pointed out, however, none of the authorities addresses the question of whether the tenant must intend to return as a tenant. They were focussed on whether the secure tenant in each case had lost that status and could be evicted rather than the secure tenant's ability to exercise the right to buy. It is necessary, therefore, to return to basic principles. As I have already stated, I do not consider that there is anything in section 81 which requires the tenant, in the sense of the individual to whom the contractual tenancy has been granted, to intend to return to a property in the capacity of tenant, or to resume using the property as the principal home in that capacity.

25 [2024] EWCA Civ 1561, [2025] WLR 1766.
26 Ibid, para 52.

I agree with Zacaroli J that it is sufficient that they genuinely believe the dwelling house to be their principal or only home and intend to return to use it as such albeit once their right to buy has been exercised. They fulfil the tenant condition because at the relevant time they are the tenant and continue to occupy the dwelling-house as their only or principal home in the extended sense which has been understood in the case law since *Brown v Brash and Ambrose* , in 1948, if not before.'

4.22 For many practitioners, this may seem a surprising result because Rabbi Weintraub openly had no intention of returning to the premises *as a tenant* and the statutory requirement to occupy demised premises as your only principal home is with reference to the secure tenancy requirements. The floodgates argument raised on behalf of the authority was always unlikely to be given much weight, however, given the unusual facts of the case.[27]

4.23 The lessons to be learned from a plethora of cases under the Rent Acts, and the Housing Acts of 1985 and 1988, are therefore:

- Evidence, as so often (and unsurprisingly), is key. If it is said that an individual is not living at the demised premises as their only or principal home, it is important, where possible, to gather evidence as to where the landlord says that individual *is* living. Credit reference reports and correspondence may, though, only take matters so far. Contemporaneous neighbour evidence may have a role to play, as will evidence from internal inspections of the premises. See Chapter 6 for further details as to evidence and information gathering.
- Whilst there is no absolute necessity to have details of where the tenant is in fact living, it may though strengthen the case if evidence of such accommodation and its enduring value to the tenant is available.
- Proper service of a valid notice to quit in a periodic tenancy case (including introductory tenancies) is key, but in many instances a landlord will also serve a notice seeking possession at the same time (expressed to be without prejudice to the primary case in reliance on the notice to quit) and rely on both in the alternative in any subsequent possession proceedings. Mr Sawyer (see **4.16**), for example, would have been in breach of his tenancy had the trial judge determined that there were periods when he had not lived at the demised premises as his only or principal home, even if at the expiry of the notice to quit it was held he did by then so reside.
- In such circumstances, the primary case is, as said, reliance on the notice to quit; but if the finding is that the tenant has 'returned home' prior to the expiry of such a notice then their behaviour and conduct may still

27 Lord Justice Males even doubted whether the Rabbi had another home – see para 73 of the judgment.

represent a breach of tenancy (see **4.4** above), allowing discretionary possession proceedings.[28]

- The remedy is, therefore, by way of Part 55 possession proceedings relying on:
  - a notice to quit in a periodic tenancy case based on the argument that security of tenure has been lost by reason of the tenant not living at the premises as their only or principal home;
  - in the alternative and if the tenant 'moves back in' prior to the expiry of the notice to quit, a notice seeking possession citing the breach of tenancy grounds of Ground 1 (secure tenancy) 'Rent lawfully due from the tenant has not been paid or an obligation of the tenancy has been broken or not performed' or Ground 12 (assured tenancy) 'Any obligation of the tenancy (other than one related to the payment of rent) has been broken or not performed' of Schedule 2 to the Housing Acts of 1985 and 1988 respectively; and
  - in flexible and (any remaining) assured fixed-term tenancy cases, action is generally by forfeiture if it is said the only or principal home breach of tenancy situation continues, otherwise by service of a section 146 notice *and* notice seeking possession (breach of tenancy ground) in the alternative if the tenant has returned.
- As a question of fact, an appeal is only likely to succeed if there has been some misapplication of the law and principles pertaining to this issue, or the trial judge's findings of primary facts are perverse and without proper, rational or indeed any basis.[29]

SUCCESSION

Right of succession: secure tenancies (overview)

4.24 The right of succession to a secure tenancy is now governed by section 86A of the Housing Act 1985 (England) and sections 73 to 83 of the Renting Homes (Wales) Act 2016 (Wales). In England, section 86A provides in the case of tenancies entered into on or after 1 April 2012:[30]

28 Housing Act 1985, Ground 1 (secure tenancies)/ Housing Act 1988, Ground 12 (assured tenancies), to be found in Sch 2 to both Acts.

29 See **4.4**(b). In *Staechelin & Ors v ACLBDD Holdings & Ors* [2019] EWCA Civ 817, [2019] 3 All ER 429 the court reminded itself that it was a question of whether the findings were ones that no reasonable judge could have reached or were rationally insupportable, Lord Justice Lewison confirming at para 30 that, 'it is a long settled principle, stated and restated in domestic and wider common law jurisprudence, that an appellate court should not interfere with the trial judge's conclusions on primary facts unless it is satisfied that he was plainly wrong'.

30 Localism Act 2011, s 160(6). As noted at **4.28**, the Housing and Planning Act 2016, Sch 8 and s 120 will, when brought into force, amend the Housing Act 1985 further so as to bring the succession provisions for pre-1 April 2012 secure tenancies into line with those for tenancies granted since that date. It will only do so where the tenant dies after the amendment has come into force.

(a) If the deceased tenant was a sole tenant then their spouse or civil partner (or person living with the tenant as a spouse or civil partner) would succeed so long as:

- they were also living at the premises as their only or principal home;[31] and
- the tenant had not themselves been a successor.[32]

(b) Second successions are though possible under the statutory scheme if the express term of the deceased tenant's agreement provides as much.[33] Otherwise, the statutory restriction to one succession has been held by the Court of Appeal to be non-discriminatory in Convention right terms.[34]

(c) If there was no spouse, civil partner, etc to succeed to the tenancy in the circumstances described above, then an extended succession right provided for in the tenancy agreement (eg carer, other family member) is enforceable as a statutory succession.[35]

(d) Since the second edition of this book, the Court of Appeal determined in *Abdelrahman v Islington LBC*[36] that the meaning of stepchild in a local authority's succession policy was a child of a person's spouse or civil partner from a previous relationship (and therefore excluded children of unmarried couples).

(e) In *Rahimi v Westminster City Council*[37] the Court of Appeal dismissed a would-be successor's appeal against a judgment on appeal to the effect that he could not succeed to his grandmother's tenancy because her tenancy had originally been a joint tenancy such that the original joint tenant, though not in occupation, was the lawful successor. An argument that after the joint tenant's departure from the premises the authority had granted a sole tenancy to the remaining tenant, such that upon their death the occupying grandchild could succeed, was rejected.

4.25 Statutory succession does not apply to joint tenancies (though see fn 32) – where one of joint tenants dies, the remaining joint tenant(s) succeed to the tenancy under the doctrine of survivorship.[38]

31 Housing Act 1985, s 86A(1), (5); see *Catalyst Housing Ltd v Martin* [2018] EWCA Civ 1206.
32 Ibid, s 88(1)(b) – remembering that, as always, a change from joint to sole tenancy upon death of a tenant counts as a succession (see s 86A(3)).
33 Ibid, s 86A(4).
34 *Haringey LBC v (1) Simawi (2) Secretary of State for Housing, Communities and Local Government* [2019] EWCA Civ 1770, [2020] 2 All ER 701.
35 Housing Act 1985, s 86A(2).
36 [2025] EWCA Civ 1038, [2025] HLR 45.
37 [2024] EWCA Civ 73, [2024] HLR 17.
38 *Cunningham-Reid v Public Trustee* [1944] KB 602 – though it is not treated as a transmission of tenancy (*Tennant v Hutton* (unreported) 9 July 1996; Court of Appeal (Civil Division) Transcript No 904 of 1996 as reported in *Solihull MBC v Hickin* [2012] UKSC 39, [2012] 1 WLR 2295, para 8 *per* Lord Sumption JSC).

4.26 For Wales, as noted at **4.24**, succession is now dealt with at sections 73 to 83 of the Renting Homes (Wales) Act 2016, and the former statutory provision at section 87 of the Housing Act 1985 has been repealed to that end.

4.27 In *Turley v (1) Wandsworth LBC (2) Secretary of State for Communities and Local Government*,[39] the Court of Appeal held that a tenancy condition which required for succession purposes the long-term partner of a secure tenant to have resided with them throughout the 12-month period immediately prior to the secure tenant's death (ie the position in **4.22**) was not discriminatory or incompatible with her rights under Articles 8 and 14 of the European Convention on Human Rights but rather was justified as the provision was not 'manifestly without reasonable foundation'. Lord Justice Underhill concluded:

> '42 I would dismiss this appeal. I am sorry for the appellant because the comparatively brief interruption in her relationship with Mr Doyle after a long period of living together has had the consequence of depriving her of the right to succeed to the tenancy of the house which has been her home for many years. But bright-line rules will sometimes have hard effects, and they are not for that reason unlawful. The Council cannot be blamed for insisting on the rules, in circumstances where there is an acute shortage of social housing, particularly no doubt of flats of the size occupied by the appellant. In that connection I should record that at an early stage, before the commencement of these proceedings, it offered her a three-bedroom flat in exchange for her current home; but she did not accept the offer.'

4.28 When (or rather, if) section 120 of, and Schedule 8 to, the Housing and Planning Act 2016 are brought into force, the more restrictive succession rights for secure tenancies brought in for post-1 April 2012 secure tenancies and set out at **4.20** will apply to *all* secure tenancies (see fn 30).

Right of succession: assured tenancies (overview)

4.29 The assured periodic tenancy succession regime, to be found at section 17 of the Housing Act 1988,[40] was always more restrictive when it came to succession compared with that applicable for secure tenancies, until the changes brought in by the Localism Act 2011 as described above.

4.30 Private registered providers of social housing, such as housing associations, frequently had and still have tenancy provisions seeking to extend or add to the statutory rule but, as a matter of statutory succession, that was previously only possible to spouses, civil partners or those living together as husband and wife or as civil partners *and* occupying the premises as their only

39 [2017] EWCA Civ 189, [2017] HLR 21.

40 At the time of writing, there are impending changes to this provision by reason of Renters' Rights Act 2025, Sch 2, para 28, largely reflecting the eventual abolition of fixed-term tenancies. See fn 44.

or principal home immediately before the tenant's death[41] (and such purported extensions were in fact an agreement to provide a new tenancy – see **4.32**).

4.31 Amendments brought in by the Localism Act 2011 changed that position for some tenancies provided for by private registered providers from 1 April 2012[42] and further alterations were made with effect from 13 March 2014 so that we now have the following position:

(a) Statutory succession still does not apply to joint tenancies – where one of joint tenants dies, the remaining joint tenant(s) succeeds to the tenancy under the doctrine of survivorship (see **4.25**).

(b) If the deceased tenant – whether periodic[43] or fixed-term (of not less than two years)[44] – was a sole tenant, then their spouse or civil partner (or person living with the tenant as a spouse or civil partner) would succeed as long as:

- they were living at the premises as their only or principal home;[45] and
- the tenant was not themselves a successor.[46]

(c) Where the assured tenancy is a periodic arrangement or fixed term of not less than two years and there was no spouse, civil partner, etc to succeed to the tenancy in the circumstances described above, then as long as the deceased tenant was not themself a successor any extended succession right provided for in the tenancy agreement (eg to a carer or family member living at the premises) is enforceable as a statutory succession.[47]

(d) Fixed-term tenancies of less than two years have no statutory succession provisions and succession is only by any provision in a will or the intestacy rules.[48]

4.32 Pre-1 April 2012, periodic assured tenancies therefore simply apply the approach set out at **4.30** above.[49] Tenancy terms (in agreements entered into from 11 May 2000 unless the agreement provides otherwise) seeking to extend rights of succession, though not statutory or enforceable as such, can be enforced by

41 Housing Act 1988, s 17.
42 Localism Act 2011, s 161 – periodic tenancies arising after the end of a fixed-term tenancy (granted prior to 1 April 2012) by virtue of Housing Act 1988, s 5 are also exempt from the Localism Act amendments.
43 Housing Act 1988, s 17(1) and (4).
44 Ibid, s 17(1B) and (4). With fixed-term tenancies to ultimately be a thing of the past for the assured tenancy regime, this will be removed on a date to be appointed by Renters' Rights Act 2025, Sch 2, para 28(c), with s 17 being more generally revised by para 28. See fn 40.
45 Ibid, s 17(1)(2) and (4).
46 Ibid, s 17(1D) – remembering that, as always, a change from joint to sole tenancy upon death of a tenant counts as a succession (see s 17(2)(b)).
47 Ibid, s 17(1A), (1C), (1D), (1E) – prior to these changes, such would-be 'successors' were not in fact successors at all and rather may have had to rely on the Contracts (Rights of Third Parties) Act 1999, s 1 – for post-11 May 2000 tenancies – to enforce the right to a new tenancy; see **4.32**.
48 The successor in these circumstances will still be treated as a successor for s 17 purposes: see s 17(2)(a).
49 Localism Act 2011, s 161(7).

the would-be successor pursuant to section 1 of the Contracts (Rights of Third Parties) Act 1999:

> '(1) Subject to the provisions of this Act, a person who is not a party to a contract (a 'third party') may in his own right enforce a term of the contract if–
>
> (a) the contract expressly provides that he may, or
>
> (b) subject to subsection (2), the term purports to confer a benefit on him.
>
> (2) Subsection (1)(b) does not apply if on a proper construction of the contract it appears that the parties did not intend the term to be enforceable by the third party.
>
> (3) The third party must be expressly identified in the contract by name, as a member of a class or as answering a particular description but need not be in existence when the contract is entered into.'

Fraudulent 'succession'

4.33 The question of succession is raised here in the context of a purported or claimed succession to a tenancy later found to have been without factual or legal merit.[50] This is an issue frequently resolved by means of the landlord taking possession action against the would-be successor (on the basis that they have not *in fact or law* succeeded to the deceased tenant's tenancy and thus have no rights of occupation).

4.34 For example, this may arise in a pre-1 April 2012 secure tenancy scenario where it is later discovered that the 'family' member was not, in fact, related to the deceased tenant or even if they were, and more commonly, then the would-be successor only moved in with the tenant, say, three months before the latter's death rather than the required and stated 12 months.

4.35 The temptation to claim succession when there is, in fact, no such entitlement is obvious for three primary reasons:

(a) the would-be successor will sometimes have been living in the subject premises as their home and a failed succession could lead to homelessness;

(b) social housing attracts lower rents than those seen in the private rented sector, along with frequently better records of management and repair; and

50 In *Thurrock BC v West* [2012] EWCA Civ 1435, [2013] HLR 5, the Court of Appeal rejected a grandchild's Art 8 defence to a possession claim in a case where he had no right to succeed to the tenancy as it was a second succession. In *R (on the application of Gangera) v Hounslow LBC* [2003] EWHC 794 (Admin), [2003] HLR 68 before Mr Justice Moses, the applicant failed in his Art 14 challenge to the succession provisions of the Housing Act 1985.

(c) depending upon the nature of the tenancy, the would-be successor may enjoy a right to buy or acquire if their request to succeed is accepted.

4.36 In terms of court action, it should be remembered that the deceased tenant's tenancy persists where there is no statutory successor, albeit security of tenure will inevitably have been lost. To that end, the remaining common law tenancy will need to be terminated which is not as straightforward as may at first be thought:

(a) *Periodic tenancy* (secure or assured) – the landlord should serve a notice to quit at the premises *and* a copy on the personal representative/public trustee.[51]

(b) *Flexible tenancy* – section 90 of the Housing Act 1985 provides that security of tenure will end if no-one is entitled to be a secure tenant (eg not living at the premises as their only or principal home and not entitled to succeed) even if they were to have the tenancy vested in them by the administration of the deceased tenant's estate. This provision also provides for a notice and possession procedure:

'(6) Subject as follows, the landlord may apply to the court for an order for possession of the dwelling-house let under the tenancy.

(7) The court may not entertain proceedings for an order for possession under this section unless—

(a) the landlord has served notice in writing on the tenant–

(i) stating that the landlord requires possession of the dwelling-house, and

(ii) specifying a date after which proceedings for an order for possession may be begun, and

(b) that date has passed without the tenant giving up possession of the dwelling-house.

(8) The date mentioned in subsection (7)(a)(ii) must fall after the end of the period of four weeks beginning with the date on which the notice is served on the tenant.

(9) On an application to the court for an order for possession under this section, the court must make such an order if it is satisfied that subsection (5) applies to the tenancy.

(10)The tenancy ends when the order is executed.'

51 Served on the executors or administrators of the deceased's estate or, if there was no will or letters of administration were taken out, on the Public Trustee: Law of Property (Miscellaneous Provisions) Act 1994, s 18; Public Trustee (Notices Affecting Land) (Title on Death) Regulations 1995 (as amended); *Wirral BC v Smith* (1982) 4 HLR 81. See *Gateway Housing Association v Ali (deceased)* [2020] EWCA Civ 1339, [2021] 1 WLR 289 concerning service and the proper interpretation of s 18, especially in intestacy cases.

(c) *Assured tenancy where will/personal representatives*[52] – the Housing Act 1988 provides for a mandatory ground for possession at Schedule 2 – Ground 7 – where the tenancy has devolved under a will or intestacy, the first paragraph of which states (at the time of writing):

> 'The tenancy is a periodic tenancy (including a statutory periodic tenancy), or a fixed term tenancy of a dwelling-house in England, which has devolved under the will or intestacy of the former tenant and the proceedings for the recovery of possession are begun not later than twelve months after the death of the former tenant or, if the court so directs, after the date on which, in the opinion of the court, the landlord or, in the case of joint landlords, any one of them became aware of the former tenant's death.'

Changes to be brought in by Renters' Rights Act 2025 amendments (see fn 2) will mean that Ground 7 will read:

> 'The tenancy has devolved on a person (the *"new tenant"*) under the will or intestacy of the former tenant and the proceedings for the recovery of possession are begun not later than twelve months after the death of the former tenant or, if the court so directs, after the date on which, in the opinion of the court, the landlord or, in the case of joint landlords, any one of them became aware of the former tenant's death.
>
> But, if the new tenant is occupying the dwelling-house as the new tenant's only or principal home immediately before the death of the former tenant, an order for possession on this Ground may not be made unless–
>
> (a) the tenancy has previously devolved on the former tenant under a will or intestacy (whenever that devolution occurred), or
>
> (b) the tenancy is a special tenancy immediately before the death of the former tenant.
>
> In this Ground *"special tenancy"* means–
>
> (a) a tenancy of social housing (within the meaning given by Part 2 of the Housing and Regeneration Act 2008) where the landlord is a private registered provider of social housing;
>
> (b) a tenancy entered into pursuant to a rent-to-buy agreement (which has the same meaning as in Ground 1B) where the landlord is a private registered provider of social housing;
>
> (c) a tenancy of supported accommodation, within the meaning given by paragraph 12 of Schedule 2;

52 Though may apply to both fixed-term and periodic assured tenancies as well where the tenancy has been devolved. As with other parts of the Housing Act 1988, this Ground will be amended by reason of the Renters' Rights Act 2025 on a date to be appointed to reflect the impending cessation of fixed-term assured tenancies in the private registered provider sector (it having already taken place in the private sector).

(d) a tenancy where the former tenant's occupation of the dwelling-house is in pursuance of a local housing authority's duty to the tenant under section 193 of the Housing Act 1996 (and here "local housing authority" has the same meaning as in Ground 5G);

(e) a tenancy which meets the conditions in paragraphs (a), (b), (d) and (e) in the first paragraph of Ground 5H.

For the purposes of this ground, the acceptance by the landlord of rent from a new tenant after the death of the former tenant shall not be regarded as creating a new tenancy, unless the landlord agrees in writing to a change (as compared with the tenancy before the death) in the amount of the rent, the period or length of term of the tenancy, the premises which are let or any other term of the tenancy.'

4.37 The proper analysis can best be summarised as follows:

Overview

Statutory succession to a tenancy is by operation of law and, as such, even if not confirmed or established for some months after the death of a tenant (or even until after contested possession proceedings), the successor becomes the tenant from the point of death of the deceased tenant.

Ground 5 or 17

If there was, in fact, no right to succession and it was 'allowed' by the landlord because of a false representation made by or on behalf of the would-be successor then Ground 5 or 17 *may*[53] apply (but see Chapter 2 and 'Trespasser action' below).

If they do have a tenancy, such as by means of the landlord granting them a fresh tenancy (see, for example, 'Trespasser action' sub-paragraph (a) below), it is not by reason of statutory succession of course but rather by agreement with the landlord. In such a case, a Ground 5 or 17 case may be arguable if they came to the tenancy by reason of a false statement or omission to 'update' the landlord of the true state of affairs.

Rescission

There is also the remote question of the landlord seeking the remedy of rescission on the basis of fraudulent misrepresentation if a tenancy has been granted despite the lack of lawful succession but there is no security of tenure (if there is then Grounds 5 and 17 must be applied instead[54] – also see 'Trespasser action' below). If there is no security of tenure it will presumably

53 For example, can it be said that the landlord had 'granted' the tenancy in such circumstances, for the purposes of Ground 5 or 17, as opposed to simply accepting the succession to the deceased tenant's tenancy?

54 *Islington LBC v Uckac* [2006] EWCA Civ 340, [2006] 1 WLR 1303.

be because the 'successor' has sub-let or parted with possession of the whole, or no longer lives at the premises as their only or principal home – in such a case the 'easier' option may be to seek recovery by possession proceedings on that ground (see Chapter 3).

It follows that rescission is not going to be a usual remedy in cases of disputed succession.

Trespasser action

Much more likely, and even before that stage is reached, however, unless:

(a) the landlord and would-be successor signed a fresh tenancy agreement (sometimes done to ensure that the current tenancy conditions, especially in a stock transfer scenario, apply to the new tenant); or

(b) it was possible to argue that a new tenancy had been created by reason of the parties' subsequent actions; or

(c) there was no statutory succession but the landlord had granted a fresh tenancy in reliance on the tenancy terms of the deceased tenant (eg pre-1 April 2012 secure tenancy),

there would have been no grant or assumption of tenancy whatsoever and the landlord would be entitled to seek possession on the basis of trespasser possession proceedings (once they had determined the deceased tenant's tenancy (eg by means of a notice to quit, section 90 notice, Ground 7 reliance – see **4.3**, **4.36** and fn 54).

This will be the usual action taken by the landlord whether or not the estate of the deceased tenant is included as a defendant along with the disputed 'successor'.

Late appeal/Set aside of order

Late appeal

If a possession trial has already been held and the court has found that the defendant *has* on the proven facts succeeded to the tenancy (or has defeated any other possession claim, such as concerning an only or principal home argument as described above) then, by way of a late appeal, it can only be re-opened by way of a re-trial where:[55]

(a) new evidence has come to light which was not reasonably available to the landlord at trial;

(b) this suggests that the defendant may have given and/or presented false evidence;

(c) the new evidence is credible and would have an important influence on the case; *and*

55 *London Borough of Brent v Smart* [2005] EWCA Civ 434, paras 27–31 *per* LJ Rix, applying the traditional *Ladd v Marshall* test.

(d) there were no other factors in the interests of justice which dictated that the matter should not be re-opened.

Set aside

The even better route (than appeal) in cases where the evidence of fraud is strong would be by means of an application to set aside any order in reliance on CPR 3.1:

> '(7) A power of the court under these Rules to make an order includes a power to vary or revoke the order.'

In *Lloyds Investment (Scandinavia) Ltd v Ager-Hanssen*,[56] Mr Justice Patten said at para 7 of the judgment about the availability of the set-aside application:[57]

> 'It seems to me that the only power available to me on this application is that contained in CPR r 3.1(7), which enables the court to vary or revoke an order. This is not confined to purely procedural orders and there is no real guidance in the White Book as to the possible limits of the jurisdiction. Although this is not intended to be an exhaustive definition of the circumstances in which the power under CPR r 3.1(7) is exercisable, *it seems to me that, for the High Court to revisit one of its earlier orders, the applicant must either show some material change of circumstances or that the judge who made the earlier order was misled in some way, whether innocently or otherwise, as to the correct factual position before him.* The latter type of case would include, for example, a case of material non-disclosure on an application for an injunction. If all that is sought is a reconsideration of the order on the basis of the same material, then that can only be done, in my judgment, in the context of an appeal. Similarly it is not, I think, open to a party to the earlier application to seek in effect to reargue that application by relying on submissions and evidence which were available to him at the time of the earlier hearing, but which, for whatever reason, he or his legal representatives chose not to deploy.' (emphasis added)

In *Royal Bank of Scotland plc v Highland Financial Partners LP*,[58] Aikens LJ confirmed the relevant set-aside principles at para 106 of his judgment:

> 'The principles are, briefly: first, there has to be a 'conscious and deliberate dishonesty' in relation to the relevant evidence given, or action taken, statement made or matter concealed, which is relevant

56 [2003] EWHC 1740 (Ch).

57 In the Court of Appeal decision of *Vodafone Group plc v IPCom GmbH and Co KG* [2023] EWCA Civ at 113, it was said: 'The overwhelming thrust of the authorities is that the court's power under CPR 3.1(7) to vary or revoke orders either cannot or should not be used to discharge a sealed final order', though see the 'exception' at **4.45**.

58 [2013] EWCA Civ 328, [2013] 1 CLC 596.

to the judgment now sought to be impugned. Secondly, the relevant evidence, action, statement or concealment (performed with conscious and deliberate dishonesty) must be 'material'. 'Material' means that the fresh evidence that is adduced after the first judgment has been given is such that it demonstrates that the previous relevant evidence, action, statement or concealment was an operative cause of the court's decision to give judgment in the way it did. Put another way, it must be shown that the fresh evidence would have entirely changed the way in which the first court approached and came to its decision. Thus the relevant conscious and deliberate dishonesty must be causative of the impugned judgment being obtained in the terms it was. Thirdly, the question of materiality of the fresh evidence is to be assessed by reference to its impact on the evidence supporting the original decision, not by reference to its impact on what decision might be made if the claim were to be retried on honest evidence.'

Considering therefore the ability of the county court to entertain such a set-aside application, in the case of *(1) Shahan Salekipour (2) Amir Saleem v Jashan Kaur Parmar (In her own right & as executrix of Mohinder Singh Parmar, Deceased) sub nom Re Parmar (Deceased)*,[59] Sir Terence Etherton MR adopted a pragmatic approach in rejecting the notion that the county court, as a creature of statute, had no jurisdiction to rescind one of its own judgments.[60] At paragraph 73 of his judgment he said:

'If however, the respondent is correct about the County Court's lack of jurisdiction, the only remedy for a litigant in the County Court who wishes to have a prior final County Court order set aside for perjury or fraud is to appeal, even though that will often not be the most appropriate course consistent with the overriding objective in CPR r.1.1. It was common ground before us that the High Court has no jurisdiction to hear independent proceedings to set aside an earlier final order of the County Court obtained by perjury or fraud. If that deprivation of a previous County Court jurisdiction was the effect of the repeal of CCR Ord. 37 r.1(1), then it appears that it would have been the result of oversight rather than intention, and, contrary to objective of the CPR, would have produced a significant difference between the High Court and the County Court and would have seriously disadvantaged County Court litigants, for no sound policy reason.'

This led to his conclusion at paragraph 74:

'I agree with the appellants that such an anomaly does not exist because, leaving to one side the CPR, including the management powers under CPR 3.1, sections 23 and 38 of the 1984 Act confer jurisdiction on a County Court judge to determine proceedings to set aside a final County Court order obtained by perjury or fraud. Such proceedings appear to

59 [2017] EWCA Civ 2141, [2018] QB 833.

60 The relevant provisions of the County Courts Act 1984 are ss 23, 38 and 70.

me to fall precisely within the wording of section 23. The right of a party to have a judgment set aside on the ground of fraud is a principle of equity: *Flower v Lloyd* (1877) 6 Ch D 297; *Noble* at [42] (Elias LJ). The present proceedings are, consistently with the terms of section 23, "proceedings for relief against fraud … where the damage sustained … does not exceed in amount or value the county court limit".'

Lord Justice Rix cautioned against this set-aside option as being seen as open-ended when he said in *Tibbles v SIG Plc (t/a Asphaltic Roofing Supplies)*[61] at para 39(vii):

> 'The cases considered above suggest that the successful invocation of the rule is rare. Exceptional is a dangerous and sometimes misleading word: however, such is the interest of justice in the finality of a court's orders that it ought normally to take something out of the ordinary to lead to variation or revocation of an order, especially in the absence of a change of circumstances in an interlocutory situation.'

This caution was repeated in *Prompt Motor Limited v HSBC Bank Plc*[62] when HHJ Paul Matthews, sitting as a Deputy High Court Judge, reviewed the authorities and set out the necessarily limited parameters of such an application:

> '31. I accept that even a final judgment obtained by fraud can be set aside. But, as at present advised, I doubt whether anything less will do. Nor do I consider that a final judgment can be set aside merely because fresh evidence comes to light or, worse, evidence that was available at the time that the final judgment was given but which was not deployed is now put forward for the first time. A party has the obligation to fight a case, and the whole case, on one occasion, and cannot deal with it in stages as and when convenient; cf *Henderson v Henderson* (1843) 3 Hare 100.'

The Supreme Court allowed an appeal from the Court of Appeal in *Takhar v Gracefield Developments Ltd*[63] when it determined that an action to set aside an earlier judgment obtained by fraud could continue and that there was no requirement for the applicant to demonstrate they had exercised reasonable diligence in not raising the issue earlier.

The hearing of that matter therefore came before Mr Steven Gasztowicz QC, sitting as a Deputy High Court Judge, in September and October 2020.[64] A judgment which had been entered against the claimant in 2010 was set

61 [2012] EWCA Civ 518, [2012] 1 WLR 2591.

62 [2017] EWHC 1487 (Ch).

63 [2019] UKSC 13, [2019] AC 450.

64 [2020] EWHC 2791 (Ch). Note that there could be an argument that proceedings to set aside transactions procured by fraud could be derailed by earlier conscious decisions not to investigate suspected fraud or not to rely on a known misrepresentation. See the Supreme Court judgment in *Takhar* at para 63 and *Park v CNH* [2021] EWCA Civ 1766, [2022] 1 WLR 860 at paras 57–60.

aside after she adduced expert evidence showing that her signature on a document, that had been material to the judge's findings, was forged. On the evidence, the defendants, who were company directors, were responsible for the forgery. The judge said at para 38:

> 'In *Royal Bank of Scotland plc v Highland Financial Partners LP* [2013] EWCA Civ 328 Aikens LJ said at para 106:
>
> "The principles are, briefly: first, there has to be a 'conscious and deliberate dishonesty' in relation to the relevant evidence given, or action taken, statement made or matter concealed, which is relevant to the judgment now sought to be impugned. Secondly, the relevant evidence, action, statement or concealment (performed with conscious and deliberate dishonesty) must be 'material'. 'Material' means that the fresh evidence that is adduced after the first judgment has been given is such that it demonstrates that the previous relevant evidence, action, statement or concealment was an operative cause of the court's decision to give judgment in the way it did. Put another way, it must be shown that the fresh evidence would have entirely changed the way in which the first court approached and came to its decision. Thus the relevant conscious and deliberate dishonesty must be causative of the impugned judgment being obtained in the terms it was. Thirdly, the question of materiality of the fresh evidence is to be assessed by reference to its impact on the evidence supporting the original decision, not by reference to its impact on what decision might be made if the claim were to be retried on honest evidence."'

CONCLUSION

4.38 'Only or principal home' cases cover a multitude of scenarios but share one quality – they represent a use of the premises not anticipated by or allowed for in the tenancy agreement (by reason of express or implied terms).

4.39 Action in respect of the same may result in anything from a warning as to future use of the premises, through to the obtaining of a possession order (whether that be suspended on terms or outright, discretionary or mandatory) and even leading potentially to criminal prosecution (see Chapter 7).

4.40 'False' succession claims also involve a misuse of property and are most commonly 'tested', where the landlord does not itself accept any succession claim (even if they have come to that conclusion belatedly), by means of possession proceedings, with the court ultimately determining whether the defendant was entitled to succeed to the tenancy in issue and, if so, any notice to quit served is then of no effect.

4.41 These issues of fact are rarely clear and straightforward, and whilst the litigation process is not inherently controversial, the evidential strength of any case is often difficult to accurately gauge in advance of any claim.

CHAPTER 5

Civil Financial Remedies

- Unlawful profit orders (UPOs)
- Damages for misrepresentation
- The tort of deceit and unjust enrichment
- [Rescission]

Key points

- UPOs allow for the recovery by the social landlord[1] of the gross profits achieved by a tenant sub-letting or parting with possession of some or all of their premises.
- UPOs do not apply to shared ownership arrangements.[2]
- Civil financial remedies for social housing fraud above and beyond a UPO are limited and, particularly in respect of housing associations, rarely used.
- Rescission as a remedy is available for cases of fraudulent misrepresentation (unless the false representation possession grounds are available)[3] and is usually considered in cases of right-to-buy/acquire or shared ownership fraud. Damages may not be awarded in lieu of rescission in such a case.
- Damages may be claimed in deceit in addition to or instead of a possession claim on the false representation ground or when claiming rescission.

INTRODUCTION

5.1 Social housing fraud has an obvious cost to landlords, particularly local authorities, as is clear from Chapter 1, and whilst the emphasis upon its discovery is often the return of the premises in issue, there is also the question of financial compensation which can and should be addressed.

1 That is, local authorities, private registered providers of social housing, registered social landlords or community landlords – see Prevention of Social Housing Fraud Act 2013 (PSHF), ss 2, 5 and 11.
2 PSHF, s 5(4)(b).
3 Housing Act 1985, Sch 2, Ground 5 (secure tenancies); Housing Act 1988, Sch 2, Ground 17 (assured tenancies) – see Chapter 2.

5.2 When criminal proceedings are brought in relation to social housing fraud the Magistrates' and Crown Courts enjoy powers to make compensation orders in favour of the social landlord, and the Crown Court can also make a confiscation order: these remedies are dealt with in more detail at Chapter 7.[4] This chapter addresses instead the options available to landlords in seeking to recover monies in civil proceedings in the county court or (more rarely) the High Court, and the remedy of rescission in so far as it is related to the question of damages for misrepresentation. The financial options may be exercised in addition to or as an alternative to proceedings for possession of the premises, particularly in the following scenarios:

- Sub-letting/parting with possession of let premises.
- Fraudulent misrepresentation and the tort of deceit.

UNLAWFUL PROFIT ORDERS (UPOs)

5.3 One of the clearest routes for a social landlord to recover financial recompense for fraudulent misuse of their properties is to be found within the provisions set down in the Prevention of Social Housing Fraud Act 2013 (PSHF).[5] This legislation applies to England and Wales[6] and is focused on the twin issues of sub-letting and the parting with possession of demised premises. Chapter 3 provides detailed analysis on the meaning of these terms and the procedure for seeking possession of premises in these circumstances. In this section we are concerned with the procedure for recovering monies received by tenants, either at the same time as, or separate to, any possession proceedings.

5.4 The PSHF has given social landlords two clear benefits in terms of their civil rights and remedies in dealing with such a misuse of their stock:

(a) It introduced a new procedure for recovering the gross profit element of the tenant's sub-letting/parting with possession activities which is very clear, simple and straightforward (PSHF, s 5).

(b) It extends to assured tenancies (other than shared ownership leases) the approach which has long applied to secure tenancies: where the *whole* of the demised premises are sub-let or the tenant(s) part with possession of the same, security of tenure is not only lost but it cannot be restored save by the grant of a fresh tenancy (Housing Act 1988, s 15A as inserted by PSHF, s 6).[7]

4 For example, on 11 September 2024 at Snaresbrook Crown Court a defendant in an unlawful sub-letting case who had pleaded guilty to four counts of fraud in December 2022 was ordered to pay £242,705 to the London Borough of Islington (see **7.79**).

5 In force from 15 October 2013 (England) and 5 November 2013 (Wales).

6 Renting Homes (Wales) Act 2016 (Consequential Amendments) Regulations 2022, SI 2022/1166, reg 33 has from 1 December 2022 led to amendments of the PSHF following the replacement of tenancies and licences with occupation contracts.

7 Previously, so long as the tenant or at least one of the joint tenants (or their spouse/civil partner) returned to live at the premises as their only or principal home prior to the expiry of the notice to quit then security of tenure was restored, even in sub-letting/parting with possession cases and the said notice was therefore then of no effect.

5.5 Earlier legislation, such as the Theft Act 1968, the Proceeds of Crime Act 2002 and the Fraud Act 2006, does still apply to social housing fraud scenarios. However, in the context of recovering 'compensation' for the types of housing fraud to which it applies, the UPO approach found in the PSHF is expressly designed to be:

(a) simpler;

(b) readily available in conjunction with existing criminal/civil proceedings; and

(c) easier to obtain.

Conditions

5.6 Where a secure or assured tenant, or in Wales a contract-holder occupying premises under a secure contract, has sub-let their premises or allowed others to stay there in their absence, then they will often have done so, at least in part, with a view to making a profit on such an enterprise. Social housing rents, even at affordable rent levels, are lower than those seen in the private rented sector (including short-term lets). The profit possibilities are all the greater if continuing (fraudulent) housing benefit and universal credit (housing costs) awards are factored in.

5.7 The PSHF provides that UPOs can be obtained in both criminal[8] and civil[9] proceedings under the Act, the former being dealt with at Chapter 7. For civil recovery, section 5 of the PSHF requires four basic conditions to be satisfied to allow for an order:[10]

(1) the sub-letting/parting with possession has taken place in breach of an express or implied condition of the tenancy (knowledge that such actions constitute a breach on the part of the tenant or dishonesty is not required);

(2) the sub-letting/parting with possession can be of the whole or part of the premises. For secure tenancies, if of part then this must be shown to have been without the landlord's written consent – with assured tenancies the tenancy condition may similarly allow the sub-letting of part *if* permission is first obtained such that (1) above is not satisfied;

(3) the tenant has ceased to occupy the premises as their only or principal home; *and*

(4) the tenant has received money as a result of the sub-letting/parting with possession.

5.8 In addition, for assured tenancy cases:

8 PSHF, s 4.
9 Ibid, s 5.
10 Ibid, s 5(3) and (4).

(a) the landlord must be a private registered provider of social housing (England)[11] or community landlord (Wales[12]),[13] invariably a housing association; and

(b) the tenancy must not be a shared ownership lease.[14]

5.9 The first two conditions at **5.7** are addressed in detail in Chapter 3 and, in reality, are unlikely to provide a difficult obstacle to obtaining a UPO – once the sub-letting or parting with possession is shown and the position of the tenant(s) or contract-holder sufficiently demonstrated to satisfy the condition at **5.7**(3) then to some extent the question of a UPO is one of mathematics.

5.10 That is not, though, to ignore the fact that if these conditions are satisfied the court '*may*' make a UPO but is not bound to do so.[15] There are no reported cases as yet to demonstrate when a court may or will decide *not* to make a UPO, despite the conditions for one being satisfied, but factors such as:

(a) length of time since the offending period occurred;

(b) some fault on the part of the landlord in not detecting the fraud earlier or either previously agreeing to the activity or ignoring the evidence;

(c) a particular joint tenant not being the main instigator of the arrangement; or

(d) the tenant's circumstances having dramatically changed for the worse since their activities came to light,

may be four examples where, on the facts of a particular case, a court declines to make a UPO.

The application

5.11 Applications for UPOs in the civil courts must be made by a landlord,[16] either by way of a Part 7 claim:

11 Housing and Regeneration Act 2008, s 80.

12 Renting Homes (Wales) Act 2016 (Consequential Amendments) Regulations 2022, SI 2022/1166, reg 33(4)(b)(ii)(bb).

13 PSHF, s 5(4)(a).

14 Ibid, s 5(4)(b). For most shared ownership leases they are not, in any event, assured tenancies following the introduction of the Renters' Rights Act 2025.

15 Ibid, s 5(1).

16 Ibid.

Separate Part 7 claim for UPO

GREENHOFF HOUSING ASSOCIATION

Claimant

-and-

MR BARRY KANE

Defendant

PARTICULARS OF CLAIM

Introduction

1. The Claimant is a private registered provider of social housing and the freehold owner of 19B Di Maria Way, Angelford, AD1 5DD ('the Premises').
2. The Defendant is an individual aged 53 years of age who on 5 May 2014 entered into an assured non-shorthold weekly periodic tenancy agreement ('the Agreement') with the Claimant in respect of the Premises.

The Agreement

3. The Agreement provided at clauses 3.4 and 3.5:

   '3.4 You must at all times live at the Premises as your only or principal home.

   3.5 You are not entitled to sub-let or part with possession of any part of the Premises without our prior written consent.'

Breach

4. On 19 March 2025 an officer of the Claimant visited the Premises for the purposes of a tenancy audit and spoke to a Mr John Evans there. Mr Evans showed the officer the tenancy agreement he had entered into on 12 June 2024 with the Defendant in respect of a bedroom therein and use of the bathroom, kitchen, lounge and hallway.
5. The said tenancy agreement is exhibited to these particulars at 'Annex A' and shows that Mr Evans was to pay to the Defendant £120.00 per week under the terms of his tenancy. He showed the officer a rent book demonstrating that he had, in fact, paid the Defendant such sums every week from 12 June 2024.
6. Mr Evans also advised that the Defendant did not live at the Premises – and no one else did aside from himself – but stayed with his partner

nearby and only visited to collect the rent each week. He further advised that the second bedroom was locked and not in use.

7. The Claimant has at no stage been asked for, or given, permission to the Defendant to sub-let part of the Premises and he is accordingly in breach of both clauses 3.4 and 3.5 of the Agreement.

Basis of claim

8. It is known that the Defendant told Mr Evans to leave the Premises shortly after the visit on 19 March 2025 and that he is now back living at the Premises.

9. The Premises were sub-let to Mr Evans from 12 June 2024 until on or around 19 March 2025 ('the sub-letting period') and during this time the Defendant was not living there as his only or principal home.

10. The conditions for an unlawful profit order provided for at section 5(4) of the Prevention of Social Housing Fraud Act 2013 are satisfied:

    (a) The Claimant is a private registered provider of social housing.
    (b) The tenancy of the Premises is not a shared ownership lease.
    (c) The Defendant sub-let part of the Premises in breach of clause 3.5 of his tenancy agreement.
    (d) During the period of the sub-letting the Defendant ceased to occupy the Premises as his only or principal home.
    (e) The Defendant received money from the sub-letting.

11. The Premises are a two-bedroom flat on the third floor of a four-storey block and the current weekly rent applicable to the Premises is £85.00 per week.

Sums claimed

12. The Defendant received 40 weeks' payment of £120.00 from Mr Evans as rent for the latter's sub-letting of the Premises. This totals £4,800.00.

13. The Defendant paid £3,000.00 to the Claimant in respect of his gross rent for the Premises during the sub-letting period.

14. The Claimant therefore claims £1,800.00 in addition to interest pursuant to section 69 of the County Courts Act 1984 at such rate as the court shall determine.

AND the Claimant claims:

1. An Unlawful Profit Order against the Defendant in the sum of £1,800.

2. Interest pursuant to section 69, County Courts Act 1984.

3. Costs.

Statement of truth

[I believe][the (claimant or as may be) believes] that the facts stated in this [name document being verified] are true. I understand] [The (claimant or as may be) understands that proceedings for contempt of court may be brought against anyone who makes, or causes to be made, a false statement in a document verified by a statement of truth without an honest belief in its truth.

or (more normally) as part of ongoing possession proceedings, whether in the original pleading or in a statement of case varied to include the UPO claim by way of an N244 Application Notice.

Example Particulars of Claim (part)

(Possession claim and UPO)

...

Unlawful profit order (UPO)

8. Paragraph 5 is repeated herein.
9. The conditions for a UPO provided for at section 5(4) of the Prevention of Social Housing Fraud Act 2013 are met:
   (a) The Premises were let to the Defendant under an assured tenancy and the Claimant is a private registered provider of social housing.
   (b) In breach of clause 3(2)(b) of the said tenancy agreement, the Defendant sub-let the whole of the Premises for the period 8 January 2024 to 23 February 2025 ('the sub-letting period') to Ms Louise Macari.
   (c) During this period he was not living at the Premises as his only or principal home and rather was residing at the Second Premises.
   (d) The Defendant received £12,545.00 from Ms Macari during the sub-letting period.
10. The Claimant seeks and is entitled to a UPO for the maximum amount in the sum of £5,500 having only received £7,045 from the Defendant during the sub-letting period in respect of what was purported to be rent.
11. The Claimant further seeks interest pursuant to section 69 of the County Courts Act 1984 at such a rate and for such a period as the court thinks fit.

AND the Claimant claims:

1. Possession of the Premises forthwith (mandatory ground).
2. A money judgment in respect of any outstanding arrears of rent and use and occupation charges as at the date of the final hearing.
3. Use and Occupation charges at the daily rate of £13.71 from the date of the final hearing until possession is given up.

4. An unlawful profit order in the sum of £5,500 with interest pursuant to section 69 of the County Courts Act 1984.
5. Costs.

Statement of Truth

[I believe][the (claimant or as may be) believes] that the facts stated in this [name document being verified] are true. I understand] [The (claimant or as may be) understands that proceedings for contempt of court may be brought against anyone who makes, or causes to be made, a false statement in a document verified by a statement of truth without an honest belief in its truth.

5.12 Although section 5(8) of PSHF provides that an application can be made to the High Court *or* county court, the usual application will be to the county court. Claims and/or applications to the High Court should be limited to cases involving unusually large sums of money or complex points of law of public importance.[17]

5.13 It is clear from section 5(2) of PSHF that the claim/application can only be made against the tenant. The conditions at section 5(3) and 5(4) expressly refer to 'a tenant under the tenancy' having 'received money as a result of the [sub-letting/parting with possession]'.

5.14 For example, if the tenant has left the premises and allowed a friend to have use of them, and that friend 'sub-lets' it and keeps all the proceeds, then a UPO is not available because the tenant has not received money as a result of this conduct. However, if the friend in fact passed all or some of the money to the tenant, then even though it may be argued that it is not the tenant who has sub-let all or part of the premises, the tenant is likely to be caught by the UPO provisions as they will likely be found to have 'parted with possession'.

The amount sought

5.15 Section 5 of PSHF provides:

> '(5) The amount payable under an unlawful profit order must be such amount as the court considers appropriate, having regard to any evidence and to any representations that are made by or on behalf of the landlord or the tenant, but subject to subsections (6) and (7).
>
> (6) The maximum amount payable under an unlawful profit order is calculated as follows–

17 Ibid, s 5(9) which states that: 'Section 110(3) of the Housing Act 1985 (by which the claimant in proceedings relating to a secure tenancy may not recover the claimant's costs if the proceedings are taken in the High Court) does not apply to proceedings under this section'.

Step 1

Determine the total amount the tenant received as a result of the conduct described in subsection (3)(a) or (4)(c) (or the best estimate of that amount).

Step 2

Deduct from the amount determined under step 1 the total amount, if any, paid by the tenant as rent to the landlord (including service charges) over the period during which the conduct described in subsection (3)(a) or (4)(c) took place.'

5.16 It follows that:

(a) the court has a wide discretion about whether to make an award at all and, if it does, its quantum. By way of example of the latter, Sovereign Network Group obtained a UPO of £136,000 in a possession action concluded in February 2024, [18]whilst three years previously the Riverside Group was awarded a UPO in the sum of £145,178;[19]

(b) precise evidence of monies received by way of the sub-letting is not always available but the courts have significant flexibility and discretion, as shown by the phrase 'best estimate' in section 5(6); and

(c) the award is subject to a maximum figure, namely the 'true profit' element (ie the amount received because of the sub-letting or parting with possession, less that paid by the tenant to her/his landlord *during the relevant period*).

5.17 A tenant who sub-lets for less than the rent they pay during the offending period cannot therefore have a UPO made against them. Similarly, no UPO is available where the tenant has parted with possession without asking for any monies from those allowed to reside in the premises in their stead.[20]

5.18 Conversely, if a tenant does not pay rent to their landlord during the sub-letting period or does not pay the full rent required, a later payment by the tenant to make-up for or exceed such a shortfall *after* any sub-letting period does not count towards step 2 of the section 5(6) calculation because it is not paid 'over a period during which the conduct … took place'. A judge would, though, have the discretion to factor it in when determining the 'appropriate' UPO, in addition to making an order for payment of arrears in the usual way.

Example calculation

A is a (sole) secure tenant of a three-bedroom property. Her landlord is a local housing authority (LHA).

18 See www.sng.org.uk/press-release/sng-secures-record-unlawful-profit-order.
19 See www.riverside.org.uk/second-largest-unlawful-profit-order-tenancy-fraud.
20 Ibid, s 5(2) – there is, by definition, no profit element in such a case.

The LHA find out in January 2024 that A has been sub-letting the property since June 2019 at a weekly rent of £230.00 (plus utility charges which remained in A's name) and since then has been living in another house which she co-owns with her partner. A notice to quit is served and A arranges for the sub-tenants to leave, then clears all arrears that had arisen on her rent account and hands in the keys to the property, which is now vacant.

A refuses to deal further with the LHA who thereupon decide against criminal prosecution under PSHF, but rather seek a UPO in a Part 7 claim brought in the county court. They assert that during the period of the sub-letting, A paid £25,000 to them towards the property's rent.

The amount sought is:

246 weeks of sub-letting × £230.00 rent received by A from sub-tenants = £56,580.00

Plus utility payments received by A from sub-tenants = £2,460.

Less £25,000 received by LHA from A *during the sub-letting period.*

Total Claim = £34,040 (plus interest)

5.19 If a criminal UPO has been made under s 4 of PSHF, then a civil court may only make an additional UPO if:

(a) the second UPO does not exceed in amount the aggregate of:

- the sum by which the tenant's profit found under section 5 of PSHF exceeds that ordered by the Magistrates' Court or Crown Court, and
- the amount that has not been recovered under the criminal UPO.[21]

(b) permission is granted by the county court or High Court when enforcement is sought to recover the sum not recovered under the criminal UPO.[22]

5.20 A UPO made by the civil courts is treated as a judgment debt. Therefore if the amount of the Order is £5,000 or more, an applicant may also seek statutory interest.[23]

5.21 The High Court authority of *Poplar HARCA v Begum and anor*,[24] referred to in Chapter 3 and still the only reported civil authority on UPOs,[25] dealt effectively with the question of how (fraudulent) housing benefit payments during the sub-letting period should be treated.

21 Ibid, s 5(7).
22 Ibid, s 5(8).
23 County Courts Act 1984, s 74; County Courts (Interest on Judgment Debts) Order 1991, SI 1991/1184 (as amended).
24 [2017] EWHC 2040 (QB), [2017] HLR 42.
25 See **3.39–3.41**.

5.22 Mr Justice Turner confirmed in *Begum* that a UPO was appropriate, and that housing benefit received during the sub-letting period should be treated as monies received:

> '42. In this case, it is evident that each and every condition under section 5(4)[26] has been fulfilled. The issue arises, however, as to the calculation of the maximum amount payable. The appellant points to the fact that a net sum of £1,550 was received by the respondents from Ms Rehana and Mr Ahmed and this is the sum which should be ordered to be paid. The Recorder, however, concluded that the rent which the respondents were collecting was less than the rent they were paying the applicants and thus assumed that the maximum payment was zero. In so doing, he left out of account the fact that the rent for the flat was covered entirely by Housing Benefit and so the monies received by the respondents from Ms Rehana and Mr Ahmed was pure profit.
>
> 43. I am satisfied that the total amount referred to under step 1 does not exclude the element of Housing Benefit. It is argued on behalf of the respondents that, on a strict interpretation of the statute, the Housing Benefit was not, in itself, received as a result of their breach of the tenancy agreement and so should be disregarded. I do not agree. The inclusion of the word "total" indicates that the gross receipts secured and consequent upon the dishonest relinquishment of possession should be considered under step 1. To hold otherwise would be to render all but nugatory the clear purpose of the section. A very considerable proportion of tenants in socially rented homes are in receipt of Housing Benefit and those who have their rents paid for them are those in the best position to be able to benefit from unlawful profiteering of this type. To disregard Housing Benefit under Step 1 but include it to the ill-gotten advantage of the fraudster under Step 2 would be to thwart the obvious intention of Parliament to provide a mechanism with which to strip him of his spoils.'

FRAUDULENT MISREPRESENTATION

Overview

5.23 Obtaining a UPO under the PSHF is, as can be seen from the Section above, a comparatively straightforward and regulated process. The situation becomes more complicated, however, where the fraud alleged does not fall within the UPO requirements and rather involves, for example, a false claim of succession, the right to buy, the right to acquire or a shared ownership transaction, or even the misrepresentation (to obtain a tenancy) factors dealt with in Chapter 2.

26 The judgment, in fact, wrongly refers to s 1(4).

5.24 Chapter 2 necessarily deals with a number of issues concerning misrepresentation, including questions as to the duty to disclose changes of circumstance and reliance, and these are further alluded to at **5.41** below. What is common ground, however, is that the proper focus here is on the fact that one of the parties to a contract, whether it be:

- a tenancy agreement or occupation contract;
- shared ownership lease; or
- right to buy/right to acquire sale,

has entered into the arrangement on the basis of a misrepresentation.

5.25 We are concerned in this book with matters of fraud and there is always a potential remedy, in cases of fraudulent misrepresentation, of rescission[27] and/or damages.[28] Rescission will have the effect of setting aside the transaction and putting the parties back into the position they were in prior to the agreement or contract. This is addressed at **5.33** onwards below, as well as being explained in Chapter 2.

5.26 For innocent and negligent misrepresentation there is no absolute right to rescission (though it is seen as the normal remedy, and damages for innocent misrepresentation will generally not be available anyway except under section 2(2) of the Misrepresentation Act 1967) because of the said legislation. Where both rescission and damages are possible the court may prefer the latter under section 2(2) of the said Act if that is seen as being more equitable (ie it will in such circumstances not award both[29]):

> '(1) Where a person has entered into a contract after a misrepresentation has been made to him by another party thereto and as a result thereof he has suffered loss, then, if the person making the misrepresentation would be liable to damages in respect thereof had the misrepresentation been made fraudulently, that person shall be so liable notwithstanding that the misrepresentation was not made fraudulently, unless he proves that he had reasonable ground to believe and did believe up to the time the contract was made the facts represented were true.
>
> (2) Where a person has entered into a contract after a misrepresentation has been made to him *otherwise than fraudulently*, and he would be entitled, by reason of the misrepresentation, to rescind the contract, then, if it is claimed, in any proceedings arising out of the contract, that the contract ought to be or has been rescinded, the court or arbitrator may declare the contract subsisting and *award damages in lieu of*

27 The court cannot refuse rescission in a fraudulent misrepresentation scenario simply on the basis that it would be seen as unjust or deny practical justice to the parties: *Patarkatsishvili v Woodward-Fisher* [2025] EWHC 265 (Ch).

28 Ibid. In addition to rescission the buyers of the property were awarded damages for consequential losses such as stamp duty land tax, legal costs and repair costs. In fraudulent misrepresentation cases this would be usual – ie rescission and damages – see *Johnson v Agnew* [1980] AC 367.

29 And both remedies are not generally available in innocent misrepresentation cases anyway.

rescission, if of opinion that it would be equitable to do so, having regard to the nature of the misrepresentation and the loss that would be caused by it if the contract were upheld, as well as to the loss that rescission would cause to the other party.' (emphasis added)

Damages may also be sought by way of the common law tort of deceit if fraudulent (**5.40–5.55**). In the latter instance, that may be in addition to or instead of any claim seeking the remedy of rescission or possession (as described in Chapter 2). For fraudulent misrepresentation (sometimes pleaded in the alternative to deceit), the following must be shown:[30]

(a) A representation was made which was false.

(b) The representor must have known the statement to be false or have been reckless as to its accuracy.

(c) There must have been intention on the part of the representor to induce the representee to act as they did.

(d) The representee must show that they understood the statement and relied on it when entering into the contract.

(e) The court must find that the representee would not have entered into the contract on the terms it did were it not for the misrepresentation.

Right to buy/acquire

5.27 Part 5 of the Housing Act 1985 gives secure tenants of more than three years' tenure (including those with the preserved right to buy[31]) in England[32] the right to buy a freehold or long leasehold interest in their homes, depending on the nature of the property and the landlord's interest in it. The previous great attraction of this right was the significant[33] statutory discounts available to such tenants.[34] As of 21 November 2024 these figures were changed. Maximum discounts are now capped at £16,000 in London (with limits ranging from £22,000 to £38,000

30 See, eg, *SK Shipping Europe Plc v Capital VLCC 3 Corp & Ors* [2020] EWHC 3448 (Comm), Foxton J at [113]–[117].

31 Housing Act 1985, s 171A. In particular, tenants of local housing authorities whose home is part of their landlord's stock transferred to a private registered provider such as a housing association become assured tenants: see Housing (Preservation of Right to Buy) Regulations 1993 (SI 1993/2241).

32 Housing Act 1985, s 119(A1) – in Wales the Abolition of the Right to Buy and Associated Rights (Wales) Act 2018 ended the right to buy, the preserved right to buy and the right to acquire in Wales.

33 The maximum discount was, before 21 November 2024, 35% rising at 1% pa for every year after the first 5 years as a public-sector tenant up to a maximum discount of 70% (not exceeding £112,800 in respect of dwelling-houses situated within the areas of London authorities, and £84,600 elsewhere), and 50% rising at 2% pa after 5 years as a public-sector tenant up to a maximum discount of 70% (not exceeding £112,800 in London and £84,600 elsewhere) in respect of flats.

34 Housing Act 1985, ss 129–131, and Sch 4.

elsewhere), with some exceptions; this is a reduction from the previous £136,400 cap in London and £102,400 elsewhere.[35]

5.28 An application to exercise the right to buy commences when the tenant serves a notice claiming the right,[36] followed by a landlord admitting or denying that right[37] and identifying the proposed price.[38]

5.29 The most obvious fraud is where a tenant seeks to exercise their apparent right to buy and yet no longer satisfies the required conditions at the time of sale (if they ever did). To give an obvious example, if the tenancy ceases to be secure at any time before completion of the right to buy (eg sub-letting of the whole of the premises or 'simply' ceasing to use it as their only or principal home) the tenant loses their entitlement to exercise the right to buy.[39]

5.30 Lord Justice Mann said in *Muir Group Housing Association Ltd v Thornley*,[40] where the tenants moved out and sub-let the subject premises after their right-to-buy application had been admitted by the landlord:

> 'I accordingly conclude that a tenant who has ceased to be a secure tenant has no right which he can enforce under section 138(3).[41] The conclusion accords with my belief that most people would find it surprising if Parliament had enacted right to buy provisions which enabled a person to acquire a house at a discount when he no longer occupied it as his only, or principal, home.'

5.31 The difficulty arising from right-to-buy cases where the fraud is *not* identified prior to the sale – where the remedies are much more obvious by way of stopping the right-to-buy process and taking any necessary action in the normal way as a result of the newly discovered sub-letting, etc – is that identified in *Haringey LBC v Hines* at **5.43** below. If there is no contract in a right-to-buy process then save for the ingenious argument, not dealt with by the Court of Appeal, that it would have to be viewed as a disposal outside of the Part 5 scheme, and thus the 'no contract' approach would not 'bite', this could rather encourage the greater reliance on criminal sanctions and activity, especially under sections 2 (false representation) and 3 (failing to disclose information) of the Fraud Act 2006. (Some companies and individuals, even family members, get local authority tenants to go through the right-to-buy process, in effect on their

35 Housing (Right to Buy) (Limits on Discounts) (England) Order 2024, SI 2024/1073.
36 Housing Act 1985, s 122(1).
37 Ibid, s 124(1).
38 Ibid, s 125.
39 *Bradford City Metropolitan Council v McMahon* [1994] 1 WLR 52, (1993) 25 HLR 534 CA (death); *Sutton LBC v Swann* (1986) 18 HLR 140 CA (no longer only or principal home); *Muir Group Housing Association Ltd v Thornley* (1993) 25 HLR 89 CA (sub-letting).
40 (1993) 25 HLR 89 CA at [97].
41 This provision allows a secure tenant, who has established the right to buy and all matters relating to the grant have been agreed or determined, to enforce the said grant of the freehold (house) or leasehold (flat) interest.

behalf, ie a deferred resale agreement. This could lead to the discount having to be repaid by the tenant pursuant to sections 155/163A of the Housing Act 1985.)

5.32 Some tenants of housing associations[42] enjoy the right to acquire their properties after three years as a public-sector tenant,[43] though the discounts were (until the 2024 changes noted at **5.27**) significantly below that for the right to buy.[44] Despite that, the same principles described above apply as for the right to buy.

Rescission

5.33 Rescission is not, of course, a financial remedy strictly speaking, but it is closely connected with the issues surrounding fraudulent misrepresentation and the tort of deceit. In broad terms, and as noted at **5.25** above, any misrepresentation which induces a party to enter a contract gives that party the right to seek the remedy of rescission of that contract. That is, a right to treat the arrangement as void, whereby the defendant in such circumstances no longer has the tenancy or right-to-buy arrangement, etc.

5.34 Rescission for fraudulent misrepresentation is in principle an absolute right and the usual and appropriate remedy,[45] though see **5.37**(f), and first requires the party affected to show that they were induced to enter into a contract as a result of a false statement made dishonestly so that they have the right to avoid and rescind that contract. In the context of tenancy fraud, therefore, it is necessary to show that there has been an incorrect statement of fact which was intended to, and did, induce the landlord to enter into a contract such as a tenancy agreement or lease.[46]

5.35 Housing practitioners will be well used to this concept when dealing with the Grounds 5 and 17 possession claims discussed in Chapter 2. This includes the rule that, where Ground 5 or 17 is available, rescission is *not* present as an alternative option for ending the tenancy.[47]

42 Registered with the Regulator of Social Housing. From the summer of 2017, the government had been running pilot schemes allowing for an extension of the right-to-buy process to housing associations on a voluntary basis, with a view to this becoming more widespread across the sector: funding arrangements to be provided for by means of Housing and Planning Act 2016, ss 64–68. This initiative is, however, not being extended with the effect that such tenants are now restricted, if qualifying, to the right to acquire.

43 See Housing and Regeneration Act 2008 (England), ss 180–184 and the Housing (Right to Acquire) Regulations 1997 (SI 1997/619).

44 Between £9,000 and £16,000: Housing (Right to Acquire) (Discount) Order 2002 (SI 2002/1091).

45 *Cavaliero v Puget* (1865) 4 F & F 537.

46 *Chitty on Contracts*, 36th edn, paras 10-055 *et seq.*

47 *Islington London Borough Council v Uckac and another* [2006] EWCA Civ 340, [2006] 1 WLR 1303. See **2.12–2.13**.

5.36 It follows from the above that this remedy is likely to be used in social housing fraud cases to recover premises obtained by fraudulent misrepresentation where the particular focus is on:

(a) right-to-buy and right-to-acquire fraudulent arrangements; and

(b) grants of tenancy where security of tenure is not retained, such that Grounds 5 and 17 are not available (see Chapter 2 at **2.8–2.19**).

5.37 Any possession claim seeking the remedy of rescission[48] would need in particular to address the following matters:

(a) If the false representation is made in an application form or similar document which warns the writer of the need to be accurate and advise of changing circumstances,[49] or if the false statement was inaccurate from the start, then such a claim starts off in a straightforward manner.

(b) Otherwise, there *may* be issues where the false statement is outside such processes and it is argued that there is no common law duty to disclose material facts.[50] This is discussed further at **2.32**; *Haringey LBC v Hines* referred to at **5.43–5.46** below is illustrative of the difficulties that can arise if the right analysis is not followed and the right questions are not asked. At the very least it confirms the common sense in local housing authorities and others making it absolutely clear on the face of any application form of the *ongoing* requirement of disclosure.

(c) The pleaded claim needs to set out the alleged fraudulent misrepresentations clearly[51] and fully.[52]

(d) In cases based on fraud:[53]

> 'The more serious the allegation the less likely it is the event occurred and hence the stronger should be the evidence before the court concludes that the allegation is established on the balance of probability. Fraud is less likely than negligence …'

(e) The tort of deceit, which is covered below at **5.40–5.55**, and damages for misrepresentation (see **5.26**) may be available in lieu of (or in addition to, especially in cases of fraudulent misrepresentation) any rescission claim.

48 Rescission is, in fact, simply communicated by the innocent party to the other, though a declaration would ordinarily be sought and (of course) if property is not voluntarily returned, possession action will be required (where one might expect the fact of rescission to be disputed).

49 Or there is a statutory requirement to disclose such as is found in the Housing Act 1996, ss 171 and 214 (re allocation and homelessness duties and powers).

50 *Ward v Hobbs* (1878) 4 App Cas 13, but see *Hurley v Dyke* [1979] RTR 265.

51 *Wallingford v Mutual Society* (1879–1880) LR 5 App Cas 685; *Abbey Forwarding Ltd (In Liquidation) v Hone* [2010] EWHC 2029 (Ch) – see CPR PD16, para 8.2(1).

52 *Lowe v Machell* [2012] 1 All ER (Comm) 153 at [74] *per* Lewison LJ; *NGM Sustainable Developments Ltd v Phillip Wallis, Lizzano Ltd, Cascina Ltd, Kevin Reardon, Hydro Properties Ltd, Hydro Property Holdings Ltd* [2015] EWHC 2089 (Ch) at [55] *per* Peter Smith J.

53 *Re: H (Sexual abuse, standard of proof)* [1996] AC 563 at [586] *per* Lord Nicholls.

(f) As an equitable remedy rescission may not always be available. For example:

- Has too long elapsed such that rescission would be inequitable?[54]
- Is it simply not possible to restore the parties to their pre-contract position?
- Has the innocent party affirmed the contract?
- Have third-party rights, such as a mortgagee, intervened?
- Would the remedy of rescission lead to an unjust enrichment?[55]

5.38 If the fact of rescission is though clear and sustainable then:

(a) In a right-to-buy/right-to-acquire scenario, it leaves the parties in their previous position of landlord and tenant. If, then, the reason for the rescission is, say, that the tenant had sub-let the whole of the premises at any time prior to the grant of the freehold/leasehold interest then a notice to quit or section 146 notice (in a flexible tenancy case) can be served and separate possession proceedings taken.[56]

(b) If the problem was that the tenant 'simply' was not living at the premises as their only or principal home, but had not sub-let or parted with possession of the whole, then again a notice to quit or section 146 notice could be served but it may be advisable to also serve a notice seeking possession (breach of tenancy) because the loss of security of tenure here – as previously explained at **4.4** – is ambulatory and the tenant may move back in prior to the expiry of any notice to quit such that it is of no effect.

(c) In a shared ownership case, once rescission is achieved the occupants would have no tenancy at all, having moved into the premises at the outset under a (now voided) shared ownership arrangement. Possession, thereafter, should then be straightforward.

Damages

5.39 As referred to at **5.26**, damages may be available to a successful claimant landlord, in particular in relation to the false representation cases dealt with in Chapter 2, though this is achievable not only under the Misrepresentation Act 1967 in a case of fraudulent misrepresentation where the inducement was into a contract (ie tenancy agreement) but also by way of the common law tort of deceit.

54 *Fisher v Brooker* [2009] UKHL 41, [2009] 1 WLR 1764 at [64] *per* Lord Neuberger.

55 *Halpern v Halpern* [2007] 1 CLC 527, [2008] QB 195 at [61–75] *per* Carnwath LJ.

56 Given that rescission is 'declared' by the innocent party prior to any possession claim, then such a claim will likely seek a declaration of the rescission as well as a possession order in reliance on the notice to quit, s 146, notice seeking possession.

DECEIT

5.40 The tort of deceit is a separate (common law) cause of action[57] which *may* provide grounds for damages in and of itself, though it is fair to report that it is not a common basis of action at all in the social housing context (particularly where the claimant is a private registered provider of social housing as opposed to a local housing authority). In 2017 the Supreme Court summarised the tort as follows:[58]

> '18 Subject to one point, the ingredients of a claim for deceit based upon an alleged fraudulent misrepresentation are not in dispute. It must be shown that the defendant made a materially false representation which was intended to, and did, induce the representee to act to its detriment. To my mind it is not necessary, as a matter of law, to prove that the representee believed that the representation was true. In my opinion there is no clear authority to the contrary. However, that is not to say that the representee's state of mind may not be relevant to the issue of inducement. Indeed, it may be very relevant. For example, if the representee does not believe that the representation is true, he may have serious difficulty in establishing that he was induced to enter into the contract or that he has suffered loss as a result … .'

5.41 Mr Justice Soole provided an equally as helpful but longer 'run through' of the necessary constituent parts of the tort of deceit when he gave judgment in *Barley v Muir*:[59]

> '1. A claimant must establish that there was
>
> (a) a representation,
>
> (b) that representation was false,
>
> (c) it was dishonestly made, **and**
>
> (d) it was intended to be relied on: *AIC Ltd v ITS Testing Services (UK) Ltd* [2006] EWCA Civ 1601, [2007] 1 All ER (Comm) 667 at para. 251 per Rix LJ.
>
> 2. The dishonest representation must be clearly identified, distinctly alleged and as distinctly proved: *AIC* at para. 254, and *Paragon Finance plc v DB Thakerar & Co* [1999] 1 All ER 400.
>
> 3. The standard of proof is the civil standard: *Re B* [2009] 1 AC 11 at para. 13 per Lord Hoffmann.

57 A claim for fraudulent misrepresentation is generally founded in the tort of deceit as well as any remedy of rescission. Jackson LJ said in *Ludsin Overseas Ltd v Eco3 Capital Ltd* [2013] EWCA Civ 413 at para 80: 'That tort can equally well be described as fraudulent misrepresentation. Regardless of what label is applied, the defendant will be liable if the four ingredients set out above are established'.

58 *Zurich Insurance Co plc v Hayward* [2016] UKSC 48, [2017] AC 142 per Lord Clarke JSC.

59 [2018] EWHC 619 (QB) at paras 173–183.

4. The representation must be one of fact. A statement of opinion will not suffice unless the deceit is in the fact that the opinion was not, or not honestly, held or in some further implicit dishonest misrepresentation of fact to be derived from the statement of opinion: *AIC* at para. 255.

5. A representation by a professional person in a position where he would be expected to have significantly greater knowledge of the facts represented then did the representee will or may carry an implied representation that the representor or has reasonable grounds for making the statement: *Barings plc (in liquidation) v Coopers & Lybrand* [2002] EWHC 461 (Ch), [2002] 2 BCLC 410 at paras. 50 to 52.

6. Whether any and if so what representation has been made has to be "judged objectively according to the impact that whatever is said may be expected to have on a reasonable representee in the position and with the known characteristics of the actual representee" … The reference to the characteristics of the representee is important. The court may regard a sophisticated commercial party who was told that no representations are being made to him quite differently than it would a consumer. In the case of an express statement, "the court has to consider what a reasonable person would have understood from the words used in the context in which they were used" … The answer to that question may depend on the nature and content of the statement, the context in which it was made, the characteristics of the maker and of the person to whom it was made, and the relationship between them': *Raiffesen Zentralbank Osterreich v Royal Bank of Scotland plc* [2010] EWHC 1392 (Comm) at paras. 80 to 82 per Christopher Clarke J.

7. As to implied representations, the court has to perform a similar task except that it has to consider what a reasonable person would have inferred was being implicitly represented by the representor's words and conduct in their context: *Raiffeisen* at para. 83.

8. As to falsity, it is not necessary for what was said to be entirely correct, provided it is substantially correct, and the difference between what is represented and what is actually correct would not have been likely to induce a reasonable person in the position of the claimant to enter into the contract. The claimant must show that the difference between what was represented and the truth would have been likely to induce a reasonable person in its position to enter into the contract: *Raiffensen* at para. 149.

9. As to dishonesty, "fraud is proved when it is shown that a false representation has been made (1) knowingly, (2) without belief in its truth, or (3) recklessly, careless whether it be true or false": *Derry v. Peek* (1889) 14 App Cas 337 at 374; see *AIC* at para. 256.

10. As to recklessness, "Not caring, in that context, did not mean not taking care, it meant indifference to the truth, the moral obliquity of which

consists in a wilful disregard of the importance of truth…": *Angus v. Clifford* [1891] 2 Ch 449 at 471; see also *AIC* at para. 257.

11. As to intent, it is possible to be fraudulent even by means of an ambiguous statement, but in such a case it is essential that the representor should have intended the statement to be understood in the sense in which it is understood by the claimant … or should have deliberately used the ambiguity for the purpose of deceiving him and succeeded in doing so: AIC at para.253; see also *Goose v. Sandford* [2001] Lloyd's Rep PN 189 at para. 41.

12. As to inducement/reliance, the misrepresentation need not be the sole or predominant cause of entering the contract. It is sufficient if it is one of the inducing causes: *Ross River v. Cambridge City Football Club* [2007] EWHC 2115 (Ch) at [200].'

The claimant must also demonstrate that they suffered loss as a consequence,[60] although Master Pester noted in *Aitsan Limited and others v Duffy and Anor*:[61]

> 'However, there is authority that where a claim proves that he has been deceived into expending money, the burden shifts to the defendant if he wishes to argue that the expenditure did not amount to a loss to the claimant: see Clerk & Lindsell , at 17-43; also *Parallel Imports (Europe) Ltd t/a Baglan Car Centre v Radivan* [2007] EWCA Civ 1373.'

5.42 As with the analysis of Grounds 5 and 17 in Chapter 2, the more material the statement, the stronger the presumption that it induced the claimant to enter into it.[62] That is clear from *Hines* referred to at **5.37**(b) above and immediately below; further, Lord Justice Hobhouse said in *Downs v Chappell*:[63]

> 'The judge was wrong to ask how they [the representees] would have acted if they had been told the truth. They were never told the truth. They were told lies in order to induce them to enter into the contract. The lies were material and successful … The judge should have concluded that the plaintiffs had proved their case on causation …'

5.43 Putting all the above in a social housing context, and appreciating the potential pitfalls of such a claim, in *Haringey LBC v Hines*[64] the defendant sought to exercise her right to buy and in the statutory notice she stated (wrongly) that the relevant premises were her only or principal home. She was granted a long

60 *Smith v Chadwick* (1883–84) LR 9 App Cas 187 HL – this is another question of fact. Fancourt J in *Patarkatsishvili, Hunyak v Woodward-Fisher* [2025] EWHC 265 (Ch) at para 250 said: 'For claims in deceit, a claimant is entitled to recover for all such damage as flows directly from the transaction, including consequential losses, without any limit on the basis of foreseeability of loss. However, the loss must be causally connected with the deceit'.

61 [2025] EWHC 1562 (Ch) at [26].

62 *Ross River Ltd v Cambridge City Football Club Ltd* [2008] 1 All ER 1004 at [241] *per* Briggs J.

63 [1997] 1 WLR 426 at [433].

64 [2010] EWCA Civ 1111, [2011] HLR 6.

lease, but six years later the local authority discovered that she had, in fact, lived elsewhere at the time of purchase.

5.44 In July 2008, the authority brought a claim in the county court against the defendant contending that, by accepting the offer to buy the flat, she had falsely represented:

(a) that she was still occupying it as her only or principal home; and

(b) that she was entitled to exercise the right to buy.

It was alleged that these representations were fraudulent because she knew that they were untrue. The authority claimed, amongst other remedies, damages for misrepresentation.

5.45 The trial judge held that the authority did not have a claim in misrepresentation because an acquisition under the right to buy was not a contract,[65] but that they had succeeded in establishing a claim in deceit. He awarded the authority damages of £38,000 plus interest.

5.46 The Court of Appeal allowed the tenant's appeal and held that the judge's finding that the defendant knew that her flat had ceased to be her only or principal home before the 16 May 2002 acceptance of the section 125 offer notice did not, of itself, establish the claim in deceit. Rather the authority had to also demonstrate that, as at that date, the defendant:

(a) knew, as a matter of law, that the flat had to remain her only or principal home throughout the right-to-buy process;

(b) knew that the flat was no longer her only or principal home; and

(c) dishonestly intended her acceptance of the authority's proposed terms of acquisition to mislead the authority so that she could acquire the flat even though she was no longer entitled to do so.

5.47 If those hurdles can be overcome, however, the correct measure of damages in deceit is an award which serves to put the claimant into the position they would have been in if the representation had not been made to them.[66] As is said in Clerk & Lindsell on *Torts*, 24th edn, 2024, at 17-45:

> '… the loss directly flowing from the claimant's reliance on the defendant's statement; that is, generally speaking, the sum that will put him in the same position as if he had not relied on it. Credit must of course be given for any gains made by the claimant, though to qualify for deduction such gains must be closely connected with the relevant transaction, and also both tangible and relatively permanent.' (citations to the authorities omitted)

65 Thereby following *Rushton v Worcester City Council* [2001] EWCA Civ 367, [2002] HLR 9.
66 *Doyle v Olby (Ironmongers) Ltd* [1969] 2 QB 158.

5.48 As the misrepresentation will have been made fraudulently, all losses flowing from it can be recovered, even if they are not reasonably foreseeable.[67] For example, if a claim in deceit is brought alongside a Ground 5 possession claim brought by a local housing authority, as described at Chapter 2, this may potentially include the cost of temporary accommodation for a third-party household who would have been granted the tenancy were it not for the defendant's fraud which led to the premises being allocated elsewhere.

5.49 To give a practical example, the Cornerstone on Social Housing Fraud blog reported on 24 April 2018 a case at the County Court at Central London concerning a damages claim for fraudulent misrepresentation.

5.50 The defendant had applied to the claimant local authority for housing assistance in 2003. In 2009 he was offered a tenancy of a flat and signed a declaration confirming that his housing circumstances had not changed since he had first applied, and that he had no other accommodation to live in.

5.51 That information was clearly wrong as he had in fact purchased a house in 2005 and when this was discovered many years later he was prosecuted under the Fraud Act 2006. In 2015, he pleaded guilty to five offences, including an offence of fraud by false representation contrary to section 2 of the Fraud Act 2006, and was sentenced to 16 months' imprisonment.

5.52 The local authority thereafter started a civil action to recover damages of £69,842.64 for the defendant's fraudulent misrepresentation. Importantly and appropriately, this sum was based on the estimated cost of securing one unit of temporary accommodation for other applicants for housing during the period in which the defendant was the tenant of the flat.

5.53 At trial HHJ Saggerson found for the local authority and ordered the defendant to pay damages of £69,842.64 (whilst also holding that rent payments made could not be taken into account as a credit by the defendant as these were payable by whoever occupied the property). The defendant was also ordered to pay the local authority's costs, which were summarily assessed.

5.54 The judge rejected challenges to the claim based, for example, on causation and remoteness of damage, though doubted whether the original pleading of breach of contract as the cause of action was sustainable. He had though no doubt that the amended statement of case introducing a fraudulent misrepresentation claim was clearly made out.

5.55 Finally, it is worth noting that, whereas in a claim under section 2(1) of the Misrepresentation Act 1967 it is for the defendant to show that they had reasonable grounds for believing the offending statement to be true, in the tort of deceit that burden (ie knowledge/recklessness as to the falsity) falls on the claimant.

67 *Royscott Trust v Rogerson* [1991] 2 QB 297, CA.

CONCLUSION

5.56 In a case covered by the PSHF, a UPO will be commonplace and, usually, advisable. As Chapter 7 makes clear and explains, there may also be criminal confiscation and compensation orders on the agenda, but rarely consideration of much else.

5.57 Having said that, the spectre of a tort of deceit/fraudulent misrepresentation claim does present a useful 'bargaining chip' where fraud is discovered, as well as, in appropriate cases, a potentially fruitful cause of action, in particular for local housing authorities seeking to recover the costs of accommodating those households in temporary accommodation because premises which should be or should have been available to them are not because of the fraud.

CHAPTER 6

Investigation and Evidence

- Witness evidence
- Data Protection Act 2018
- Data sharing
- Covert surveillance
- PSHF Regulations
- Court powers
- 'Missing' witnesses

Key points

- Data Protection legislation – the Data Protection Act 2018 (DPA) and UK GDPR – should not be seen as a bar to a social landlord obtaining third party information about possible fraudulent activity in respect of their premises. There are sufficient provisions to allow 'processing' (ie disclosure) and the bigger issue is 'persuading' the third party of this.
- Because of these practical difficulties of *in fact* receiving requested information, local authorities have particular powers to request and obtain information from banks, utility providers, etc, as provided for in the Prevention of Social Housing Fraud Act 2013 (PSHF) and attendant regulations.
- Local Authorities further frequently interview, under caution, those tenants suspected of benefit fraud and for offences under the PSHF/ Fraud Act 2006.
- Covert surveillance is not common in housing fraud investigations but may be used (with, for local authorities, the proper authorisation).
- The Civil Procedure Rules 1998 provide a social landlord with the tools to obtain further details of a defendant's case and its evidential basis before trial, such as by way of an application for specific disclosure/third party disclosure or a Part 18 request for further information.
- The Rules also require the landlord to ensure that they themselves comply with any relevant provisions, such as the service of a CPR 32.19 notice, if they want the other side to prove the authenticity of a disclosed document (see **6.75**).

INTRODUCTION

6.1 The successful detection and prosecution of social housing fraud invariably depends on good and reliable information. You often hear the phrase 'something smells', particularly when it comes to potential sub-letting and only or principal home cases, and the social landlord concerned frequently has a sound basis for investigation. But will they ultimately have enough evidence to proceed to court?

6.2 Some information is easily come by, such as reports from neighbours or the social landlord's own records. For example, the landlord may have received complaints of anti-social behaviour in one of their properties, yet the alleged perpetrators do not match the expected occupants.

6.3 Similarly, by way of further example, the social landlord's gas contractor may have visited premises to carry out an annual inspection and been met by an individual other than the tenant who states that *they* are living there with their family and not the tenant. Annual tenancy audits by social landlords are, of course, a deliberate means of detecting any such inconsistencies with their records.

6.4 Obtaining *sufficient* evidence to justify further action, such as a claim for possession of residential premises or an unlawful profit order, can though be more difficult and requires ingenuity, persistence and a sound understanding of the tools at the social landlord's (and their partners') disposal.

6.5 This chapter considers those 'tools' and their legislative underpinning, both in the context of pre- and post-court issue activity. If used effectively, they may ensure the relevant disclosure and obtaining of data such as:

- housing benefit/universal credit/council tax support records;
- electoral roll information;
- credit applications and use;
- ownership of other property;
- utility bills and usage;
- police information; and
- bank statements.

6.6 They may also ensure that the defendant in any claim is required to provide more information and explanation than a bare denial, however eloquently put.[1]

1 Bearing in mind that CPR 16.5 does require more than a bare denial in many instances such that a failure to address or explain their responses to pleaded allegations in any particulars claim may lead to an application to strike out the defence (and probably an unless order being sought for a fully compliant statement of case by a specified date).

WITNESS EVIDENCE

6.7 Before considering the obtaining of documentary evidence to support the action by or on behalf of a social landlord, it is worth briefly addressing the value of lay witnesses in any trial. To give a few examples of where this may be useful:

- as evidence of other persons staying at the demised premises than the tenant(s);
- to show that the tenant is living elsewhere;
- to illustrate relevant conversations in meetings, at visits or in interview; or
- by a sub-tenant in support of sub-letting allegations.

6.8 The impact of not calling witnesses or particular witnesses is dealt with later in this chapter. Here we are concerned with the value of evidence heard and tested at trial (though note the final observation of Mr Justice Trower at **6.10**).

6.9 In *Gestmin SGPS SA v Credit Suisse (UK) Ltd*[2] Leggatt J (as he then was) said about the difficulties of memory recollection:

> 'In the light of these considerations, the best approach for a judge to adopt in the trial of a commercial case is, in my view, to place little if any reliance at all on witnesses' recollections of what was said in meetings and conversations, and to base factual findings on inferences drawn from the documentary evidence and known or probable facts. This does not mean that oral testimony serves no useful purpose – though its utility is often disproportionate to its length. But its value lies largely, as I see it, in the opportunity which cross-examination affords to subject the documentary record to critical scrutiny and to gauge the personality, motivations and working practices of a witness, rather than in testimony of what the witness recalls of particular conversations and events. Above all, it is important to avoid the fallacy of supposing that, because a witness has confidence in his or her recollection and is honest, evidence based on that recollection provides any reliable guide to the truth.'

6.10 Similarly, in *JSC Commercial Bank Privatbank v Kolomoisky & Ors*[3] Mr Justice Trower explained:

> 'There was no dispute at the trial that the general approach to proving a case in fraud was comprehensively summarised by Bryan J in *JSC BM Bank v. Kekhman* [2018] EWHC 791 (Comm) ("*Kekhman*") at [41] – [92] and *Yurov* at [50]. For present purposes, it is not necessary to recite those passages in full. The following headline points suffice:

2 [2013] EWHC 3560 (Comm) at para 22.
3 [2025] EWHC 1987 (Ch) at para 47.

i) Fraud or dishonesty must be distinctly alleged and distinctly proved; it must be sufficiently particularised, and it is not sufficiently particularised if the facts pleaded are consistent with innocence or negligence.

ii) As in an ordinary civil claim, the burden of proof is on the claimant and the fact that fraud is alleged does not change the standard of proof from being the balance of probability. When assessing the probabilities, the court will have in mind, to whatever extent is appropriate in the particular case, that the more serious the allegation the less likely it is that the event occurred and, hence, the stronger should be the evidence before the court concludes that the allegation is established.

iii) Inherent probabilities can be weighed alongside or against specific evidence from a particular case. But care must be taken in working out what in a particular case is inherently probable or improbable. It is generally correct that absent other information, the more serious the wrongdoing, the less likely it is that it was carried out, because most people are not serious wrongdoers. The standard of proof remains the same, but more cogent evidence is required to prove fraud than to prove negligence or innocence because the evidence has to outweigh the countervailing inherent improbability.

iv) Memories are fallible, people can convince themselves of the veracity of false recollections of events and retain confidence in their false recollection, and a judge's ability to evaluate honesty and reliability merely from a witness's demeanour is also fallible. Therefore, where possible, a court should rely on documentary evidence and any other objectively provable facts.

v) The nature of circumstantial evidence is that its effect is cumulative, and the essence of a successful case based on circumstantial evidence is that the whole is stronger than individual parts.

vi) Hearsay evidence of a witness who has not been cross-examined is generally given less weight than the evidence of a witness who has been called and cross-examined and had their evidence tested in cross-examination.'

6.11 The last case reference in this section concerns the judgment of Mr Justice Picken in *McLaren Indy LLC, McLaren Racing Ltd v Alpha Racing USA LLC and others*[4] in which he considered the proper approach to the consideration of witness testimony and other evidential matters. This included the following observations:

(a) The *Gestmin* approach may not be open to a Judge, or will only be of limited assistance, where there is no or limited contemporaneous documentary evidence (para 84).

4 [2026] EWHC 110 (Comm) at paras 81–135.

(b) '... evasive or argumentative evidence, straining the meaning of plain words, self-contradiction, the making of speeches instead of answering questions and a changing position upon cross-examination are all factors that go to credibility' (para 85).

DATA PROTECTION ACT 2018

Introduction

6.12 Section 2 of the DPA explains:

'(1) The UK GDPR[5] and this Act protect individuals with regard to the processing of personal data, in particular by–

(a) requiring personal data to be processed lawfully and fairly, on the basis of the data subject's consent or another specified basis,

(b) conferring rights on the data subject to obtain information about the processing of personal data and to require inaccurate personal data to be rectified, and

(c) conferring functions on the Commissioner, giving the holder of that office responsibility for monitoring and enforcing their provisions.'

6.13 The DPA,[6] along with the UK GDPR, has heightened and updated the data protection previously enshrined in its 1998 predecessor. To cite from a guide (for organisations) for lawful use of data on the Information Commissioner's Office's (ICO's) website:[7]

'• You **must** have a valid lawful basis to handle personal information.

• There are seven lawful bases available for you to use. No single basis is 'better' or more important than the others. The most appropriate basis depends on your purpose and relationship with the person.

• Most lawful bases say that what you want to do **must** be 'necessary'. If you can reasonably achieve the same purpose without the processing, you won't have a lawful basis.

5 Regulation (EU) 2016/679 of the European Parliament and of the Council of 27 April 2016 on the protection of natural persons with regard to the processing of personal data and on the free movement of such data (United Kingdom General Data Protection Regulation), as it forms part of the law of England and Wales, Scotland and Northern Ireland by virtue of s 3 of the European Union (Withdrawal) Act 2018 (and see s 205(4)).

6 As amended in particular by the Data Protection, Privacy and Electronic Communications (Amendments etc) (EU Exit) Regulations 2019, the Data Protection, Privacy and Electronic Communications (Amendments etc) (EU Exit) Regulations 2020 and the Data (Use and Access) Act 2025.

7 See https://ico.org.uk/for-organisations/uk-gdpr-guidance-and-resources/lawful-basis/a-guide-to-lawful-basis.

- You **must** determine your lawful basis before you start using the personal information and you **must** document it.
- Take care to get it right first time – you **should not** swap to a different lawful basis at a later date without good reason. In particular, you can't usually swap from consent to a different basis.
- You **must** include your lawful basis and your purposes for using the personal information in your privacy information.
- If your purposes change, you **must** identify a lawful basis for the new purpose. Your original lawful basis may not always be appropriate.
- If you want to use special category data, you **must** identify both a lawful basis and an additional condition for using this type of information.
- If you want to use criminal conviction data or information about offences, you **must** identify both a lawful basis and an additional condition for using this type of information (if you don't have official authority to use the information).'

6.14 The ICO is the regulator responsible for making sure that organisations comply with the DPA. It also has a remit for promoting good practice in information handling. For example, the ICO has provided invaluable guidance on data protection and data sharing[8] which is discussed below.

6.15 In terms of social housing fraud, data protection issues impact most obviously upon what information the social landlord can obtain from third parties – directly or through another body – about an allegedly errant tenant or others (such as their partner or supposed sub-tenants) and, to a lesser degree relevance-wise to the topic of housing fraud, what data a social landlord can hold on their tenants and others. *Experience has shown that the difficulties encountered have less to do with the operation of the DPA and UK GDPR, but more to do with the willingness of companies being prepared to co-operate in providing requested information regardless.*

6.16 Having said that it is helpful to have an overview of data protection legislation, if only to be able to better respond to its improper invoking as an excuse not to assist. The four main areas covered by the said legislation are:

(a) General data processing;

(b) Law enforcement data processing;

(c) Data processing by the Intelligence Services; and

(d) Regulatory oversight and enforcement.

8 See https://ico.org.uk/for-organisations/uk-gdpr-guidance-and-resources/data-sharing. Due to the Data (Use and Access) Act 2025 coming into law on 19 June 2025 the Guidance is under review at the time of writing.

Data protection: personal data

6.17 Before addressing the first of those issues it is helpful to clarify what is encompassed by 'personal data', the processing of which is being protected by the data protection legislation:

(a) It means any information relating to an identified or identifiable living individual[9] (such as a tenant). This includes, for example, an identifier such as a name, an identification number, IP address, cookie identifier or location data, or one or more factors specific to the physical, physiological, genetic, mental, economic, cultural or social identity of the individual.

(b) It applies to the *processing* of such data wholly or partly by automated means, *or* otherwise forms part of, or is intended to form part of, a filing system (eg case files).

(c) Information about companies, public authorities or a deceased person is not 'personal data'.

6.18 Lord Justice Auld considered the breadth of the definition of 'personal data', at the time of the Data Protection Act 1998, in *Durant v Financial Services Authority*[10] and concluded, in an analysis which holds good today:

(a) not all information retrieved from a computer search against an individual's name or unique identifier is personal data within the DPA;

(b) mere mention of the data subject in a document held by a data controller does not necessarily amount to her or his 'personal data';

(c) whether it does so in any particular instance depends on *'where it falls in a continuum of relevance or proximity to the data subject as distinct, say, from transactions or matters in which he may have been involved to a greater or lesser degree'*;

(d) it may be relevant to consider whether the information is biographical in a significant sense (ie it goes beyond the recording of the putative data subject's involvement in a matter or an event that has no personal connotations, a life event in respect of which his privacy could not be said to be compromised);

(e) the information should have the putative data subject as its focus rather than some other person with whom they may have been involved or some transaction or event in which they may have figured or have had an interest; and

(f) in essence, it should be information that affects her or his privacy, whether in their personal or family life, business or professional capacity.[11]

9 DPA, s 3(2), following the UK GDPR definition at Art 4(1): 'any information relating to an identified or identifiable natural person (data subject)'.

10 [2003] EWCA Civ 1746, [2004] FSR 28 at para 28.

11 In Case C-101/01 *Criminal Proceedings against Lindquist* (6 November 2003), the court held, at para 27, that 'personal data' covered the name of a person or identification of him by some other means (eg by giving his telephone number or information regarding his working conditions or hobbies).

6.19 The meaning of 'personal data' was reconsidered by the Court of Appeal in *Edem v Information Commissioner*.[12] Mr Edem wished to know the name of the FSA staff members who had dealt with his complaint. The First-tier Tribunal held that the information did not constitute personal data because the way in which it was used did not satisfy the test of biological significance or focus set out in *Durant*. The Court of Appeal disagreed and considered that the FSA staff members' names were personal because in the relevant context, their names were sufficient to identify them. The Court of Appeal, in the judgment of Moses LJ at [21], further endorsed the ICO's technical guidance to assist in determining what is personal data, where it stated:

> 'It is important to remember that it is not always necessary to consider "biographical significance" to determine whether data is personal data. In many cases data may be personal data simply because its content is such that it is "obviously about" an individual. Alternatively, data may be personal data because it is clearly "linked to" an individual because it is about his activities and is processed for the purpose of determining or influencing the way in which that person is treated. You need to consider "biographical significance" only where information is not "obviously about" an individual or clearly "linked to" him.'

6.20 More recently, in *Ashley v Revenue and Customs Commissioners*,[13] Mrs Justice Heather Williams considered 'personal data' in a somewhat different legislative context at paragraphs 74 to 124 of her judgment and said of *Durant*:[14]

> 'The general proposition that whether information "relates to" the data subject may be a question of degree on a continuum of relevance is not, as I understand it, contentious. Whilst Auld LJ's two "notions" have been cited in a number of the later cases, looked at in context, it is apparent that he was not laying down an exhaustive list of the ways in which information may "relate to" a data subject, as opposed to providing suggested indicators that were at least partly prompted by the circumstances of the particular case before the court. By way of example, Auld LJ does not refer in terms to the impact of the information in question upon the data subject; albeit his reference to the "focus" of the information may be wide enough to accommodate this. As I will return to, Ms Proops also points out that it is now clear that the purpose of the exercise of data access rights extends beyond affording protection to a data subject's right to privacy.'

'As I have observed when undertaking my chronological review of the authorities, ***Durant*** was clearly a correct decision on its facts and the indicators or "notions" identified by Auld LJ as to when information would "relate to" a data subject stemmed from the circumstances of that case and were not advanced as or intended to be an exhaustive account of how the statutory test could be met (paras

12 [2014] EWCA Civ 92.

13 [2025] EWHC 134 (KB), [2025] 4 WLR 29.

14 Paragraphs 83 and 164.

82–83 and 88 above). In any event the second of Auld LJ's notions—whether the data subject is the "focus" of the information—is not necessarily out of step with the later authorities, if it is applied in a manner that reflects the broad way in which the concept of "personal data" has subsequently been interpreted in those authorities, including that this focus may come not only from the content of the information, but from its purpose or effect.'6.21
In reality, the definition of 'personal data' causes little pause for thought in the majority of social housing fraud investigations – trying to find out where the tenant in fact lives or lived, whether they owned property at the time of their housing application, etc is invariably going to involve the identification of an individual from the information sought/provided (and indeed that is its purpose) and thus constitute the seeking of 'personal data'.

Retention of information

6.22 Whatever the precise definition of 'personal data', or indeed 'data', it is good practice for a social landlord to make clear to tenants and others that certain data is collected by them and may be shared in certain circumstances. This is usually done in the form of what is commonly known as a 'fair processing notice' and examples can be seen on a number of social landlords' websites.[15]

6.23 What information can be retained, however, in what form and for how long will be informed by data protection principles referred to at **6.29**. There are *some* supplementary provisions to be found in the DPA for particular purposes:

(a) Part 3 of the DPA, sections 34–42A, for law enforcement processing; and

(b) Part 4 of the DPA, sections 85–91A, for intelligence services processing.

Obtaining of information: introduction

6.24 As for the important issue of the obtaining of information from a third party, *save for freely given responses* to enquiries from people such as:

(a) neighbours of the premises under investigation or of where the tenant is thought to be living in cases of only or principal home or sub-letting/parting with possession concerns;

(b) family of the tenant;

(c) sub-tenants in a sub-letting case; and occasionally

15 See, eg, Birmingham City Council's Privacy Statement available at www.birmingham.gov.uk/info/50333/privacy/2926/privacy_statement. See also that used by the Hyde Group available at: www.hyde-housing.co.uk/privacy/#:~:text=We%20may%20use%20your%20personal%20data%20to%20carry%20out%20internal,legitimate%20interests%20for%20these%20purposes.

(d) the person(s) under investigation themselves given voluntarily to the social landlord or those investigating on their behalf (whether under caution or not),

the difficulty can often be, as already noted, 'persuading' the third party that the legitimate data protection rights of the subject individual concerned do not in fact or law prevent the information's disclosure.

6.25 In the context of a social housing fraud investigation and the gathering of evidence, the DPA and UK GDPR may be said to provide a potential 'hurdle' to obtaining access to information held by other bodies about that person, but one which is not necessarily or indeed (often) insurmountable.

6.26 As indicated at **6.5**, in addressing this issue we are concerned with data held by organisations such as the police, utility companies, employers and the banks, as well as more general and widespread information such as may be secured by credit reference agencies and other companies. In short, information commonly seen in housing fraud trial bundles.

6.27 This is in addition to the personal information already held by the social landlords themselves in respect of their tenants (see **6.2–6.3**), such as:

(a) household names, date of birth, contact details, religion, ethnicity, etc;

(b) complaints and correspondence;

(c) support contact details and physical/mental health information;

(d) tenancy agreements, repair requests, details of family members living at premises;

and the question of what can be 'processed' therefore has to be next considered having satisfied the definition of 'data' and 'personal data'.

Obtaining of information: processing

6.28 As noted at **6.17**, it is the 'processing' of 'personal data' that is protected under the DPA and UK GDPR. The meaning of 'personal data' is explained at **6.17–6.21**, so what is meant by 'processing'? Section 3(4) of the DPA defines 'processing', with regard to information, as the:

(a) collection, recording, organisation, structuring or storage;

(b) adaptation or alteration;

(c) retrieval, consultation or use;

(d) disclosure by transmission, dissemination or otherwise making available;

(e) alignment or combination; or

(f) restriction, erasure or destruction.[16]

16 Subject to ss 3(14)(c), 5(7), 29(2) and 82(3), which make provision about references to processing in the different Parts of the DPA.

6.29 In addressing the question of 'processing' and its operation for the purposes for which a social landlord would be concerned, regard must be had, in particular, to the six data protection principles set out in the UK GDPR in respect of personal data.[17] These will need to be complied with and they are set out in full in Appendix A. In summary they are as follows:

(1) The first data protection principle – requirement that processing be lawful, fair and transparent.

(2) The second data protection principle – requirement that purposes of processing be specified, explicit and legitimate.

(3) The third data protection principle – requirement that personal data be adequate, relevant and not excessive.

(4) The fourth data protection principle – requirement that personal data be accurate and, where necessary, kept up to date.

(5) The fifth data protection principle – requirement that personal data be kept for no longer than is necessary for the purpose for which it was processed.

(6) The sixth data protection principle – requirement that personal data be processed in a secure manner.

6.30 Most crucially, Article 6(1) of the UK GDPR sets out the conditions referred to in the First Principle, at least one of which must be met so that information can be lawfully processed:

- The data subject has given their consent to the processing of his or her personal data for one or more specific purposes:[18] para (a).
- The processing is necessary for the performance of a contract to which the data subject is a party or in order to take steps at the request of the data subject prior to entering into a contract: para (b).
- The processing is necessary for compliance with any legal obligation to which the data controller is subject: para (c).
- The processing is necessary to protect the vital interests of the data subject or of another natural person: para (d).
- The processing is necessary for the performance of a task carried out in the public interest or in the exercise of official authority vested in the controller: para (e).[19]

17 UK GDPR, Art 5(1), as amended by the Data (Use and Access) Act 2025.

18 See UK GDPR, Arts 7–8.

19 DPA, s 8 makes it clear that this includes processing of personal data that is necessary for the administration of justice, the exercise of a function of either House of Parliament, the exercise of a function conferred on a person by an enactment or rule of law, the exercise of a function of the Crown, a Minister of the Crown or a government department, or an activity that supports or promotes democratic engagement.

- The process is necessary for the purposes of a recognised legitimate interest: para (ea).[20]
- The processing is necessary for the purposes of legitimate interests pursued by the controller or by a third party, except where such interests are overridden by the interests or fundamental rights and freedoms of the data subject which require protection of personal data, in particular where the data subject is a child: para (f).

6.31 There is an additional requirement when it comes to what is referred to as 'special categories of personal data'.[21] This latter term is defined at Article 9 of the UK GDPR as consisting of information as to:

(a) the racial or ethnic origin of the data subject;

(b) their political opinions;

(c) their religious or philosophical beliefs;

(d) trade union membership;

(e) the processing of genetic data, biometric data for the purpose of uniquely identifying a natural person, data concerning health or data concerning a natural person's sex life or sexual orientation.

6.32 In those cases processing of personal data is prohibited unless at least one of the ten conditions set down at Article 9(2) of the UK GDPR[22] is satisfied for the First Principle to be capable of being satisfied. These conditions include explicit consent, it being necessary 'for the establishment, exercise or defence of legal claims or whenever courts or tribunals are acting in their judicial capacity' and personal data 'manifestly made public by the data subject'.

6.33 As for criminal convictions, section 10(5), (6) of the DPA provides – with regard to the processing of personal data relating to criminal convictions and offences or related security measures that is not carried out under the control of official authority – that they must meet a condition in Part 1, 2 or 3 of Schedule 1.[23] This includes:

> '(a) Processing is necessary for the administration of justice: para 7(a).
>
> (b) Processing is necessary to prevent fraud and consists of the disclosure and processing of personal data by a member of an anti-fraud organisation[24], or in accordance with arrangements made by an anti-fraud organisation: para 14.

20 UK GDPR, Art 6(1)(ea) (inserted 19 June 2025 for the purposes of making regulations, otherwise prospectively) by Data (Use and Access) Act 2025, ss 70(2)(b), 142(1), (2)(h).

21 See DPA, ss 10–11.

22 As amended by the Data (Use and Access) Act 2025.

23 See UK GDPR, Art 10. Some of these conditions are subject to prospective amendments to be brought in by the Data (Use and Access) Act 2025.

24 Serious Crime Act 2007, s 68(8) – 'an anti-fraud organisation' means any unincorporated association, body corporate or other person which enables or facilitates any sharing of information to prevent fraud or a particular kind of fraud or which has any of these functions as its purpose or one of its purposes.

(c) Processing is necessary for the purpose of, or in connection with, any legal proceedings (including prospective legal proceedings), for the purpose of obtaining legal advice or is otherwise necessary for the purposes of establishing, exercising or defending legal rights: para 33.'

6.34 For example, this could allow the police to disclose information to a social landlord where confirmation is sought for the purposes of an absolute ground for possession[25] (condition 1 – serious offence). Disclosure of convictions, records and summaries of police activity are, after all, common in anti-social behaviour and absolute ground cases.

6.35 Indeed, this may be of use in confirming an individual's address or their claimed address at various times (eg the tenant may have given the police a different address to that of the demised premises).

6.36 Under these principles and conditions therefore, information cannot be obtained from a third party in a social fraud investigation:

- without the consent of the individual;
- *unless* the PSHF Regulations are being used (as described in **6.59** onwards below);
- *unless* and otherwise save as is described above (such as is referred to at **6.30** above);
- *unless* and otherwise save as is described in the 'Exemptions' section below.

This requires consideration of the exemptions to some or all of the data protection principles to be found in Schedules 2 to 4 to the DPA.

Exemptions

6.37 Section 15(1) of the DPA provides:

> 'Schedules 2, 3 and 4 make provision for exemptions from, and restrictions and adaptations of the application of, rules of the GDPR.'

6.38 The two provisions which are frequently cited as allowing the obtaining of such information about an individual without their consent or even knowledge in cases of social housing fraud are:

Schedule 2, para 2	Crime and taxation
Schedule 2, para 5	Disclosures required to be disclosed by law or made in connection with legal proceedings etc.

25 Housing Act 1985, s 84A (secure tenancies)/Housing Act 1988, Sch 2, Ground 7A (assured tenancies).

Crime and taxation (Schedule 2, para 2)

6.39 Schedule 2 of the DPA provides, at paragraph 2, an exemption from the relevant UK GDPR provisions:

> '(1) The listed GDPR provisions and Article 34(1) and (4) of the GDPR (communication of personal data breach to the data subject) do not apply to personal data processed for any of the following purposes–
>
> (a) the prevention or detection of crime,
>
> (b) the apprehension or prosecution of offenders, or
>
> (c) the assessment or collection of a tax or duty or an imposition of a similar nature,
>
> to the extent that the application of those provisions would be likely to prejudice any of the matters mentioned in paragraphs (a) to (c).'

6.40 Given that sub-letting and parting with the possession of the whole or part of let premises may well constitute a crime[26] and activities surrounding acquiring a tenancy, right to buy, shared ownership and right to acquire involving false representations may similarly be a criminal offence,[27] it is not surprising that information is more readily disclosable in such cases.

6.41 This exemption is therefore frequently used by local authority and accredited fraud investigators.

Disclosure required by law (Schedule 2, para 5)

6.42 A further exemption is where disclosure of data 'is required by an enactment, a rule of law or an order of a court or tribunal', or where:

> '5(1) The listed GDPR provisions do not apply to personal data consisting of information that the controller is obliged by an enactment to make available to the public, to the extent that the application of those provisions would prevent the controller from complying with that obligation.
>
> (2) The listed GDPR provisions do not apply to personal data where disclosure of the data is required by an enactment, a rule of law or an order of a court or tribunal, to the extent that the application of those provisions would prevent the controller from making the disclosure.
>
> (3) The listed GDPR provisions do not apply to personal data where disclosure of the data–

26 PSHF, ss 1 and 2.

27 See Chapter 7 and, in particular, the reference to the Fraud Act 2006 and offences under Parts 6 and 7 of the Housing Act 1996.

(a) *is necessary for the purpose of, or in connection with, legal proceedings (including prospective legal proceedings),*

(b) is necessary for the purpose of obtaining legal advice, or

(c) is otherwise necessary for the purposes of establishing, exercising or defending legal rights,

to the extent that the application of those provisions would prevent the controller from making the disclosure.' (emphasis added)

6.43 These provisions in essence replicate the exemptions previously found under sections 29 and 35 of the 1998 Act.

6.44 To give an obvious example of the paragraph 5 exemption, a local authority seeking information from a bank as to a tenant's statements pursuant to the Prevention of Social Housing Fraud (Power to Require Information) (England) Regulations 2014, described further below, can do so without the restriction of the DPA by reason of this provision.

6.45 It follows that there is a proper and effective data protection response to many refusals by third parties to disclose information about the data subject tenant, etc. Whether that is acknowledged by the third party raises a different question, though the court procedures highlighted later in this chapter may further assist in obtaining the requested information.

DATA SHARING

> 'There is a general obligation to evidence your compliance and justify your approach, so you should maintain relevant documentation and adopt additional measures as necessary. A data sharing agreement is one example of good practice to demonstrate you are meeting your accountability obligations. If you are unable to justify your approach, it is likely you will fail to meet those obligations.'[28]

6.46 Data sharing is not in itself inherently controversial or commercially unusual. For example, a social landlord will, as a matter of course, provide necessary disclosures of information about a tenant and their premises to maintenance and gas contractors.

6.47 It is also not uncommon for local authorities and housing associations (and others) to enter into data-sharing protocols and agreements,[29] and even for

28 See *Data Sharing: A Code of Practice* (Information Commissioner's Office, 17 October 2022), p 33. This is, as already noted above, subject at the time of writing to review following the coming into law of the Data (Use and Access) Act 2025.

29 See Chartered Institute of Housing *Tenancy Fraud and Data Sharing: A Guide for Housing Associations* (Feb 2012) for some examples. Many social landlords are members of the National Anti-Fraud Network (NAFN) which gives them access to a database along with other services. This can assist in a range of circumstances, such as right to buy fraudulent applications and general data sharing.

different departments in, say, a local authority to do the same (though the Code referred to in the paragraph below is not intended to cover data sharing with processors or within an organisation. It is not therefore treated as data sharing though other data protection obligations may apply).[30] The purpose will be to explain *what, why* and *when* specified personal data can be shared, though it should be stressed that the DPA still applies and such protocols are not a 'way around' the statutory disclosure restrictions. Most public sector organisations, assuming they have identified an express or implied power to share data, will rely on the public interest task lawful basis in Article 6 of the UK GDPR (though a privacy notice, and even some tenancy agreements, advise of data sharing practices such as to bring in the possibility of the consent lawful basis).

6.48 These protocols will invariably be informed by the (statutory) Data Sharing Code of Practice prepared by the Information Commissioner's Office.[31] The Code states:

> 'This is a statutory code of practice prepared under section 121 of the Data Protection Act 2018.
>
> It is a practical guide for organisations about how to share personal data in a way that complies with data protection law.
>
> It aims to give you confidence to share data fairly and proportionately.'[32]

6.49 Annex A to the Code provides a step-by-step checklist on whether to share personal data. This includes the following:

Key points to consider:

- What is the sharing meant to achieve?
- Have you assessed the potential benefits and risks to individuals and/or society of sharing or not sharing?
- Is it fair to share data in this way?
- Is the sharing necessary and proportionate to the issue you are addressing?
- What is the minimum data you can share to achieve the aim?
- Could the objective be achieved without sharing personal data, or by sharing less personal data?
- What safeguards can you put in place to minimise the risks or potential adverse effects of the sharing?
- Is there an applicable exemption in the DPA 2018?

30 See p 19 of the Code.

31 Prepared and published under DPA, s 121 and available at *Data Sharing: A Code of Practice*. See fn 28.

32 Ibid, p 9.

COVERT SURVEILLANCE

6.50 Though this book is not intended to explain in any detail the methods of evidence gathering, it is worth acknowledging the possible obtaining of evidence by covert surveillance.

6.51 Data protection laws do not apply, for example, to CCTV cameras that only cover the user's own private property, and to the extent that they go further than this there would ordinarily be signs displayed saying that recording is taking place, and why. The ICO has produced a helpful CCTV Code of Practice which you can find on its website.

6.52 Sometimes, social landlords will want to use covert surveillance techniques to garner the necessary (further) information to enable them to determine the reality of a case and their legal options, particularly with regard to the questions of who is living at the subject premises. Examples of such activity include use of (hidden) CCTV, a listening device in a neighbouring property or surveillance from a vehicle.

6.53 One of the Home Office's Codes of Practice (updated 22 February 2024) referred to below – 'Covert Surveillance and Property Interference' – explains at paragraph 2.4:

> 'Specifically, covert surveillance may be authorised under the 2000 Act if it is either directed or intrusive:
>
> - Directed surveillance is covert surveillance that is not intrusive and is carried out in relation to a specific investigation or operation in such a manner as is likely to result in the obtaining of private information about any person (other than by way of an immediate response to events or circumstances such that it is not reasonably practicable to seek authorisation under the 2000 Act);
> - Intrusive surveillance is covert surveillance that is carried out in relation to anything taking place on residential premises or in any private vehicle (and that involves the presence of an individual on the premises or in the vehicle or is carried out by a means of a surveillance device).'

6.54 A private registered provider of social housing, such as a housing association, would need to be aware of the constraints impose by the DPA, UK GDPR and Human Rights Act 1998 (Article 8 – right to respect for private and family life), and the documents referred to in the paragraph below by way of guidance (though not strictly bound it is 'industry practice' to comply). A local authority also has the ability to engage in such covert surveillance but only if they comply not only with those aforementioned legislative 'restrictions' but also with, amongst other legislation, the provisions of the Regulation of Investigatory Powers Act 2000 (RIPA) and the Investigatory Powers Act 2016. Part II of RIPA provides for such required authorisation of covert surveillance by public authorities, which include local authorities,[33] where that surveillance is likely to result in the obtaining of private information about a person.

6.55 Before doing so, close regard should be had to three guidance documents:[34]

(1) Investigatory Powers Act: codes of practice (Home Office – November 2023).

(2) Covert Human Intelligence Sources revised codes of practice (Home Office – 13 December 2022).

(3) Code of Practice for investigation of protected electronic information (Home Office – August 2018).

6.56 In *Lopez Ribalda v Spain*[35] the court rejected the applicants' claims against their dismissals for theft, which followed the use of covert video surveillance at their workplace, and held that the Spanish courts had not breached their right to respect for their private life under ECHR Article 8 or their right to a fair trial under Article 6.

6.57 What though happens if evidence is improperly obtained? In *Jones v University of Warwick*[36] the Court of Appeal held, in respect of secretly filmed evidence, that the trial judge had a discretion to exclude evidence that would otherwise be admissible, pursuant to the Criminal Procedure Rules, rule 32.1 and a decision made in the exercise of this discretion was only to be interfered with if the discretion had been exercised wrongly. The fact that W's insurers had committed a trespass in entering J's home and had infringed her right to privacy under Article 8(1) was a relevant circumstance for the court to consider when deciding whether to exercise its discretion. However, W's insurers had not acted so outrageously that the evidence should be struck out. The exclusion of the video evidence, which was relevant and otherwise admissible, would create an artificial and undesirable situation. Accordingly it was not appropriate to interfere with the judge's decision but the court was entitled to show its disapproval of the improper conduct of W's insurers when making orders for costs.

6.58 More recently in *Perrin v Walsh*[37] HHJ Grimshaw, sitting as a Deputy Master, referenced *Jones* and reminded himself (in dealing with a road traffic accident damages claim) that the court has the power to control evidence under CPR 32.1 and further that:

> 'The issue of fairness, in the context of ambush, was considered in *Rall v Hume* [2001] EWCA Civ 146, where Potter LJ said, at [19]:

33 RIPA, Sch 1, para 17.
34 There is also the Office of Surveillance Commissioners Procedures and Guidance booklet.
35 (2020) 71 EHRR 7.
36 [2003] EWCA Civ 151, [2003] 1 WLR 954.
37 [2025] EWHC 2536 (KB) at paras. 12 and 19.

> "In principle, as it seems to me, the starting point on any application of this kind must be that, where video evidence is available which, according to the defendant, undermines the case of the claimant to an extent that would substantially reduce the award of damages to which she is entitled, it will usually be in the overall interests of justice to require that the defendant should be permitted to cross-examine the plaintiff and her medical advisors upon it, so long as this does not amount to trial by ambush."'
>
> 'As I stated within the *ex tempore* judgment that I gave at a previous hearing of this case, the Court has a power to restrict evidence and, in particular, refuse permission for the Defendant to rely on surveillance evidence, where it is appropriate to do so. This is an exercise of judicial discretion having made an evaluative judgment considering the competing public interests outlined by the Court in *Jones*. Having reached that conclusion, the parties agree that the Court needs to consider the probative value of the surveillance evidence and how that is weighed against the prejudice created by the failings alleged by the Claimant.'

PSHF REGULATIONS

6.59 The Prevention of Social Housing Fraud (Power to Require Information) (England) Regulations 2014[38] ('the Regulations') came into force on 6 April 2014. They make express provision for powers to be given to an 'authorised officer'[39] to *require* information from third parties for housing fraud investigation purposes.

6.60 There remain for social landlords, as outlined above, the more general information gathering activities under the auspices of the DPA and UK GDPR, and at times the surveillance powers to be found under legislation such as RIPA.

6.61 The Regulations, however, essentially create a distinct power, under regulation 4, to require information from certain identified third parties, *but only for housing fraud investigation purposes*,[40] a definition which extends beyond simply the PSHF sub-letting/parting with possession offences.

6.62 Section 7(7) of the PSHF defines 'housing fraud investigation purposes' as purposes relating to the prevention, detection or securing of evidence for a conviction of:

(a) a PSHF offence;

38 SI 2014/899 – made under PSHF, ss 7, 8 and 9(2)(b) and (c). There are also the Prevention of Social Housing Fraud (Detection of Fraud)(Wales) Regulations 2014/826 – made under PSHF, ss 7 and 8 to similar effect and in force from 28 March 2014.

39 Defined in reg 2 as 'a person acting in accordance with any authorisation for the purposes of these Regulations which is for the time being in force in relation to that person'.

40 See reg 4(1).

(b) an offence under the Fraud Act 2006 relating to the unlawful sub-letting or parting with possession of the whole or part of a dwelling-house let by a local authority, a private registered provider of social housing or a registered social landlord;

(c) an offence under the Fraud Act 2006 relating to an application for an allocation of housing accommodation under Part 6 of the Housing Act 1996;

(d) an offence under the Fraud Act 2006 relating to an application for accommodation or for assistance in obtaining accommodation, under Part 7 of the Housing Act 1996 or under Part 2 of the Housing (Wales) Act 2014;

(e) an offence under the Fraud Act 2006 relating to–

(i) a claim to exercise the right to buy under Part 5 of the Housing Act 1985,

(ii) a claim to exercise the right to acquire under section 16 of the Housing Act 1996 before the repeal of that section by the Abolition of the Right to Buy and Associated Rights (Wales) Act 2017 came into force,

(iii) a claim to exercise the right to acquire under section 180 of the Housing and Regeneration Act 2008, or

(f) an associated offence in relation to an offence mentioned in any of paragraphs (a) to (e).

6.63 Chapter 7 deals with some of these offences in more detail.

6.64 The local authority can grant authorisation to an individual to exercise the regulation 4 investigation powers – which can relate to matters beyond the authority's geographical boundary – if:[41]

(a) the authorisation is in writing; and

(b) the individual is employed by that or another local authority or by a joint committee that carries out functions relating to housing fraud investigation purposes on behalf of that authority.

6.65 To then exercise these powers under the Regulations, regulation 4 merely requires the authorised officer to have reasonable grounds for suspecting that:

(a) the person they require information from is a bank, building society, other provider of credit or utilities company (or employee of any of these bodies); and

(b) they either have or may have, possession of or access to, any information about any matter that is relevant to housing fraud investigation purposes.

6.66 Common examples of information obtained by this means are:

(a) Bank statements demonstrating:

41 See reg 3.

- regular payments going into the account (eg the allegation being that they are rent payments from a sub-letting);
- regular payments of mortgage and (other) rent suggesting a second property;
- address(es) used for bank purposes; and
- activity on the account and geographical location of the same.

(b) Utility accounts demonstrating:

- whose name the account is in;
- method of payment; and
- utility usage (especially useful in only or principal home cases).

6.67 For telecommunications information, which had previously been included in the Regulations, one now has to look to the Investigatory Powers Act 2016.

6.68 The operation of the regulation 4 power is unsurprisingly not without caveats and 'hurdles'. For example and most obviously, regulation 4 states (with emphasis added in italics):

> '(5) An authorised officer shall not, in exercise of those powers, require any information from any person by virtue of that person falling within paragraph (3) unless *it appears to that officer that there are reasonable grounds for believing that the person to whom it relates is–*
>
> *(a) a person who has committed, is committing or intends to commit an offence listed in section 7(7)*[42] *of the Prevention of Social Housing Fraud Act 2013; or*
>
> *(b) a person who is* ***a member of the family*** *of a person falling within sub-paragraph (a).*' (emphasis added)

6.69 It does not, therefore, assist in obtaining information from third parties, such as a 'reluctant' sub-tenant, who is unrelated to the tenant. Nor does it allow for a 'fishing expedition' as the relevant officer must have 'reasonable grounds' for believing that the individual in question has committed, is committing or intends to commit one of the offences set out at **6.62**.

6.70 Unlike general requests for information, those made under the Regulations have real 'bite'. It is an offence under regulation 5 to not provide, intentionally delay, etc the information requested and conviction makes any defendant liable to a fine (ongoing breach thereafter is punishable by a fine not exceeding £40 per day).[43] The Regulations also provide in this respect a limitation on such action:

42 See **6.62**.
43 The Regulations also deal with the liability of directors (reg 6).

'7.— Legal proceedings

(1) Proceedings for an offence under regulation 5 may be brought within the period of 6 months beginning with the date on which evidence sufficient in the opinion of the prosecutor to warrant the proceedings came to the prosecutor's knowledge.

(2 But no such proceedings may be brought more than three years —

(a) after the commission of the offence, or

(b) in the case of a continuous contravention, after the last date on which the offence was committed.

(3) A certificate signed by the prosecutor and stating the date on which such evidence came to the prosecutor's knowledge is conclusive evidence of that fact; and a certificate to that effect and purporting to be signed is to be treated as being so signed unless the contrary is proved.'

COURT PROCESSES

6.71 Obtaining information via the routes described earlier in this chapter is largely, though by no means exclusively, confined to pre-court activities. Effective use of court procedures after the issue of proceedings may further help to 'fill in the gaps' and strengthen the evidence available to the social landlord to its optimum effect.

Pre-action

6.72 Most of the actions available through the civil courts relate to the post-issue period, though pre-action disclosure is available pursuant to Rule 31.16 of the Civil Procedure Rules 1998 (CPR).[44]

6.73 Any application for pre-action disclosure:

(a) can only be made against a likely would-be party;

(b) must identify the documents or class of documents to be disclosed (which would have been disclosable under standard disclosure if proceedings had been issued); and

(c) will only be considered if it is desirable to:

- dispose fairly of the anticipated proceedings;
- assist the dispute to be resolved without proceedings; or
- save costs.

44 An application for disclosure before proceedings have started is permitted under s 33 of the Senior Courts Act 1981 (for the High Court) or s 52 of the County Courts Act 1984 (for the County Court).

6.74 This option is unlikely to be taken up in social housing fraud cases very often, not only because of the powers already available to a social landlord to obtain information (see above) but also because it is unlikely that such evidence will 'tip the balance' between issuing or not issuing proceedings in most instances.

6.75 One pre-issue rule that is important in certain housing fraud cases is CPR 32.19:

> '(1) A party shall be deemed to admit the authenticity of a document disclosed to him under Part 31 (disclosure and inspection of documents) unless he serves notice that he wishes the document to be proved at trial.
>
> (2) A notice to prove a document must be served–
>
> (a) by the latest date for serving witness statements; or
>
> (b) within 7 days of disclosure of the document, whichever is later.'

6.76 In a world where AI is having an ever-growing impact, the prevalence of false information in documentary form is likely to increase – eg 'doctored' bank accounts, forged death certificates and altered GP letters. The rule in CPR 32.19 essentially requires the party disclosing such documents to be put on (sufficient) notice that they will be required to prove the authenticity of the document in issue.

6.77 The provision does require a notice (ie putting the other party to proof in a statement of case would not be sufficient)[45] though it has been said that, though there is no general duty on parties to point out to their opponents any procedural errors, if they wish to rely on CPR 32.19 they should make the point promptly (bearing in mind the duty at CPR 1.3 for parties 'to help the court to further the overriding objective').[46]

6.78 If a party is late with any CPR 32.19 notice, then it is a question of seeking relief from sanctions under CPR 3.19.[47] If a notice is accepted then the burden turns to the party producing the document to provide credible evidence that it is genuine.

Post-issue

6.79 A social landlord has four primary options available to them after proceedings have been issued in the County Court or High Court, all of which are generally under-used:

45 *Mumford v HMRC* [2017] UKFTT 19 (TC) at para 50.

46 *Anthony McGann v Michael Bisping* [2017] EWHC 2951 (Comm) at para 24. In *Lionwalk Ltd v Singh* [2018] EWHC 1513 (QB), HHJ Walden-Smith, sitting as a Judge of the High Court, held that the interests of justice and the possibility of fraud meant that the disputed documents should be produced to a handwriting expert despite the breach of CPR 32.19.

47 See *Tuke v J D Classics Ltd* [2018] EWHC 531 (QB).

- Part 18 Request for Further Information;
- Specific disclosure;
- Disclosure against third party;
- Witness summons.

Part 18 request

6.80 Firstly, therefore, there is the Part 18 Request for Further Information procedure, whose purpose is to clarify a party's case. For example, it may be helpful where the defence is, in essence, a bare denial of sub-letting, but does not respond in substance or at all to the pleaded matters used to support the landlord's case, such as statements provided by the alleged sub-tenant, evidence of the defendant living elsewhere, credit reference information, etc.

6.81 The provision of a defence may therefore still leave unknown in such cases, to give three actual examples known to the author, the following information:

(1) What the defendant says about monthly (rent level) payments going into their account.

(2) How long they spend (and what they do) in another country, where their partner and business are.

(3) What the tenant lived on between 2012 and 2015 when they were not working and were not in receipt of social security benefits (the suspicion being it was from the income obtained from sub-letting her local authority flat).

6.82 It is important to note the following when considering use of the Part 18 process:[48]

(a) A preliminary written request should always be made first, providing a date when a response is expected and confirming that the request is made under Part 18. This should usually be served by e-mail if reasonably practicable.

(b) The request should be proportionate and with a genuine purpose of knowing the case the first party has to meet.

(c) Such a request should comply in full with the Practice Direction to Part 18.

(d) Any response should be verified by a statement of truth.

(e) If the second party objects to complying with the request (including on the basis that it would be disproportionately expensive) or any part of it, then they should inform the first party promptly.

48 See the Practice Direction to CPR 18, paras 1 to 5.

(f) If no response at all is made, then the first party can seek an order requiring a response without a hearing and without serving the application on the second party (assuming at least 14 days was given to respond). It is worth noting what DHCJ Richard Salter QC in *Al Saud and another v Gibbs and another* said:[49]

> '45. The burden must nevertheless always be on the party seeking an order under CPR Pt 18, both to demonstrate that the threshold conditions identified in para 35 above are met and (to the extent not already implicit in the satisfaction of those conditions) to satisfy the court that, in all the circumstances, the making of such an order would assist in dealing with the case justly in accordance with the overriding objective.
>
> 46. One of the complaints made by the claimants about Mr Gibbs's responses to the RFI is that they show that he has failed to exercise reasonable diligence in examining relevant documents and undertaking reasonable enquiries. Mr Atrill invited my attention to the following passage in paras 20.96, 20.98 and 20.101 of Matthews and Malek, *Disclosure*, 5th ed (2017):
>
>> "It is incumbent upon a party responding to a request to a Part 18 order to exercise reasonable diligence in formulating a response."
>>
>> "… the court is likely to regard a party [as] being under a duty to undertake reasonable enquiries, but what constitutes reasonable enquiries will depend on the circumstances … a party is not bound to make enquiries to the extent that such enquiries place an unfair or oppressive burden on him."
>>
>> "If it is necessary for the purposes of responding to a request, the party must examine the documents in his control … or that of his servants or agents held in that capacity. If a such search would be unduly burdensome, then that may be a ground for objecting to the request."
>
> 47. In my judgment, those passages accurately state the law in this area. I would, however, add this rider. Where, as in the present case, a request under Part 18 has already been answered, and the objection is that the answer given is inadequate because reasonable diligence has not been exercised, the proper way forward will not usually be to ask the court (as the claimants in the present case have done) simply to order that the original generally worded request should be answered again. Such a course will often just postpone until an application for sanctions for non-compliance or for relief from such sanctions is made the inevitable issue of what reasonable diligence in formulating a response to that request—and thus compliance with the order—actually requires. By that time it is likely to be too late to consider the appropriateness of the scope of the original order: see e g *In re Bankside Hotels Ltd* [2015] EWHC 1080 (Ch) at [40] and [54(1)].

49 [2022] EWHC 706 (Comm), [2022] 1 WLR 3082.

48. The better course will usually be, wherever possible, to ask the court to specify in its order precisely what further enquiries the party responding to the Part 18 request should carry out, so that the issue of what proper compliance requires is plainly defined from the outset.'

(g) A court granting an order under Part 18 can make it subject to conditions, and with the application of a sanction, such as a striking out of the defence, for failure to comply.

(h) The court can make a Part 18 order of its own initiative or upon application by the requesting party (ie where the other party has failed to respond to the preliminary request identified at (a) or failed to respond adequately).

(i) A request is necessarily made post-statement of case but may be made prior to witness statements being served and more than once. A response may necessitate a further follow-up request for further information.

(j) As referenced at **6.6**, an alternative strategy could be to require the defendant to provide a properly pleaded defence, seeking the striking out of the existing version and an unless order in respect of any new defence. CPR 16.5 provides:

'(1) In the defence, the defendant must deal with every allegation in the particulars of claim, stating–

(a) which of the allegations are denied;

(b) which allegations they are unable to admit or deny, but which they require the claimant to prove; and

(c) which allegations they admit.

(2) Where the defendant denies an allegation–

(a) they must state their reasons for doing so; and

(b) if they intend to put forward a different version of events from that given by the claimant, they must state their own version.'

Preliminary Request for Further Information or Clarification – PD18

1.1 Before making an application to the court for an order under Part 18, the party seeking clarification or information (the first party) should first serve on the party from whom it is sought (the second party) a written request for that clarification or information (a Request) stating a date by which the response to the Request should be served. The date must allow the second party a reasonable time to respond.

1.2 A Request should be concise and strictly confined to matters which are reasonably necessary and proportionate to enable the first party to prepare his own case or to understand the case he has to meet.

1.3 Requests must be made as far as possible in a single comprehensive document and not piecemeal.

1.4 A Request may be made by letter if the text of the Request is brief and the reply is likely to be brief; otherwise the Request should be made in a separate document.

1.5 If a Request is made in a letter, the letter should, in order to distinguish it from any other that might routinely be written in the course of a case,
(1) state that it contains a Request made under Part 18, and
(2) deal with no matters other than the Request.

1.6
(1) A Request (whether made by letter or in a separate document) must –
(a) be headed with the name of the court and the title and number of the claim,
(b) in its heading state that it is a Request made under Part 18, identify the first party and the second party and state the date on which it is made,
(c) set out in a separate numbered paragraph each request for information or clarification,
(d) where a Request relates to a document, identify that document and (if relevant) the paragraph or words to which it relates,
(e) state the date by which the first party expects a response to the Request.

(2)
(a) A Request which is not in the form of a letter may, if convenient, be prepared in such a way that the response may be given on the same document.
(b) To do this the numbered paragraphs of the Request should appear on the left hand half of each sheet so that the paragraphs of the response may then appear on the right.
(c) Where a Request is prepared in this form an extra copy should be served for the use of the second party.

1.7 Subject to the provisions of rule 6.23(5) and (6) and paragraphs 4.1 to 4.3 of Practice Direction 6A, a request should be served by e-mail if reasonably practicable.

Responding to a Request

2.1 A response to a Request must be in writing, dated and signed by the second party or his legal representative.

2.2
(1) Where the Request is made in a letter the second party may give his response in a letter or in a formal reply.
(2) Such a letter should identify itself as a response to the Request and deal with no other matters than the response.

2.3

(1) Unless the Request is in the format described in paragraph 1.6(2) and the second party uses the document supplied for the purpose, a response must:
   (a) be headed with the name of the court and the title and number of the claim,
   (b) in its heading identify itself as a response to that Request,
   (c) repeat the text of each separate paragraph of the Request and set out under each paragraph the response to it,
   (d) refer to and have attached to it a copy of any document not already in the possession of the first party which forms part of the response.

(2) A second or supplementary response to a Request must identify itself as such in its heading.

2.4

The second party must when he serves his response on the first party serve on every other party and file with the court a copy of the Request and of his response.

Statements of Truth

3 Attention is drawn to Part 22 and to the definition of a statement of case in Part 2 of the rules; a response should be verified by a statement of truth.

General matters

4.1

(1) If the second party objects to complying with the Request or part of it or is unable to do so at all or within the time stated in the Request he must inform the first party promptly and in any event within that time.

(2) He may do so in a letter or in a separate document (a formal response), but in either case he must give reasons and, where relevant, give a date by which he expects to be able to comply.

4.2

(1) There is no need for a second party to apply to the court if he objects to a Request or is unable to comply with it at all or within the stated time. He need only comply with paragraph 4.1(1) above.

(2) Where a second party considers that a Request can only be complied with at disproportionate expense and objects to comply for that reason he should say so in his reply and explain briefly why he has taken that view.

Applications for Orders under Part 18

5.1 Attention is drawn to Part 23 (Applications) and to Practice Direction 23A.

5.2 An application notice for an order under Part 18 should set out or have attached to it the text of the order sought and in particular should specify the matter or matters in respect of which the clarification or information is sought.

5.3

(1) If a Request under paragraph 1 for the information or clarification has not been made, the application notice should, in addition, explain why not.

(2) If a Request for clarification or information has been made, the application notice or the evidence in support should describe the response, if any.

5.4 Both the first party and the second party should consider whether evidence in support of or in opposition to the application is required.

5.5

(1) Where the second party has made no response to a Request served on him, the first party need not serve the application notice on the second party, and the court may deal with the application without a hearing.

(2) Sub-paragraph (1) above only applies if at least 14 days have passed since the Request was served and the time stated in it for a response has expired.

5.6 Unless paragraph 5.5 applies the application notice must be served on the second party and on all other parties to the claim.

5.7 An order made under Part 18 must be served on all parties to the claim.

5.8 Costs:

(1) Attention is drawn to the Practice Directions 44 to 48 on costs and, in particular, Subsections 8 and 9 of Practice Direction 44, which relate to the court's power to make a summary assessment of costs.

(2) Attention is also drawn to rule 44.10(1) which provides that the general rule is that if an order does not mention costs no party is entitled to costs relating to that order.

Request for Further Information

IN THE COUNTY COURT AT TRAFFORD

CLAIM NO: OT7456

BETWEEN:

PEARSON HEIGHTS HOUSING ASSOCIATION

Claimant

-and-

MR BRIAN GREENHOFF

Defendant

---

18 REQUEST

The Claimant requires the Defendant to respond to the questions below by **4.00pm on Thursday 29 October 20XX**.

1. In paragraph 4 of the Defence dated 21 September 20XX it is said 'No admissions are made as to paragraph 5 of the Annex to the Particulars of Claim'.

   (a) Does the Defendant know Timothy Hill referred to at paragraph 5(b) of the Annex to the Particulars of Claim'?

   (b) Has the said Timothy Hill ever stayed overnight at Flat 3, Rosebush Avenue, Trafford, TF3 3DD ('the Premises') since the Defendant's tenancy commenced on 10 April 20XX? If so when and was payment received for the stay?

   (c) Did the Defendant ever provide the said Timothy Hill with a tenancy agreement in respect of the Premises? If so:

- When?
- Can the Defendant please provide a copy to the Claimant's solicitors?
- What were the terms of the tenancy?

   (d) Has the Defendant ever visited 12 Broom Heights, Manchester M13 1TT ('the Second Premises')?

   (e) Has the Defendant ever stayed overnight at the Second Premises? If so, when and how often?

   (f) Does the Defendant admit:

- He was on the electoral register at the Second Premises from 20XX? If so, why?

- He used the Second Premises as his address for bank and correspondence purposes? If so, why?
- He has use of the Second Premises? If so, under what arrangement?

The response to this Part 18 Request for Further Information should be sent to: Gotcha Solicitors, Parting Way, Manchester MXX 2KH. The Defendant is referred to paragraphs 2 and 3 of the Practice Direction to CPR 18, which is exhibited to this document.

28 September 20XX

Specific disclosure

6.83 In many instances, allied to the Part 18 process, there is the availability of powers under CPR Part 31 for a court to order *specific disclosure* of identified documents or classes of documents (CPR 31.12), or *disclosure against a person who is not a party* (CPR 31.17).

6.84 With respect to the former, the order will require the defendant to disclose the identified documents and carry out a search to the extent provided in the order. To give one example of the latter, it may be that the tenant does not, in fact, retain their bank statements or housing benefit decision letters but an order under CPR 31.12 (and see **6.86**) can require them to seek copies from the bank and local authority respectively and then disclose the results of their request.

6.85 The court, on considering such an application, is concerned with two primary issues – whether the requested documents are relevant to the proceedings,[50] and whether they are (or have been) in the other party's control. Where a claim is likely to turn on particular documents, there is obviously a stronger case for an order to be made.[51]

6.86 It is worth noting here that CPR 35.9 provides with respect to expert evidence provisions:[52]

> 'Where a party has access to information which is not reasonably available to another party, the court may direct the party who has access to the information to–
>
> (a) prepare and file a document recording the information; and
>
> (b) serve a copy of that document on the other party.'

50 *Harrods Ltd v Times Newspaper Ltd* [2006] EWCA Civ 294, [2006] All ER (D) 302 (Feb) at para 12.

51 *Chantrey Vellacott v Convergence Group Plc* [2006] EWHC 490 (Ch).

52 The White Book 2026 says at 35.9.1: 'It does not provide the means to obtain access to a party's expert report. It simply provides the means to obtain information, which is presumably derived from a source of expertise accessible to the other party'.

Third-party disclosure

6.87 As for third-party disclosure, the court must be satisfied that:

(a) the documents for which disclosure is sought are likely to support the case of the applicant or adversely affect the case of one of the other parties to the proceedings; and

(b) disclosure is necessary to dispose fairly of the claim or to save costs.

6.88 For example, the claimant social landlord may seek the bank accounts of the alleged sub-tenant, not available under the PSHF Regulations, or details in relation to where the tenant claims to have lived at the relevant time (such as household bills).

6.89 It is fair to note that, in 'fraud' possession claims, applications under CPR 31.17 are not usual, not least because the courts have warned that disclosure against non-parties is the exception rather than the rule[53] and the jurisdiction should be exercised with caution.[54]

6.90 Related to this process is the *Norwich Pharmacal* application, referred to in the authority referenced below as 'a pre-proceedings order for disclosure against a third party who has potentially innocently been caught up in wrongdoing'.

6.91 This was successfully sought in *Kensington & Chelsea RBC v Airbnb Payments UK Ltd*[55] where Zacaroli J, as he then was, went through the conditions:

> '8. It is now well-established that an applicant for a Norwich Pharmacal order must satisfy four conditions, most recently summarised in a case called *Collier v Bennett* [2020] EWHC 1884 (QB), a decision of Saini J at [31] to [41]. First, the applicant must establish a good arguable case that a form of legally recognised wrong has been committed against it by a person. That is, it must be a case that is more than barely capable of serious argument but need not necessarily reach the threshold of 50 per cent likely to succeed.
>
> 9. I have no doubt that the unlawful subletting of the claimant's properties is a wrong committed against it, giving the claimant the right to bring civil or criminal proceedings under the Prevention of Social Housing Fraud Act 2013, or the Fraud Act 2006, or to take steps to evict the tenant and recover the property so that it can be used for social housing purposes.
>
> 10. There is compelling evidence that such fraud is being committed on a fairly wide scale, both nationally and within the claimant's borough. The

53 *Frankson v Home Office* [2003] EWCA Civ 655, [2003] 1 WLR 1952 at para 10.
54 *Re Howglen Ltd* [2001] 1 All ER 376 at [382h].
55 [2022] EWHC 2209 (Ch).

two target blocks are likely locations for the committing of tenancy fraud for the reasons given in evidence to which I have already alluded.

11. The second requirement is that the respondent to the application must be mixed up in [*the activity*][56] so as to have facilitated the wrongdoing. This requirement is intended to distinguish the mere witness from someone who is more than that: see, for example, the decision of Mann J in *Various Claimants v News Group Newspapers (No.2)* [2013] EWHC 2119 (Ch) at [52] and [54]. He held the relevant question is whether the respondent is a mere witness to wrongdoing or whether its engagement with the wrongdoing makes it more than a mere witness and therefore susceptible to an order.

12. It is clear that the respondent's conduct need not itself involve any wrongdoing. Orders may be made against wholly innocent persons. A relevant example, in quite a close area to this case, is RFU v Consolidated Information Services *Limited (Formerly Viagogo Limited)* [2012] UKSC 55, in which the respondent's website facilitated private individuals anonymously advertising and selling tickets to England rugby matches at inflated prices.

13. The defendant's conduct in this case, that is of enabling payments to hosts of AirBnB properties, is in my judgment conduct that undoubtedly facilitates the wrongdoing that it is fairly believed is being committed by some of the tenants of the two target blocks. The subletting is no doubt for reward and, without payment, it would not occur. The payment process is effected by the defendant and therefore an integral, albeit wholly innocent, part of the fraud being committed.

14. The third requirement is that the respondent must be able or likely to be able to provide the information or documents necessary to enable the ultimate wrongdoer to be pursued. Necessary in this context does not imply that this must be the last resort, rather the question is whether in all the circumstances justice requires from the facilitator the co-operation demanded by the claimant with a view to righting the facilitator's wrong: see Burford Capital v LSE [2020] EWHC 1183 (Comm).

15. There is no doubt that the respondent had the relevant information and documents. Indeed, it has started preparing the same in anticipation of an order being made. As I have already summarised, while there may be other methods which the claimant could follow to try to identify wrongdoers amongst its tenants, these are not reasonably practicable.

16. The fourth and final condition is whether it is just in all the circumstances to make the order. A number of factors have been identified as relevant to this question, see for example, the ten factors identified by the Supreme

56 The judgment clearly contains a typographical error so the words in italics have been added.

Court in the RFU case, but it boils down to a simple question: a fact-specific judicial assessment of whether the remedy is required to do justice. Factors of particular relevance here include whether the claimant already has sufficient information to bring proceedings without the order, and whether the order would, in reality, be a wide-ranging exercise in seeking discovery and evidence, rather than a focused application to obtain information necessary to bring proceedings.'

Witness summons

6.92 Finally, there is the question of witnesses and, in particular, the ability to *witness summons* an individual to attend court to give evidence or produce documents in court (CPR 34.2) by use of Form N20 or obtain the court's permission to call the other party's (identified) witness where they were not otherwise going to be called so that they may be cross-examined (CPR 33.4):

'34.2

(1) A witness summons is a document issued by the court requiring a witness to–

(a) attend court to give evidence; or

(b) produce documents to the court.

(2) A witness summons must be in the relevant practice form.

(3) There must be a separate witness summons for each witness.

(4) A witness summons may require a witness to produce documents to the court either–

(a) on the date fixed for a hearing; or

(b) on such date as the court may direct.

(5) The only documents that a summons under this rule can require a person to produce before a hearing are documents which that person could be required to produce at the hearing.'

'33.4

(1) Where a party–

(a) proposes to rely on hearsay evidence; and

(b) does not propose to call the person who made the original statement to give oral evidence,

the court may, on the application of any other party, permit that party to call the maker of the statement to be cross-examined on the contents of the statement.

(2) An application for permission to cross-examine under this rule must be made not more than 14 days after the day on which a notice of intention to rely on the hearsay evidence was served on the applicant.'[57]

6.93 A witness summons, which will be served by the Court unless the party advises otherwise,[58] does not require the permission of the Court unless it is issued less than seven days before trial or requires attendance of the witness on a day other than that fixed for the trial: CPR 34.3.

6.94 The party issuing the witness summons must pay in advance the witness's reasonable travel expenses and (extremely modest[59]) compensation for loss of time.

6.95 One has to be careful in the use of witness summonses because it can backfire and end up strengthening the case of the defendant. For example, if in a sub-letting case you want to hear evidence from neighbours of the relevant premises and decide to witness summons such people who have previously indicated they do not want to get involved, then they could end up not supporting the case that other persons than the tenant(s) were living at the premises.

6.96 An application under CPR 33.4 – to call the maker of a statement, who a party does not intend to call, to be cross-examined on it – must be made not more than 14 days after the day on which a notice of intention to rely on the hearsay evidence was served on the applicant, though a party can seek permission to do so outside of this time.[60]

MISSING WITNESSES

6.97 This chapter has considered, in part, some issues of evidence obtained and submitted. In a housing fraud case it is not infrequently true that the greater

57 A party who does not apply for the court's permission to call witnesses for the purpose of cross-examination, when they could have done so, should not be taken to have accepted the evidence because they have not done so: *Parsons v Atkinson* [2024] EWHC 888 (KB).

58 See CPR 34.6: '(1) A witness summons is to be served by the court unless the party on whose behalf it is issued indicates in writing, when he asks the court to issue the summons, that he wishes to serve it himself. (2) Where the court is to serve the witness summons, the party on whose behalf it is issued must deposit, in the court office, the money to be paid or offered to the witness under rule 34.7'.

59 In addition to 'conduct money' at the time of service the witness must be offered or paid 'such sum by way of compensation for loss of time as may be specified in Practice Direction 34A'. Paragraph 3.3 of the Practice Direction states that the sum in respect of the period during which earnings or benefit are lost, or such lesser sum as it may be proved that the witness will lose as a result of their attendance at court, is to be based on the sums payable to witnesses attending the Crown Court. (Fixed pursuant to the Prosecution of Offences Act 1985 and the Costs in Criminal Cases (General) Regulations 1986 (SI 1986/1335).) A helpful guide and summary of sums payable can be found at: www.cps.gov.uk/legal-guidance/witness-expenses-and-allowances.

60 See CPR 3.1: '(2) Except where these Rules provide otherwise, the court may– (a) extend or shorten the time for compliance with any rule, practice direction or court order (even if an application for extension is made after the time for compliance has expired)'.

surprise is what evidence is *not* provided by a defendant more than what is. For example, in trying to show that they are living at the demised premises why has the defendant not called any of the neighbours, friends, etc who are said to have visited there or even relatives?

6.98 In December 2017 the High Court had cause to consider a claim by an insurance company for damages based on the assertion that the defendant had fraudulently represented to them that his car had been in collision with another vehicle driven by someone who they insured. Mr Justice Teare handed down judgment in *UK Insurance Ltd v Stuart John Gentry*[61] on 18 January 2018 and awarded the Claimant damages of £19,179 in addition to interest and costs.

6.99 One of the most interesting aspects of the judgment was a reminder of the court's approach to 'missing' witnesses, and at paragraph 68 of the judgment it was said:

> 'Mr. Grant on behalf of the Claimant invited the Court to draw adverse inferences from the failure of Mr. Gentry to give evidence (or to call evidence from Mr. Miller, Mr. Ebbs, and Mr. Toms). The circumstances in which inferences may be drawn have been summarised by the Court of Appeal in *Wisnewski v Central Manchester Health Authority* [1998] PIQR P324 at p.14 in these terms:
>
> "(1) In certain circumstances a court may be entitled to draw adverse inferences from the absence or silence of a witness who might be expected to have material evidence to give on an issue in an action.
>
> (2) If a court is willing to draw such inferences, they may go to strengthen the evidence adduced on that issue by the other party or to weaken the evidence, if any, adduced by the party who might reasonably have been expected to call the witness.
>
> (3) There must, however, have been some evidence, however weak, adduced by the former on the matter in question before the court is entitled to draw the desired inference: in other words, there must be a case to answer on that issue.
>
> (4) If the reason for the witness's absence or silence satisfies the court, then no such adverse inference may be drawn. If, on the other hand, there is some credible explanation given, even if it is not wholly satisfactory, the potentially detrimental effect of his/her absence or silence may be reduced or nullified."'

6.100 In *Ahuja Investments Ltd v Victorygame Ltd*[62] HHJ Hodge QC, sitting as a Deputy Judge of the High Court, addressed the issue, where relevant, in this manner:

61 [2018] EWHC 37 (QB).
62 [2021] EWHC 2382 (Ch).

'32. The omission to call a material witness or witnesses without reasonable explanation may have a significance that goes beyond the drawing of appropriate adverse inferences. Three particular aspects are of particular relevance to the present case. First, in a case where there are contemporary documents which appear on their face to provide cogent evidence on an issue which is contrary to the evidence of one of the parties to the litigation, the court may decide to take the documents at their face value, and decline to accept that party's evidence to the contrary, where this is unsupported by the evidence of a non-party witness who clearly could have given evidence material to that issue and who might have, but has not, been called by that party as a witness. The same may apply where the evidence of one of the parties to the litigation is contrary to the known or probable facts.

33. Second, the failure to call a witness who might have been able to give evidence on a material issue may mean that the court is left with no direct evidence at all on that issue. In that situation, the party who might be expected to have called that witness cannot complain if the court rejects that party's case on that issue and either makes a finding based on the inherent probabilities presented by the limited evidence that is before the court, or simply concludes that it is unable to make any finding of fact at all on that issue …'

6.101 This judgment had expressly in mind the remarks of Lord Leggatt JSC in *Efobi v Royal Mail Group* where he said:[63]

'The question whether an adverse inference may be drawn from the absence of a witness is sometimes treated as a matter governed by legal criteria … I think there is a risk of making overly legal and technical what really is or ought to be just a matter of ordinary rationality. So far as possible, tribunals should be free to draw, or to decline to draw, inferences from the facts of the case before them using their common sense without the need to consult law books when doing so. Whether any positive significance should be attached to the fact that a person has not given evidence depends entirely on the context and particular circumstances. Relevant considerations will naturally include such matters as whether the witness was available to give evidence, what relevant evidence it is reasonable to expect that the witness would have been able to give, what other relevant evidence there was bearing on the point(s) on which the witness could potentially have given relevant evidence, and the significance of those points in the context of the case as a whole. All these matters are inter-related and how these and any other relevant considerations should be assessed cannot be encapsulated in a set of legal rules.'

6.102 To give one example of how this might operate in a housing context, consider a possession claim where the landlord seeks to show that the tenant did not live at the demised premises as their only or principal home at the expiry

63 [2021] UKSC 33, [2021] 1 WLR 3863 at para 41.

of a notice to quit. They have credit reference evidence linking the tenant to an alternative address which proves to be their partner's. The tenant does not call their partner to give evidence, or the partner has provided a witness statement but does not attend trial.

6.103 The two-stage assessment approach will then be:

(a) why has the partner not been called or not attended trial?

(b) if there is no good reason, should the court draw an adverse inference such as to diminish the defendant's evidence or bolster that of the claimant?

6.104 Submissions on the absence of 'expected' people at trial can be a powerful and decisive tool for a social landlord.

CONCLUSION

6.105 This chapter promotes the truism that 'a claim is only as good as the evidence in support of it'. Sometimes though, documentary evidence will be scarce and the case will turn upon the credibility of the witnesses and their performance, in particular, under cross-examination.

6.106 At other times, the evidence is so overwhelming one wonders why the defendant bothers to defend the proceedings. A successful conclusion for the social landlord should be then easily achievable.

6.107 More likely, however, is something in between the two extremes; and it is foolhardy not to ensure that the best evidence possible is put before the court. This is likely to require all or some of the following:

(a) proactive efforts to obtain information from relevant third parties;

(b) the application and invoking of data-sharing arrangements;

(c) if the social landlord is not a local housing authority, the engagement with and use of the local authority to obtain information as part of any 'housing fraud investigation' (including by the undertaking of 'under caution' interviews); and

(d) a proactive use of court procedures, in particular the Part 18 Request for Further Information, and close regard to questions of disclosure and its adequacy.

CHAPTER 7

Criminal Sanctions

- Sub-letting offences
- Right-to-buy/right-to-acquire/shared ownership fraud
- Allocation and homelessness offences

Key points

- There are specific criminal offences relating to sub-letting and parting with possession, and the failure to provide accurate information for social housing allocation and homelessness purposes, to be found in the Prevention of Social Housing Fraud Act 2013 (PSHF), applying now solely to England,[1] and Parts 6 and 7 of the Housing Act 1996 respectively.
- The Fraud Act 2006 creates a series of fraud offences and will be used, especially in a housing context, in false statement, right-to-buy, right-to-acquire and shared ownership cases.
- The making of an unlawful profit order (UPO) should be considered by the court upon conviction for an offence under the PSHF.
- A local authority can prosecute an offence under the PSHF even if the premises concerned are not let by them or are not even in their area.
- The Sentencing Act 2020, s 134(1) allows a criminal court to make a compensation order to cover loss or damage resulting from the criminal offence of which the defendant has been convicted.
- The Proceeds of Crime Act 2002 (POCA) also provides for the availability of confiscation orders in the Crown Court in respect of the defendant's financial benefits from their criminal lifestyle.

INTRODUCTION

7.1 Any book on social housing fraud is inevitably going to deal with the criminal aspect of such activity in addition to the more immediate and well-

1 Until 1 December 2022 this offence applied to England and Wales but that was revised to England alone by the Renting Homes (Wales) Act 2016 (Consequential Amendments) Regulations 2022, SI 2022/1166, reg 33(2).

trodden civil remedy route of possession, damages and, perhaps, declaration.[2] It is a matter treated seriously by the criminal courts, one example being shown by the remarks of HHJ Dawson referred to on appeal by McCombe LJ in *R v Abokede*:[3]

> 'As I have said before in these cases, council accommodation is what I would call sensitive accommodation. There is a huge waiting list for accommodation. People wait sometimes generations for such accommodation to become available. It is subsidised accommodation. It is public property and therefore, clearly, the courts take a view as to the public view of the crimes being committed and in this case, my view is that it is a serious matter to abuse the system of providing accommodation for those in need and indeed creating a situation where now for many years because you are still in the accommodation, someone who was in that queue did not get the accommodation that they should have obtained and therefore had to wait longer or perhaps did not get it at all. It is a serious matter.'

7.2 This chapter does not purport to be a definitive guide to all the criminal sanctions that may be available – for example, it does not deal with any related benefit fraud offences, the common law conspiracy to defraud or issues of false accounting under section 17 of the Theft Act 1968. However, it does seek to demonstrate the range of the most likely options available to prosecutors when faced with a social housing fraud case.

7.3 In particular, the PSHF has brought into sharp focus the inter-relationship between criminal sanctions and civil remedies, although alongside the more general Fraud Act 2006 offences there had been (and remain) earlier targeted criminal offences created, such as can be found at sections 171 and 214 of the Housing Act 1996 and which are dealt with below.

7.4 As a preliminary point, it is always worth remembering that in criminal proceedings the general rule is that the prosecution bears the legal burden of proving *all* elements of the offence[4] and that guilt must be established to the criminal standard of proof (that is, beyond reasonable doubt).[5]

7.5 Those offences most obviously relevant to social housing fraud are identified and discussed below and, if a conviction is achieved, this will provide

2 Ie for rescission.

3 [2013] EWCA Crim 947 at [11].

4 This is in contrast to civil proceedings where, for example, the burden of proving the right to succession is on the would-be successor (*Governors of the Peabody Donation Fund v Grant* (1983) 6 HLR 41 at [44] *per* Donaldson LJ) and sufficient absence from a premises may lead to an explanation being required from the tenant in an only or principal home case: *Lambeth LBC v Vandra* [2005] EWCA Civ 1801; [2006] HLR 19 at [8]–[10] *per* Mummery LJ; *Islington LBC v Boyle* [2011] EWCA Civ 1450; [2012] PTSR 1093 at [65] *per* Etherton LJ.

5 *Woolmington v DPP* [1935] AC 462.

conclusive proof of any of the matters that need to be proved for any civil action, particularly bearing in mind section 11 of the Civil Evidence Act 1968:[6]

> '(1) In any civil proceedings the fact that a person has been convicted of an offence by or before any court in the United Kingdom or of a service offence (anywhere) shall (subject to subsection (3) below) be admissible in evidence for the purpose of proving, where to do so is relevant to any issue in those proceedings, that he committed that offence, whether he was so convicted upon a plea of guilty or otherwise and whether or not he is a party to the civil proceedings; but no conviction other than a subsisting one shall be admissible in evidence by virtue of this section.
>
> (2) In any civil proceedings in which by virtue of this section a person is proved to have been convicted of an offence by or before any court in the United Kingdom or of a service offence–
>
> (a) he shall be taken to have committed that offence unless the contrary is proved; and
>
> (b) without prejudice to the reception of any other admissible evidence for the purpose of identifying the facts on which the conviction was based, the contents of any document which is admissible as evidence of the conviction, and the contents of the information, complaint, indictment or charge-sheet on which the person in question was convicted, shall be admissible in evidence for that purpose.
>
> (3) Nothing in this section shall prejudice the operation of section 13 of this Act or any other enactment whereby a conviction or a finding of fact in any criminal proceedings is for the purposes of any other proceedings made conclusive evidence of any fact.
>
> (4) Where in any civil proceedings the contents of any document are admissible in evidence by virtue of subsection (2) above, a copy of that document, or of the material part thereof, purporting to be certified or otherwise authenticated by or on behalf of the court or authority having custody of that document shall be admissible in evidence and shall be taken to be a true copy of that document or part unless the contrary is shown.'

7.6 If a party wishes to use spent convictions as evidence in civil proceedings, they must first seek to rely on section 7 of the Rehabilitation of Offenders Act 1974 which provides:

> '(3) If at any stage in any proceedings before a judicial authority in England and Wales (not being proceedings to which, by virtue of any of paragraphs (a) to (e) of subsection (2) above[7] or of any order for the time being in force under subsection (4) below, section 4(1) above has no application, or

6 In *Re Q (A Child) (Fact finding Rehearing)* [2019] EWFC 60, Baker LJ determined that the purpose of s 11 was principally to establish a rule to be applied in circumstances in which the criminal trial and conviction occurred before the civil fact-finding process. It could not have been Parliament's intention that a subsequent conviction would lead to a presumption that a prior, contrary finding in civil proceedings would be overturned on appeal. Rather, the proper interpretation of s 11 was that the weight to be attached to a conviction in such circumstances would vary depending on all the circumstances.

7 None of the exceptions are relevant to a housing fraud scenario.

proceedings to which section 8 below applies) the authority is satisfied, in the light of any considerations which appear to it to be relevant (including any evidence which has been or may thereafter be put before it), *that justice cannot be done in the case except by admitting or requiring evidence relating to a person's spent convictions or to circumstances ancillary thereto, that authority may admit or, as the case may be, require the evidence in question* notwithstanding the provisions of subsection (1) of section 4 above, and may determine any issue to which the evidence relates in disregard, so far as necessary, of those provisions.' (emphasis added)

ALLOCATION FRAUD

'(1) A person commits an offence if, in connection with the exercise by a local housing authority of their functions under this Part–

(a) he knowingly or recklessly makes a statement which is false in a material particular, or

(b) he knowingly withholds information which the authority have reasonably required him to give in connection with the exercise of those functions.'

Housing Act 1996, s 171

7.7 Chapter 2 discusses the route to recovery of a social housing unit procured by a fraudulent misrepresentation. However, not only is such activity a ground for possession of the premises but it may also represent a specific criminal offence even if it does not result in an actual allocation of housing.

7.8 The criminal offence, set out in section 171 above, requires the false statement(s) or withholding of information to be in relation to the operation by a local housing authority (LHA) of its allocation scheme. The following should, therefore, be appreciated:

(a) An LHA is required to comply with the provisions of Part 6 when allocating accommodation.[8]

(b) This includes nominations by an LHA to a private registered provider of social housing or registered social landlord (primarily, housing associations).[9]

8 Housing Act 1996, s 159(1).

9 Ibid, s 159(2)(c) – this would cover the nomination arrangements many LHAs have with housing associations in their area (see s 159(4)) and it also includes, in Wales, where the LHA 'select a person to be a tenant under a secure contract or an introductory standard contract of housing accommodation held by them' or 'nominate a person to be a tenant under a secure contract or an introductory standard contract of housing accommodation held by another person' (see s 159(2)(d) and (e)). Sub-paragraph (5) goes on to say: 'The provisions of this Part do not apply to an allocation of housing accommodation by a local housing authority in Wales to a person who is already a tenant under a secure contract or an introductory standard contract unless the allocation involves a transfer of housing accommodation for that person and is made on his application'.

7.9 The section 171 offence can be committed in two different ways, broadly by giving or withholding information, and can best be explained by way of some questions:

- *First*, is the LHA exercising its functions under Part 6 of the Housing Act 1996? If not, then section 171 is of no application.
- *Second,* has the defendant made a false statement? This is obviously a central requirement for the section 171 offence but needs to be refined by way of two further questions that require an affirmative answer,
  - Did the defendant knowingly or recklessly make the statement?
  - Was the statement false in a material sense?
- *Third*, as an alternative to the second requirement, has the applicant knowingly withheld information which the LHA have reasonably required in the exercise of their allocation functions?

False statement

7.10 The most obvious starting point in considering the issue of false statement is to make the point that the applicant does not need to be both the maker of the statement and the potential defendant (though usually they are in fact one and the same). Someone assisting the applicant to complete the form may therefore be caught by this provision.

7.11 The mere copying down of false information would not, however, be sufficient and:

- absent any further evidence that the maker of the statement knew that it was false, or was reckless as to its accuracy, and
- absent evidence that they intended the LHA to believe in its accuracy,

no offence will have been committed.

7.12 The *Allocation of Accommodation: Guidance for Local Housing Authorities in England* (June 2012)[10] helpfully confirms:[11]

> '5.15 The circumstances in which an offence is committed could include providing false information:
>
> - on an application form for social housing
> - in response to a request for further information in support of the application
> - during review proceedings.'

10 Produced by the Ministry of Housing, Communities and Local Government under the Housing Act 1996, s 169 and, at the time of preparing this chapter, was last updated on 1 April 2026.

11 The above guidance states in relation to staff fraud or negligence: '5.17 Authorities may also wish to take action to minimise the risk of staff allocating incorrectly or even fraudulently, for example to applicants who do not have sufficient priority under the allocation scheme or do not meet the authority's qualification criteria. Appropriate steps might include vetting staff who take allocation decisions or providing for decisions to be validated by employing senior staff to undertake random checks'.

Withholding information

7.13 As with the making of a false statement, the offence of withholding relevant information can be committed by a person other than the applicant. The most obvious examples of who such other person may be are a partner, employer or landlord. It should be stressed, however, that a mere failure to answer a request for information from such third parties is unlikely to be sufficient.

Sentence

7.14 The sentencing for a section 171 offence is dealt with at **7.20** below.

7.15 To give a practical example of a prosecution for this offence, in 2018 a tenant of South Oxfordshire District Council had failed to disclose, when applying to go on the Council's housing register, that she in fact owned a property (which she was letting out). She had been living in the allocated property for a number of years by the time of the discovery and conviction, and the authority had been alerted to the situation by means of an anonymous tip-off. Following her guilty plea she was fined £250 and ordered to pay £1,250 and a £30 victim surcharge.[12]

7.16 Four years later and by way of further example, Tewkesbury Borough Council successfully prosecuted an individual, who had just been offered social housing, after he had failed to advise them of a change in circumstances (he had moved into private rented accommodation). On 27 July 2022, he pleaded guilty to three offences under section 171 at Cheltenham Magistrates' Court. He was fined £1,062.00, reduced to £708.00 for an early guilty plea, given a victim surcharge of £71.00 and ordered to pay costs to the council of £515.50.[13]

7.17 As a footnote to this discussion on allocation 'fraud', it is worth noting that the grant of a secure tenancy to someone to whom accommodation has been allocated inconsistently with the authority's allocation scheme does not of itself render the tenancy void or ineffective.[14]

HOMELESSNESS FRAUD

> '(1) It is an offence for a person, with intent to induce a local housing authority to believe in connection with the exercise of their functions under this Part that he or another person is entitled to accommodation or assistance in accordance with the provisions of this Part or is entitled to accommodation or assistance of a particular description–
>
> (a) knowingly or recklessly to make a statement which is false in a material particular, or

12 *Oxford Mail*, 12 February 2018.

13 Reported by the Council on 29 July 2022.

14 *Birmingham City Council v Qasim* [2009] EWCA Civ 1080; [2010] PTSR 471 at [37] *per* Lord Neuberger and [46]–[48] *per* Lord Justice Sedley – see **2.14–2.16**.

(b) knowingly to withhold information which the authority have reasonably required him to give in connection with the exercise of those functions.

(2) If before an applicant receives notification of the local housing authority's decision on his application there is any change of facts material to his case, he shall notify the authority as soon as possible.

The authority shall explain to every applicant, in ordinary language, the duty imposed on him by this subsection and the effect of subsection (3).

(3) A person who fails to comply with subsection (2) commits an offence unless he shows that he was not given the explanation required by that subsection or that he had some other reasonable excuse for non-compliance.'

Housing Act 1996, s 214

7.18 The first two offences under section 214(1)(a) and (1)(b) mirror those seen above for allocation fraud. This is with the 'addition' of the need to demonstrate an intention to induce the LHA, in connection with the exercise of their homelessness (Part 7) functions, to believe that the homeless applicant is entitled to accommodation or assistance under the homelessness provisions of Part 7.

7.19 There is, though, an *additional* offence, under sub-paragraph (2), of failing to notify the LHA of material changes, which *is* restricted to the applicant. The reason is apparent when one considers the various elements of the offence:

(a) An applicant is under a positive duty to inform the LHA as soon as possible of any change of facts material to their application prior to the LHA's decision.[15]

(b) What is a 'change of material fact' is a moot point and may provide a line of defence where the change is not of obvious relevance or import.

(c) Before such an offence can be committed, an LHA must explain to an applicant, in ordinary language, the nature of his duty to notify them of material changes and that any failure to do so is a criminal offence. If the applicant can show that this advice was not given then it provides an absolute defence. The *Homelessness Code of Guidance for Local Authorities* (February 2018) records at paragraph 18.10:

> 'Under section 214, it is an offence for a person, knowingly or recklessly to make a false statement, or knowingly to withhold information, with intent to induce the housing authority to believe that they, or another person, are entitled to accommodation or assistance under Part 7. If, before the applicant receives notification of a decision, there is any change of facts

15 In the first edition it was suggested that 'decision' meant the original (section 184) determination but there is a credible argument that the duty also extends to the statutory review process as the review decision entails 'the local housing authority's decision on his application' as well.

material to their case, they must inform the housing authority of this as soon as possible. Housing authorities must ensure that all applicants are made aware of these obligations and that they are explained in ordinary language. Housing authorities are advised to ensure that the obligations are conveyed sensitively to avoid intimidating applicants.'

(d) Similarly, if the applicant can show that they had some other reasonable excuse for non-compliance then, again, this could constitute a complete defence to the charge: section 214(3).

Sentence[16]

7.20 Offences under the allocation and homelessness provisions explained above are prosecuted in the magistrates' court and carry an unlimited fine.[17]

PREVENTION OF SOCIAL HOUSING FRAUD ACT 2013

7.21 The PSHF creates two criminal offences relating to the sub-letting or parting with possession of the whole of, or part of, demised premises let by a local authority or private registered provider of social housing[18] without the landlord's consent. There are broad similarities between the provisions concerning secure tenancies (s 1) and assured tenancies (s 2).[19]

7.22 There is nothing to prevent a social landlord seeking both a criminal remedy by way of conviction[20] and a civil remedy through possession action and/or UPO application in the county court (see Chapters 3 and 5, and **7.5** above).

7.23 It follows that not only is a conviction admissible evidence in the civil courts of the sub-letting and parting with possession claimed by the landlord, see **7.5–7.6**, but also and conversely, because of the higher standard of proof required in the criminal courts, a failure to secure a conviction is not necessarily fatal to a claim for possession of premises or an application for a UPO reliant on the same facts.[21]

16 See Housing Act 1996, ss 171(2) and 214(4).

17 See Sentencing Act 2020, s 118; Legal Aid, Sentencing and Punishment of Offenders Act 2012, s 85 removed the £5,000 fine limit previously found in this (and other) relevant offences.

18 PSHF, s 2(3) (or registered social landlord or community landlord in Wales) – a shared ownership lease is excluded from these provisions and is, in any event, for those shared ownership agreements that are no longer assured tenancies as a result of amendments introduced to Housing Act 1988, Sch 1 with effect from 27 December 2025 by Renters' Rights Act 2025, s 31(1).

19 At the time of writing, there are amendments to these provisions proposed in the Victims and Courts Bill 2024–26 in respect of sentencing.

20 The prosecution, though, can be by a local authority even if the premises are owned or otherwise let by a housing association – PSHF, s 3(5).

21 Indeed, the author has previously represented a local authority where that happened – an acquittal in the magistrates' court followed by, a few months later, an outright possession order in the county court.

Major offence

7.24 A tenant will commit an offence if:[22]

(a) they sub-let or part with possession of the whole of the premises, or part thereof, without the landlord's written consent (for assured tenancies there is no reference to consent although this is likely to be a breach of tenancy: see **7.26–7.27**);

(b) this is done dishonestly and in breach of an express or implied term of the tenancy; and

(c) the tenant ceases to occupy the premises as their only or principal home. Of course, if the arrangement is a joint tenancy then no offence is committed if the joint tenant remains in occupation.

Lodgers

7.25 As has been made clear in Chapter 3, lodger and most licensee arrangements do not constitute either sub-letting or parting with possession.

Consent

7.26 Most tenancy agreements have express terms which prohibit sub-letting or parting with possession of the whole of the demised premises, only allowing the same in respect of part with the landlord's written consent.

7.27 In any event, it is an implied term of every secure and (periodic) assured tenancy agreement that the tenant will not sub-let or part with possession of part of the dwelling without the landlord's (written for secure tenancies) consent,[23] which must not be unreasonably withheld (and will be treated as given if it is unreasonably withheld).[24]

Dishonesty

7.28 The test for 'dishonesty' is as confirmed by the Supreme Court in *Ivey v Genting Casinos (UK) Ltd t/a Crockfords*.[25] This is referred to in more detail at **7.56** below.

22 PSHF, ss 1(2), 2(2).

23 Housing Act 1985, s 93(1)(b) (secure tenancies); HA 1988, s 15(1) (periodic assured tenancies – which also implies a term preventing, without the landlord's consent, a sub-letting or parting with possession of the whole). Of course, ultimately, all assured tenancies will be periodic tenancies by reason of the Renters' Rights Act 2025.

24 Housing Act 1985, s 94(2). For periodic assured tenancies, the Housing Act 1988 expressly provides at s 15(2) that the usual statutory provision implying a condition that consent may not be unreasonably withheld (Landlord and Tenant Act 1927, s 19) does not apply.

25 [2017] UKSC 67, [2018] AC 391.

Only or principal home

7.29 This is considered in more detail at Chapter 4 but suffice to say here:

(a) it is a question of fact and degree;

(b) if the sub-letting or parting with possession is of the whole of the demised premises then this will be treated as being inconsistent with the premises still being the tenant's only or principal home;[26]

(c) physical occupation of the premises is not necessarily required to retain security of tenure, but the tenant will have to have an objective[27] intention to return to the premises (which must remain their only or principal home notwithstanding the tenant's physical non-occupation and must not be sub-let as a whole);[28]

(d) a sufficiently lengthy or continuous absence from the premises could compel the inference that the tenant had ceased to occupy the property as his only or principal home, the onus then being on the tenant to rebut it.[29]

Less serious offence

7.30 For the less serious offence of 'knowingly' sub-letting or parting with possession, which does not require dishonesty, the prosecution must show that the tenant:[30]

(a) has, in breach of an express or implied term of the tenancy, sub-let or parted with possession of the whole or part of the premises without the landlord's written consent (for assured tenancies there is again no reference to consent);

(b) no longer lives at the premises as their only or principal home; and

(c) knows that this is contrary to the express or implied terms of his tenancy.

7.31 Knowledge that any sub-letting is a breach of tenancy can include where a defendant has 'deliberately shut their eyes' to the truth.[31]

Defences

7.32 There are two specified defences to the less serious crime.

26 *Ujima Housing Association v Ansah* (1998) 30 HLR 831, CA.
27 *Amoah v Barking and Dagenham LBC* (2001) 82 P & CR DG6, Ch D.
28 *Crawley BC v Sawyer* (1988) 20 HLR 98, CA.
29 *London Borough of Islington v (1) Boyle (2) Collier* [2011] EWCA Civ 1450, [2012] HLR 19.
30 PSHF, s 1(1) for secure tenancies; s 2(1) for assured tenancies.
31 *Warner v Metropolitan Police Commr* [1969] 2 AC 256 at 279 *per* Lord Reid; *Atwal v Massey* (1972) 56 Cr App R 6, DC.

7.33 First, where the tenant's actions are due to violence, or threats of violence, by a person either residing in, or in the locality[32] of, the premises.[33] The violence or threats of violence must either be towards:

- the tenant; or
- a member of the tenant's family[34] who was residing with the tenant immediately before they ceased to occupy the premises.

7.34 Though 'violence' is not formally defined in the PSHF it is apparent from section 1(3) that it can concern domestic violence[35] as well as, for example, gang activity.[36]

7.35 The second defence is where a person who occupies the dwelling is a person entitled[37] to apply to the court for an order giving that person a right to occupy the dwelling to have the tenancy transferred to them, or a person in respect of whom an application may be made to have the tenancy transferred to them or to another person for their benefit.[38] This usually applies to the tenant's current or former spouse, civil partner, co-habitant or child.

32 Not defined in the Act but see the anti-social behaviour injunction case of *Manchester City Council v Lawler* (1998) 31 HLR 119 – Butler Sloss LJ said at [124]: 'One purpose of the phrase "in the locality" was to avoid the often difficult, unrewarding and sometimes lengthy discussion of whether to identify one road rather than another which would meet the general need to keep the tiresome and obstreperous tenant under some control in the area where he/she was likely to be the most troublesome. That area may be the part or the whole of a housing estate. It may straddle parts of two housing estates or include local shops serving the housing estate but within its boundaries. In my view, if one asked a resident in Broadoak Drive if Haveley Circle and Haveley Road were in the locality, the answer would be "yes of course"'.

33 Section 1(3).

34 Section 11(4) defines this term by reference to Housing Act 1985, s 113(5) – spouse or civil partner or person living together with another as if they were his spouse or civil partner, parent, grandparent, child, grandchild, brother, sister, uncle, aunt, nephew or niece. In this context: a relationship by marriage or civil partnership shall be treated as a relationship by blood; a relationship of half-blood shall be treated as a relationship of the whole blood; the stepchild of a person shall be treated as his child (including the stepchild of a civil partner) and an illegitimate child shall be treated as the legitimate child of his mother and reputed father. A foster child is not a 'child' for the purposes of s 113: *Sheffield City Council v Wall* [2010] EWCA Civ 922, [2011] 1 WLR 1342, [2010] HLR 47. In *Abdelrahman v Islington LBC* [2025] EWCA Civ 1038 the Court of Appeal held that the meaning of 'stepchild' in a local authority's policy concerning those entitled to succeed to secure tenancies, ascertained at the date when the policy had been issued, was a child of a person's spouse or civil partner by a previous marriage or civil partnership. Excluding the children of unmarried couples from the definition of 'stepchild' was a proportionate means of pursuing a legitimate aim and the policy was ECHR-compliant.

35 See *Yemshaw v Hounslow London Borough Council (Secretary of State for Communities and Local Government and another intervening)* [2011] UKSC 3, [2011] 1 WLR 433, [2011] HLR 16.

36 This type of behaviour was referred to by Jack Dromey MP during the passage of the PSHF Bill, *Hansard*, HC, Deb, 23 October 2012, Vol 551, col 891.

37 Eg under the Family Law Act 1996, ss 33–41, s 53, Sch 7.

38 PSHF, s 1(4).

Proceedings

7.36 The major (dishonesty) offence can be tried summarily in the magistrates' court or on indictment in the Crown Court, whereas the lesser offence is summary only and heard in the magistrates' court. Precedents 7.1, 7.2 and 7.3 shown below set out the documents and their required contents that will be needed to begin proceedings in the magistrates' court (though careful reference should also be made to Part 7 of the Criminal Procedure Rules 2025 to ensure compliance).

Precedent 7.1

PSHF Information[39]
IN THE STILLOPEN MAGISTRATES' COURT (1910)
INFORMATION

Prosecutor: Stillopen Borough Council, 7 Trafford Place, Stillopen, ST1 2BM
Defendant: Mr Stuart Pearson, of 33 Devereux Close, Stillopen, ST17 1RR

1. Between 29 July 20XX to 18 July 20XX *(Date of Information)*, Mr Stuart Pearson, being a tenant of 33 Devereux Close, Stillopen, ST17 1RR ('the Premises'), a dwelling-house owned by the Ferguson Heights Housing Association and let to him under an assured shorthold tenancy, did, knowing that it was in breach of the tenancy and in breach of an express or implied term of the tenancy (clause 7.2), sub-let or part with possession of the whole of the Premises and ceased to occupy the Premises as his only or principal home **contrary to** section 2(1) of the Prevention of Social Housing Fraud Act 2013

2. Between 29 July 20XX to 18 July 20XX *(Date of Information)*, Mr Stuart Pearson being a tenant of 33 Devereux Close, Stillopen, ST17 1RR ('the Premises'), a dwelling-house owned by the Ferguson Heights Housing Association and let to him under an assured shorthold tenancy, did dishonestly and in breach of an express or implied term of the tenancy (clause 7.2), sub-let or part with possession of the whole of the Premises and ceased to occupy the Premises as his only or principal home **contrary to** section 2(2) of the Prevention of Social Housing Fraud Act 2013

DATED THE EIGHTEENTH DAY OF OCTOBER 20XX

....

Ms Fiona Best
Borough Solicitor
Stillopen Borough Council,
7 Trafford Place,
Stillopen,
ST1 2BM

39 This leads to the magistrates' court issuing a summons or warrant: Magistrates' Courts Act 1980, s 1(1); Criminal Procedure Rules 2025, r 7.2.

Precedent 7.2

PSHF Summons
IN THE STILLOPEN MAGISTRATES' COURT (1910)

To: Mr Stuart Pearson

Of: 33 Devereux Close, Stillopen, ST17 1RR

INFORMATION was on 18 February 20XX laid before me, the undersigned Justice of the Peace, by Fiona Giggs, Borough Solicitor for Stillopen Borough Council for and on behalf of the Council of such Borough of 7 TRAFFORD PLACE, STILLOPEN, ST1 2BM

1. Between 29 July 20XX to 18 July 20XX *(Date of Information)*, Mr Stuart Pearson being a tenant of 33 Devereux Close, Stillopen, ST17 1RR ('the Premises'), a dwelling-house owned by the Ferguson Heights Housing Association and let to him under an assured shorthold tenancy, did, knowing that it was in breach of the tenancy, and in breach of an express or implied term of the tenancy (clause 7.2), sub-let or part with possession of the whole of the Premises and ceased to occupy the Premises as his only or principal home **contrary to** section 2(1) of the Prevention of Social Housing Fraud Act 2013

2. Between 29 July 20XX to 18 July 20XX *(Date of Information)*, Mr Stuart Pearson being a tenant of 33 Devereux Close, Stillopen, ST17 1RR ('the Premises'), a dwelling-house owned by the Ferguson Heights Housing Association and let to him under an assured shorthold tenancy, did dishonestly and in breach of an express or implied term of the tenancy (clause 7.2), sub-let or part with possession of the whole of the Premises and ceased to occupy the Premises as his only or principal home **contrary to** section 2(2) of the Prevention of Social Housing Fraud Act 2013

YOU ARE THEREFORE HEREBY SUMMONSED to appear on Friday, 6 November 20XX at the hour of 10am before the Stillopen Magistrates' Court sitting at The Civic Centre, Carrington Street, Stillopen, ST1 7DB to answer to the said Information.

DATED THE EIGHTEENTH DAY OF OCTOBER 20XX

Delegated Legal Adviser for the Area first above mentioned

Precedent 7.3

PSHF Certificate
CERTIFICATE
Prevention of Social Housing Fraud Act 2013
Stillopen Borough Council v Stuart Pearson

Evidence that was sufficient to warrant these proceedings in Stillopen Magistrates' Court came to the prosecutor's knowledge on 15 June 20XX

Fiona Giggs
Borough Solicitor
Stillopen Borough Council
18.10.20XX

7.37 It should be noted:

(a) A local authority can prosecute section 1 *and* section 2 (and associated) offences even if the premises are not theirs (eg it is a housing association let) and even if the property is not in their area.[40]

(b) For a summary offence, such as the lesser offence under sections 1(1) and 2(1) of the PSHF, a magistrates' court may ordinarily not try a person unless the information was 'laid' (served on) the court within six months of the time that the offence was committed.[41]

However, section 3(1) of the PSHF provides that this six-month period does not start to run until 'the date on which evidence sufficient in the opinion of the prosecutor to warrant the proceedings came to the prosecutor's knowledge'. This is subject to a long-stop of three years from the commission of the offence after which no prosecution of the lesser offence is possible.[42]

Example: A tenant has been sub-letting his one-bedroom flat since November 2020 to various sub-tenants under six-month lets. His landlord housing association only finds out about this in January 2024. He can be prosecuted then for *all* this activity under section 2(1) even though the offences started more than six months ago and, for example, the latest arrangement has been running for nine months. The contravention is continuous as the time runs from the last day.

Criminal Procedure Rules 2025

'7.2(3) An application for the issue of a summons or warrant must–

(a) set out the allegation or allegations made by the applicant in terms that comply with 7.3(1) (Allegation of offence in application or charge); and

40 PSHF, s 3(5), (6).
41 Magistrates' Courts Act 1980, s 127; Criminal Procedure Rules 2025, para 7.2(10).
42 PSHF, s 3(2).

(b) demonstrate–
   (i) that the application is made in time, if legislation imposes a time limit, and
   (ii) that the applicant has the necessary consent, if legislation requires it.'[43]

'7.3(1) An allegation of an offence in an application for the issue of a summons or warrant or in a charge must contain–

(a) a statement of the offence that–
   (i) describes the offence in ordinary language, and
   (ii) identifies any legislation that creates it; and

(b) such particulars of the conduct constituting the commission of the offence as to make clear what the prosecutor alleges against the defendant, including the value of any damage or theft alleged where that value is known and where it affects the exercise of the court's powers.

(2) More than one incident of the commission of the offence may be included in the allegation if those incidents taken together amount to a course of conduct having regard to the time, place or purpose of commission.'

(d) Precedent 7.3 (set out above) is an example certificate confirming when the prosecutor had knowledge, in their view, of sufficient evidence to warrant the prosecution of the lesser offence (see (b) above). This is provided for under section 3(3) of the PSHF and is conclusive proof of its contents.

(e) The more serious dishonesty offences at sections 1(2) and 2(2) are either-way offences – so can be tried in either the magistrates' court or the Crown Court. As such, they avoid the six-month limitation to prosecute provided for under section 127 of the Magistrates' Courts Act 1980.[44] Note that 'either way' offences must still begin with information 'laid' in a magistrates' court, from which they may then be committed to the Crown Court for trial on indictment.

Trial

7.38 For those used to civil proceedings, a PSHF trial in the criminal courts has some significant differences, not least in the areas of disclosure, the production of the defendant's case, hearsay evidence and, of course, the standard of proof. It is important in particular to have proper regard to the Criminal Procedure Rules

43 There may be other requirements but not if the prosecutor is the CPS or local authority (amongst others): Prosecution of Offences Act 1985, s 17(6); Criminal Procedure Rules 2025, r 7.2(4)–(6).

44 *Kemp v Leibherr (Great Britain) Ltd* [1987] 1 WLR 607 at [615B] *per* Glidewell LJ; delay though can lead to the court refusing to issue the summons – see *R v Clerk to the Medway Justices, ex parte DHSS* [1986] Crim LR 686.

2025 (the paragraphs that follow are just by way of an overview of some of the issues to note).

7.39 The standard of proof is straightforward. As noted at **7.4**, the prosecution must prove its case beyond reasonable doubt.

7.40 Yet while the prosecutor in the magistrates' court will have been required to serve initial details of their case where the defendant was in custody in relation to the offence charged prior to the first hearing:[45]

- a summary of the circumstances of the offence;
- the defendant's criminal record, and

if the defendant was not in police custody at that time, also:

- any account given by the defendant in interview (this may be in the summary of the circumstances);
- any written statement or exhibit that the prosecutor has available and considers material to plea, allocation of the case for trial, or to sentence; and
- any available statement as to the effect of the offence on a victim, their family or others,

as early as possible (and in any event no later than the beginning of the day of the first hearing),[46] that is not necessarily the case with the defendant.

7.41 Indeed, for a trial in the magistrates' court, unlike in the Crown Court,[47] a defendant does not even need to give a defence statement setting out their position, although they may do so.[48] What they must do, however, is give a witness notice indicating if they will be calling witnesses other than themselves and, if so, who those witnesses will be.[49]

7.42 Much of the evidence in a sub-letting case frequently relies on hearsay evidence, which is dealt with at Part 20 of the Criminal Procedure Rules 2025 and Chapter 2 of Part 11 of the Criminal Justice Act 2003.

7.43 Hearsay evidence – ie a statement not made in oral evidence – may include for example:

(a) bank account details and statements obtained from the bank of either the defendant or a third party;

45 Criminal Procedure Rules 2025, r 8.3.
46 Criminal Procedure Rules 2025, r 8.2.
47 Criminal Procedure and Investigations Act 1996, s 5.
48 Ibid, s 6; Criminal Procedure Rules 2025, r 15.4 – one advantage to a defendant of serving a defence statement may be that this then allows them, under r 15.5 and s 8 of the Criminal Procedure and Investigations Act 1996, to seek further prosecution disclosure. Forms are available for the defence statement and defence witness notice, provided by the Criminal Procedure Rule Committee and Ministry of Justice.
49 Criminal Procedure and Investigations Act 1996, s 6C subject to transitional provisions specified in SI 2010/1183, art 4(2).

(b) utility accounts; and

(c) reports of visits to the subject premises by the social landlord or their contractors.

7.44 Hearsay evidence is not generally admissible in criminal proceedings, unless it is a statement[50] the admissibility of which is agreed by the parties[51] or it can fit through one of the gateways provided by the 2003 Act. These include:

(a) evidence admissible where the court is satisfied it is in the interests of justice to so admit or a statutory provision makes it admissible (s 114(1)(a), (d));

(b) unavailability of witness (health, out of UK and not reasonably practicable to secure their attendance, due to fear of giving evidence, cannot be found or dead) (s 116);

(c) evidence created in the course of a trade, business or profession where the maker of the statement had no personal knowledge of the matters dealt with (such as a statement from a bank worker exhibiting the defendant's bank statements)(s 117(1)(b), (2)); and

(d) a rule of law preserved by section 118 of the Criminal Justice Act 2003 makes it admissible (eg evidence relating to a person's age or date or place of birth).

7.45 Reliance on hearsay by the prosecutor must generally[52] be indicated by the service and lodging of a hearsay notice – to be found online[53] – served not more than 20 business days after a not guilty plea has been entered by the defendant (10 business days in the Crown Court).[54]

7.46 Once the prosecution's evidence has been heard then – either of its own motion or upon application by the defendant – the court may, after hearing any representations from the prosecution, acquit prior to the defendant's case opening (or in the Crown Court direct the jury to acquit) on the ground that the prosecution evidence is insufficient for any reasonable court to properly convict.[55]

7.47 If the procedure at **7.46** does not apply the defendant is able to then present their case, having first been advised of their right to give evidence and the potential effect of not so doing or refusing to answer a question if they do.[56]

50 Under Criminal Justice Act 2003, s 115, (a) a 'statement' means any representation of fact or opinion, by any means, and includes a representation in pictorial form; and (b) a 'matter stated' is something stated by someone with the apparent purpose of causing another person to believe it, or causing another person, or a machine, to act or operate on the basis that the matter is as stated.

51 Ibid, s 114(1)(c).

52 Criminal Procedure Rules 2025, r 20.2(1) – Where admission is sought under the Criminal Justice Act 2003, ss 114(1)(d), 116, 117(1)(c) and 121 (multiple hearsay).

53 Search for 'Criminal hearsay notice'.

54 Criminal Procedure Rules 2025, r 20.2(3).

55 Ibid, r 24.3(3)(d) (magistrates' court) or 25.9(2)(e) (Crown Court).

56 Ibid, r 24.3(3)(e) (magistrates' court) or 25.9(2)(f) (Crown Court).

7.48 Unlike the procedure usually adopted in the county court, it is the defendant who has the right to make the final representations.[57]

Sentence

7.49 A person convicted on summary conviction in the magistrates' court for the lesser offence can be liable for a fine not exceeding level 5 (unlimited for offences committed on or after 12 March 2015 or £5,000 if earlier).[58]

7.50 In respect of the major (dishonesty) offence, on summary conviction in the magistrates' court, the defendant will be liable to a maximum of six months' imprisonment and/or a fine not exceeding the statutory maximum (or both; if convicted on indictment in the Crown Court, they can be sentenced to a maximum of two years' imprisonment and/or a fine).[59]

7.51 UPOs, which are dealt with in Chapter 5 in respect of civil remedies, are available if the defendant is convicted under section 1 or 2 of the PSHF (or an associated offence[60]).[61] Section 4(3) of the PSHF defines the UPO in this way:

> '(3) An "unlawful profit order" is an order requiring the offender to pay the landlord[62] an amount representing the profit made by the offender as a result of the conduct constituting the offence.'

7.52 The court can either make such an order of its own motion, if it considers it appropriate to do so, or accede to an application by the prosecution for a UPO.[63] If the court declines to make such an order they must give reasons during the sentencing.[64]

7.53 Section 4 further provides as follows:

57 Ibid, r 24.3(3)(i) (magistrates' court) or 25.9(2)(k) (Crown Court).
58 PSHF, s 1(5) (secure tenancies); s 2(6) (assured tenancies) – see n 16.
59 PSHF, s 1(6) (secure tenancies); s 2(7) (assured tenancies).
60 Defined in PSHF, s 11(10) as (a) an offence of aiding, abetting, counselling or procuring the commission of that offence, (b) an offence of attempting or conspiring to commit that offence, or (c) an offence under Part 2 of the Serious Crime Act 2007 (encouraging or assisting crime) in relation to that offence.
61 See PSHF, s 4.
62 Which s 4(13) explains 'means the landlord under the tenancy in respect of which the offence was committed'. Section 11(6) also states: 'References in this Act to the landlord under a secure or an assured tenancy include— (a) in a case where the tenancy has ended, a person who was the landlord under the tenancy, and (b) in a case where the tenancy has ceased to be a secure or an assured tenancy, the person who was the landlord under the tenancy when it was a secure or an assured tenancy'.
63 A section 4 UPO is enforced in the same way as for costs and compensation – see Administration of Justice Act 1970, s 41 and Sch 9, para 12B, and Magistrates' Courts Act 1980, ss 75–91 (eg attachment of earnings, benefits reduction, means inquiry, distress warrant, imprisonment and the taking of civil proceedings).
64 PSHF, s 4(4).

(a) There is a maximum UPO that can be ordered which mirrors that for civil UPOs (see Chapter 5). In essence, it is the 'profit element' of the activity after deducting what the tenant has paid in rent during the sub-letting period.

(b) If a civil UPO has already been made then the criminal UPO may only consist of the 'profit element' over and above the amount ordered in the civil court in addition to any unpaid portion of that earlier order. Enforcement of that latter element by the landlord requires the leave of the court.[65]

(c) UPOs take priority over fines. If the defendant cannot afford both, then only a UPO will be made.[66]

(d) Interest is payable at the usual civil judgment rate if the UPO is not paid by the time ordered.[67]

FRAUD ACT 2006

> 'The Act provides for a general offence of fraud with three ways of committing it, which are by false representation, by failing to disclose information and by abuse of position.'
>
> *Paragraph 7 of the Explanatory Notes to the Fraud Act 2006*

7.54 The Housing Act 1996 and the PSHF deal with many of the primary areas of social housing fraud. However, a lacuna would certainly arise if they were the only pieces of legislation providing for criminal offences in this area, not least with respect to:

(a) right-to-buy fraud (and that relating to right to acquire and shared ownership), and

(b) fraud involving employees of the landlord.

7.55 The Fraud Act 2006, which received Royal Assent on 8 November 2006, outlines a general either way offence of fraud at section 1 if a person is guilty of fraud:

(a) by false representation (s 2);

(b) by failing to disclose information (s 3); and

(c) by abuse of position (s 4).

7.56 All these fraud offences require dishonesty to be shown. This is determined by answering the question – would the defendant's behaviour be regarded as dishonest by the ordinary standards of reasonable and honest people? Lord Hughes rejected, therefore, the long-standing two-stage *Ghosh* test:[68]

65 Ibid, s 4(7).
66 Ibid, s 4(8)–(9).
67 Ibid, s 4(10)–(11) – see Judgments Act 1838, s 17.
68 *R v Ghosh* [1982] QB 1053.

(1) Would the defendant's behaviour be regarded as dishonest by the ordinary standards of reasonable and honest people?

(2) Was the defendant aware that his conduct was dishonest and would be regarded as dishonest by reasonable and honest people?

in the *Ivey v Genting Casinos* case referred to at **7.28** above, and he rather preferred Lord Hoffmann's analysis in *Barlow Clowes International v Eurotrust International Ltd*:[69]

> '10 The judge stated the law in terms largely derived from the advice of the Board given by Lord Nicholls of Birkenhead in *Royal Brunei Airlines Sdn Bhd v Tan* [1995] 2 AC 378. In summary, she said that liability for dishonest assistance requires a dishonest state of mind on the part of the person who assists in a breach of trust. Such a state of mind may consist in knowledge that the transaction is one in which he cannot honestly participate (for example, a misappropriation of other people's money) or it may consist in suspicion combined with a conscious decision not to make inquiries which might result in knowledge: *Manifest Shipping Co Ltd v Uni-Polaris Insurance Co Ltd* [2003] 1 AC 469. Although a dishonest state of mind is a subjective mental state, the standard by which the law determines whether it is dishonest is objective. If by ordinary standards a defendant's mental state would be characterised as dishonest, it is irrelevant that the defendant judges by different standards. The Court of Appeal held this to be a correct state of the law and their Lordships agree.'

False representation (section 2)

> '(1) A person is in breach of this section if he–
>
> (a) dishonestly makes a false representation, and
>
> (b) intends, by making the representation–
>
> (i) to make a gain for himself or another, or
>
> (ii) to cause loss to another or to expose another to a risk of loss.'
>
> *Fraud Act 2006, s 2*

7.57 The section 2 offence of fraud by false representation requires four elements:

(a) a false (ie untrue or misleading) representation must be made;[70]

(b) it must be made 'dishonestly';[71]

(c) the maker of the statement must know that it is false (or might be so);[72]

69 [2005] UKPC 37, [2006] 1 WLR 1476 at [1479]–[1480].
70 Fraud Act 2006, s 2(1)(a), (2)(a).
71 Ibid, s 2(1)(a).
72 Ibid, s 2(2)(b).

(d) it was made for the purpose of gain, or to cause loss to another (or expose them to it).[73]

7.58 An obvious example of a section 2 offence in a right-to-buy scenario is where the supposed tenant maintains in their application that they live at the relevant premises as their only or principal home, when that is not the case.

7.59 Indeed, to give one example of the particulars of an offence in a right-to-buy case:[74]

> '[The appellants] on or about 31 January 2011, dishonestly and intending thereby to make a gain for themselves or another, made a representation to the London Borough of Lewisham in a "Notice Claiming the Right to Buy," in relation to the council property at 43 Frankham House, Crossfield Estate, London, SE8, which was and which they knew was or might be untrue or misleading, namely that the said property was their only or principal home, which was false because they were, in fact, the joint owners of a residential property at 102 Brookehowse Road, Bellingham, London, SE6 which was their principal home, in breach of section 2 of the Fraud Act 2006.'

7.60 The section 2 representation can be either of fact or law[75] and can be express or implied.[76] Attempts to argue that the (obvious) fraud had nothing to do with the beneficiary may also be difficult for any defendant to pursue successfully.

7.61 In *Mohammed Idrees v Director of Public Prosecutions*,[77] the defendant had sought to argue that he had nothing to do with the fact that someone impersonating him had taken the theory driving test, which he had failed 15 times previously. Lord Justice Moses said:

> '5 The issue on this appeal, as the magistrates posed in the question they asked, was whether there was sufficient evidence at the close of the prosecution case. In my judgment there plainly was. Indeed, any contrary view would have been perverse. The magistrates rightly focused upon the fact that the only person who could possibly have benefited from this attempt by the unknown person to impersonate Mr Idrees was Mr Idrees himself. No other sensible explanation has been advanced. Courageously Mr Smith today, landed with this brief, sought to submit that somebody might have taken pity on Mr Idrees' plight in failing to pass his test on 15 previous occasions and had arranged for the unknown man to impersonate him without Mr Idrees' knowledge. Anything is possible. The magistrates are required to confine their deliberations on the facts to that which is not fanciful. Such a possibility advanced by Mr Smith was wholly fanciful. If

73 Ibid, s 1(b)(ii).
74 *R v (1) Krissene Offormezie (2) Ngozika Eze* [2015] EWCA Crim 324 – the defendants both successfully appealing against conviction.
75 Fraud Act 2006, s 2(3).
76 Ibid, s 2(4).
77 [2011] EWHC 624 (Admin).

one adds to that benefit the circumstance that the test had been booked for Mr Idrees in English on this occasion, whereas previously he [had] taken it 15 times in Urdu, the evidence becomes overwhelming.'

Failure to disclose information (section 3)

> 'A person is in breach of this section if he–
>
> (a) dishonestly fails to disclose to another person information which he is under a legal duty to disclose, and
>
> (b) intends, by failing to disclose the information–
>
> (i) to make a gain for himself or another, or
>
> (ii) to cause loss to another or to expose another to a risk of loss.'
>
> *Fraud Act 2006, s 3*

7.62 The section 3 offence of fraud by failing to disclose information can extend to obligations imposed by contract, such (arguably) as a housing association accommodation application.

7.63 This offence is generally straightforward. It is the concept of 'legal duty to disclose', which requires some explanation. The *Law Commission Report on Fraud*[78] explained it in this way:

> '7.28 … Such a duty may derive from statute (such as the provisions governing company prospectuses) from the fact that the transaction in question is one of the utmost good faith (such as a contract of insurance), from the express or implied terms of a contract, from the custom of a particular trade or market, or from the existence of a fiduciary relationship between the parties (such as that of agent and principal).
>
> 7.29 For this purpose there is a legal duty to disclose information not only if the defendant's failure to disclose it gives the victim a cause of action for damages, but also if the law gives the victim a right to set aside any change in his or her legal position to which he or she may consent as a result of the non-disclosure. For example, a person in a fiduciary position has a duty to disclose material information when entering into a contract with his or her beneficiary, in the sense that a failure to make such disclosure will entitle the beneficiary to rescind the contract and to reclaim any property transferred under it.'

7.64 Establishing this legal duty in the housing context can be difficult. Whilst an obligation to provide information may be apparent in either a contract of employment or a tenancy agreement, it may be more tenuous to argue that

78 Number 276 of 2002 – referred to by Lord Justice Pitchford in *R v Forrest (Nathan)* [2014] EWCA Crim 308 at [10].

legal obligations arise in an application for housing, in which case a different offence (such as fraud by false representation) may prove to be a more natural fit.

7.65 In *R v D*[79] the Court of Appeal (Criminal Division) agreed with the trial judge that the defendant was, for council tax purposes, not under a legal duty to disclose to the relevant local authority the fact of her residence at a particular address. Lord Justice Davis said, in delivering the judgment of the court:

> '15. Section 3, however, is specific that for criminal culpability to attach there must be a "legal duty" to disclose such information …
>
> 26. … As Mr Dennis inevitably conceded, there was no common law relationship between the local authority and the defendant which could give rise to any such duty of notification; nor was there any relevant fiduciary duty or other equitable obligation existing in this regard so as to require notification. The local authority is itself a creature of statute; and if it is to be able to recover council tax from those resident within its area then it must look to statutory authority for so doing …
>
> 33. Moreover, a conclusion that such an implied duty of notification does not arise under the statutory scheme relating to payment of council tax by no means leaves a local authority without remedy. A local authority is in a good position to get the information which it needs. For example, it will almost invariably know who the registered owner of the property is and can always seek, in appropriate circumstances, information under *reg.3*. Moreover, where failure to pay council tax has arisen, the local authority will have a remedy in the form of civil recovery in the civil courts.'

Abuse of position (section 4)

> '(1) A person is in breach of this section if he–
>
> (a) occupies a position in which he is expected to safeguard, or not to act against, the financial interests of another person,
>
> (b) dishonestly abuses that position, and
>
> (c) intends, by means of the abuse of that position–
>
> (i) to make a gain for himself or another, or
>
> (ii) to cause loss to another or to expose another to a risk of loss.
>
> (2) A person may be regarded as having abused his position even though his conduct consisted of an omission rather than an act.'

Fraud Act 2006, s 4

79 [2019] EWCA Crim 209, [2019] 2 Cr App R 15.

7.66 Section 4 makes it an offence to commit a fraud by dishonestly abusing one's position. It follows that this is the section usually applied where a staff member has, for example, been involved in right-to-buy, right-to-acquire, shared ownership or allocation fraud.

7.67 It applies in situations where the defendant has been put in a privileged position and, by virtue of this position, is expected positively to safeguard another's financial interests or at least not to act against those interests.

7.68 In the same report, referred to at **7.63** above, the Law Commission explained the meaning of 'position':

> '7.38 The necessary relationship will be present between trustee and beneficiary, director and company, professional person and client, agent and principal, employee and employer, or between partners. It may arise otherwise, for example within a family, or in the context of voluntary work, or in any context where the parties are not at arm's length. In nearly all cases where it arises, it will be recognised by the civil law as importing fiduciary duties, and any relationship that is so recognised will suffice. We see no reason, however, why the existence of such duties should be essential. This does not of course mean that it would be entirely a matter for the fact-finders whether the necessary relationship exists. The question whether the particular facts alleged can properly be described as giving rise to that relationship will be an issue capable of being ruled upon by the judge and, if the case goes to the jury, of being the subject of directions.'

7.69 In the context of allocation fraud, this may include cases where an employee of an LHA fraudulently allocates its properties outside the lawful allocation scheme, with the caveat provided by Lord Neuberger in *Birmingham City Council v Qasim*:[80]

> '43 Equally, it should be emphasised, that this is a case where the selection of the applicants in breach of the terms of the allocation scheme was made by a person to whom, as Mr Arden accepts, the Council had properly delegated the tasks of granting residential tenancies on its behalf. Different considerations would presumably apply where a tenancy had been purportedly granted by a person with no such authority, even if he had been employed by the Council.'

Sentence[81]

7.70 Section 1 of the Fraud Act 2006 provides:

80 Ibid. See also Lord Justice Sedley: '48 What then is the effect of a departure from the scheme? Clearly if an allocation bears what Lord Radcliffe in *Smith v East Elloe Rural DC* [1956] A.C. 736 called the brand of invalidity on its forehead (if, for example, it was issued by the doorkeeper) it is of no legal effect'.

81 See Sentencing Act 2020 and the Sentencing Guidelines (Sentencing Council).

'(3) A person who is guilty of fraud is liable–

(a) on summary conviction, to imprisonment for a term not exceeding the general limit in a magistrates' court or to a fine not exceeding the statutory maximum (or to both);

(b) on conviction on indictment, to imprisonment for a term not exceeding 10 years or to a fine (or to both).

(4) Subsection (3)(a) applies in relation to Northern Ireland as if the reference to 12 months were a reference to 6 months.'

7.71 In *R v Hamza & Ahmed*,[82] the defendants had pleaded guilty to eight counts of fraud pursuant to section 1 of the Fraud Act 2006. They had made two right-to-buy applications, in 2011 and 2012, to Sandwell Metropolitan Borough Council concerning 245 Thimblemill Road in Smethwick. The first defendant was the tenant of this property. To be entitled to proceed with such an application:

(a) it had to be the first defendant's sole or principal residence (it was not and representations to the contrary were false); and

(b) the second defendant had to be related to her and to have lived at the property for the previous 12 months (both these representations were untrue).

Each defendant was sentenced to concurrent terms of 20 months' imprisonment on each of the counts applicable to them, down from 30 months because of the guilty pleas.

7.72 In 2021 there was an appeal against sentence in *R v Gerald Kenyon*,[83] which is also referred to at the conclusion to Chapter 1 at **1.38**. Mr Kenyon had been sentenced to 18 months' imprisonment in July 2019 having been convicted of five offences of fraud for failure to disclose information (sub-letting his flat and later seeking to purchase it, unsuccessfully as it turned out, with a right-to-buy application). Mrs Justice Yip, in delivering the court's judgment rejecting the renewed permission application, said:

'10. By his grounds of appeal, the applicant contends that the judge failed to make sufficient allowance for his mitigation, including his health problems. He also challenged the judge's conclusion that only a custodial sentence could be justified. Further, he suggested that the claimed losses and profit were inadequately evidenced and that he was accordingly sentenced on an improper basis.

11.In refusing leave the single judge noted that the judge was well placed to assess the applicant's criminality, having presided over the trial. She concluded that the judge correctly placed the offending in category 3A of the relevant Sentencing Council guideline. It was category A harm as the fraud was perpetrated over six years, which is on any view is a sustained

82 [2014] EWCA Crim 2378.
83 [2021] EWCA Crim 68.

period of time. The applicant's activities also included a significant degree of planning, requiring him to find somewhere else to live, create a system for documents to be sent elsewhere, and direct those he sublet the property to about what to say if any official attended. There was both the risk of and actual harm, the amount of which justified placing the offending into category 3. The judge reflected the figure which the applicant actually obtained, his mitigation and totality by reducing the term that he imposed to the lowest end of the range for offences within category 3A.

12.We entirely agree with the single judge's conclusions that the offences were too serious to justify a suspended sentence order and that the sentence was not arguably manifestly excessive. We also agree with the reasons she gave for so concluding. In the circumstances this renewed application for permission to appeal against sentence must be refused.'

PROCEEDS OF CRIME ACT 2002

Confiscation orders

7.73 Section 6 of POCA provides for confiscation orders to be made by the Crown Court with the purpose of depriving the defendant of the benefit that they have obtained from crime:[84]

'(1) The Crown Court must proceed under this section if the following two conditions are satisfied.

(2) The first condition is that a defendant falls within any of the following paragraphs–

(a) he is convicted of an offence or offences in proceedings before the Crown Court;

(b) he is committed to the Crown Court for sentence in respect of an offence or offences under any provision of sections 14 to 20 of the Sentencing Code;

(c) he is committed to the Crown Court in respect of an offence or offences under section 70 below (committal with a view to a confiscation order being considered).

(3) The second condition is that–

(a) the prosecutor asks the court to proceed under this section, or

(b) the court believes it is appropriate for it to do so.

(4) The court must proceed as follows–

(a) it must decide whether the defendant has a criminal lifestyle;

84 There are amendments proposed at the time of writing by reason of the Crime and Policing Bill 2024–26.

(b) if it decides that he has a criminal lifestyle it must decide whether he has benefited from his general criminal conduct;

(c) if it decides that he does not have a criminal lifestyle it must decide whether he has benefited from his particular criminal conduct.

(5) If the court decides under subsection (4)(b) or (c) that the defendant has benefited from the conduct referred to it must–

(a) decide the recoverable amount, and

(b) make an order (a confiscation order) requiring him to pay that amount.

Paragraph (b) applies only if, or to the extent that, it would not be disproportionate to require the defendant to pay the recoverable amount.

(6) But the court must treat the duty in subsection (5) as a power if it believes that any victim of the conduct has at any time started or intends to start proceedings against the defendant in respect of loss, injury or damage sustained in connection with the conduct.

(6A) The court must also treat the duty in subsection (5) as a power if–

(a) an order has been made, or it believes an order may be made, against the defendant under section 4 (criminal unlawful profit orders) of the Prevention of Social Housing Fraud Act 2013 in respect of profit made by the defendant in connection with the conduct, or

(b) it believes that a person has at any time started or intends to start proceedings against the defendant under section 5 (civil unlawful profit orders) of that Act in respect of such profit.

(7) The court must decide any question arising under subsection (4) or (5) on a balance of probabilities.

(8) The first condition is not satisfied if the defendant absconds (but section 27 may apply).

(9) References in this Part to the offence (or offences) concerned are to the offence (or offences) mentioned in subsection (2).' (emphasis added)

7.74 Chapter 5 deals with the UPO that may be obtained by a landlord under the PSHF, along with other potential civil remedies allowing for some financial 'compensation' to be paid to the landlord as a result of social housing fraud.

7.75 Paragraphs **7.51–7.53** above also deal with UPOs in criminal proceedings in cases brought under the PSHF.

7.76 As well as providing for civil remedies for unlawful conduct under Part 5 of POCA (recovery orders: see **7.89–7.92**), section 6 also allows the court to make a confiscation order in the following circumstances:[85]

85 POCA, s 6 – the legitimate aim of the penalty is to remove the financial proceeds of the crime from the criminal: *R v Waya* (Terry) [2012] UKSC 51, [2012] 3 WLR 1188.

(1) The matter is before the Crown Court (either after trial and conviction, or committal to the Crown Court for sentence) – see section 6(2).

(2) The prosecutor has asked for a confiscation order or the Court believes it appropriate to make such an order – see section 6(3).

(3) The Court decides, on the balance of probabilities,[86] that the defendant has a criminal lifestyle and has benefited from his criminal conduct or has simply so benefited from the particular criminal conduct before them – see section 6(4).[87]

7.77 If those conditions are satisfied then the Court must decide, again on the balance of probabilities, the just recoverable amount – based on the benefit from the conduct concerned[88] – and make an order (unless civil recovery is being or is likely to be sought, when this duty becomes a power).

7.78 In *R v Andrewes*[89] the Supreme Court allowed an appeal against the refusal of a confiscation order and held that an order may be disproportionate where value for an arrangement was given by the defendant but that it would be proportionate to confiscate the difference between, on the facts of the case, the higher earnings made as a result of the fraud and the lower earnings that the offender would have made had they not committed the fraud. Lord Hodge DPSC and Lord Burrows gave the judgment of the court and noted:

> '44 … Mr Andrewes has performed valuable services for the hospice and the two trusts in return for the net earnings and, if one were to focus solely on his performance of the services (before his fraud was uncovered), it would be hard to deny that the hospice and the two trusts were receiving full value in exchange for the salary paid. But the hospice and the two trusts sought to employ or engage in a senior managerial position a person of honesty and integrity and Mr Andrewes would not have obtained the employment or office, which would have gone to another candidate, if the truth about his qualifications had been known. In that sense, the fraudster would be profiting from his crime if no confiscation order were made. How then should the proportionality proviso be interpreted so as to take into account the analogy to restoration while ensuring that the fraudster does not profit from his criminal conduct?'

7.79 In practice, the court will typically only invoke its confiscation powers if the prosecution invites it to do so. The prosecution must do this after conviction but before sentence and need not give any indication of its intention to take this step. POCA proceedings can only be dealt with in the Crown Court; the magistrates' court will commit summary proceedings to the Crown Court for

86 Ibid, s 6(7).

87 Rental income from a criminally obtained house or flat constituted a 'benefit': see *R v Oyebola (Folarin)* [2013] EWCA Crim 1052, [2014] 1 Cr App R (S) 58.

88 POCA, s 7(1).

89 [2022] UKSC 24, [2022] 1 WLR 3878.

this purpose upon the invitation of the prosecution under section 70(1), POCA.[90] This is in contrast to UPOs, which can be made by the magistrates' court. To give a recent example, on 11 September 2024 at Snaresbrook Crown Court a confiscation order in the sum of £242,705 was made in a housing fraud case. As the London Borough of Islington reported at the time:[91]

> 'Mr Deb fraudulently took on a council tenancy in 2011 without telling the council he had bought a home in nearby Haringey in the time between applying for council housing and being offered a home.
>
> Throughout his tenancy, Mr Deb then failed to tell the council he owned the three-bedroom property – which was big enough for his family – and instead, let it for up to £2,000 a month while claiming for full housing benefit for the council tenancy and pocketing the proceeds.
>
> The council discovered the fraud when Mr Deb applied to buy his council home, at a significant discount, through the national Right to Buy scheme.'

7.80 POCA orders can be a time-consuming and costly process, involving disclosure by the defence and investigation by the prosecution, with exchange of reports and information with a view to agreeing two main figures: the 'benefit figure' (how much profit has been derived from criminality) and the 'available amount' (what assets are available for confiscation). A confiscation order is then made in the lower sum of these two amounts.

7.81 Under the Home Office Asset Recovery Incentivisation Scheme (ARIS), authorities that investigate and prosecute offences are entitled to recover approximately one-third of the total amount recovered by the court under a confiscation order. By contrast the UPO regime, however, provides for all monies recovered to be paid directly to the landlord.

7.82 The principal financial advantage of POCA proceedings over the UPO procedure is that there should be no deductions for expenditure incurred by offending. However, it is unlikely to be appropriate to pursue confiscation proceedings where a UPO would be readily available.

SENTENCING ACT 2020

Compensation orders

7.83 The criminal court must consider making a compensation order in any case where personal injury, loss or damage has resulted from the offence, and

90 '70 Committal by magistrates' court
(1) This section applies if—
(a) a defendant is convicted of an offence by a magistrates' court, and
(b) the prosecutor asks the court to commit the defendant to the Crown Court with a view to a confiscation order being considered under section 6.'

91 See www.islington.media/news/islington-council-wins-back-gbp-260-000-in-landmark-tenancy-fraud-case.

the court must also (as with the UPO) give reasons if it decides *not* to order such compensation.[92] Any such order is effectively a requirement for a convicted party to pay compensation for personal injury, loss or damage resulting from the (in this instance, fraud) offence or other offences taken into account by the court in sentencing.[93]

7.84 Section 134 of the Sentencing Act 2020 provides:

> '(1) A compensation order is available to a court by or before which an offender is convicted of an offence. This is subject to section 136 (road accidents).
>
> (2) Where a compensation order is available, the court may make such an order whether or not it also deals with the offender for the offence in any other way.'

7.85 As for the operation of such orders, section 135 goes on to state:

> '(1) A compensation order must specify the amount to be paid under it.
>
> (2) That amount must be the amount that the court considers appropriate, having regard to any evidence and any representations that are made by or on behalf of the offender or the prosecution. But see also sections 136 to 139.
>
> (3) In determining—
>
> (a) whether to make a compensation order against an offender, or
>
> (b) the amount to be paid under such an order,
>
> the court must have regard to the offender's means, so far as they appear or are known to the court.
>
> (4) Where the court considers—
>
> (a) that it would be appropriate both to impose a fine and to make a compensation order, but
>
> (b) that the offender has insufficient means to pay both an appropriate fine and appropriate compensation,
>
> the court must give preference to compensation (though it may impose a fine as well).
>
> (5) For modifications of this section where the court also makes an order under section 380 (power to order parent or guardian to pay fine, costs, compensation or surcharge), see section 140.

92 Sentencing Act 2020, s 55.
93 Ibid, s 133.

(6) For the effect of proceedings in relation to confiscation orders on the court's powers in relation to compensation orders, see the following provisions of the Proceeds of Crime Act 2002—

(a) section 13(4) (where confiscation order has been made);

(b) section 15 (where proceedings on a confiscation order have been postponed).'

7.86 Mr Justice Cranston said in *R v Stapylton (Ben)* in relation to the predecessor compensation order legislation:[94]

> '11 Since the first legislation enabling compensation to be awarded by the criminal courts was enacted, section 1(1) of the Criminal Justice Act 1972, the courts have laid down a number of principles about the making of compensation orders. First, the court has no jurisdiction to make an order where there are real issues as to whether those to benefit have suffered any, and if so, what loss: *R v Horsham Justices ex p Richards* [1985] 1 WLR 986, 993. Thus in *R v Christopher Paul Watson* (1990–91) 12 Cr App R (S) 508 no award was made in favour of insurers because there was no evidence as to the loss. Coupled with that is that because compensation orders are for straightforward cases: *R v Donovan* (1981) 3 Cr App R (S) 192, a court should not embark on a detailed inquiry as to the extent of any injury, loss or damage. If the matter demands such attention it is better left for civil proceedings. *Further, compensation orders must not be made unless there is a realistic possibility of compliance* (*R v Webb* (1979) 1 Cr App R (S) 16). Orders should not be made if they will be protracted in effect, although much will turn on the nature of the offence and the offender: *R v Olliver* (1989) 1 Cr App R (S) 10.' (emphasis added)

7.87 The amount of the loss will need to be agreed by the defendant or established by evidence. Any such 'evidence hearings' should be straightforward and simple (see *Hyde v Emery*).[95] In appropriate cases, the court can award a sum representing the loss of interest if the compensation order is large and the period long: *R v Schofield*.[96]

7.88 By way of example as to the appropriateness of the sums awarded under a compensation order, in *R v Mohammed Hossain & Ors*[97] the three appellants appealed against what they said were excessive compensation orders (£6,695.55, £23,031.12 and £19,739.39). The Court of Appeal (Criminal Division) found that there was no evidence that the appellants could pay those sums and varied the orders to:

94 [2012] EWCA Crim 728, [2013] 1 Cr App R (S) 12. The Powers of Criminal Courts (Sentencing) Act 2000 was the Act then in force.
95 (1984) Cr App R (S) 206.
96 [1978] 2 All ER 705.
97 [2016] EWCA Crim 1099.

- £1,800 at £50 pcm: 3 years.
- £3,600 at £75 pcm: 4 years.
- £3,600 at £75 pcm: 4 years.

Civil recovery orders

7.89 As noted at **7.76**, POCA allows, in Part 5,[98] for the recovery in civil proceedings before the High Court of property obtained either through unlawful conduct[99] or the forfeiting of cash which is (or represents) property obtained through unlawful conduct (or which is intended to be so used) through the magistrates' court.[100] Section 240 says:

> '(1) This Part has effect for the purposes of–
>
> (a) enabling the enforcement authority to recover, in civil proceedings before the High Court or Court of Session, property which is, or represents, property obtained through unlawful conduct,
>
> (b) enabling property which is, or represents, property obtained through unlawful conduct, or which is intended to be used in unlawful conduct, to be forfeited in civil proceedings before a magistrates' court or (in Scotland) the sheriff [and, in certain circumstances, to be forfeited by the giving of a notice].
>
> (2) The powers conferred by this Part are exercisable in relation to any property (including cash) whether or not any proceedings have been brought for an offence in connection with the property.'

7.90 To give one example of the application of a recovery order, in *Serious Organised Crime Agency v Olden*[101] Mr Olden was said to have engaged in mortgage fraud and other deception. In February 2006, he was convicted of a number of offences, including three counts of obtaining property by deception. His conviction was set aside by the Court of Appeal (Criminal Division) on 9 March 2007 and thereafter the Assets Recovery Agency successfully applied to the High Court for a property freezing order and for an order for possession of a number of assets.

7.91 Mr Olden won his appeal in part, in relation to the possession order of the properties (although not in relation to recoveries of identified money sources). It was found that POCA did not provide power for a possession order but rather a recovery order vesting any property in the trustee (who could then seek a possession order in the usual way under CPR Part 55).

98 Recovery orders and, from s 245A, property freezing orders.
99 POCA, s 240(1)(a).
100 Ibid, s 240(1)(b).
101 [2010] EWCA Civ 143, [2010] CP Rep 29.

7.92 This book does not go into any further detail as to the POCA civil remedies because they are exercisable in England not by the social landlord but by the Financial Conduct Authority, HMRC, the National Crime Agency, the Director of Public Prosecutions or the Director of the Serious Fraud Office.[102]

PRIVATE PROSECUTIONS

7.93 Sometimes, legislation, such as section 3 of the PSHF, makes express provision as to who may prosecute the criminal offences created thereunder:

> '(5) A local authority may prosecute an offence under section 1 or 2 in relation to a dwelling-house–
>
> (a) whether or not the dwelling-house is or was let under a tenancy under which the local authority is or was the landlord, and
>
> (b) whether or not the dwelling-house is located in the local authority's area.'

7.94 In any event there is, in most instances,[103] nothing to prevent any individual or organisation, such as a Housing Association for example, from bringing a private prosecution (and some, such as the RSPCA, exercise this right regularly). Section 6(1) of the Prosecution of Offences Act 1985 confirms:

> '(1) Subject to subsection (2) below, nothing in this Part shall preclude any person from instituting any criminal proceedings or conducting any criminal proceedings to which the Director's duty to take over the conduct of proceedings does not apply.
>
> (2) Where criminal proceedings are instituted in circumstances in which the Director is not under a duty to take over their conduct, he may nevertheless do so at any stage.'

7.95 Section 1 of the Magistrates' Courts Act 1980 provides:

> **'Issue of summons to accused or warrant for his arrest**
>
> (1) On an information being laid before a justice of the peace that a person has, or is suspected of having, committed an offence, the justice may issue–
>
> (a) a summons directed to that person requiring him to appear before a magistrates' court to answer the information, or
>
> (b) a warrant to arrest that person and bring him before a magistrates' court.'

102 The enforcement authority being so defined for England and Wales at POCA 2002, s 316(1).

103 The Director of Public Prosecutions (DPP) has power under POA 1985, s 6(2) to take over private prosecutions and, in some cases, the private prosecutor must seek the consent of the Attorney General or of the DPP before the commencement of proceedings.

7.96 The test used by the magistrates' court when considering an application by a private prosecutor for a summons was explained by the Divisional Court (Gross LJ and Sweeney J) in R (on the application of Kay and Anor) v Leeds Magistrates' Court.[104] Sweeney J said:

> '(1) The magistrate must ascertain whether the allegation is an offence known to the law, and if so whether the essential ingredients of the offence are prima facie present; that the offence alleged is not time-barred; that the court has jurisdiction; and whether the informant has the necessary authority to prosecute.
>
> (2) If so, generally the magistrate ought to issue the summons, unless there are compelling reasons not to do so – most obviously that the application is vexatious (which may involve the presence of an improper ulterior purpose and/or long delay); or is an abuse of process; or is otherwise improper.
>
> (3) Hence the magistrate should consider the whole of the relevant circumstances to enable him to satisfy himself that it is a proper case to issue the summons and, even if there is evidence of the offence, should consider whether the application is vexatious, an abuse of process, or otherwise improper.
>
> (4) Whether the applicant has previously approached the police may be a relevant circumstance.
>
> (5) There is no obligation on the magistrate to make enquiries, but he may do so if he thinks it necessary.
>
> (6) A proposed defendant has no right to be heard, but the magistrate has a discretion to: (a) Require the proposed defendant to be notified of the application. (b) Hear the proposed defendant if he thinks it necessary for the purpose of making a decision.'

7.97 In *R (Virgin Media Ltd) v Zinga*[105] the Court of Appeal (Criminal Division) confirmed that such a power to initiate criminal prosecutions extends to confiscation proceedings as well, in holding as follows:

(a) A private prosecutor could institute confiscation proceedings by inviting the court to proceed under section 6 of POCA. In the overwhelming majority of cases involving a private prosecutor, initiation of confiscation proceedings would also serve the public interest.

(b) The DPP may use the power under section 6(2) of the Prosecution of Offences Act 1985 to take over a private prosecution when the court asks for assistance from the CPS in dealing with confiscation proceedings that involve compensation or other recompense from a defendant. Alternatively, the court may simply ask the CPS to assist the court.

104 [2018] EWHC 1233 (Admin), [2018] 2 Cr App R 27 at [22].
105 [2014] EWCA Crim 52, [2014] 1 WLR 2228.

7.98 As for costs, the Practice Direction (Costs in Criminal Proceedings) 2015 (as amended) says at 1.2.1:

> 'The powers enabling the court to award costs in criminal proceedings are primarily contained in Part II of the Prosecution of Offences Act 1985 ("the Act") (sections 16 to 19B), the Access to Justice Act 1999 and the Legal Aid, Sentencing and Punishment of Offenders Act 2012 (in relation to funded clients) and in regulations made under those Acts including the Costs in Criminal Cases (General) Regulations 1986, as amended ("the General Regulations").'

Further:

- Paragraph 1.3.1 goes on to state that where the court orders that the costs of a private prosecutor should be paid from central funds, the order will be for such amount as the court considers 'sufficient reasonably to compensate the party for expenses incurred by him in the proceedings'; unless the court considers that there are circumstances that make it inappropriate to allow the full amount, in which event the court will allow 'such lesser sum as it considers just and reasonable'.
- Paragraph 1.4.1 states that where the court makes an order in favour of a private prosecutor, but is of the opinion that there are circumstances which make it inappropriate that the prosecutor should recover the full amount of the costs:

  > '... the court may assess the lesser amount that would in its opinion be just and reasonable, and specify that amount in the order. If the court is not in a position to specify the amount payable, the judge may make remarks which the appropriate authority will take into account as a relevant circumstance when determining the costs payable.'

- Paragraph 2.6.1 states that in a case in which the costs of a private prosecutor may be awarded out of central funds:

  > 'An order should be made save where there is good reason for not doing so, for example, where proceedings have been instituted or continued without good cause.'

7.99 There are various options and variations therefore provided for, especially in the Prosecution of Offences Act 1985:

(a) Defence costs to be paid out of central funds: section 16.[106]

(b) Prosecution costs to be paid out of central funds in limited circumstances (eg no order is possible in favour of a public authority): section 17.[107]

106 The Costs in Criminal Cases (General) Regulations 1986 (made under s 20 of the 1985 Act) contain provisions in Part 3 relating to costs out of central funds.

107 The Court of Appeal (Criminal Division) provided guidance in the form of principles of general application regarding the making of an order under s 17 for the payment from central funds of the costs of private prosecutions undertaken by an individual or entity other than the police or a state prosecuting authority in *R v BDI* [2025] EWCA Crim 1289.

(c) Award of costs to the prosecutor and payable by the defendant 'as [the court] considers just and reasonable':[108] section 18.

(d) To award costs against a party where the court is satisfied that the other party has incurred costs 'as a result of an unnecessary or improper act or omission by, or on behalf of, another party to the proceedings': section 19;

(e) Wasted costs provision against a legal or other representative: section 19A.

(f) Provision for award of costs against third parties: section 19B.

7.100 It may be thought that a prosecutor would always seek their costs but there will be instances where there is no point because of the defendant's means, particularly when any compensation order or other financial penalty is factored in as these will be given priority.

7.101 To give four examples from press reports highlighted in the Cornerstone on Social Housing Fraud blog:

1. 'A woman who sublet her Plymouth Community Homes property for around seven years has been ordered to pay £580 by Plymouth magistrates.'
2. 'Marita Head of Lower Trevivian, St Clether, Launceston, pleaded guilty to knowingly subletting a social housing property in Swinburne Gardens between 15 January 2013 and 16 October 2018. She was fined £100 and ordered to pay £450 costs and £50 victim surcharge.'
3. 'For sub-letting the property, Ketch was ordered to pay £1,796.30 back to Durham County Council. He must also pay £600 towards court costs and was given to separate penalty for failing to notify the council of his change in circumstances relating to council tax payment reductions.'
4. 'Both defendants were each ordered to undertake 120 hours of unpaid work, with Harry Harriman ordered to pay the council's costs of £3,000 and Louisa Harriman £2,250.'

7.102 Part 45 of the Criminal Procedure Rules 2025 supplements the legislative cost provisions and confirms at rule 45.5(3)(b) that if the prosecutor is seeking their costs following a successful prosecution then 'the general rule is that the court must make an order if it is satisfied that the defendant can pay'.

7.103 In *R v Adedeji (Katheryn)*[109] the Court of Appeal set aside a prosecution costs order, made against a defendant who had unlawfully sub-let a social housing property, as procedural defects had led the judge to apply an arbitrary and overly broad-brush approach to the question of costs. A new prosecution costs order was made for £32,000, with the defendant liable for 50% of that figure (she was one of two appellants). Green LJ delivered the judgment of the court, including with regard to the award of costs, and stated at [42]–[45]:

108 The Practice Direction says that an order for costs in such circumstances should be made where the defendant has the means to pay.

109 [2019] EWCA Crim 804, [2019] 4 WLR 136.

'… There are three particular aspects of the principles that are of relevance which we summarise as follows.

43 *First*, the prosecution is under an obligation to serve upon the defence, at the earliest time, full details of its costs in order to give the defendant a proper opportunity to make representations upon them, if appropriate.

44 *Second*, costs awarded should not ordinarily be greatly at variance with any fine imposed. We take this as imposing a general obligation to ensure that costs are broadly proportionate to the financial sanctions imposed. In *R v Northallerton Magistrates' Court, Ex parte Dove* [2000] 1 Cr App R (S) 136 Lord Bingham CJ emphasised that an order for costs should never exceed the sum which the prosecutors actually and reasonably incurred. Lord Bingham also acknowledged that whilst there was no requirement that a sum ordered should stand in any "arithmetical relationship to any fine imposed" but, none the less, the order should not be grossly disproportionate to the fine.

45 *Third*, when setting costs, a judge should take into account that the prosecution might be seeking to defray costs incurred by the officers of a third party (such as a Council) which might be said to be "*routine*" and would have to be incurred in any event, in the normal way.'

7.104 As for the assessment of costs under section 19 of the Prosecution of Offences Act 1985, Hickinbottom J said in *Evans v Serious Fraud Office*[110], at [20]:

'i) If making a s 19 order, the court has to order that a specified amount is paid by one party to another party … This requires the judge to assess the costs to be paid …

ii) Unless the judge considers it appropriate to depart from the general rule (and gives reasons for doing so), the assessment must be of an amount that reasonably compensates the receiving party for costs 'actually, reasonably and properly incurred' as a result of the unnecessary or improper act or omission identified, and 'reasonable in amount', in this context, 'reasonableness' incorporating a degree of proportionality …

iii) The statutory scheme envisages a summary assessment, adopting a broad-brush approach. Unlike a summary assessment of costs in civil proceedings, there is no fixed procedure; and the judge may adopt any procedure that gives all relevant parties a fair opportunity to make representations.

iv) The judge must satisfy himself that the amounts claimed do not offend the indemnity principle …

110 [2015] EWHC 1525 (QB), [2015] 3 Costs LR 557.

v) In making the assessment, the judge must take into account all relevant factors …

vii) In making the assessment, the judge has a very wide discretion. There is no appeal: his determination will only be subject to challenge on public law grounds.

viii) The judge is required to give reasons for his decision; but in the context of the fact that he is making a broad-brush summary assessment. His reasons need therefore cover only the main issues between the parties. The judge does not explain why he has come to the precise figure to which he has come – let alone descend to the consideration of individual items that would be appropriate in an assessment by a taxing authority – so long as the parties can understand broadly why he considers that figure reasonably to compensate the receiving party for costs reasonably incurred as a result of the identified unnecessary or improper act(s) or omission(s). There is simply no requirement that a receiving party should give the detail required on a detailed assessment, and the judge should not be drawn into performing anything akin to a detailed assessment …'

CONCLUSION

7.105 Social landlords will be familiar by now with the criminal sanction possibilities of the PSHF and no doubt will be aware, too, of its 'predecessor' the Fraud Act 2006 which, as made clear in this chapter, remains very much in force. They may also have had some success in recovery of monies pursuant to the Sentencing Act 2020 (compensation orders), in particular to cover any losses resulting from the offence.

7.106 Criminal prosecution potentially allows a social landlord to 'send out a message' about their being tough on housing fraud, 'recover' monies in some instances and, upon any conviction, provide incontrovertible evidence of wrongdoing for any civil action. However, it inevitably represents a small part of their activity in this area and they will naturally be more interested in recovering the properties relevant to the fraud or misuse, and the costs of so doing, as well as any civil orders available to recoup the perpetrators' illicit gains.

7.107 Yet the criminal options and procedures available are important not only to put the seriousness of social housing fraud into its proper context, it is a criminal act, but also because civil remedies alone may not always encourage this fact to be sufficiently appreciated.

APPENDIX A

Statutes

References

Law of Property Act 1925
s 146

Protection from Eviction Act 1977
ss 2, 3, 3A, 5

Housing Act 1996
ss 124–143, 171, 214

Commonhold and Leasehold Reform Act 2002
ss 76–77, 168–169

Proceeds of Crime Act 2002
ss 6–13B, 240–245G

Data Protection Act 2018
ss 1–11, 15–16, 29-42A, 82, 114-117, 121, Sch 1-2

Sentencing Act 2020
Part 7, Chapter 2

Full-Text Provisions
Housing Act 1985

PART IV
SECURE TENANCIES AND RIGHTS OF SECURE TENANTS

Security of tenure

79 Secure tenancies.

(1) A tenancy under which a dwelling-house [in England][1] is let as a separate dwelling is a secure tenancy at any time when the conditions described in sections 80 and 81 as the landlord condition and the tenant condition are satisfied.

(2) Subsection (1) has effect subject to—

(a) the exceptions in Schedule 1 (tenancies which are not secure tenancies),

(b) sections 89(3) and (4) and 90(3) and (4) (tenancies ceasing to be secure after death of tenant), and

(c) sections 91(2) and 93(2) (tenancies ceasing to be secure in consequence of assignment of subletting).

(3) The provisions of this Part apply in relation to a licence to occupy a dwelling-house [in England][1] (whether or not granted for a consideration) as they apply in relation to a tenancy.

(4) Subsection (3) does not apply to a licence granted as a temporary expedient to a person who entered the dwelling-house or any other land as a trespasser (whether or not, before the grant of that licence, another licence to occupy that or another dwelling-house had been granted to him).

Amendments

1 Inserted by the Renting Homes (Wales) Act 2016 (Consequential Amendments) Regulations 2022, SI 2022/1166, reg 11(1), (9).

80 The landlord condition.

(1) The landlord condition is that the interest of the landlord belongs to one of the following authorities or bodies—

a local authority,

a [development][1] corporation,

[a housing action trust,][2]

[a Mayoral development corporation,][3]

an urban development corporation,

[in the case of a tenancy falling within subsections (2A) to (2E), the Homes and Communities Agency[, the Greater London Authority][4] or the Welsh Ministers (as the case may be),][5]

...[6]

...[7]

...[7] housing co-operative to which this section applies.

(2) ...[7]

[(2A) A tenancy falls within this subsection if the interest of the landlord is transferred to—

(a) the Homes and Communities Agency as mentioned in section 52(1)(a) to (d) of the Housing and Regeneration Act 2008,

[(aa) the Greater London Authority as mentioned in section 333ZI(2)(a) to (d) of the Greater London Authority Act 1999, or][8]

(b) the Welsh Ministers as mentioned in section 36(1)(a)(i) to (iii) of the New Towns Act 1981.

(2B) A tenancy falls within this subsection if it is entered into pursuant to a contract under which the rights and liabilities of the prospective landlord are transferred to the Homes and Communities Agency[, the Greater London Authority][4] or the Welsh Ministers as mentioned in subsection (2A)(a)[, (aa)][4] or (b) (as the case may be).

(2C) A tenancy falls within this subsection if it is granted by the Homes and Communities Agency[, the Greater London Authority][4] or the Welsh Ministers to a person (alone or jointly with others) who, immediately before it was entered into, was a secure tenant of the Homes and Communities Agency[, the Greater London Authority][4] or the Welsh Ministers (as the case may be).

(2D) A tenancy falls within this subsection if—

(a) it is granted by the Homes and Communities Agency[, the Greater London Authority][4] or the Welsh Ministers to a person (alone or jointly with others),

(b) before the grant of the tenancy, an order for possession of a dwelling-house let under a secure tenancy was made against the person (alone or jointly with others) and in favour of the Homes and Communities Agency[, the Greater London Authority][4] or the Welsh Ministers (as the case may be) on the court being satisfied as mentioned in section 84(2)(b) or (c), and

(c) the tenancy is of the premises which constitute the suitable accommodation as to which the court was so satisfied.

(2E) A tenancy falls within this subsection if it is granted by the Homes and Communities Agency[, the Greater London Authority][4] or the Welsh Ministers pursuant to an obligation under section 554(2A).][5]

(3) If a co-operative housing association ceases to be [a private registered provider of social housing or][9] [a registered social landlord][10], it shall, within the period of 21 days beginning with the date on which it ceases to be [such a body][11], notify each of its tenants who thereby becomes a secure tenant, in writing, that he has become a secure tenant.

[(4) This section applies to a housing co-operative within the meaning of section 27B (agreements under certain superseded provisions) where the dwelling-house is comprised in a housing co-operative agreement within the meaning of that section.][12]

[(5) In this Act and in any provision made under this Act, or made by or under any other enactment, a reference to—

(a) a person within section 80 or 80(1) of this Act, or

(b) a person who satisfies the landlord condition under this section,

includes a reference to the Homes and Communities Agency[, to the Greater London Authority][4] or to the Welsh Ministers so far as acting in their capacity as landlord (or, in the case of disposals, former landlord) in respect of a tenancy which falls within subsections (2A) to (2E) above but, subject to this, does not include the Homes and Communities Agency[, the Greater London Authority][4] or the Welsh Ministers.

(6) Subsection (5)—

(a) applies whether the person is described as an authority, body or landlord or in any other way and whether the reference is otherwise expressed in a different way, and

(b) is subject to any provision to the contrary.][5]

Amendments

1 Substituted by the Housing and Regeneration Act 2008 (Consequential Provisions) Order 2008, SI 2008/3002, art 4, Sch 1, paras 2, 10(1), (2)(a).

2 Inserted by the Housing Act 1988, s 83(1), (2).

3 Inserted by the Localism Act 2011, s 222, Sch 22, paras 9, 11.

4 Inserted by the Localism Act 2011, s 195(1), Sch 19, paras 10, 13(1), (2), (4)–(8).

5 Inserted by the Housing and Regeneration Act 2008 (Consequential Provisions) Order 2008, SI 2008/3002, art 4, Sch 1, paras 2, 10(1), (2)(b), (3), (4).

6 Repealed by the Government of Wales Act 1998, s 152, Sch 18, Pt IV.

7 Repealed by the Housing Act 1988, s 140(2), Sch 18.

8 Substituted by the Localism Act 2011, s 195(1), Sch 19, paras 10, 13(1), (3).

9 Inserted by the Housing and Regeneration Act 2008 (Consequential Provisions) Order 2010, SI 2010/866, art 5, Sch 2, paras 15, 19(1), (4)(a).

10 Substituted by the Housing Act 1996 (Consequential Provisions) Order 1996, SI 1996/2325, art 5(1), Sch 2, para 14(1), (8)(b).

11 Substituted by the Housing and Regeneration Act 2008 (Consequential Provisions) Order 2010, SI 2010/866, art 5, Sch 2, paras 15, 19(1), (4)(b).

12 Substituted by the Housing and Planning Act 1986, s 24(2), Sch 5, para 26.

81 The tenant condition.

The tenant condition is that the tenant is an individual and occupies the dwelling-house as his only or principal home; or, where the tenancy is a joint tenancy, that each of the joint tenants is an individual and at least one of them occupies the dwelling-house as his only or principal home.

[81ZA Grant of secure tenancies in cases of domestic abuse

(1) This section applies where a local housing authority grants a secure tenancy of a dwelling-house in England before the day on which paragraph 4 of Schedule 7 to the Housing and Planning Act 2016 (grant of new secure tenancies in England) comes fully into force.

(2) The local housing authority must grant a secure tenancy that is not a flexible tenancy if—

(a) the tenancy is offered to a person who is or was a tenant of some other dwelling-house under a qualifying tenancy (whether as the sole tenant or as a joint tenant), and

(b) the authority is satisfied that—

(i) the person or a member of the person's household is or has been a victim of domestic abuse carried out by another person, and

(ii) the new tenancy is granted for reasons connected with that abuse.

(3) The local housing authority must grant a secure tenancy that is not a flexible tenancy if—

(a) the tenancy is offered to a person who was a joint tenant of the dwelling-house under a qualifying tenancy, and

(b) the authority is satisfied that—

(i) the person or a member of the person's household is or has been a victim of domestic abuse carried out by another person, and

(ii) the new tenancy is granted for reasons connected with that abuse.

(4) In this section—

'abuse' means—

(a) physical or sexual abuse;

(b) violent or threatening behaviour;

(c) controlling or coercive behaviour;

(d) economic abuse (within the meaning of section 1(4) of the Domestic Abuse Act 2021);

(e) psychological, emotional or other abuse;

'domestic abuse' means abuse carried out by a person who is personally connected to the victim of the abuse (within the meaning of section 2 of the Domestic Abuse Act 2021);

'qualifying tenancy' means a tenancy of a dwelling-house in England which is—

(a) a secure tenancy other than a flexible tenancy, or

(b) an assured tenancy—

(i) which is not an assured shorthold tenancy, and

(ii) which is granted by a private registered provider of social housing, by the Regulator of Social Housing or by a housing trust which is a charity.

(5) For the purposes of this section, a person may be a victim of domestic abuse despite the fact that the abuse is directed at another person (for example, the person's child).][1]

Amendment

1 Inserted by the Domestic Abuse Act 2021, s 79(1), (2).

82 Security of tenure.

(1) A secure tenancy which is either—

(a) a weekly or other periodic tenancy, or

(b) a tenancy for a term certain but subject to termination by the landlord,

cannot be brought to an end by the landlord except [as][1] [mentioned in subsection (1A)][2].

[(1A) The tenancy may be brought to an end by the landlord—

(a) obtaining—

(i) an order of the court for the possession of the dwelling-house, and

(ii) the execution of the order,

(b) obtaining an order under subsection (3), or

(c) obtaining a demotion order under section 82A.

(2) In the case mentioned in subsection (1A)(a), the tenancy ends when the order is executed.][1]

(3) Where a secure tenancy is a tenancy for a term certain but with a provision for re-entry or forfeiture, the court shall not order possession of the dwelling-house in pursuance of that provision, but in a case where the court would have made such an order it shall instead make an order terminating the tenancy on a date specified in the order and section 86 (periodic tenancy arising on termination of fixed term) shall apply.

(4) Section 146 of the Law of Property Act 1925 (restriction on and relief against forfeiture), except subsection (4) (vesting in under-lessee), and any other enactment or rule of law relating to forfeiture, shall apply in relation to proceedings for an order under subsection (3) of this section as if they were proceedings to enforce a right of re-entry or forfeiture.

Amendments

1 Substituted by the Housing and Regeneration Act 2008, s 299, Sch 11, paras 1, 2.

2 Substituted by the Anti-social Behaviour Act 2003, s 14(1)(a).

[83 Proceedings for possession or termination: [general][1] notice requirements.

[(A1) This section applies in relation to proceedings for an order mentioned in section 82(1A) other than—

(a) proceedings for possession of a dwelling-house under section 84A (absolute ground for possession for anti-social behaviour), including proceedings where possession is also sought on one or more of the grounds set out in Schedule 2, or

(b) proceedings for possession of a dwelling-house under section 107D (recovery of possession on expiry of flexible tenancy).][1]

(1) The court shall not entertain [proceedings to which this section applies][2] unless—

(a) the landlord has served a notice on the tenant complying with the provisions of this section, or

(b) the court considers it just and equitable to dispense with the requirement of such a notice.

(2) A notice under this section shall—

(a) be in a form prescribed by regulations made by the Secretary of State,

(b) specify the ground on which the court will be asked to make [the order][3] and

(c) give particulars of that ground.

(3) Where the tenancy is a periodic tenancy and the ground or one of the grounds specified in the notice is Ground 2 in Schedule 2 (nuisance or other anti-social behaviour), the notice—

(a) shall also—

(i) state that proceedings for the possession of the dwelling-house may be begun immediately, and

(ii) specify the date sought by the landlord as the date on which the tenant is to give up possession of the dwelling-house, and

(b) ceases to be in force twelve months after the date so specified.

(4) Where the tenancy is a periodic tenancy and Ground 2 in Schedule 2 is not specified in the notice, the notice—

(a) shall also specify the date after which proceedings for the possession of the dwelling-house may be begun, and

(b) ceases to be in force twelve months after the date so specified.

[(4A) If the proceedings are for a demotion order under section 82A the notice—

(a) must specify the date after which the proceedings may be begun;

(b) ceases to be in force twelve months after the date so specified.][4]

(5) The date specified in accordance with subsection (3), [(4) or (4A)][3] must not be earlier than the date on which the tenancy could, apart from this Part, be brought to an end by notice to quit given by the landlord on the same date as the notice under this section.

(6) Where a notice under this section is served with respect to a secure tenancy for a term certain, it has effect also with respect to any periodic tenancy arising on the termination of that tenancy by virtue of section 86; and subsections (3) to (5) of this section do not apply to the notice.

(7) Regulations under this section shall be made by statutory instrument and may make different provision with respect to different cases or descriptions of case, including different provision for different areas.][5]

Amendments

1 Inserted by the Anti-social Behaviour, Crime and Policing Act 2014, s 181(1), Sch 11, para 7(1)–(3).

2 Substituted by the Anti-social Behaviour, Crime and Policing Act 2014, s 181(1), Sch 11, para 7(1), (4).

3 Substituted by the Anti-social Behaviour Act 2003, s 14(3)(b), (d).

4 Inserted by the Anti-social Behaviour Act 2003, s 14(3)(c).

5 Substituted by the Housing Act 1996, s 147(1).

[83A Additional requirements in relation to certain proceedings for possession.

(1) Where a notice under section 83 has been served on a tenant containing the information mentioned in subsection (3)(a) of that section, the court shall not entertain proceedings for the possession of the dwelling-house unless they are begun at a time when the notice is still in force.

(2) Where—

(a) a notice under section 83 [or 83ZA][1] has been served on a tenant, and

(b) a date after which proceedings may be begun has been specified in the notice in accordance with [section 83(4)(a) or section 83ZA(9)(a)][2],

the court shall not entertain proceedings for the possession of the dwelling-house unless they are begun after the date so specified and at a time when the notice is still in force.

(3) Where—

(a) the ground or one of the grounds specified in a notice under section 83 [or 83ZA][1] is Ground 2A in Schedule 2 (domestic violence), and

(b) the partner who has left the dwelling-house as mentioned in that ground is not a tenant of the dwelling-house, the court shall not entertain proceedings for the possession of the dwelling-house unless it is satisfied that the landlord has served a copy of the notice on the partner who has left or has taken all reasonable steps to serve a copy of the notice on that partner.

This subsection has effect subject to subsection (5).

(4) Where—

(a) Ground 2A in Schedule 2 is added to a notice under section 83 [or 83ZA][1] with the leave of the court after proceedings for possession are begun, and

(b) the partner who has left the dwelling-house as mentioned in that ground is not a party to the proceedings,

the court shall not continue to entertain the proceedings unless it is satisfied that the landlord has served a notice under subsection (6) on the partner who has left or has taken all reasonable steps to serve such a notice on that partner.

This subsection has effect subject to subsection (5).

(5) Where subsection (3) or (4) applies and Ground 2 in Schedule 2 (nuisance or other anti-social behaviour) is also specified in [a notice][2] under section 83 [or a notice is served under section 83ZA][1], the court may dispense with the requirements as to service in relation to the partner who has left the dwelling-house if it considers it just and equitable to do so.

(6) A notice under this subsection shall—

(a) state that proceedings for the possession of the dwelling-house have begun,

(b) specify the ground or grounds on which possession is being sought, and

(c) give particulars of the ground or grounds.][3]

Amendments

1 Inserted by the Anti-social Behaviour, Crime and Policing Act 2014, s 181(1), Sch 11, para 8(1), (2), (4), (5), (6)(b).

2 Substituted by the Anti-social Behaviour, Crime and Policing Act 2014, s 181(1), Sch 11, para 8(1), (3), (6)(a).

3 Substituted by the Housing Act 1996, s 147(1).

84 Grounds and orders for possession.

(1) The court shall not make an order for the possession of a dwelling-house let under a secure tenancy except on one or more of the grounds set out in Schedule 2 [or in accordance with [section 84A (absolute ground for possession for anti-social behaviour) or][1] section 107D (recovery of possession on expiry of flexible tenancy)][2].

(2) The court shall not make an order for possession—

(a) on the grounds set out in Part I of [Schedule 2][3] (grounds 1 to 8), unless it considers it reasonable to make the order,

(b) on the grounds set out in Part II of that Schedule (grounds 9 to 11), unless it is satisfied that suitable accommodation will be available for the tenant when the order takes effect,

(c) on the grounds set out in Part III of that Schedule (grounds 12 to 16), unless it both considers it reasonable to make the order and is satisfied that suitable accommodation will be available for the tenant when the order takes effect;

and Part IV of that Schedule has effect for determining whether suitable accommodation will be available for a tenant.

[(3) Where a notice under section 83 [or 83ZA][1] has been served on the tenant, the court shall not make [an order on any of the grounds mentioned in subsection (2)][3] unless the ground is specified in the notice; but the grounds so specified may be altered or added to with the leave of the court.

(4) Where a date is specified in a notice under section 83 in accordance with subsection (3) of that section, the court shall not make an order which requires the tenant to give up possession of the dwelling-house in question before the date so specified.][4]

Amendments

1 Inserted by the Anti-social Behaviour, Crime and Policing Act 2014, s 181(1), Sch 11, para 9(1), (2), (4)(a).

2 Inserted by the Localism Act 2011, s 155(2).

3 Substituted by the Anti-social Behaviour, Crime and Policing Act 2014, s 181(1), Sch 11, para 9(1), (3), (4)(b).

4 Substituted by the Housing Act 1996, s 147(2).

85 Extended discretion of court in certain proceedings for possession.

(1) Where proceedings are brought for possession of a dwelling-house let under a secure tenancy on any of the grounds set out in Part I or Part III of Schedule 2 (grounds 1 to 8 and 12 to 16: cases in which the court must be satisfied that it is reasonable to make a possession order), the court may adjourn the proceedings for such period or periods as it thinks fit.

(2) On the making of an order for possession of such a dwelling-house on any of those grounds, or at any time before the execution of the order, the court may—

(a) stay or suspend the execution of the order, or

(b) postpone the date of possession,

for such period or periods as the court thinks fit.

(3) On such an adjournment, stay, suspension or postponement the court—

(a) shall impose conditions with respect to the payment by the tenant of arrears of rent (if any) and rent ...[1] unless it considers that to do so would cause exceptional hardship to the tenant or would otherwise be unreasonable, and

(b) may impose such other conditions as it thinks fit.

[(4) The court may discharge or rescind the order for possession if it thinks it appropriate to do so having had regard to—

(a) any conditions imposed under subsection (3), and

(b) the conduct of the tenant in connection with those conditions.][2]

(5) ...[1]

[(5A) ...[1]][3]

Amendments

1 Repealed by the Housing and Regeneration Act 2008, ss 299, 321(1), Sch 11, para 3(1), (2), (4), Sch 16.

2 Substituted by the Housing and Regeneration Act 2008, s 299, Sch 11, para 3(1), (3).

3 Inserted by the Family Law Act 1996, s 66(1), Sch 8, para 53(1), (3).

86 Periodic tenancy arising on termination of fixed term.

(1) Where a secure tenancy ('the first tenancy') is a tenancy for a term certain and comes to an end—

(a) by effluxion of time, or

(b) by an order of the court under section 82(3) (termination in pursuance of provision for re-entry or forfeiture),

a periodic tenancy of the same dwelling-house arises by virtue of this section, unless the tenant is granted another secure tenancy of the same dwelling-house (whether a tenancy for a term certain or a periodic tenancy) to begin on the coming to an end of the first tenancy.

(2) Where a periodic tenancy arises by virtue of this section—

(a) the periods of the tenancy are the same as those for which rent was last payable under the first tenancy, and

(b) the parties and the terms of the tenancy are the same as those of the first tenancy at the end of it;

except that the terms are confined to those which are compatible with a periodic tenancy and do not include any provision for re-entry or forfeiture.

Succession on death of tenant

[86A Persons qualified to succeed tenant: England

(1) A person ('P') is qualified to succeed the tenant under a secure tenancy of a dwelling-house in England if—

(a) P occupies the dwelling-house as P's only or principal home at the time of the tenant's death, and

(b) P is the tenant's spouse or civil partner.

(2) A person ('P') is qualified to succeed the tenant under a secure tenancy of a dwelling-house in England if—

(a) at the time of the tenant's death the dwelling-house is not occupied by a spouse or civil partner of the tenant as his or her only or principal home,

(b) an express term of the tenancy makes provision for a person other than such a spouse or civil partner of the tenant to succeed to the tenancy, and

(c) P's succession is in accordance with that term.

(3) Subsection (1) or (2) does not apply if the tenant was a successor as defined in section 88.

(4) In such a case, a person ('P') is qualified to succeed the tenant if—

(a) an express term of the tenancy makes provision for a person to succeed a successor to the tenancy, and

(b) P's succession is in accordance with that term.

[(5) For the purposes of this section, a person who was living with the tenant as if they were a married couple or civil partners is to be treated as the tenant's spouse or civil partner.][1]

(6) Subsection (7) applies if, on the death of the tenant, there is by virtue of subsection (5) more than one person who fulfils the condition in subsection (1)(b).

(7) Such one of those persons as may be agreed between them or as may, where there is no such agreement, be selected by the landlord is for the purpose of this section to be treated …[2] as the tenant's spouse or civil partner.][3]

Amendments

1 Substituted by the Civil Partnership (Opposite-sex Couples) Regulations 2019, SI 2019/1458, reg 41(1), Sch 3, para 10(1), (2)(a).

2 Repealed by the Civil Partnership (Opposite-sex Couples) Regulations 2019, SI 2019/1458, reg 41(1), Sch 3, para 10(1), (2)(b)

3 Inserted by the Localism Act 2011, s 160(1).

87 …[1]

Amendment

1 Repealed by the Renting Homes (Wales) Act 2016 (Consequential Amendments) Regulations 2022, SI 2022/1166, reg 11(1), (12).

88 Cases where the tenant is a successor.

(1) The tenant is himself a successor if—

(a) the tenancy vested in him by virtue of section 89 (succession to a periodic tenancy), or

(b) he was a joint tenant and has become the sole tenant, or

(c) the tenancy arose by virtue of section 86 (periodic tenancy arising on ending of term certain) and the first tenancy there mentioned was granted to another person or jointly to him and another person, or

(d) he became the tenant on the tenancy being assigned to him (but subject to subsections [(2) to (3)][1], or

(e) he became the tenant on the tenancy being vested in him on the death of the previous tenant [or

(f) the tenancy was previously an introductory tenancy and he was a successor to the introductory tenancy.][2]

(2) A tenant to whom the tenancy was assigned in pursuance of an order under section 24 of the Matrimonial Causes Act 1973 (property adjustment orders in connection with matrimonial proceedings) [or section 17(1) of the Matrimonial and Family Proceedings Act 1984 (property adjustment orders after overseas divorce, &c.)][3] is a successor only if the other party to the marriage was a successor.

[(2A) A tenant to whom the tenancy was assigned in pursuance of an order under Part 2 of Schedule 5, or paragraph 9(2) or (3) of Schedule 7, to the Civil Partnership Act 2004 (property adjustment orders in connection with civil partnership proceedings or after overseas dissolution of civil partnership, etc.) is a successor only if the other civil partner was a successor.][4]

(3) A tenant to whom the tenancy was assigned by virtue of section 92 (assignments by way of exchange) is a successor only if he was a successor in relation to the tenancy which he himself assigned by virtue of that section.

(4) Where within six months of the coming to an end of a secure tenancy which is a periodic tenancy ('the former tenancy') the tenant becomes a tenant under another secure tenancy which is a periodic tenancy, and—

(a) the tenant was a successor in relation to the former tenancy, and

(b) under the other tenancy either the dwelling-house or the landlord, or both, are the same as under the former tenancy,

the tenant is also a successor in relation to the other tenancy unless the agreement creating that tenancy otherwise provides.

Amendments

1 Substituted by the Civil Partnership Act 2004, s 81, Sch 8, para 21(1), (2).

2 Inserted by the Housing Act 1996, s 141(1), Sch 14, para 1.

3 Inserted by the Housing Act 1996, s 222, Sch 18, para 9.

4 Inserted by the Civil Partnership Act 2004, s 81, Sch 8, para 21(1), (3).

89 Succession to periodic tenancy.

(1) This section applies where a secure tenant dies and the tenancy is a periodic tenancy.

[(1A) Where there is a person qualified to succeed the tenant under section 86A, the tenancy vests by virtue of this section—

(a) in that person, or

(b) if there is more than one such person, in such one of them as may be agreed between them or as may, where there is no agreement, be selected by the landlord.][1]

(2) Where there is a person qualified to succeed the tenant [under section 87][1], the tenancy vests by virtue of this section in that person, or if there is more than one such person in the one to be preferred in accordance with the following rules—

(a) the tenant's spouse [or civil partner][2] is to be preferred to another member of the tenant's family;

(b) of two or more other members of the tenant's family such of them is to be preferred as may be agreed between them or as may, where there is no such agreement, be selected by the landlord.

[(3) Where there is no person qualified to succeed the tenant, the tenancy ceases to be a secure tenancy—

(a) when it is vested or otherwise disposed of in the course of the administration of the tenant's estate, unless the vesting or other disposal is in pursuance of an order made under—

(i) section 24 of the Matrimonial Causes Act 1973 (property adjustment orders made in connection with matrimonial proceedings),

(ii) section 17(1) of the Matrimonial and Family Proceedings Act 1984 (property adjustment orders after overseas divorce, &c.), …[3]

(iii) paragraph 1 of Schedule 1 to the Children Act 1989 (orders for financial relief against parents)[, or

(iv) Part 2 of Schedule 5, or paragraph 9(2) or (3) of Schedule 7, to the Civil Partnership Act 2004 (property adjustment orders in connection with civil partnership proceedings or after overseas dissolution of civil partnership, etc.)][2]

(b) when it is known that when the tenancy is so vested or disposed of it will not be in pursuance of such an order.][4]

(4) A tenancy which ceases to be a secure tenancy by virtue of this section cannot subsequently become a secure tenancy.

Amendments

1 Inserted by the Localism Act 2011, s 160(3)–(5).

2 Inserted by the Civil Partnership Act 2004, s 81, Sch 8, para 22.

3 Repealed by the Civil Partnership Act 2004, s 261(4), Sch 30.

4 Substituted by the Housing Act 1996, s 222, Sch 18, para 10.

90 Devolution of term certain.

(1) This section applies where a secure tenant dies and the tenancy is a tenancy for a term certain.

(2) The tenancy remains a secure tenancy until—

(a) it is vested or otherwise disposed of in the course of the administration of the tenant's estate, as mentioned in subsection (3), or

(b) it is known that when it is so vested or disposed of it will not be a secure tenancy.

(3) The tenancy ceases to be a secure tenancy on being vested or otherwise disposed of in the course of administration of the tenant's estate, unless—

[(a) the vesting or other disposal is in pursuance of an order made under—

(i) section 24 of the Matrimonial Causes Act 1973 (property adjustment orders in connection with matrimonial proceedings),

(ii) section 17(1) of the Matrimonial and Family Proceedings Act 1984 (property adjustment orders after overseas divorce, &c.), …[1]

(iii) paragraph 1 of Schedule 1 to the Children Act 1989 (orders for financial relief against parents), or

[(iv) Part 2 of Schedule 5, or paragraph 9(2) or (3) of Schedule 7, to the Civil Partnership Act 2004 (property adjustment orders in connection with civil partnership proceedings or after overseas dissolution of civil partnership, etc), or][2]][3]

(b) the vesting or other disposal is to a person qualified to succeed the tenant.

(4) A tenancy which ceases to be a secure tenancy by virtue of this section cannot subsequently become a secure tenancy.

[(5) The following provisions apply where a tenancy that was a secure tenancy of a dwelling-house in England—

(a) has been vested or otherwise disposed of in the course of the administration of the secure tenant's estate, and

(b) has ceased to be a secure tenancy by virtue of this section.

(6) Subject as follows, the landlord may apply to the court for an order for possession of the dwelling-house let under the tenancy.

(7) The court may not entertain proceedings for an order for possession under this section unless—

(a) the landlord has served notice in writing on the tenant—

(i) stating that the landlord requires possession of the dwelling-house, and

(ii) specifying a date after which proceedings for an order for possession may be begun, and

(b) that date has passed without the tenant giving up possession of the dwelling-house.

(8) The date mentioned in subsection (7)(a)(ii) must fall after the end of the period of four weeks beginning with the date on which the notice is served on the tenant.

(9) On an application to the court for an order for possession under this section, the court must make such an order if it is satisfied that subsection (5) applies to the tenancy.

(10) The tenancy ends when the order is executed.][4]

Amendments

1 Repealed by the Civil Partnership Act 2004, s 261(4), Sch 30.

2 Inserted by the Civil Partnership Act 2004, s 81, Sch 8, para 23.

3 Substituted by the Housing Act 1996, s 222, Sch 18, para 11.

4 Inserted by the Localism Act 2011, s 162(1).

Assignment, lodgers and subletting

91 Assignment in general prohibited.

(1) A secure tenancy which is—

(a) a periodic tenancy, or

(b) a tenancy for a term certain granted on or after 5th November 1982, is not capable of being assigned except in the cases mentioned in subsection (3).

(2) If a secure tenancy for a term certain granted before 5th November 1982 is assigned, then, except in the cases mentioned in subsection (3), it ceases to be a secure tenancy and cannot subsequently become a secure tenancy.

(3) The exceptions are—

(a) an assignment in accordance with section 92 (assignment by way of exchange);

[(b) an assignment in pursuance of an order made under—

(i) section 24 of the Matrimonial Causes Act 1973 (property adjustment orders in connection with matrimonial proceedings),

(ii) section 17(1) of the Matrimonial and Family Proceedings Act 1984 (property adjustment orders after overseas divorce, &c.), …[1]

(iii) paragraph 1 of Schedule 1 to the Children Act 1989 (orders for financial relief against parents)[, or

(iv) Part 2 of Schedule 5, or paragraph 9(2) or (3) of Schedule 7, to the Civil Partnership Act 2004 (property adjustment orders in connection with civil partnership proceedings or after overseas dissolution of civil partnership, etc.)][2]][3]

(c) an assignment to a person who would be qualified to succeed the tenant if the tenant died immediately before the assignment.

Amendments

1 Repealed by the Civil Partnership Act 2004, s 261(4), Sch 30.

2 Inserted by the Civil Partnership Act 2004, s 81, Sch 8, para 24.

3 Substituted by the Housing Act 1996, s 222, Sch 18, para 12.

92 Assignments by way of exchange.

(1) It is a term of every secure tenancy that the tenant may, with the written consent of the landlord, assign the tenancy to another secure tenant who satisfies the condition in subsection (2) [or to an assured tenant who satisfies the conditions in subsection (2A)][1].

(2) The condition is that the other secure tenant has the written consent of his landlord to an assignment of his tenancy either to the first-mentioned tenant or to another secure tenant who satisfies the condition in this subsection.

[(2A) The conditions to be satisfied with respect to an assured tenant are—

(a) that the landlord under his assured tenancy is [the Regulator of Social Housing, a private registered provider of social housing,][2] …[3] [a registered social landlord][4] or a housing trust which is a charity; and

(b) that he intends to assign his assured tenancy to the secure tenant referred to in subsection (1) or to another secure tenant who satisfies the condition in subsection (2).][1]

(3) The consent required by virtue of this section shall not be withheld except on one or more of the grounds set out in Schedule 3, and if withheld otherwise than on one of those grounds shall be treated as given.

(4) The landlord may not rely on any of the grounds set out in Schedule 3 unless he has, within 42 days of the tenant's application for the consent, served on the tenant a notice specifying the ground and giving particulars of it.

(5) Where rent lawfully due from the tenant has not been paid or an obligation of the tenancy has been broken or not performed, the consent required by virtue of this section may be given subject to a condition requiring the tenant to pay the outstanding rent, remedy the breach or perform the obligation.

(6) Except as provided by subsection (5), a consent required by virtue of this section cannot be given subject to a condition, and a condition imposed otherwise than as so provided shall be disregarded.

Amendments

1 Inserted by the Local Government and Housing Act 1989, s 163(1)–(3).

2 Substituted by the Housing and Regeneration Act 2008 (Consequential Provisions) Order 2010, SI 2010/866, art 5, Sch 2, paras 15, 21.

3 Repealed by the Government of Wales Act 1998, ss 140, 152, Sch 16, paras 4, 10, Sch 18, Pt VI.

4 Substituted by the Housing Act 1996 (Consequential Provisions) Order 1996, SI 1996/2325, art 5(1), Sch 2, para 14(1), (9).

93 Lodgers and subletting.

(1) It is a term of every secure tenancy that the tenant—

(a) may allow any persons to reside as lodgers in the dwelling-house, but

(b) will not, without the written consent of the landlord, sublet or part with possession of part of the dwelling-house.

(2) If the tenant under a secure tenancy parts with the possession of the dwelling-house or sublets the whole of it (or sublets first part of it and then the remainder), the tenancy ceases to be a secure tenancy and cannot subsequently become a secure tenancy.

94 Consent to subletting.

(1) This section applies to the consent required by virtue of section 93(1)(b) (landlord's consent to subletting of part of dwelling-house).

(2) Consent shall not be unreasonably withheld (and if unreasonably withheld shall be treated as given), and if a question arises whether the withholding of consent was unreasonable it is for the landlord to show that it was not.

(3) In determining that question the following matters, if shown by the landlord, are among those to be taken into account—

(a) that the consent would lead to overcrowding of the dwelling-house within the meaning of Part X (overcrowding);

(b) that the landlord proposes to carry out works on the dwelling-house, or on the building of which it forms part, and that the proposed works will affect the accommodation likely to be used by the sub-tenant who would reside in the dwelling-house as a result of the consent.

(4) Consent may be validly given notwithstanding that it follows, instead of preceding, the action requiring it.

(5) Consent cannot be given subject to a condition (and it purporting to be given subject to a condition shall be treated as given unconditionally).

(6) Where the tenant has applied in writing for consent, then—

(a) if the landlord refuses to give consent, it shall give the tenant a written statement of the reasons why consent was refused, and

(b) if the landlord neither gives nor refuses to give consent within a reasonable time, consent shall be taken to have been withheld.

95 Assignment or subletting where tenant condition not satisfied.

(1) This section applies to a tenancy which is not a secure tenancy but would be if the tenant condition referred to in section 81 (occupation by the tenant) were satisfied.

(2) Sections 91 and 93(2) (restrictions on assignment or sub-letting of whole dwelling-house) apply to such a tenancy as they apply to a secure tenancy, except that—

(a) section 91(3)(b) and (c) (assignments excepted from restrictions) do not apply to such a tenancy for a term certain granted before 5th November 1982, and

(b) references to the tenancy ceasing to be secure shall be disregarded, without prejudice to the application of the remainder of the provisions in which those references occur.

[Flexible tenancies

107A Flexible tenancies

(1) For the purposes of this Act, a flexible tenancy is a secure tenancy to which any of the following subsections applies.

(2) This subsection applies to a secure tenancy if—

(a) it is granted by a landlord in England for a term certain of not less than two years, and

(b) before it was granted the person who became the landlord under the tenancy served a written notice on the person who became the tenant under the tenancy stating that the tenancy would be a flexible tenancy.

(3) This subsection applies to a secure tenancy if—

(a) it becomes a secure tenancy by virtue of a notice under paragraph 4ZA(2) of Schedule 1 (family intervention tenancies becoming secure tenancies),

(b) the landlord under the family intervention tenancy in question was a local housing authority in England,

(c) the family intervention tenancy was granted to a person on the coming to an end of a flexible tenancy under which the person was a tenant,

(d) the notice states that the tenancy is to become a secure tenancy that is a flexible tenancy for a term certain of the length specified in the notice, and sets out the other express terms of the tenancy, and

(e) the length of the term specified in the notice is at least two years.

(4) The length of the term of a flexible tenancy that becomes such a tenancy by virtue of subsection (3) is that specified in the notice under paragraph 4ZA(2) of Schedule 1.

(5) The other express terms of the flexible tenancy are those set out in the notice, so far as those terms are compatible with the statutory provisions relating to flexible tenancies; and in this subsection 'statutory provision' means any provision made by or under an Act.

(6) This subsection applies to a secure tenancy if—

(a) it is created by virtue of section 137A of the Housing Act 1996 (introductory tenancies becoming flexible tenancies), or

(b) it arises by virtue of section 143MA of that Act (demoted tenancies becoming flexible tenancies).][1]

Amendments

1 Inserted by the Localism Act 2011, s 154.

[107B Review of decisions relating to flexible tenancies

(1) This section applies if a person ('the prospective landlord')—

(a) offers to grant a flexible tenancy (whether or not on the coming to an end of an existing tenancy of any kind), or

(b) serves a notice under section 137A of the Housing Act 1996 stating that, on the coming to an end of an introductory tenancy, it will become a flexible tenancy.

(2) A person to whom the offer is made or on whom the notice is served ('the person concerned') may request a review of the prospective landlord's decision about the length of the term of the tenancy.

(3) The review may only be requested on the basis that the length of the term does not accord with a policy of the prospective landlord as to the length of the terms of the flexible tenancies it grants.

(4) A request for a review must be made before the end of—

(a) the period of 21 days beginning with the day on which the person concerned first receives the offer or notice, or

(b) such longer period as the prospective landlord may in writing allow.

(5) On a request being duly made to it, the prospective landlord must review its decision.

(6) The Secretary of State may by regulations make provision about the procedure to be followed in connection with a review under this section.

(7) The regulations may, in particular, make provision—

(a) requiring the decision on the review to be made by a person of appropriate seniority who was not involved in the original decision, and

(b) as to the circumstances in which the person concerned is entitled to an oral hearing, and whether and by whom the person may be represented at such a hearing.

(8) The prospective landlord must notify the person concerned in writing of the decision on the review.

(9) If the decision is to confirm the original decision, the prospective landlord must also notify the person of the reasons for the decision.

(10) Regulations under this section—

(a) may contain transitional or saving provision;

(b) are to be made by statutory instrument which is subject to annulment in pursuance of a resolution of either House of Parliament.][1]

Amendments

1 Inserted by the Localism Act 2011, s 154.

[107C Termination of flexible tenancy by tenant

(1) It is a term of every flexible tenancy that the tenant may terminate the tenancy in accordance with the following provisions of this section.

(2) The tenant must serve a notice in writing on the landlord stating that the tenancy will be terminated on the date specified in the notice.

(3) That date must be after the end of the period of four weeks beginning with the date on which the notice is served.

(4) The landlord may agree with the tenant to dispense with the requirement in subsection (2) or (3).

(5) The tenancy is terminated on the date specified in the notice or (as the case may be) determined in accordance with arrangements made under subsection (4) only if on that date—

(a) no arrears of rent are payable under the tenancy, and

(b) the tenant is not otherwise materially in breach of a term of the tenancy.][1]

Amendments

1 Inserted by the Localism Act 2011, s 154.

[107D Recovery of possession on expiry of flexible tenancy

(1) Subject as follows, on or after the coming to an end of a flexible tenancy a court must make an order for possession of the dwelling-house let on the tenancy if it is satisfied that the following conditions are met.

(2) Condition 1 is that the flexible tenancy has come to an end and no further secure tenancy (whether or not a flexible tenancy) is for the time being in existence, other than a secure tenancy that is a periodic tenancy (whether or not arising by virtue of section 86).

(3) Condition 2 is that the landlord has given the tenant not less than six months' notice in writing—

(a) stating that the landlord does not propose to grant another tenancy on the expiry of the flexible tenancy,

(b) setting out the landlord's reasons for not proposing to grant another tenancy, and

(c) informing the tenant of the tenant's right to request a review of the landlord's proposal and of the time within which such a request must be made.

(4) Condition 3 is that the landlord has given the tenant not less than two months' notice in writing stating that the landlord requires possession of the dwelling-house.

(5) A notice under subsection (4) may be given before or on the day on which the tenancy comes to an end.

(6) The court may refuse to grant an order for possession under this section if—

(a) the tenant has in accordance with section 107E requested a review of the landlord's proposal not to grant another tenancy on the expiry of the flexible tenancy, and

(b) the court is satisfied that the landlord has failed to carry out the review in accordance with provision made by or under that section or that the decision on the review is otherwise wrong in law.

(7) If a court refuses to grant an order for possession by virtue of subsection (6) it may make such directions as to the holding of a review or further review under section 107E as it thinks fit.

(8) This section has effect notwithstanding that, on the coming to an end of the flexible tenancy, a periodic tenancy arises by virtue of section 86.

(9) Where a court makes an order for possession of a dwelling-house by virtue of this section, any periodic tenancy arising by virtue of section 86 on the coming to an end of the flexible tenancy comes to an end (without further notice and regardless of the period) in accordance with section 82(2).

(10) This section is without prejudice to any right of the landlord under a flexible tenancy to recover possession of the dwelling-house let on the tenancy in accordance with this Part.][1]

Amendments

1 Inserted by the Localism Act 2011, s 154.

[107E Review of decision to seek possession

(1) A request for a review of a landlord's decision to seek an order for possession of a dwelling-house let under a flexible tenancy must be made before the end of the period of 21 days beginning with the day on which the notice under section 107D(3) is served.

(2) On a request being duly made to it, the landlord must review its decision.

(3) The review must, in particular, consider whether the decision is in accordance with any policy of the landlord as to the circumstances in which it will grant a further tenancy on the coming to an end of an existing flexible tenancy.

(4) The Secretary of State may by regulations make provision about the procedure to be followed in connection with a review under this section.

(5) The regulations may, in particular, make provision—

(a) requiring the decision on the review to be made by a person of appropriate seniority who was not involved in the original decision, and

(b) as to the circumstances in which the person concerned is entitled to an oral hearing, and whether and by whom the person may be represented at such a hearing.

(6) The landlord must notify the tenant in writing of the decision on the review.

(7) If the decision is to confirm the original decision, the landlord must also notify the tenant of the reasons for the decision.

(8) The review must be carried out, and the tenant notified, before the date specified in the notice of proceedings as the date after which proceedings for the possession of the dwelling-house may be begun.

(9) Regulations under this section—

(a) may contain transitional or saving provision;

(b) are to be made by statutory instrument which is subject to annulment in pursuance of a resolution of either House of Parliament.][1]

Amendments

1 Inserted by the Localism Act 2011, s 154.

Miscellaneous

109 Provisions not applying to tenancies of co-operative housing associations.

Sections 91 to 108 (assignment and subletting, repairs and improvements, variation of terms, provision of information and consultation, contributions to costs of transfers and heating charges) do not apply to a tenancy when the interest of the landlord belongs to a co-operative housing association.

Supplementary provisions

112 Meaning of 'dwelling-house'.

(1) For the purposes of this Part a dwelling-house may be a house or a part of a house.

(2) Land let together with a dwelling-house shall be treated for the purposes of this Part as part of the dwelling-house unless the land is agricultural land (as defined in section 26(3)(a) of the General Rate Act 1967) exceeding two acres.

113 Members of a person's family.

(1) A person is a member of another's family within the meaning of this Part if—

(a) he is the spouse [or civil partner][1] of that person, or he and that person live together [as if they were a married couple or][2] [civil partners][1], or

(b) he is that person's parent, grandparent, child, grand-child, brother, sister, uncle, aunt, nephew or niece.

(2) For the purpose of subsection (1)(b)—

(a) a relationship by marriage [or civil partnership][1] shall be treated as a relationship by blood,

(b) a relationship of the half-blood shall be treated as a relationship of the whole blood,

(c) the stepchild of a person shall be treated as his child, and

(d) an illegitimate child shall be treated as the legitimate child of his mother and reputed father.

Amendments

1 Inserted by the Civil Partnership Act 2004, s 81, Sch 8, para 27.

2 Substituted by the Civil Partnership (Opposite-sex Couples) Regulations 2019, SI 2019/1458, reg 41(1), Sch 3, para 10(1), (3).

PART V
THE RIGHT TO BUY

The right to buy

118 The right to buy.

(1) A secure tenant [of a dwelling-house in England][1] has the right to buy, that is to say, the right, in the circumstances and subject to the conditions and exceptions stated in the following provisions of this Part—

(a) if the dwelling-house is a house and the landlord owns the freehold, to acquire the freehold of the dwelling-house;

(b) if the landlord does not own the freehold or if the dwelling-house is a flat (whether or not the landlord owns the freehold), to be granted a lease of the dwelling-house.

(2) Where a secure tenancy is a joint tenancy then, whether or not each of the joint tenants occupies the dwelling-house as his only or principal home, the right to buy belongs jointly to all of them or to such one or more of them as may be agreed between them; but such an agreement is not valid unless the person or at least one of the persons to whom the right to buy is to belong occupies the dwelling-house as his only or principal home.

[(3) For the purposes of this Part, a dwelling-house which is a commonhold unit (within the meaning of the Commonhold and Leasehold Reform Act 2002) shall be treated as a house and not as a flat.][2]

Amendments

1 Inserted by the Abolition of the Right to Buy and Associated Rights (Wales) Act 2018 (Consequential Amendments and Savings Provisions) Regulations 2019, SI 2019/110, reg 3(b).

2 Inserted by the Commonhold and Leasehold Reform Act 2002, s 68, Sch 5, para 5.

119 Qualifying period for right to buy.

[(A1) [The][1] right to buy does not arise unless the period which, in accordance with Schedule 4, is to be taken into account for the purposes of this section is at least three years.][2]

(1) …[3]

(2) Where the secure tenancy is a joint tenancy the condition in subsection [(A1) …[3]][2] …[3] need be satisfied with respect to one only of the joint tenants.

Amendments

1 Substituted by the Abolition of the Right to Buy and Associated Rights (Wales) Act 2018 (Consequential Amendments and Savings Provisions) Regulations 2019, SI 2019/110, reg 3(c)(i).

2 Inserted by the Deregulation Act 2015, s 28(1), (2), (4).

3 Repealed by the Abolition of the Right to Buy and Associated Rights (Wales) Act 2018 (Consequential Amendments and Savings Provisions) Regulations 2019, SI 2019/110, reg 3(c)(ii), (iii).

120 Exceptions to the right to buy

The right to buy does not arise in the cases specified in Schedule 5 (exceptions to the right to buy).

121 Circumstances in which the right to buy cannot be exercised.

[(1) The right to buy cannot be exercised if the tenant is subject to an order of the court for possession of the dwelling-house.][1]

(2) The right to buy cannot be exercised if the person, or one of the persons, to whom the right to buy belongs—

(a) [has made a bankruptcy application that has not been determined or][2] has a bankruptcy petition pending against him,

(b) …[3]

(c) is an undischarged bankrupt, …[4]

(d) has made a composition or arrangement with his creditors the terms of which remain to be fulfilled, [or

(e) is a person in relation to whom a moratorium period under a debt relief order applies (under Part 7A of the Insolvency Act 1986).][5]

[(3) The right to buy cannot be exercised at any time during the suspension period under an order made under section 121A in respect of the secure tenancy.][6]

Amendments

1 Substituted by the Housing and Regeneration Act 2008, s 304(1).

2 Inserted by the Enterprise and Regulatory Reform Act 2013 (Consequential Amendments) (Bankruptcy) and the Small Business, Enterprise and Employment Act 2015 (Consequential Amendments) Regulations 2016, SI 2016/481, reg 2(1), Sch 1, para 6.

3 Repealed by the Insolvency Act 1985, s 235(3), Sch 10, Pt III.

4 Repealed by the Tribunals, Courts and Enforcement Act 2007 (Consequential Amendments) Order 2012, SI 2012/2404, art 3(2), Sch 2, para 21(a).

5 Inserted by the Tribunals, Courts and Enforcement Act 2007 (Consequential Amendments) Order 2012, SI 2012/2404, art 3(2), Sch 2, para 21(b).

6 Inserted by the Housing Act 2004, s 192(1).

[121A Order suspending right to buy because of anti-social behaviour

(1) The court may, on the application of the landlord under a secure tenancy, make a suspension order in respect of the tenancy.

(2) A suspension order is an order providing that the right to buy may not be exercised in relation to the dwelling-house during such period as is specified in the order ('the suspension period').

(3) The court must not make a suspension order unless it is satisfied—

(a) that the tenant, or a person residing in or visiting the dwelling-house, has engaged or threatened to [engage in—

[(i) conduct that is capable of causing nuisance or annoyance to some person (who need not be a particular identified person) and that directly or indirectly relates to or affects the landlord's housing management functions, or

(ii) conduct that consists of or involves using housing accommodation owned or managed by the landlord for an unlawful purpose, and][1]][2]

(b) that it is reasonable to make the order.

(4) When deciding whether it is reasonable to make the order, the court must consider, in particular—

(a) whether it is desirable for the dwelling-house to be managed by the landlord during the suspension period; and

(b) where the conduct mentioned in subsection (3)(a) consists of conduct by a person which is capable of causing nuisance or annoyance, the effect that the conduct (or the threat of it) has had on other persons, or would have if repeated.

(5) Where a suspension order is made—

(a) any existing claim to exercise the right to buy in relation to the dwelling-house ceases to be effective as from the beginning of the suspension period, and

(b) section 138(1) shall not apply to the landlord, in connection with such a claim, at any time after the beginning of that period, but

(c) the order does not affect the computation of any period in accordance with Schedule 4.

(6) The court may, on the application of the landlord, make (on one or more occasions) a further order which extends the suspension period under the suspension order by such period as is specified in the further order.

(7) The court must not make such a further order unless it is satisfied—

(a) that, since the making of the suspension order (or the last order under subsection (6)), the tenant, or a person residing in or visiting the dwelling-house, has engaged or threatened to [engage in—

[(i) conduct that is capable of causing nuisance or annoyance to some person (who need not be a particular identified person) and that directly or indirectly relates to or affects the landlord's housing management functions, or

(ii) conduct that consists of or involves using housing accommodation owned or managed by the landlord for an unlawful purpose, and][1]][2]

(b) that it is reasonable to make the further order.

(8) When deciding whether it is reasonable to make such a further order, the court must consider, in particular—

(a) whether it is desirable for the dwelling-house to be managed by the landlord during the further period of suspension; and

(b) where the conduct mentioned in subsection (7)(a) consists of conduct by a person which is capable of causing nuisance or annoyance, the effect that the conduct (or the threat of it) has had on other persons, or would have if repeated.

(9) In this section any reference to the tenant under a secure tenancy is, in relation to a joint tenancy, a reference to any of the joint tenants.

[(10) In this section 'housing accommodation' includes—

(a) flats, lodging-houses and hostels;

(b) any yard, garden, outhouses and appurtenances belonging to the accommodation or usually enjoyed with it;

(c) any common areas used in connection with the accommodation.][1]][3]

Amendments

1 Substituted by the Anti-social Behaviour, Crime and Policing Act 2014, s 181(1), Sch 11, para 11.

2 Substituted by the Police and Justice Act 2006, s 52, Sch 14, para 13(1), (2).

3 Inserted by the Housing Act 2004, s 192(2).

[121AA Information to help tenants decide whether to exercise right to buy etc.

(1) Every body which lets dwelling-houses [in England][1] under secure tenancies shall prepare a document that contains information for its secure tenants about such matters as are specified in an order made by the Secretary of State.

(2) The matters that may be so specified are matters which the Secretary of State considers that it would be desirable for secure tenants to have information about when considering whether to exercise the right to buy or the right to acquire on rent to mortgage terms.

(3) The information contained in the document shall be restricted to information about the specified matters, and the information about those matters—

(a) shall be such as the body concerned considers appropriate, but

(b) shall be in a form which the body considers best suited to explaining those matters in simple terms.

(4) Once a body has prepared the document required by subsection (1), it shall revise it as often as it considers necessary in order to ensure that the information contained in it—

(a) is kept up to date so faras is reasonably practicable, and

(b) reflects any changes in the matters for the time being specified in an order under this section.

(5) An order under this section shall be made by statutory instrument which shall be subject to annulment in pursuance of a resolution of either House of Parliament.][2]

Amendments

1 Inserted by the Abolition of the Right to Buy and Associated Rights (Wales) Act 2018 (Consequential Amendments and Savings Provisions) Regulations 2019, SI 2019/110, reg 3(d).

2 Inserted by the Housing Act 2004, s 189(1).

[121B Provision of information

(1) This section sets out when the document prepared by a body under section 121AA is to be published or otherwise made available.

(2) The body shall—

(a) publish the document (whether in its original or a revised form), and

(b) supply copies of it to the body's secure tenants [of dwelling-houses in England][1],

at such times as may be prescribed by, and otherwise in accordance with, an order made by the Secretary of State.

(3) The body shall make copies of the current version of the document available to be supplied, free of charge, to persons requesting them.

(4) The copies must be made available for that purpose—

(a) at the body's principal offices, and

(b) at such other places as it considers appropriate,

at reasonable hours.

(5) The body shall take such steps as it considers appropriate to bring to the attention of its secure tenants [of dwelling-houses in England][1] the fact that copies of the current version of the document can be obtained free of charge from the places where, and at the times when, they are made available in accordance with subsection (4).

(6) In this section any reference to the current version of the document is to the version of the document that was last published by the body in accordance with subsection (2)(a).

(7) An order under this section shall be made by statutory instrument which shall be subject to annulment in pursuance of a resolution of either House of Parliament.][2]

Amendments

1 Inserted by the Abolition of the Right to Buy and Associated Rights (Wales) Act 2018 (Consequential Amendments and Savings Provisions) Regulations 2019, SI 2019/110, reg 3(e).

2 Inserted by the Housing Act 2004, s 189(1).

Claim to exercise right to buy

122 Tenant's notice claiming to exercise right to buy.

(1) [A][1] secure tenant claims to exercise the right to buy by written notice to that effect served on the landlord.

(2) In this Part 'the relevant time', in relation to an exercise of the right to buy, means the date on which that notice is served.

(3) The notice may be withdrawn at any time by notice in writing served on the landlord.

Amendments

1 Substituted by the Abolition of the Right to Buy and Associated Rights (Wales) Act 2018 (Consequential Amendments and Savings Provisions) Regulations 2019, SI 2019/110, reg 3(f).

123 Claim to share right to buy with members of family.

(1) A secure tenant may in his notice under section 122 require that not more than three members of his family who are not joint tenants but occupy the dwelling-house as their only or principal home should share the right to buy with him.

(2) He may validly do so in the case of any such member only if—

(a) that member is his spouse[, is his civil partner][1] or has been residing with him throughout the period of twelve months ending with the giving of the notice, or

(b) the landlord consents.

(3) Where by such a notice any members of the tenant's family are validly required to share the right to buy with the tenant, the right to buy belongs to the tenant and those members jointly and he and they shall be treated for the purposes of this Part as joint tenants.

Amendments

1 Inserted by the Civil Partnership Act 2004, s 81, Sch 8, para 28.

124 Landlord's notice admitting or denying right to buy.

(1) Where a notice under section 122 (notice claiming to exercise right to buy) has been served by the tenant, the landlord shall, unless the notice is withdrawn, serve on the tenant within the period specified in subsection (2) ...[1] a written notice either—

(a) admitting his right, or

(b) denying it and stating the reasons why, in the opinion of the landlord, the tenant does not have the right to buy.

(2) The period for serving a notice under this section is four weeks where the requirement of section 119 (qualifying period for the right to buy) is satisfied by a period or periods during which the landlord was the landlord on which the tenant's notice under section 122 was served, and eight weeks in any other case.

(3) ...[1]

Amendments

1 Repealed by the Abolition of the Right to Buy and Associated Rights (Wales) Act 2018 (Consequential Amendments and Savings Provisions) Regulations 2019, SI 2019/110, reg 3(i).

125 Landlord's notice of purchase price and other matters.

(1) Where a secure tenant has claimed to exercise the right to buy and that right has been established (whether by the landlord's admission or otherwise), the landlord shall—

(a) within eight weeks where the right is that mentioned in section 118(1)(a) (right to acquire freehold), and

(b) within twelve weeks where the right is that mentioned in section 118(1)(b) (right to acquire leasehold interest).

serve on the tenant a notice complying with this section.

(2) The notice shall describe the dwelling-house, shall state the price at which, in the opinion of the landlord, the tenant is entitled to have the freehold conveyed or, as the case may be, the lease granted to him and shall, for the purpose of showing how the price has been arrived at, state—

(a) the value at the relevant time,

(b) the improvements disregarded in pursuance of section 127 (improvements to be disregarded in determining value), and

(c) the discount to which the tenant is entitled, stating the period to be taken into account under section 129 (discount) and, where applicable, the amount mentioned in section 130(1) (reduction for previous discount) or section 131(1) or (2) (limits on amount of discount).

(3) The notice shall state the provisions which, in the opinion of the landlord, should be contained in the conveyance or grant.

[(4) Where the notice states provisions which would enable the landlord to recover from the tenant—

(a) service charges, or

(b) improvement contributions,

the notice shall also contain the estimates and other information required by section 125A (service charges) or 125B (improvement contributions).][1]

[(4A) The notice shall contain a description of any structural defect known to the landlord affecting the dwelling-house or the building in which it is situated or any other building over which the tenant will have rights under the conveyance or lease.][2]

[(5) The notice shall also inform the tenant of—

(a) the effect of sections 125D and 125E(1) and (4) (tenant's notice of intention, landlord's notice in default and effect of failure to comply),

(b) his right under section 128 to have the value of the dwelling-house at the relevant time determined or re-determined by the district valuer,

(c) the effect of section 136(2) (change of tenant after service of notice under section 125),

(d) the effect of sections 140 and 141(1), (2) and (4) (landlord's notices to complete and effect of failure to comply),

(e) the effect of the provisions of this Part relating to the right to acquire on rent to mortgage terms, and

(f) the relevant amount and multipliers for the time being declared by the Secretary of State for the purposes of section 143B.][3]

Amendments

1 Substituted by the Housing and Planning Act 1986, s 4(1).

2 Inserted by the Housing and Planning Act 1986, s 24(1), Sch 5, para 3.

3 Substituted by the Leasehold Reform, Housing and Urban Development Act 1993, s 104.

[125A Estimates and information about service charges.

(1) A landlord's notice under section 125 shall state as regards service charges (excluding, in the case of a flat, charges to which subsection (2) applies)—

(a) the landlord's estimate of the average annual amount (at current prices) which would be payable in respect of each head of charge in the reference period, and

(b) the aggregate of those estimated amounts,

and shall contain a statement of the reference period adopted for the purpose of the estimates.

(2) A landlord's notice under section 125 given in respect of a flat shall, as regards service charges in respect of repairs (including works for the making good of structural defects), contain—

(a) the estimates required by subsection (3), together with a statement of the reference period adopted for the purpose of the estimates, and

(b) a statement of the effect of—

paragraph 16B of Schedule 6 (which restricts by reference to the estimates the amounts payable by the tenant), and

section 450A and the regulations made under that section (right to a loan in respect of certain service charges).

(3) The following estimates are required for works in respect of which the landlord considers that costs may be incurred in the reference period—

(a) for works itemised in the notice, estimates of the amount (at current prices) of the likely cost of, and of the tenant's likely contribution in respect of, each item, and the aggregate amounts of those estimated costs and contributions, and

(b) for works not so itemised, an estimate of the average annual amount (at current prices) which the landlord considers is likely to be payable by the tenant.][1]

Amendments

1 Inserted by the Housing and Planning Act 1986, s 4(2).

[125B Estimates and information about improvement contributions.

(1) A landlord's notice under section 125 given in respect of a flat shall, as regards improvement contributions, contain—

(a) the estimates required by this section, together with a statement of the reference period adopted for the purpose of the estimates, and

(b) a statement of the effect of paragraph 16C of Schedule 6 (which restricts by reference to the estimates the amounts payable by the tenant).

(2) Estimates are required for works in respect of which the landlord considers that costs may be incurred in the reference period.

(3) The works to which the estimates relate shall be itemised and the estimates shall show—

(a) the amount (at current prices) of the likely cost of, and of the tenant's likely contribution in respect of, each item, and

(b) the aggregate amounts of those estimated costs and contributions.][1]

Amendments

1 Inserted by the Housing and Planning Act 1986, s 4(2).

[125C Reference period for purposes of ss. 125A and 125B.

(1) The reference period for the purposes of the estimates required by section 125A or 125B is the period—

(a) beginning on such date not more than six months after the notice is given as the landlord may reasonably specify as being a date by which the conveyance will have been made or the lease granted, and

(b) ending five years after that date or, where the notice states that the conveyance or lease will provide for a service charge or improvement contribution to be calculated by reference to a specified annual period, with the end of the fifth such period beginning after that date.

(2) For the purpose of the estimates it shall be assumed that the conveyance will be made or the lease granted at the beginning of the reference period on the terms stated in the notice.][1]

Amendments

1 Inserted by the Housing and Planning Act 1986, s 4(2).

[125D Tenant's notice of intention.

(1) Where a notice under section 125 has been served on a secure tenant, he shall within the period specified in subsection (2) either—

(a) serve a written notice on the landlord stating either that he intends to pursue his claim to exercise the right to buy or that he withdraws that claim, or

(b) serve a notice under section 144 claiming to exercise the right to acquire on rent to mortgage terms.

(2) The period for serving a notice under subsection (1) is the period of twelve weeks beginning with whichever of the following is the later—

(a) the service of the notice under section 125, …[1]

(b) where the tenant exercises his right to have the value of the dwelling-house determined or re-determined by the district valuer [(or where the landlord exercises his right to have the value of the dwelling-house re-determined by the district valuer), the relevant event][2].

[(3) In subsection (2)(b) 'the relevant event' means—

(a) where a review notice was capable of being served under section 128A in relation to the determination or re-determination but no such notice was served during the period permitted by that section, the service of the notice under section 128(5) stating the effect of the determination or re-determination,

(b) where a review notice was served under section 128A in relation to the determination or re-determination and section 128B(3) applied, the service on the tenant of the notice under section 128B(3), and

(c) where a review notice was served under section 128A in relation to the determination or re-determination and section 128B(5) applied, the service of the notice under section 128B(7).][3]][4]

Amendments

1 Repealed by the Housing and Regeneration Act 2008, s 321(1), Sch 16.

2 Substituted by the Housing and Regeneration Act 2008, s 306(1), (3).

3 Inserted by the Housing and Regeneration Act 2008, s 306(1), (4).

4 Inserted by the Leasehold Reform, Housing and Urban Development Act 1993, s 105(1).

[125E Landlord's notice in default.

(1) The landlord may, at any time after the end of the period specified in section 125D(2) or, as the case may require, section 136(2), serve on the tenant a written notice—

(a) requiring him, if he has failed to serve the notice required by section 125D(1), to serve that notice within 28 days, and

(b) informing him of the effect of this subsection and subsection (4).

(2) At any time before the end of the period mentioned in subsection (1)(a) (or that period as previously extended) the landlord may by written notice served on the tenant extend it (or further extend it).

(3) If at any time before the end of that period (or that period as extended under subsection (2)) the circumstances are such that it would not be reasonable to expect the tenant to comply with a notice under this section, that period (or that period as so extended) shall by virtue of this subsection be extended (or further extended) until 28 days after the time when those circumstances no longer obtain.

(4) If the tenant does not comply with a notice under this section, the notice claiming to exercise the right to buy shall be deemed to be withdrawn at the end of that period (or, as the case may require, that period as extended under subsection (2) or (3)).][1]

Amendments

1 Inserted by the Leasehold Reform, Housing and Urban Development Act 1993, s 105(1).

Purchase price

126 Purchase price

(1) The price payable for a dwelling-house on a conveyance or grant in pursuance of this Part is—

(a) the amount which under section 127 is to be taken as its value at the relevant time, less

(b) the discount to which the purchaser is entitled under this Part.

(2) References in this Part to the purchase price include references to the consideration for the grant of a lease.

127 Value of dwelling-house.

(1) The value of a dwelling-house at the relevant time shall be taken to be the price which at that time it would realise if sold on the open market by a willing vendor—

(a) on the assumptions stated for a conveyance in subsection (2) and for a grant in subsection (3), …[1]

(b) disregarding any improvements made by any of the persons specified in subsection (4) and any failure by any of those persons to keep the dwelling-house in good internal repair[, and

(c) on the assumption that any service charges or improvement contributions payable will not be less than the amounts to be expected in accordance with the estimates contained in the landlord's notice under section 125.][2]

(2) For a conveyance the assumptions are—

(a) that the vendor was selling for an estate in fee simple with vacant possession,

(b) that neither the tenant nor a member of his family residing with him wanted to buy, and

(c) that the dwelling-house was to be conveyed with the same rights and subject to the same burdens as it would be in pursuance of this Part.

(3) For the grant of a lease the assumptions are—

(a) that the vendor was granting a lease with vacant possession for the appropriate term defined in paragraph 12 of Schedule 6 (but subject to sub-paragraph (3) of that paragraph).

(b) that neither the tenant nor a member of his family residing with him wanted to take the lease,

(c) that the ground rent would not exceed £10 per annum [or, if the lease would be a regulated lease within the meaning of the Leasehold Reform (Ground Rent) Act 2022, the rent permitted by that Act][3], and

(d) that the grant was to be made with the same rights and subject to the same burdens as it would be in pursuance of this Part.

(4) The persons referred to in subsection (1)(b) are—

(a) the secure tenant,

(b) any person who under the same tenancy was a secure tenant [or an introductory tenant][4] before him, and

[(c) any member of his family who, immediately before the secure tenancy was granted (or, where an introductory tenancy has become the secure tenancy, immediately before the introductory tenancy was granted), was a secure tenant or, an introductory tenant of the same dwelling-house under another tenancy,][5]

but do not include, in a case where the secure tenant's tenancy has at any time been assigned by virtue of section 92 (assignments by way of exchange), a person who under that tenancy was a secure tenant [or an introductory tenant][4] before the assignment.

[(5) In this section 'introductory tenant' and 'introductory tenancy' have the same meaning as in Chapter I of Part V of the Housing Act 1996.][4]

Amendments

1 Repealed by the Housing and Planning Act 1986, s 24(2), (3), Sch 5, para 28, Sch 12, Pt I.

2 Inserted by the Housing and Planning Act 1986, s 4(3).

3 Inserted by the Leasehold Reform (Ground Rent) Act 2022, s 19(1).

4 Inserted by the Housing Act 1996 (Consequential Amendments) Order 1997, SI 1997/74, art 2, Schedule, para 3(j)(i), (iii), (k).

5 Substituted by the Housing Act 1996 (Consequential Amendments) Order 1997, SI 1997/74, art 2, Schedule, para 3(j)(ii).

128 Determination of value by district valuer.

(1) Any question arising under this Part as to the value of a dwelling-house at the relevant time shall be determined by the district valuer in accordance with this section.

(2) A tenant may require that value to be determined …[1] by a notice in writing served on the landlord not later than three months after the service on him of the notice under section 125 (landlord's notice of purchase price and other matters) or, if proceedings are then pending between the landlord and the tenant for the determination of any other question arising under this Part, within three months of the final determination of the proceedings.

(3) If such proceedings are begun after a previous determination under this section—

(a) the tenant may, by notice in writing served on the landlord within four weeks of the final determination of the proceedings, require the value of the dwelling-house at the relevant time to be re-determined, and

(b) the landlord may at any time within those four weeks, whether or not a notice under paragraph (a) is served, require the district valuer to re-determine that value;

and where the landlord requires a re-determination to be made in pursuance of this subsection, it shall serve on the tenant a notice stating that the requirement is being or has been made.

(4) Before making a determination or re-determination in pursuance of this section, the district valuer shall consider any representation made to him by the landlord or the tenant within four weeks from the service of the tenant's notice under this section or, as the case may be, from the service of the landlord's notice under subsection (3).

(5) As soon as practicable after a determination or re-determination has been made in pursuance of this section, the landlord shall serve on the tenant a notice [stating—

(a) the effect of the determination or re-determination,

(b) the matters mentioned in section 125(2) and (3) (terms for exercise of right to buy), and

(c) the effect of section 128A(2) (right of district valuer to serve review notice and of landlord and tenant to request that such a notice is served).][2]

[(5A) The landlord shall, as soon as practicable, serve a copy of the notice on the district valuer if—

(a) the district valuer requests it; or

(b) the landlord requests a review of the determination or re-determination under section 128A(2)(b).

(5B) The tenant shall, as soon as practicable, serve a copy of the notice on the district valuer if the tenant requests a review of the determination or re-determination under section 128A(2)(b).

(5C) For the purposes of subsections (5A) and (5B) it does not matter whether the request in question was made before, on or after the service of the notice in accordance with subsection (5).][3]

(6) …[4]

Amendments

1 Repealed by the Housing and Regeneration Act 2008, s 321(1), Sch 16.

2 Substituted by the Housing and Regeneration Act 2008, s 306(1), (6).

3 Inserted by the Housing and Regeneration Act 2008, s 306(1), (7).

4 Repealed by the Leasehold Reform, Housing and Urban Development Act 1993, s 187(2), Sch 22.

[128A Determination of value: review notices

(1) Subsection (2) applies if the value of a dwelling-house has been determined or re-determined under section 128 ('the section 128 determination').

(2) The district valuer may—

(a) on the valuer's own initiative; or

(b) at the request of the landlord or the tenant of the dwelling-house;

serve on the landlord and the tenant a notice of intention to review the section 128 determination giving reasons for the intention ('a review notice').

(3) A request under subsection (2)(b) must—

(a) be in writing;

(b) state the reason it is being made; and

(c) confirm that the landlord has not made to the tenant a grant of the kind mentioned in section 138(1) in respect of the claim by the tenant to exercise the right to buy in respect of the dwelling-house.

(4) The landlord or the tenant may not make a request under subsection (2)(b) after the end of the period of 28 days beginning with the section 128(5) service date.

(5) The district valuer must, before the end of the period of 14 days beginning with the day on which such a request is made, serve on the landlord and the tenant—

(a) a review notice; or

(b) a notice stating—

(i) that the request was made;

(ii) that the district valuer has decided not to comply with it; and

(iii) the reasons for the decision.

(6) A review notice may not be served after the end of the period of 42 days beginning with the section 128(5) service date.

(7) A review notice may not be served in relation to a determination which is subject to a re-determination required in pursuance of section 128(3) (but this does not prevent the service of a review notice in relation to the re-determination).

(8) A review notice may not be served if the landlord has made a grant of the kind mentioned in subsection (3)(c).

(9) A person who makes a request under subsection (2)(b) must inform the district valuer if a grant of the kind mentioned in subsection (3)(c) is made during the period of 14 days mentioned in subsection (5).

(10) Subsection (11) applies if the district valuer is considering whether to serve a review notice on the valuer's own initiative.

(11) The landlord or the tenant must, if requested by the district valuer, inform the valuer whether a grant of the kind mentioned in subsection (3)(c) has been made.

(12) In this section and section 128B—

'a review notice' has the meaning given by subsection (2);

'the section 128 determination' has the meaning given by subsection (1);

'the section 128(5) service date' means the day on which the landlord serves a notice on the tenant under section 128(5) in relation to the section 128 determination.][1]

Amendments

1 Inserted by the Housing and Regeneration Act 2008, s 306(1), (2).

[128B Review of determination of value

(1) The district valuer must review the section 128 determination as soon as reasonably practicable after serving a review notice.

(2) Subsection (3) applies if, following the review, the district valuer decides that neither of the withdrawal conditions is met.

(3) The district valuer must, as soon as reasonably practicable, serve on the landlord and the tenant a notice stating—

(a) the decision;

(b) the reasons for it; and

(c) that no further determination or (as the case may be) re-determination is to be made under this section.

(4) Subsection (5) applies if, following the review, the district valuer decides that either withdrawal condition is met or both are met.

(5) The district valuer must—

(a) as soon as reasonably practicable, withdraw the section 128 determination by serving a further determination notice on the landlord and the tenant; and

(b) make a further determination or (as the case may be) re-determination of the value of the dwelling-house at the relevant time.

(6) Before making such a determination or re-determination, the district valuer must consider any representation made to the valuer by the landlord or the tenant before the end of the period of 14 days beginning with the day on which the further determination notice was served.

(7) As soon as practicable after such a determination or re-determination has been made, the landlord must serve on the tenant a determination effect notice.

(8) A determination effect notice is a notice stating—

(a) the effect of the further determination or (as the case may be) re-determination; and

(b) the matters mentioned in section 125(2) and (3).

(9) For the purposes of this section, the withdrawal conditions are—

(a) that a significant error was made in the section 128 determination; or

(b) that the district valuer did not comply with section 128(4) in relation to the section 128 determination.

(10) This section does not apply to a determination which is subject to a re-determination required in pursuance of section 128(3) (but this does not prevent this section applying to the re-determination).

(11) In this section—

'a further determination notice' is a notice stating—

(a) that the section 128 determination is withdrawn;

(b) the reasons for the withdrawal; and

(c) that a further determination or (as the case may be) re-determination of the value of the dwelling-house at the relevant time will be made;

'significant error', in relation to the section 128 determination, means an error of fact, or a number of such errors, made in the section 128 determination as a result of which the value of the dwelling-house determined or (as the case may be) re-determined was at least 5% more or less than it would otherwise have been.][1]

Amendments

1 Inserted by the Housing and Regeneration Act 2008, s 306(1), (2).

129 Discount.

[(1) Subject to the following provisions of this Part, a person exercising the right to buy is entitled to a discount of a percentage calculated by reference to the period which is to be taken into account in accordance with Schedule 4 (qualifying period for right to buy and discount).

(2) The discount is, subject to any order under subsection (2A)—

(a) in the case of a house, [35 per cent][1] plus one per cent. for each complete year by which the qualifying period exceeds [five][1] years, up to a maximum of 60 per cent.;

(b) in the case of a flat, [50 per cent][1] plus two per cent. for each complete year by which the qualifying period exceeds [five][1] years, up to a maximum of 70 per cent.

(2A) The Secretary of State may by order made with the consent of the Treasury provide that, in such cases as may be specified in the order—

(a) the minimum percentage discount,

(b) the percentage increase for each complete year of the qualifying period after the first [five][1], or

(c) the maximum percentage discount,

shall be such percentage, higher than that specified in subsection (2), as may be specified in the order.

(2B) An order—

(a) may make different provision with respect to different cases or descriptions of case,

(b) may contain such incidental, supplementary or transitional provisions as appear to the Secretary of State to be necessary or expedient, and

(c) shall be made by statutory instrument and shall not be made unless a draft of it has been laid before and approved by resolution of each House of Parliament.][2]

(2) The discount shall not exceed 60 per cent.

(3) Where joint tenants exercise the right to buy, Schedule 4 shall be construed as if for the secure tenant there were substituted that one of the joint tenants whose substitution will produce the largest discount.

Amendments

1 Substituted by the Housing Act 2004, s 180(2)–(4).

2 Substituted by the Housing and Planning Act 1986, s 2(1).

130 Reduction of discount where previous discount given.

(1) There shall be deducted from the discount an amount equal to any previous discount qualifying, or the aggregate of previous discounts qualifying, under the provisions of this section.

(2) A 'previous discount' means a discount given before the relevant time—

(a) on conveyance of the freehold, or a grant or assignment of a long lease, of a dwelling-house by a person within paragraph 7 [or 7A][1] of Schedule 4 (public sector landlords) or, in such circumstances as may be prescribed by order of the Secretary of State, by a person so prescribed, or

[(aa) on conveyance of the freehold, or a grant or assignment of a long lease of a dwelling-house by a person against whom the right to buy was exercisable by virtue of section 171A (preservation of right to buy on disposal to private sector landlord) to a person who was a qualifying person for the purposes of the preserved right to buy and in relation to whom that dwelling-house was the qualifying dwelling-house, or][1]

[(ab) in pursuance of the provision required by paragraphs 3 to 5 or paragraph 7 of Schedule 6A (redemption of landlord's share), or][2]

(b) in pursuance of the provision required by paragraph 1 of Schedule 8 (terms of shared ownership lease: right to acquire additional shares), or any other provision to the like effect [or

(c) in pursuance of any provision of, or required by, this Part …[3] by virtue of section 17 of the Housing Act 1996 (the right to acquire).][4]

(3) A previous discount qualifies for the purposes of this section if it was given—

(a) to the person or one of the persons exercising the right to buy, or

(b) to the spouse[, or civil partner,][5] of that person or one of those persons (if they are living together at the relevant time), or

(c) to a deceased spouse[, or deceased civil partner,][5] of that person or one of those persons (if they were living together at the time of the death);

and where a previous discount was given to two or more persons jointly, this section has effect as if each of them had been given an equal proportion of the discount.

(4) Where the whole or part of a previous discount has been recovered by the person by whom it was given (or a successor in title of his)—

(a) by the receipt of a payment determined by reference to the discount, or

(b) by a reduction so determined of any consideration given by that person (or a successor in title of his), or

(c) in any other way,

then, so much of the discount as has been so recovered shall be disregarded for the purposes of this section.

(5) An order under this section—

(a) may make different provision with respect to different cases or descriptions of case, including different provision for different areas, and

(b) shall be made by statutory instrument which shall be subject to annulment in pursuance of a resolution of either House of Parliament.

(6) In this section 'dwelling-house' includes any yard, garden, outhouses and appurtenances belonging to the dwelling-house or usually enjoyed with it.

Amendments

1 Inserted by the Housing and Planning Act 1986, s 24(2), Sch 5, para 29.

2 Inserted by the Leasehold Reform, Housing and Urban Development Act 1993, s 187(1), Sch 21, para 11.

3 Repealed by the Abolition of the Right to Buy and Associated Rights (Wales) Act 2018 (Consequential Amendments and Savings Provisions) Regulations 2019, SI 2019/110, reg 3(j).

4 Inserted by the Housing Act 1996 (Consequential Amendments) (No. 2) Order 1997, SI 1997/627, art 2, Schedule, para 3(1), (3)

5 Inserted by the Civil Partnership Act 2004, s 81, Sch 8, para 29.

131 Limits on amount of discount

(1) Except where the Secretary of State so determines, the discount shall not reduce the price below the amount which, in accordance with a determination made by him, is to be taken as representing so much of the costs incurred in respect of the dwelling-house as, in accordance with the determination—

[(a) is to be treated as incurred at or after the beginning of that period of account of the landlord in which falls the date which is eight years, or such other period of time as may be specified in an order made by the Secretary of State, earlier than the relevant time, and][1]

(b) is to be treated as relevant for the purposes of this sub-section;

and if the price before discount is below that amount, there shall be no discount.

[(1A) In subsection (1)(a) above 'period of account', in relation to any costs, means the period for which the landlord made up those of its accounts in which account is taken of those costs.][2]

(2) The discount shall not in any case reduce the price by more than such sum as the Secretary of State may by order prescribe.

(3) An order or determination under this section may make different provision for different cases or descriptions of case, including different provision for different areas.

(4) An order under this section shall be made by statutory instrument which shall be subject to annulment in pursuance of a resolution of either House of Parliament.

Amendments

1 Substituted by the Housing Act 1988, s 122(1), (2).

2 Inserted by the Housing Act 1988, s 122(1), (3).

Change of tenant or landlord after service of notice claiming right to buy

136 Change of secure tenant after notice claiming right to buy.

(1) Where, after a secure tenant ('the former tenant') has given a notice claiming the right to buy, another person ('the new tenant')—

(a) becomes the secure tenant under the same secure tenancy, otherwise than on an assignment made by virtue of section 92 (assignments by way of exchange), or

(b) becomes the secure tenant under a periodic tenancy arising by virtue of section 86 (periodic tenancy arising on termination of fixed term) on the coming to an end of the secure tenancy, the new tenant shall be in the same position as if the notice had been given by him and he had been the secure tenant at the time it was given.

[(2) If a notice under section 125 (landlord's notice of purchase price and other matters) has been served on the former tenant, then, whether or not the former tenant has served a notice under subsection (1) of section 125D (tenant's notice of intention), the new tenant shall serve a notice under that subsection within the period of twelve weeks beginning with whichever of the following is the later—

(a) his becoming the secure tenant, ...[1]

(b) where the right to have the value of the dwelling-house determined or re-determined by the district valuer is or has been exercised by him or the former tenant [(or where the right to have the value of the dwelling-house re-determined by the district valuer is or has been exercised by the landlord), the relevant event][2].][3]

[(2A) In subsection (2)(b) 'the relevant event' means—

(a) where a review notice was capable of being served under section 128A in relation to the determination or re-determination but no such notice was served during the period permitted by that section, the service of the notice under section 128(5) stating the effect of the determination or re-determination,

(b) where a review notice was served under section 128A in relation to the determination or re-determination and section 128B(3) applied, the service on the new tenant or (as the case may be) the former tenant of the notice under section 128B(3), and

(c) where a review notice was served under section 128A in relation to the determination or re-determination and section 128B(5) applied, the service of the notice under section 128B(7).][4]

(6) The preceding provisions of this section do not confer any right on a person required in pursuance of section 123 (claim to share right to buy with members of family) to share the right to buy, unless he could have been validly so required had the notice claiming to exercise the right to buy been given by the new tenant.

(7) The preceding provisions of this section apply with the necessary modifications if there is a further change in the person who is the secure tenant.

Amendments

1 Repealed by the Housing and Regeneration Act 2008, s 321(1), Sch 16

2 Substituted by the Housing and Regeneration Act 2008, s 306(1), (8).

3 Substituted for subsections (2) to(5) by the Leasehold Reform, Housing and Urban Development Act 1993, s 105(2).

4 Inserted by the Housing and Regeneration Act 2008, s 306(1), (9).

137 Change of landlord after notice claiming right to buy or right to a mortgage.

[(1)][1] Where the interest of the landlord in the dwelling-house passes from the landlord to another body after a secure tenant has given a notice claiming to exercise the right to buy ...[2], all parties shall[, subject to subsection (2),][1] be in the same position as if the other body had become the landlord before the notice was given and had been given that notice and any further notice given by the tenant to the landlord and had taken all steps which the landlord had taken.

[(2) If the circumstances after the disposal differ in any material respect, as for example where—

(a) the interest of the disponee in the dwelling-house after the disposal differs from that of the disponor before the disposal, or

(b) ...[2]

(c) any of the provisions of Schedule 5 (exceptions to the right to buy) becomes or ceases to be applicable,

all those concerned shall, as soon as practicable after the disposal, take all such steps (whether by way of amending or withdrawing and re-serving any notice or extending any period or otherwise) as may be requisite for the purpose of securing that all parties are, as nearly as may be, in the same position as they would have been if those circumstances had obtained before the disposal.][1]

Amendments

1 Inserted by the Housing and Planning Act 1986, s 24(1), Sch 5, para 4.

2 Repealed by the Leasehold Reform, Housing and Urban Development Act 1993, s 187(2), Sch 22.

Completion of purchase in pursuance of right to buy

138 Duty of landlord to convey freehold or grant lease

(1) Where a secure tenant has claimed to exercise the right to buy and that right has been established, then, as soon as all matters relating to the grant ...[1] have been agreed or determined, the landlord shall make to the tenant—

(a) if the dwelling-house is a house and the landlord owns the freehold, a grant of the dwelling-house for an estate in fee simple absolute, or

(b) if the landlord does not own the freehold or if the dwelling-house is a flat (whether or not the landlord owns the freehold), a grant of a lease of the dwelling-house,

in accordance with the following provisions of this Part.

(2) If the tenant has failed to pay the rent or any other payment due from him as a tenant for a period of four weeks after it has been lawfully demanded from him, the landlord is not bound to comply with subsection (1) while the whole or partof that payment remains outstanding.

[(2A) Subsection (2B) applies if an application is pending before any court—

(a) for a demotion[, Ground 2 or 2ZA possession order or section 84A possession order][2] to be made in respect of the tenant, or

(b) for a suspension order to be made in respect of the tenancy.

(2B) The landlord is not bound to comply with subsection (1) until such time (if any) as the application is determined without—

(a) a demotion order[, an operative Ground 2 or 2ZA possession order or an operative section 84A possession order][2] being made in respect of the tenant, or

(b) a suspension order being made in respect of the tenancy,

or the application is withdrawn.

(2C) For the purposes of subsection (2A) and (2B)—

'demotion order' means a demotion order under section 82A;

['Ground 2 or 2ZA possession order' means an order for possession under Ground 2 or Ground 2ZA in Schedule 2;][2]

['operative Ground 2 or 2ZA possession order' means an order made under Ground 2 or Ground 2ZA in Schedule 2 which requires possession of the dwelling-house to be given up on a date specified in the order;][2]

['operative section 84A possession order' means an order under section 84A which requires possession of the dwelling-house to be given up on a date specified in the order;

'section 84A possession order' means an order for possession under section 84A;][3]

'suspension order' means a suspension order under section 121A.

(2D) Subsection (1) has effect subject to section 121A(5) (disapplication of subsection (1) where suspension order is made).][4]

[(2E) Subsection (1) also has effect subject to—

(a) section 138A(2) (operation of subsection (1) suspended while initial demolition notice is in force), and

(b) section 138B(2) (subsection (1) disapplied where final demolition notice is served).][5]

(3) The duty imposed on the landlord by subsection (1) is enforceable by injunction.

Amendments

1 Repealed by the Leasehold Reform, Housing and Urban Development Act 1993, s 187(2), Sch 22.

2 Substituted by the Anti-social Behaviour, Crime and Policing Act 2014, s 100(1)(a)-(d).

3 Inserted by the Anti-social Behaviour, Crime and Policing Act 2014, s 100(1)(e).

4 Inserted by the Housing Act 2004, s 193(1).

5 Inserted by the Housing Act 2004, s 183(1).

[138A Effect of initial demolition notice served before completion

(1) This section applies where—

(a) an initial demolition notice is served on a secure tenant under Schedule 5A, and

(b) the notice is served on the tenant before the landlord has made to him such a grant as is required by section 138(1) in respect of a claim by the tenant to exercise the right to buy.

(2) In such a case the landlord is not bound to comply with section 138(1), in connection with any such claim by the tenant, so long as the initial demolition notice remains in force under Schedule 5A.

(3) Section 138C provides a right to compensation in certain cases where this section applies.][1]

Amendments

1 Inserted by the Housing Act 2004, s 183(2).

[138B Effect of final demolition notice served before completion

(1) This section applies where—

(a) a secure tenant has claimed to exercise the right to buy, but

(b) before the landlord has made to the tenant such a grant as is required by section 138(1) in respect of the claim, a final demolition notice is served on the tenant under paragraph 13 of Schedule 5.

(2) In such a case—

(a) the tenant's claim ceases to be effective as from the time when the final demolition notice comes into force under that paragraph, and

(b) section 138(1) accordingly does not apply to the landlord, in connection with the tenant's claim, at any time after the notice comes into force.

(3) Section 138C provides a right to compensation in certain cases where this section applies.][1]

Amendments

1 Inserted by the Housing Act 2004, s 183(2).

[138C Compensation where demolition notice served

(1) This section applies where—

(a) a secure tenant has claimed to exercise the right to buy,

(b) before the landlord has made to the tenant such a grant as is required by section 138(1) in respect of the claim, either an initial demolition notice is served on the tenant under Schedule 5A or a final demolition notice is served on him under paragraph 13 of Schedule 5, and

(c) the tenant's claim is established before that notice comes into force under Schedule 5A or paragraph 13 of Schedule 5 (as the case may be).

(2) If, within the period of three months beginning with the date when the notice comes into force ('the operative date'), the tenant serves on the landlord a written notice claiming an amount of compensation under subsection (3), the landlord shall pay that amount to the tenant.

(3) Compensation under this subsection is compensation in respect of expenditure reasonably incurred by the tenant before the operative date in respect of legal and other fees, and other professional costs and expenses, payable in connection with the exercise by him of the right to buy.

(4) A notice under subsection (2) must be accompanied by receipts or other documents showing that the tenant incurred the expenditure in question.][1]

Amendments

1 Inserted by the Housing Act 2004, s 183(2).

139 Terms and effect of conveyance or grant and mortgage.

(1) A conveyance of the freehold executed in pursuance of the right to buy shall conform with Parts I and II of Schedule 6; a grant of a lease so executed shall conform with Parts I and III of that Schedule; and Part IV of that Schedule has effect in relation to certain charges.

(2) The secure tenancy comes to an end on the grant to the tenant of an estate in fee simple, or of a lease, in pursuance of the provisions of this Part relating to the right to buy; and if there is then a subtenancy section 139 of the Law of Property Act 1925 (effect of extinguishment of reversion) applies as on a merger or surrender.

(3) …[1]

Amendments

1 Repealed by the Leasehold Reform, Housing and Urban Development Act 1993, s 187(2), Sch 22.

140 Landlord's first notice to complete.

(1) The landlord may, subject to the provisions of this section, serve on the tenant at any time a written notice requiring him—

(a) if all relevant matters have been agreed or determined, to complete the transaction within a period stated in the notice, or

(b) if any relevant matters are outstanding, to serve on the landlord within that period a written notice to that effect specifying the matters,

and informing the tenant of the effect of this section and of section 141(1), (2) and (4) landlord's second notice to complete).

(2) The period stated in a notice under this section shall be such period (of at least 56 days) as may be reasonable in the circumstances.

[(3) A notice under this section shall not be served earlier than [three][1] months after—

(a) the service of the landlord's notice under section 125 (notice of purchase price and other matters), or

(b) where a notice has been served under section 146 (landlord's notice admitting or denying right to acquire on rent to mortgage terms), the service of that notice.][2]

(4) A notice under this section shall not be served if—

(a) a requirement for the determination or re-determination of the value of the dwelling-house by the district valuer has not been complied with,

[(aa) a review notice (within the meaning of section 128A) has been served in relation to such a determination or re-determination, section 128B applies and the district valuer has neither—

(i) served a notice under section 128B(3) (refusal to make further determination), nor

(ii) served a notice under section 128B(7) (a determination effect notice),

(ab) no such review notice has been served but such a notice may still be served under section 128A,][3]

(b) proceedings for the determination of any other relevant matter have not been disposed of, or

(c) any relevant matter stated to be outstanding in a written notice served on the landlord by the tenant has not been agreed in writing or determined.

(5) In this section 'relevant matters' means matters relating to the grant …[4].

Amendments

1 Substituted by the Housing Act 2004, s 184(1), (2).

2 Substituted by the Leasehold Reform, Housing and Urban Development Act 1993, s 187(1), Sch 21, para 12.

3 Inserted by the Housing and Regeneration Act 2008, s 306(1), (10).

4 Repealed by the Leasehold Reform, Housing and Urban Development Act 1993, s 187(2), Sch 22.

141 Landlord's second notice to complete.

(1) If the tenant does not comply with a notice under section 140 (landlord's first notice to complete), the landlord may serve on him a further written notice—

(a) requiring him to complete the transaction within a period stated in the notice, and

(b) informing him of the effect of this section in the event of his failing to comply.

(2) The period stated in a notice under this section shall be such period (of at least 56 days) as may be reasonable in the circumstances.

(3) At any time before the end of that period (or that period as previously extended) the landlord may by a written notice served on the tenant extend it (or further extend it).

(4) If the tenant does not comply with a notice under this section the notice claiming to exercise the right to buy shall be deemed to be withdrawn at the end of that period (or as the case may require, that period as extended under subsection (3)).

(5) If a notice under this section has been served on the tenant and by virtue of section 138(2) (failure of tenant to pay rent, etc.) the landlord is not bound to complete, the tenant shall be deemed not to comply with the notice.

142 ...[1]

Amendments

1 Repealed by the Leasehold Reform, Housing and Urban Development Act 1993, s 187(2), Sch 22.

[142A Termination of the right to acquire on rent to mortgage terms

(1) As from the termination date, the right to acquire on rent to mortgage terms is not exercisable except in pursuance of a notice served under section 144 before that date.

(2) In this section 'the termination date' means the date falling 8 months after the date of the passing of the Housing Act 2004.][1]

Amendments

1 Inserted by the Housing Act 2004, s 190(1).

[Right to acquire on rent to mortgage terms

143 Right to acquire on rent to mortgage terms.

(1) Subject to subsection (2) and sections [142A,][1] 143A and 143B, where—

(a) a secure tenant has claimed to exercise the right to buy, and

(b) his right to buy has been established and his notice claiming to exercise it remains in force,

he also has the right to acquire on rent to mortgage terms in accordance with the following provisions of this Part.

(2) The right to acquire on rent to mortgage terms cannot be exercised if the exercise of the right to buy is precluded by section 121 (circumstances in which right to buy cannot be exercised).

(3) Where the right to buy belongs to two or more persons jointly, the right to acquire on rent to mortgage terms also belongs to them jointly.][2]

Amendments

1 Inserted by the Housing Act 2004, s 190(2).

2 Substituted by the Leasehold Reform, Housing and Urban Development Act 1993, s 108.

[143A Right excluded by entitlement to housing benefit.

(1) The right to acquire on rent to mortgage terms cannot be exercised if—

(a) it has been determined that the tenant is or was entitled to housing benefit in respect of any part of the relevant period, or

(b) a claim for housing benefit in respect of any part of that period has been made (or is treated as having been made) by or on behalf of the tenant and has not been determined or withdrawn.

(2) In this section 'the relevant period' means the period—

(a) beginning twelve months before the day on which the tenant claims to exercise the right to acquire on rent to mortgage terms, and

(b) ending with the day on which the conveyance or grant is executed in pursuance of that right.][1]

Amendments

1 Substituted by the Leasehold Reform, Housing and Urban Development Act 1993, s 108.

[143B Right excluded if minimum initial payment exceeds maximum initial payment.

(1) The right to acquire on rent to mortgage terms cannot be exercised if the minimum initial payment in respect of the dwelling-house exceeds the maximum initial payment in respect of it.

(2) The maximum initial payment in respect of a dwelling-house is 80 per cent. of the price which would be payable if the tenant were exercising the right to buy.

(3) Where, in the case of a dwelling-house which is a house, the weekly rent at the relevant time did not exceed the relevant amount, the minimum initial payment shall be determined by the formula—

$P = R \times M$

where—

P = the minimum initial payment;

R = the amount of the weekly rent at the relevant time;

M = the multiplier which at that time was for the time being declared by the Secretary of State for the purposes of this subsection.

(4) Where, in the case of a dwelling-house which is a house, the weekly rent at the relevant time exceeded the relevant amount, the minimum initial payment shall be determined by the formula—

$P = Q + (E \times M)$

where—

P = the minimum initial payment;

Q = the qualifying maximum for the year of assessment which included the relevant time;

E = the amount by which the weekly rent at that time exceeded the relevant amount;

M = the multiplier which at that time was for the time being declared by the Secretary of State for the purposes of this subsection.

(5) The minimum initial payment in respect of a dwelling-house which is a flat is 80 per cent. of the amount which would be the minimum initial payment in respect of the dwelling-house if it were a house.

(6) The relevant amount and multipliers for the time being declared for the purposes of this section shall be such that, in the case of a dwelling-house which is a house, they will produce a minimum initial payment equal to the capital sum which, in the opinion of the Secretary of State, could be raised on a 25 year repayment mortgage in the case of which the net amount of the monthly mortgage payments was equal to the rent at the relevant time calculated on a monthly basis.

(7) For the purposes of subsection (6) the Secretary of State shall assume—

(a) that the interest rate applicable throughout the 25 year term were the standard national rate for the time being declared by the Secretary of State under paragraph 2 of Schedule 16 (local authority mortgage interest rates); and

(b) that the monthly mortgage payments represented payments of capital and interest only.

(8) In this section—

'net amount', in relation to monthly mortgage payments, means the amount of such payments after deduction of tax under section 369 of the Income and Corporation Taxes Act 1988 (mortgage interest payable under deduction of tax);

'qualifying maximum' means the qualifying maximum defined in section 367(5) of that Act (limit on relief for interest on certain loans);

'relevant amount' means the amount which at the relevant time was for the time being declared by the Secretary of State for the purposes of this section;

'relevant time' means the time of the service of the landlord's notice under section 146 (landlord's notice admitting or denying right);

'rent' means rent payable under the secure tenancy, but excluding any element which is expressed to be payable for services, repairs, maintenance or insurance or the landlord's costs of management.][1]

Amendments

1 Substituted by the Leasehold Reform, Housing and Urban Development Act 1993, s 108.

[144 Tenant's notice claiming right.

(1) [Subject to section 142A, a secure tenant][1] claims to exercise the right to acquire on rent to mortgage terms by written notice to that effect served on the landlord.

(2) The notice may be withdrawn at any time by notice in writing served on the landlord.

(3) On the service of a notice under this section, any notice served by the landlord under section 140 or 141 (landlord's notices to complete purchase in pursuance of right to buy) shall be deemed to have been withdrawn; and no such notice may be served by the landlord whilst a notice under this section remains in force.

(4) Where a notice under this section is withdrawn, the tenant may complete the transaction in accordance with the provisions of this Part relating to the right to buy.][2]

Amendments

1 Substituted by the Housing Act 2004, s 190(3)

2 Substituted by the Leasehold Reform, Housing and Urban Development Act 1993, s 109.

145 ...[1]

Amendments

1 Substituted by the Leasehold Reform, Housing and Urban Development Act 1993, s 109.

[146 Landlord's notice admitting or denying right.

(1) Where a notice under section 144 (notice claiming to exercise the right to acquire on rent to mortgage terms) has been served by the tenant, the landlord shall, unless the notice is withdrawn, serve on the tenant as soon as practicable a written notice either—

(a) admitting the tenant's right and informing him of the matters mentioned in subsection (2), or

(b) denying it and stating the reasons why, in the opinion of the landlord, the tenant does not have the right to acquire on rent to mortgage terms.

(2) The matters are—

(a) the relevant amount and multipliers for the time being declared by the Secretary of State for the purposes of section 143B;

(b) the amount of the minimum initial payment;

(c) the proportion which that amount bears to the price which would be payable if the tenant exercised the right to buy;

(d) the landlord's share on the assumption that the tenant makes the minimum initial payment;

(e) the amount of the initial discount on that assumption; and

(f) the provisions which, in the landlord's opinion, should be contained in the conveyance or grant and the mortgage required by section 151B (mortgage for securing redemption of landlord's share).][1]

Amendments

1 Substituted by the Leasehold Reform, Housing and Urban Development Act 1993, s 110.

[146A Tenant's notice of intention.

(1) Where a notice under section 146 has been served on a secure tenant, he shall within the period specified in subsection (2) serve a written notice on the landlord stating either—

(a) that he intends to pursue his claim to exercise the right to acquire on rent to mortgage terms and the amount of the initial payment which he proposes to make, or

(b) that he withdraws that claim and intends to pursue his claim to exercise the right to buy, or

(c) that he withdraws both of those claims.

(2) The period for serving a notice under subsection (1) is the period of twelve weeks beginning with the service of the notice under section 146.

(3) The amount stated in a notice under subsection (1)(a)—

(a) shall not be less than the minimum initial payment and not more than the maximum initial payment, and

(b) may be varied at any time by notice in writing served on the landlord.][1]

Amendments

1 Inserted by the Leasehold Reform, Housing and Urban Development Act 1993, s 111.

[146B Landlord's notice in default.

(1) The landlord may, at any time after the end of the period specified in section 146A(2), serve on the tenant a written notice—

(a) requiring him, if he has failed to serve the notice required by section 146A(1), to serve that notice within 28 days, and

(b) informing him of the effect of this subsection and subsection (4).

(2) At any time before the end of the period mentioned in subsection (1)(a) (or that period as previously extended) the landlord may by written notice served on the tenant extend it (or further extend it).

(3) If at any time before the end of that period (or that period as extended under subsection (2)) the circumstances are such that it would not be reasonable to expect the tenant to comply with a notice under this section, that period (or that period as so extended) shall by virtue of this subsection be extended (or further extended) until 28 days after the time when those circumstances no longer obtain.

(4) If the tenant does not comply with a notice under this section the notice claiming to exercise the right to acquire on rent to mortgage terms shall be deemed to be withdrawn at the end of that period (or, as the case may require, that period as extended under subsection (2) or (3)).][1]

Amendments

1 Inserted by the Leasehold Reform, Housing and Urban Development Act 1993, s 111.

[147 Notice of landlord's share and initial discount.

(1) Where a secure tenant has served—

(a) a notice under section 146A(1)(a) stating that he intends to pursue his claim to exercise the right to acquire on rent to mortgage terms, and the amount of the initial payment which he proposes to make, or

(b) a notice under section 146A(3)(b) varying the amount stated in a notice under section 146A(1)(a),

the landlord shall, as soon as practicable, serve on the tenant a written notice complying with this section.

(2) The notice shall state—

(a) the landlord's share on the assumption that the amount of the tenant's initial payment is that stated in the notice under section 146A(1)(a) or, as the case may be, section 146A(3)(b), and

(b) the amount of the initial discount on that assumption,

determined in each case in accordance with section 148.][1]

Amendments

1 Substituted by the Leasehold Reform, Housing and Urban Development Act 1993, s 112.

[148 Determination of landlord's share, initial discount etc.

The landlord's share shall be determined by the formula—

$$S = \{(P - IP) / P\} \times 100$$

the amount of the initial discount shall be determined by the formula—

$$ID = (IP / P) \times D$$

and the amount of any previous discount which will be recovered by virtue of the transaction shall be determined by the formula—

$$RD = (IP / P) \times PD$$

where—

S = the landlord's share expressed as a percentage;

P = the price which would be payable if the tenant were exercising the right to buy;

IP = the amount of the tenant's initial payment (but disregarding any reduction in pursuance of section 153B(3));

ID = the amount of the initial discount;

D = the amount of the discount which would be applicable if the tenant were exercising the right to buy;

RD = the amount of any previous discount which will be recovered by virtue of the transaction;

PD = the amount of any previous discount which would be recovered if the tenant were exercising the right to buy.][1]

Amendments

1 Substituted by the Leasehold Reform, Housing and Urban Development Act 1993, s 113.

[149 Change of landlord after notice claiming right.

(1) Where the interest of the landlord in the dwelling-house passes from the landlord to another body after a secure tenant has given a notice claiming to exercise the right to acquire on rent to mortgage terms, all parties shall subject to subsection (2) be in the same position as if the other body—

(a) had become the landlord before the notice was given, and

(b) had been given that notice and any further notice given by the tenant to the landlord, and

(c) had taken all steps which the landlord had taken.

(2) If the circumstances after the disposal differ in any material respect, as for example where—

(a) the interest of the disponee in the dwelling-house after the disposal differs from that of the disponor before the disposal, or

(b) any of the provisions of Schedule 5 (exceptions to the right to buy) becomes or ceases to be applicable,

all those concerned shall, as soon as practicable after the disposal, take all such steps (whether by way of amending or withdrawing and re-serving any notice or extending any period or otherwise) as may be requisite for the purpose of securing that all parties are, as nearly as may be, in the same position as they would have been if those circumstances had obtained before the disposal.][1]

Amendments

1 Substituted by the Leasehold Reform, Housing and Urban Development Act 1993, s 114.

[150 Duty of landlord to convey freehold or grant lease.

(1) Where a secure tenant has claimed to exercise the right to acquire on rent to mortgage terms and that right has been established, then, as soon as all matters relating to the grant and to securing the redemption of the landlord's share have been agreed or determined, the landlord shall make to the tenant—

(a) if the dwelling-house is a house and the landlord owns the freehold, a grant of the dwelling-house for an estate in fee simple absolute, or

(b) if the landlord does not own the freehold or if the dwelling-house is a flat (whether or not the landlord owns the freehold), a grant of a lease of the dwelling-house,

in accordance with the following provisions of this Part.

(2) If the tenant has failed to pay the rent or any other payment due from him as a tenant for a period of four weeks after it has been lawfully demanded from him, the landlord is not bound to comply with subsection (1) while the whole or part of that payment remains outstanding.

(3) The duty imposed on the landlord by subsection (1) is enforceable by injunction.][1]

Amendments

1 Substituted by the Leasehold Reform, Housing and Urban Development Act 1993, s 115.

[151 Terms and effect of conveyance or grant: general.

(1) A conveyance of the freehold executed in pursuance of the right to acquire on rent to mortgage terms shall conform with Parts I and II of Schedule 6; a grant of a lease so executed shall conform with Parts I and III of that Schedule; and Part IV of that Schedule applies to such a conveyance or lease as it applies to a conveyance or lease executed in pursuance of the right to buy.

(2) The secure tenancy comes to an end on the grant to the tenant of an estate in fee simple, or of a lease, in pursuance of the right to acquire on rent to mortgage terms; and if there is then a sub-tenancy section 139 of the Law of Property Act 1925 (effect of extinguishment of reversion) applies as on a merger or surrender.][1]

Amendments

1 Substituted by the Leasehold Reform, Housing and Urban Development Act 1993, s 116(1).

[151A Redemption of landlord's share.

Schedule 6A (which makes provision for the redemption of the landlord's share) shall have effect; and a conveyance of the freehold or a grant of a lease executed in pursuance of the right to acquire on rent to mortgage terms shall conform with that Schedule.][1]

Amendments

1 Inserted by the Leasehold Reform, Housing and Urban Development Act 1993, s 117(1).

[151B Mortgage for securing redemption of landlord's share.

(1) The liability that may arise under the covenant required by paragraph 1 of Schedule 6A (covenant for the redemption of the landlord's share in the circumstances there mentioned) shall be secured by a mortgage.

(2) Subject to subsections (3) and (4), the mortgage shall have priority immediately after any legal charge securing an amount advanced to the secure tenant by an approved lending institution for the purpose of enabling him to exercise the right to acquire on rent to mortgage terms.

(3) The following, namely—

(a) any advance which is made otherwise than for the purpose mentioned in subsection (2) and is secured by a legal charge having priority to the mortgage, and

(b) any further advance which is so secured,

shall rank in priority to the mortgage if, and only if, the landlord by written notice served on the institution concerned gives its consent; and the landlord shall so give its consent if the purpose of the advance or further advance is an approved purpose.

(4) The landlord may at any time by written notice served on an approved lending institution postpone the mortgage to any advance or further advance which—

(a) is made to the tenant by that institution, and

(b) is secured by a legal charge not having priority to the mortgage;

and the landlord shall serve such a notice if the purpose of the advance or further advance is an approved purpose.

(5) The approved lending institutions for the purposes of this section are—

the [Relevant Authority][1],

[an authorised deposit taker

an authorised insurer][2]

[an authorised mortgage lender.][3]

[(5A) In subsection (5) 'the Relevant Authority' does not include the Regulator of Social Housing but does include the Homes and Communities Agency.][4]

[(5B) In subsection (5) 'the Relevant Authority' also includes the Greater London Authority.][5]

(6) The approved purposes for the purposes of this section are—

(a) to enable the tenant to make an interim or final payment,

(b) to enable the tenant to defray, or to defray on his behalf, any of the following—

(i) the cost of any works to the dwelling-house,

(ii) any service charge payable in respect of the dwelling-house for works, whether or not to the dwelling-house, and

(iii) any service charge or other amount payable in respect of the dwelling-house for insurance, whether or not of the dwelling-house, and

(c) to enable the tenant to discharge, or to discharge on his behalf, any of the following—

(i) so much as is still outstanding of any advance or further advance which ranks in priority to the mortgage,

(ii) any arrears of interest on such an advance or further advance, and

(iii) any costs and expenses incurred in enforcing payment of any such interest, or repayment (in whole or in part) of any such advance or further advance.

(7) Where different parts of an advance or further advance are made for different purposes, each of those parts shall be regarded as a separate advance or further advance for the purposes of this section.

(8) The Secretary of State may by order prescribe—

(a) matters for which the deed by which the mortgage is effected must make provision, and

(b) terms which must, or must not, be contained in that deed,

but only in relation to deeds executed after the order comes into force.

(9) The deed by which the mortgage is effected may contain such other provisions as may be—

(a) agreed between the mortgagor and the mortgagee, or

(b) determined by the county court to be reasonably required by the mortgagor or the mortgagee.

(10) An order under this section—

(a) may make different provision with respect to different cases or descriptions of case, including different provision for different areas, and

(b) shall be made by statutory instrument which shall be subject to annulment in pursuance of a resolution of either House of Parliament.][6]

Amendments

1 Substituted by the Government of Wales Act 1998, s 140, Sch 16, paras 4, 5.

2 Substituted by the Financial Services and Markets Act 2000 (Consequential Amendments and Repeals) Order 2001, SI 2001/3649, art 299(1), (3).

3 Substituted by the Housing and Regeneration Act 2008, s 307(5).

4 Inserted by the Housing and Regeneration Act 2008 (Consequential Provisions) Order 2010, SI 2010/866, art 4, Sch 1, paras 1, 2.

5 Inserted by the Localism Act 2011, s 195(1), Sch 19, paras 10, 14.

6 Inserted by the Leasehold Reform, Housing and Urban Development Act 1993, s 118.

152 Landlord's first notice to complete.

(1) The landlord may, subject to the provisions of this section, serve on the tenant at any time a written notice requiring him—

(a) if all relevant matters have been agreed or determined, to complete the transaction within a period stated in the notice, or

(b) if any relevant matters are outstanding, to serve on the landlord within that period a written notice to that effect specifying the matters,

and informing the tenant of the effect of this section and of section 153(1), (2) and (4) (landlord's second notice to complete and its effect).

(2) The period stated in a notice under this section shall be such period (of at least 56 days) as may be reasonable in the circumstances.

[(3) A notice under this section shall not be served earlier than twelve months after the service of the notice under section 146 (landlord's notice admitting or denying right).][1]

(4) A notice under this section shall not be served if—

(a) a requirement for the determination or re-determination of the value of the dwelling-house by the district valuer has not been complied with,

(b) proceedings for the determination of any other relevant matter have not been disposed of, or

(c) any relevant matter stated to be outstanding in a written notice served on the landlord by the tenant has not been agreed in writing or determined.

(5) In this section 'relevant matters' means matters relating to the grant and to [securing the redemption of the landlord's share][1].

Amendments

1 Substituted by the Leasehold Reform, Housing and Urban Development Act 1993, s 119(1), (2).

153 Landlord's second notice to complete.

(1) If the tenant does not comply with a notice under section 152 (landlord's first notice to complete), the landlord may serve on him a further written notice—

(a) requiring him to complete the transaction within a period stated in the notice, and

(b) informing him of the effect of this section in the event of his failing to comply.

(2) The period stated in a notice under this section shall be such period (of at least 56 days) as may be reasonable in the circumstances.

(3) At any time before the end of that period (or that period as previously extended) the landlord may by a written notice served on the tenant extend it (or further extend it).

(4) If the tenant does not comply with a notice under this section, the notice claiming to exercise [the right to acquire on rent to mortgage terms][1] and the notice claiming to exercise the right to buy shall be deemed to have been withdrawn at the end of that period (or, as the case may require, that period as extended under subsection (3)).

(5) If a notice under this section has been served on the tenant and by virtue of section 150(2) (failure of tenant to pay rent, etc.) the landlord is not bound to complete, the tenant shall be deemed not to comply with the notice.

Amendments

1 Substituted by the Leasehold Reform, Housing and Urban Development Act 1993, s 119(3).

[Tenant's sanction for landlord's delays][1]

[153A Tenant's notices of delay.

(1) Where a secure tenant has claimed to exercise the right to buy, he may serve on his landlord a notice (in this section referred to as an 'initial notice of delay') in any of the following cases, namely,—

(a) where the landlord has failed to serve a notice under section 124 within the period appropriate under subsection (2) …[2] of that section;

(b) where the tenant's right to buy has been established and the landlord has failed to serve a notice under section 125 within the period appropriate under subsection (1) of that section;

(c) …[3]

(d) …[3]

(e) where the tenant considers that delays on the part of the landlord are preventing him from exercising expeditiously his right to buy or his [right to acquire on rent to mortgage terms][4];

and where an initial notice of delay specifies [either of the cases in paragraphs (a) and (b)][4], any reference in this section or section 153B to the default date is a reference to the end of the period referred to in the paragraph in question or, if it is later, the day appointed for the coming into force of section 124 of the Housing Act 1988.

(2) An initial notice of delay—

(a) shall specify the most recent action of which the tenant is aware which has been taken by the landlord pursuant to this Part of this Act; and

(b) shall specify a period (in this section referred to as 'the response period'), not being less than one month, beginning on the date of service of the notice, within which the service by the landlord of a counter notice under subsection (3) will have the effect of cancelling the initial notice of delay.

(3) Within the response period specified in an initial notice of delay or at any time thereafter, the landlord may serve on the tenant a counter notice in either of the following circumstances—

(a) if the initial notice specifies [either of the cases in paragraphs (a) and (b)][4] of subsection (1) and the landlord has served, or is serving together with the counter notice, the required notice under section 124, [or section 125][4], as the case may be; or

(b) if the initial notice specifies the case in subsection (1)(e) and there is no action under this Part which, at the beginning of the response period, it was for the landlord to take in order to allow the tenant expeditiously to exercise his right to buy or his [right to acquire on rent to mortgage terms][4] and which remains to be taken at the time of service of the counter notice.

(4) A counter notice under subsection (3) shall specify the circumstances by virtue of which it is served.

(5) At any time when—

(a) the response period specified in an initial notice of delay has expired, and

(b) the landlord has not served a counter notice under subsection (3),

the tenant may serve on the landlord a notice (in this section and section 153B referred to as an 'operative notice of delay') which shall state that section 153B will apply to payments of rent made by the tenant on or after the default date or, if the initial notice of delay specified the case in subsection (1)(e), the date of the service of the notice.

(6) If, after a tenant has served an initial notice of delay, a counter notice has been served under subsection (3), then, whether or not the tenant has also served an operative notice of delay, if any of the cases in subsection (1) again arises, the tenant may serve a further initial notice of delay and the provisions of this section shall apply again accordingly.][5]

Amendments

1 Inserted by the Leasehold Reform, Housing and Urban Development Act 1993, s 187(1), Sch 21, para 13(1).

2 Repealed by the Abolition of the Right to Buy and Associated Rights (Wales) Act 2018 (Consequential Amendments and Savings Provisions) Regulations 2019, SI 2019/110, reg 3(k).

3 Repealed by the Leasehold Reform, Housing and Urban Development Act 1993, s 187(2), Sch 22.

4 Substituted by the Leasehold Reform, Housing and Urban Development Act 1993, s 187(1), Sch 21, para 13(2), (3).

5 Inserted by the Housing Act 1988, s 124.

[153B Payments of rent attributable to purchase price etc.

(1) Where a secure tenant has served on his landlord an operative notice of delay, this section applies to any payment of rent which is made on or after the default date or, as the case may be, the date of the service of the notice and before the occurrence of any of the following events (and, if more than one event occurs, before the earliest to occur)—

(a) the service by the landlord of a counter notice under section 153A(3);

(b) the date on which the landlord makes to the tenant the grant required by section 138 or, as the case may be, section 150;

(c) ...[1]

(d) the date on which the tenant withdraws or is deemed to have withdrawn the notice claiming to exercise the right to buy or, as the case may be, the notice claiming to exercise the [right to acquire on rent to mortgage terms][2]; and

(e) the date on which the tenant ceases to be entitled to exercise the right to buy.

(2) Except where this section ceases to apply on a date determined under [paragraph (d) or (e)][2] of subsection (1), so much of any payment of rent to which this section applies as does not consist of—

(a) a sum due on account of rates [or council tax][3], or

(b) a service charge (as defined in section 621A),

shall be treated not only as a payment of rent but also as a payment on account by the tenant which is to be taken into account in accordance with subsection (3).

(3) In a case where subsection (2) applies, the amount which, apart from this section, would be the purchase price or, as the case may be, [the tenant's initial payment][2] shall be reduced by an amount equal to the aggregate of—

(a) the total of any payments on account treated as having been paid by the tenant by virtue of subsection (2); and

(b) if those payments on account are derived from payments of rent referable to a period of more than twelve months, a sum equal to the appropriate percentage of the total referred to in paragraph (a).

(4) In subsection (3)(b) 'the appropriate percentage' means 50 per cent. or such other percentage as may be prescribed.][4]

Amendments

1 Repealed by the Leasehold Reform, Housing and Urban Development Act 1993, s 187(2), Sch 22.

2 Substituted by the Leasehold Reform, Housing and Urban Development Act 1993, s 187(1), Sch 21, para 14.

3 Inserted by the Local Government Finance (Housing) (Consequential Amendments) Order 1993, SI 1993/651, art 2(1), Sch 1, para 14.

4 Inserted by the Housing Act 1988, s 124.

Registration of title

154 Registration of title.

(1) ...[1]

(2) Where the landlord's title to the dwelling-house is not registered, the landlord shall give the tenant a certificate stating that the landlord is entitled to convey the freehold or make the grant subject only to such incumbrances, rights and interests as are stated in the conveyance or grant or summarised in the certificate.

(3) Where the landlord's interest in the dwelling-house is a lease, the certificate under subsection (2) shall also state particulars of that lease and, with respect to each superior title—

(a) where it is registered, the title number;

(b) where it is not registered, whether it was investigated in the usual way on the grant of the landlord's lease.

(4) A certificate under subsection (2) shall be—

(a) in a form approved by the Chief Land Registrar, and

(b) signed by such officer of the landlord or such other person as may be approved by the Chief Land Registrar.

(5) The Chief Land Registrar shall, for the purpose of the registration of title, accept such a certificate as sufficient evidence of the facts stated in it; but if as a result he has to meet a claim against him under the [Land Registration Act 2002][2] the landlord is liable to indemnify him.

(6) ...[1]

(7) ...[1]

Amendments

1 Repealed by the Land Registration Act 2002, s 135, Sch 13.

2 Substituted by the Land Registration Act 2002, s 133, Sch 11, para 18(1), (3).

Provisions affecting future disposals

155 Repayment of discount on early disposal.

(1) A conveyance of the freehold or grant of a lease in pursuance of this Part shall contain (unless, in the case of a conveyance or grant in pursuance of the right to buy, there is no discount) a covenant binding on the secure tenant and his successors in title to the following effect.

[(2) In the case of a conveyance or grant in pursuance of the right to buy, the covenant shall be to pay the landlord such sum (if any) as the landlord may demand in accordance with section 155A on the occasion of the first relevant disposal (other than an exempted disposal) which takes place within the period of five years beginning with the conveyance or grant.

(3) In the case of a conveyance or grant in pursuance of the right to acquire on rent to mortgage terms, the covenant shall be to pay the landlord such sum

(if any) as the landlord may demand in accordance with section 155B on the occasion of the first relevant disposal (other than an exempted disposal) which takes place within the period of five years beginning with the making of the initial payment.][1]

[(3A) Where a secure tenant has served on his landlord an operative notice of delay, as defined in section 153A,—

(a) the [five years][1] referred to in subsection (2) shall begin from a date which precedes the date of the conveyance of the freehold or grant of the lease by a period equal to the time (or, if there is more than one such notice, the aggregate of the times) during which, by virtue of section 153B, any payment of rent falls to be taken into account in accordance with subsection (3) of that section; and

[(b) any reference in subsection (3) (other than paragraph (a) thereof) to the making of the initial payment shall be construed as a reference to the date which precedes that payment by the period referred to in paragraph (a) of this subsection.][2]][3]

Amendments

1 Substituted by the Housing Act 2004, s 185(1)-(3).

2 Substituted by the Leasehold Reform, Housing and Urban Development Act 1993, s 120(2).

3 Inserted by the Housing Act 1988, s 140(1), Sch 17, para 41.

[155A Amount of discount which may be demanded by landlord: right to buy

(1) For the purposes of the covenant mentioned in section 155(2), the landlord may demand such sum as he considers appropriate, up to and including the maximum amount specified in this section.

(2) The maximum amount which may be demanded by the landlord is a percentage of the price or premium paid for the first relevant disposal which is equal to the discount to which the secure tenant was entitled, where the discount is expressed as a percentage of the value which under section 127 was taken as the value of the dwelling-house at the relevant time.

(3) But for each complete year which has elapsed after the conveyance or grant and before the disposal the maximum amount which may be demanded by the landlord is reduced by one-fifth.

(4) This section is subject to section 155C.][1]

Amendments

1 Inserted by the Housing Act 2004, s 185(4).

[155B Amount of discount which may be demanded by landlord: right to acquire on rent to mortgage terms

(1) For the purposes of the covenant mentioned in section 155(3), the landlord may demand such sum as he considers appropriate, up to and including the maximum amount specified in this section.

(2) The maximum amount which may be demanded by the landlord is the discount (if any) to which the tenant was entitled on the making of—

(a) the initial payment,

(b) any interim payment made before the disposal, or

(c) the final payment if so made,

reduced, in each case, by one-fifth for each complete year which has elapsed after the making of the initial payment and before the disposal.][1]

Amendments

1 Inserted by the Housing Act 2004, s 185(4).

[155C Increase attributable to home improvements

(1) In calculating the maximum amount which may be demanded by the landlord under section 155A, such amount (if any) of the price or premium paid for the disposal which is attributable to improvements made to the dwelling-house—

(a) by the person by whom the disposal is, or is to be, made, and

(b) after the conveyance or grant and before the disposal,

shall be disregarded.

(2) The amount to be disregarded under this section shall be such amount as may be agreed between the parties or determined by the district valuer.

(3) The district valuer shall not be required by virtue of this section to make a determination for the purposes of this section unless—

(a) it is reasonably practicable for him to do so; and

(b) his reasonable costs in making the determination are paid by the person by whom the disposal is, or is to be, made.

(4) If the district valuer does not make a determination for the purposes of this section (and in default of an agreement), no amount is required to be disregarded under this section.][1]

Amendments

1 Inserted by the Housing Act 2004, s 186(1).

156 Liability to repay is a charge on the premises.

(1) The liability that may arise under the covenant required by section 155 is a charge on the dwelling-house, taking effect as if it had been created by deed expressed to be by way of legal mortgage.

[(2) Subject to subsections (2A) and (2B), the charge has priority as follows—

(a) if it secures the liability that may arise under the covenant required by section 155(2), immediately after any legal charge securing an amount advanced to the secure tenant by an approved lending institution for the purpose of enabling him to exercise the right to buy;

(b) if it secures the liability that may arise under the covenant required by section 155(3), immediately after the mortgage—

(i) which is required by section 151B (mortgage for securing redemption of landlord's share), and

(ii) which, by virtue of subsection (2) of that section, has priority immediately after any legal charge securing an amount advanced to the secure tenant by an approved lending institution for the purpose of enabling him to exercise the right to acquire on rent to mortgage terms.

(2A) The following, namely—

(a) any advance which is made otherwise than for the purpose mentioned in paragraph (a) or (b) of subsection (2) and is secured by a legal charge having priority to the charge taking effect by virtue of this section, and

(b) any further advance which is so secured,

shall rank in priority to that charge if, and only if, the landlord by written notice served on the institution concerned gives its consent; and the landlord shall so give its consent if the purpose of the advance or further advance is an approved purpose.

(2B) The landlord may at any time by written notice served on an approved lending institution postpone the charge taking effect by virtue of this section to any advance or further advance which—

(a) is made to the tenant by that institution, and

(b) is secured by a legal charge not having priority to that charge;

and the landlord shall serve such a notice if the purpose of the advance or further advance is an approved purpose.][1]

(3) …[2]

[(3A) The covenant required by section 155 (covenant for repayment of discount) does not, by virtue of its binding successors in title of the tenant, bind a person exercising rights under a charge having priority over the charge taking effect by virtue of this section, or a person deriving title under him; and a provision of the conveyance or grant, or of a collateral agreement is void in so far as it purports to authorise a forfeiture, or to impose a penalty or disability, in the event of any such person failing to comply with that covenant.][3]

(4) The approved lending institutions for the purposes of this section are—

the [Relevant Authority][4],

[an authorised deposit taker

an authorised insurer][5]

[an authorised mortgage lender.][6] …[7]

[(4ZA) In subsection (4) 'the Relevant Authority' does not include the Regulator of Social Housing but does include the Homes and Communities Agency.][8]

[(4ZB) In subsection (4) 'the Relevant Authority' also includes the Greater London Authority.][9]

[(4A) The approved purposes for the purposes of this section are—

(a) to enable the tenant to make an interim or final payment,

(b) to enable the tenant to defray, or to defray on his behalf, any of the following—

(i) the cost of any works to the dwelling-house,

(ii) any service charge payable in respect of the dwelling-house for works, whether or not to the dwelling-house, and

(iii) any service charge or other amount payable in respect of the dwelling-house for insurance, whether or not of the dwelling-house, and

(c) to enable the tenant to discharge, or to discharge on his behalf, any of the following—

(i) so much as is still outstanding of any advance or further advance which ranks in priority to the charge taking effect by virtue of this section,

(ii) any arrears of interest on such an advance or further advance, and

(iii) any costs and expenses incurred in enforcing payment of any such interest, or repayment (in whole or in part) of any such advance or further advance.

(4B) Where different parts of an advance or further advance are made for different purposes, each of those parts shall be regarded as a separate advance or further advance for the purposes of this section.][10]

(5) …[11]

(6) …[11]

Amendments

1 Substituted by the Leasehold Reform, Housing and Urban Development Act 1993, s 120(3).

2 Repealed by the Land Registration Act 2002, s 135, Sch 13.

3 Inserted by the Housing and Planning Act 1986, s 24(1), Sch 5, para 1(2).

4 Substituted by the Government of Wales Act 1998, s 140, Sch 16, paras 4, 5.

5 Substituted by the Financial Services and Markets Act 2000 (Consequential Amendments and Repeals) Order 2001, SI 2001/3649, art 299(1), (4)

6 Substituted by the Housing and Regeneration Act 2008, s 307(1)(a).

7 Repealed by the Housing Act 1996, ss 222, 227, Sch 18, para 22(1)(c), Sch 19, Pt XIII.

8 Inserted by the Housing and Regeneration Act 2008 (Consequential Provisions) Order 2010, SI 2010/866, art 4, Sch 1, paras 1, 3.

9 Inserted by the Localism Act 2011, s 195(1), Sch 19, paras 10, 15.

10 Inserted by the Leasehold Reform, Housing and Urban Development Act 1993, s 120(4).

11 Repealed by the Housing and Regeneration Act 2008, ss 307(1)(b), 321(1), Sch 16.

[156A Right of first refusal for landlord etc.

(1) A conveyance of the freehold or grant of a lease in pursuance of this Part shall contain the following covenant, which shall be binding on the secure tenant and his successors in title.

This is subject to subsection (8).

(2) The covenant shall be to the effect that, until the end of the period of ten years beginning with the conveyance or grant, there will be no relevant disposal which is not an exempted disposal, unless the prescribed conditions have been satisfied in relation to that or a previous such disposal.

(3) In subsection (2) 'the prescribed conditions' means such conditions as are prescribed by regulations under this section at the time when the conveyance or grant is made.

(4) The Secretary of State may by regulations prescribe such conditions as he considers appropriate for and in connection with conferring on—

(a) a landlord who has conveyed a freehold or granted a lease to a person ('the former tenant') in pursuance of this Part, or

(b) such other person as is determined in accordance with the regulations,

a right of first refusal to have a disposal within subsection (5) made to him for such consideration as is mentioned in section 158.

(5) The disposals within this subsection are—

(a) a reconveyance or conveyance of the dwelling-house; and

(b) a surrender or assignment of the lease.

(6) Regulations under this section may, in particular, make provision—

(a) for the former tenant to offer to make such a disposal to such person or persons as may be prescribed;

(b) for a prescribed recipient of such an offer to be able either to accept the offer or to nominate some other person as the person by whom the offer may be accepted;

(c) for the person who may be so nominated to be either a person of a prescribed description or a person whom the prescribed recipient considers, having regard to any prescribed matters, to be a more appropriate person to accept the offer;

(d) for a prescribed recipient making such a nomination to give a notification of the nomination to the person nominated, the former tenant and any other prescribed person;

(e) for authorising a nominated person to accept the offer and for determining which acceptance is to be effective where the offer is accepted by more than one person;

(f) for the period within which the offer may be accepted or within which any other prescribed step is to be, or may be, taken;

(g) for the circumstances in which the right of first refusal lapses (whether following the service of a notice to complete or otherwise) with the result that the former tenant is able to make a disposal on the open market;

(h) for the manner in which any offer, acceptance or notification is to be communicated.

(7) In subsection (6) any reference to the former tenant is a reference to the former tenant or his successor in title.

Nothing in that subsection affects the generality of subsection (4).

(8) In a case to which section 157(1) applies—

(a) the conveyance or grant may contain a covenant such as is mentioned in subsections (1) and (2) above instead of a covenant such as is mentioned in section 157(1), but

(b) it may do so only if the Secretary of State or, where the conveyance or grant is executed by a housing association within section 6A(3) or (4), the Relevant Authority consents.

(9) Consent may be given in relation to—

(a) a particular disposal, or

(b) disposals by a particular landlord or disposals by landlords generally,

and may, in any case, be given subject to conditions.

(10) Regulations under this section—

(a) may make different provision with respect to different cases or descriptions of case; and

(b) shall be made by statutory instrument which shall be subject to annulment in pursuance of a resolution of either House of Parliament.

(11) The limitation imposed by a covenant within subsection (2) (whether the covenant is imposed in pursuance of subsection (1) or (8)) is a local land charge.

(12) The Chief Land Registrar must enter in the register of title a restriction reflecting the limitation imposed by any such covenant.][1]

Amendments

1 Inserted by the Housing Act 2004, s 188(1).

157 Restriction on disposal of dwelling-houses in National Parks, etc.

(1) Where in pursuance of this Part a conveyance or grant is executed by a local authority …[1] or a housing association ('the landlord') of a dwelling-house situated in—

(a) a National Park,

(b) an area designated under [section 82 of the Countryside and Rights of Way Act 2000][2] as an area of outstanding natural beauty, or

(c) an area designated by order of the Secretary of State as a rural area,

the conveyance or grant may [(subject to section 156A(8)][3] contain a covenant limiting the freedom of the tenant (including any successor in title of his and any person deriving title under him or such a successor) to dispose of the dwelling-house in the manner specified below.

(2) The limitation is …[4] that until such time (if any) as may be notified in writing by the landlord to the tenant or a successor in title of his

[(a)][5] there will be no relevant disposal which is not an exempted disposal without the written consent of the landlord; but that consent shall not be withheld if the disposal is to a person satisfying the condition stated in subsection (3) [and—

(b) there will be no disposal by way of tenancy or licence without the written consent of the landlord unless the disposal is to a person satisfying that condition or by a person whose only or principal home is and, throughout the duration of the tenancy or licence, remains the dwelling-house][5].

(3) The condition is that the person to whom the disposal is made (or, if it is made to more than one person, at least one of them) has, throughout the period of three years immediately preceding the application for consent [or, in the case of a disposal by way of tenancy or licence, preceding the disposal][5]—

(a) had his place of work in a region designated by order of the Secretary of State which, or part of which, is comprised in the National Park or area, or

(b) had his only or principal home in such a region;

or has had the one in part or parts of that period and the other in the remainder; but the region need not have been the same throughout the period.

(4) …[4]

(5) …[4]

(6) A disposal in breach of such a covenant as is mentioned in subsection (1) is void [and, so far as it relates to disposals by way of tenancy or licence, such a covenant may be enforced by the landlord as if—

(a) the landlord were possessed of land adjacent to the house concerned; and

(b) the covenant were expressed to be made for the benefit of such adjacent land][5].

[(6A) Any reference in the preceding provisions of this section to a disposal by way of tenancy or licence does not include a reference to a relevant disposal or an exempted disposal.][5]

(7) Where such a covenant imposes the limitation specified in subsection (2), the limitation is a local land charge and the Chief Land Registrar shall enter [a restriction in the register of title reflecting the limitation][6].

(8) An order under this section—

(a) may make different provision with respect to different cases or descriptions of case, including different provision for different areas, and

(b) shall be made by statutory instrument which shall be subject to annulment in pursuance of a resolution of either House of Parliament.

Amendments

1 Repealed by the Government of Wales Act 1998, s 152, Sch 18, Pt IV.

2 Substituted by the Countryside and Rights of Way Act 2000, s 93, Sch 15, para 9.

3 Inserted by the Housing Act 2004, s 188(2)(a).

4 Repealedby the Housing Act 2004, ss 188(2)(b), (c), 266, Sch 16.

5 Inserted by the Housing Act 1988, s 126(1)-(5).

6 Substituted by the Land Registration Act 2002, s 133, Sch 11, para 18(1), (4).

158 Consideration for [disposal under section 156A][1]

[(1) The consideration for such a disposal as is mentioned in section 156A(4) shall be such amount as may be agreed between the parties, or determined by the district valuer, as being the amount which is to be taken to be the value of the dwelling-house at the time when the offer is made (as determined in accordance with regulations under that section).][1]

(2) That value shall be taken to be the price which, at that time, the interest to be reconveyed[, conveyed, surrendered or assigned][1] would realise if sold on the open market by a willing vendor, on the assumption that any liability under—

(a) the covenant required by section 155 (repayment of discount on early disposal), and

[(aa) any covenant required by paragraph 1 of Schedule 6A (obligation to redeem landlord's share where conveyance or grant executed in pursuance of right to acquire on rent to mortgage terms), and][2]

(b) any covenant required by paragraph 6 of Schedule 8 (payment for outstanding share on disposal of dwelling-house subject to shared ownership lease),

would be discharged by the vendor.

(3) If the [the offer is accepted in accordance with regulations under section 156A,][1] no payment shall be required in pursuance of any such covenant as is mentioned in subsection (2), but the consideration shall be reduced[, subject to subsection (4),][3] by such amount (if any) as, on a disposal made at the time the offer was made, being a relevant disposal which is not an exempted disposal, would fall to be paid under that covenant.

[(4) Where there is a charge on the dwelling-house having priority over the charge to secure payment of the sum due under the covenant mentioned in subsection (2), the consideration shall not be reduced under subsection (3) below the amount necessary to discharge the outstanding sum secured by the first-mentioned charge at the date of the offer to [(as determined in accordance with regulations under section 156A).][1]][3]

Amendments

1 Substituted by the Housing Act 2004, s 188(3).

2 Inserted by the Leasehold Reform, Housing and Urban Development Act 1993, s 187(1), Sch 21, para 15.

3 Inserted by the Housing and Planning Act 1986, s 24(1), Sch 5, para 1(3).

159 Relevant disposals.

(1) A disposal, whether of the whole or part of the dwelling-house, is a relevant disposal for the purposes of this Part if it is—

(a) a further conveyance of the freehold or an assignment of the lease, or

(b) the grant of a lease (other than a mortgage term) for a term of more than 21 years otherwise than at a rack rent.

(2) For the purposes of subsection (1)(b) it shall be assumed—

(a) that any option to renew or extend a lease or sub-lease, whether or not forming part of a series of options, is exercised, and

(b) that any option to terminate a lease or sub-lease is not exercised.

160 Exempted disposals.

(1) A disposal is an exempted disposal for the purposes of this Part if—

(a) it is a disposal of the whole of the dwelling-house and a further conveyance of the freehold or an assignment of the lease and the person or each of the persons to whom it is made is a qualifying person (as defined in subsection (2));

(b) it is a vesting of the whole of the dwelling-house in a person taking under a will or on an intestacy;

[(c) it is a disposal of the whole of the dwelling-house in pursuance of any such order as is mentioned in subsection (3);][1]

(d) it is a compulsory disposal (as defined in section 161); or

(e) it is a disposal of property consisting of land included in the dwelling-house by virtue of section 184 (land let with or used for the purposes of the dwelling-house).

(2) For the purposes of subsection (1)(a), a person is a qualifying person in relation to a disposal if—

(a) he is the person, or one of the persons, by whom the disposal is made,

(b) he is the spouse or a former spouse[, or the civil partner or a former civil partner,][2] of that person, or one of those persons, or

(c) he is a member of the family of that person, or one of those persons, and has resided with him throughout the period of twelve months ending with the disposal.

[(3) The orders referred to in subsection (1)(c) are orders under—

(a) section 24 or 24A of the Matrimonial Causes Act 1973 (property adjustment orders or orders for the sale of property in connection with matrimonial proceedings),

(b) section 2 of the Inheritance (Provision for Family and Dependants) Act 1975 (orders as to financial provision to be made from estate),

(c) …[3]

(d) paragraph 1 of Schedule 1 to the Children Act 1989 (orders for financial relief against parents)[, or

(e) Part 2 or 3 of Schedule 5, or paragraph 9 of Schedule 7, to the Civil Partnership Act 2004 (property adjustment orders, or orders for the sale of property, in connection with civil partnership proceedings or after overseas dissolution of civil partnership, etc.).][4]][5]

Amendments

1 Substituted by the Housing Act 1996, s 222, Sch 18, para 15(1), (2).

2 Inserted by the Civil Partnership Act 2004, s 81, Sch 8, para 18.

3 Repealed by the Civil Partnership Act 2004, s 261(4), Sch 30.

4 Inserted by the Civil Partnership Act 2004, s 81, Sch 8, para 30.

5 Inserted by the Housing Act 1996, s 222, Sch 18, para 15(1), (3).

161 Meaning of 'compulsory disposal'.

In this Part a 'compulsory disposal' means a disposal of property which is acquired compulsorily, or is acquired by a person who has made or would have made, or for whom another person has made or would have made, a compulsory purchase order authorising its compulsory purchase for the purposes for which it is acquired.

162 Exempted disposals which end liability under covenants.

Where there is a relevant disposal which is an exempted disposal by virtue of section 160(1)(d) or (e) (compulsory disposals or disposals of land let with or used for purposes of dwelling-house)—

(a) the covenant required by section 155 (repayment of discount on early disposal) is not binding on the person to whom the disposal is made or any successor in title of his and that covenant and the charge taking effect by virtue of section 156 cease to apply in relation to the property disposed of, and

[(aa) the covenant required by section 156A (right of first refusal for landlord etc.) is not binding on the person to whom the disposal is made or any successor in title of his, and that covenant ceases to apply in relation to the property disposed of, and][1]

(b) any such covenant as is mentioned in section 157 (restriction on disposal of dwelling-houses in National Parks, etc.) ceases to apply in relation to the property disposed of.

Amendments

1 Inserted by the Housing Act 2004, s 188(4).

163 Treatment of options.

(1) For the purposes of this Part the grant of an option enabling a person to call for a relevant disposal which is not an exempted disposal shall be treated as such a disposal made to him.

(2) For the purposes of section 157(2) (requirement of consent to disposal of dwelling-house in National Park, etc.) a consent to such a grant shall be treated as a consent to a disposal in pursuance of the option.

[163A Treatment of deferred resale agreements for purposes of section 155

(1) If a secure tenant or his successor in title enters into an agreement within subsection (3), any liability arising under the covenant required by section 155 shall be determined as if a relevant disposal which is not an exempted disposal had occurred at the appropriate time.

(2) In subsection (1) 'the appropriate time' means—

(a) the time when the agreement is entered into, or

(b) if it was made before the beginning of the discount repayment period, immediately after the beginning of that period.

(3) An agreement is within this subsection if it is an agreement between the secure tenant or his successor in title and any other person—

(a) which is made (expressly or impliedly) in contemplation of, or in connection with, the tenant exercising, or having exercised, the right to buy,

(b) which is made before the end of the discount repayment period, and

(c) under which a relevant disposal (other than an exempted disposal) is or may be required to be made to any person after the end of that period.

(4) Such an agreement is within subsection (3)—

(a) whether or not the date on which the disposal is to take place is specified in the agreement, and

(b) whether or not any requirement to make the disposal is or may be made subject to the fulfilment of any condition.

(5) The Secretary of State may by order provide—

(a) for subsection (1) to apply to agreements of any description specified in the order in addition to those within subsection (3);

(b) for subsection (1) not to apply to agreements of any description so specified to which it would otherwise apply.

(6) An order under subsection (5)—

(a) may make different provision with respect to different cases or descriptions of case; and

(b) shall be made by statutory instrument which shall be subject to annulment in pursuance of a resolution of either House of Parliament.

(7) In this section—

'agreement' includes arrangement;

'the discount repayment period' means the period of three or five years that applies for the purposes of section 155(2) or (3) (depending on whether the tenant's notice under section 122 was given before or on or after the date of the coming into force of section 185 of the Housing Act 2004).][1]

Amendments

1 Inserted by the Housing Act 2004, s 187.

Powers of Secretary of State

164 Secretary of State's general power to intervene.

(1) The Secretary of State may use his powers under this section where it appears to him that tenants generally, a tenant or tenants of a particular landlord, or tenants of a description of landlords, have or may have difficulty in exercising effectively and expeditiously the right to buy or the [right to acquire on rent to mortgage terms][1].

(2) The powers may be exercised only after he has given the landlord or landlords notice in writing of his intention to do so and while the notice is in force.

(3) Such a notice shall be deemed to be given 72 hours after it has been sent.

(4) Where a notice under this section has been given to a landlord or landlords, no step taken by the landlord or any of the landlords while the notice is in force or before it was given has any effect in relation to the exercise by a secure tenant of the right to buy, [or the right to acquire on rent to mortgage terms][1], except in so far as the notice otherwise provides.

(5) While a notice under this section is in force the Secretary of State may do all such things as appear to him necessary or expedient to enable secure tenants of the landlord or landlords to which the notice was given to exercise the right to buy, [and the right to acquire on rent to mortgage terms][1]; and he is not bound to take the steps which the landlord would have been bound to take under this Part.

(6) …[2]

Amendments

1 Substituted by the Leasehold Reform, Housing and Urban Development Act 1993, s 187(1), Sch 21, para 16.

2 Repealed by the Leasehold Reform, Housing and Urban Development Act 1993, s 187(2), Sch 22.

165 Vesting orders for purposes of s. 164.

(1) For the purpose of conveying a freehold or granting a lease in the exercise of his powers under section 164 the Secretary of State may execute a document, to be known as a vesting order, containing such provisions as he may determine; and for the purposes of stamp duty the vesting order shall be treated as a document executed by the landlord.

(2) A vesting order has the like effect, except so far as it otherwise provides, as a conveyance or grant duly executed in pursuance of this Part, and, in particular, binds both the landlord and its successors in title and the tenant and his successors in title (including any person deriving title under him or them) to the same extent as if the covenants contained in it and expressed to be made on their behalf had been entered into by them.

(3) If the landlord's title to the dwelling-house in respect of which a vesting order is made is not registered, the vesting order shall contain a certificate stating that the freehold conveyed or grant made by it is subject only to such incumbrances, rights and interests as are stated elsewhere in the vesting order or summarised in the certificate.

(4) The Chief Land Registrar shall, on a vesting order being presented to him, register the tenant as proprietor of the title concerned; and if the title has not previously been registered—

(a) he shall so register him with an absolute title, or as the case may require a good leasehold title, and

(b) he shall, for the purpose of the registration, accept any such certificate as is mentioned in subsection (3) as sufficient evidence of the facts stated in it.

(5) ...[1]

(6) If a person suffers loss in consequence of a registration under this section in circumstances in which he would have been entitled to be indemnified under [Schedule 8 to the Land Registration Act 2002][2] by the Chief Land Registrar had the registration of the tenant as proprietor of the title been effected otherwise than under this section, he is instead entitled to be indemnified by the Secretary of State and section 166(4) of this Act (recovery of Secretary of State's costs from landlord) applies accordingly.

Amendments

1 Repealed by the Land Registration Act 1988, s 2, Schedule.

2 Substituted by the Land Registration Act 2002, s 133, Sch 11, para 18(1), (5).

166 Other provisions supplementary to s. 164.

(1) A notice under section 164 may be withdrawn by a further notice in writing, either completely or in relation to a particular landlord or a particular case or description of case.

(2) The further notice may give such directions as the Secretary of State may think fit for the completion of a transaction begun before the further notice was given; and such directions are binding on the landlord, and may require the taking of steps different from those which the landlord would have been required to take if the Secretary of State's powers under section 164 had not been used.

(3) Where in consequence of the exercise of his powers under section 164 the Secretary of State receives sums due to a landlord, he may retain them while a notice under that section is in force in relation to the landlord and is not bound to account to the landlord for interest accruing on them.

(4) Where the Secretary of State exercises his powers under section 164 with respect to secure tenants of a landlord, he may—

(a) calculate, in such manner and on such assumptions as he may determine, the costs incurred by him in doing so, and

(b) certify a sum as representing those costs;

and a sum so certified is a debt from the landlord to the Secretary of State payable on a date specified in the certificate, together with interest from that date at a rate so specified.

(5) sums payable under subsection (4) may, without prejudice to any other method of recovery, be recovered from the landlord by the withholding of sums due from the Secretary of State, including sums payable to the landlord and received by the Secretary of State in consequence of his exercise of his powers under section 164.

(6) …[1]

Amendments

1 Repealed by the Leasehold Reform, Housing and Urban Development Act 1993, s 187(2), Sch 22.

167 Power to give directions as to covenants and conditions.

(1) Where it appears to the Secretary of State that, if covenants or conditions of any kind were included in conveyances or grants of dwelling-houses of any description executed in pursuance of this Part—

(a) the conveyances would not conform with Parts I and II of Schedule 6, or

(b) the grants would not conform with Parts I and III of that Schedule [or

(c) in the case of conveyances or grants executed in pursuance of the right to acquire on rent to mortgage terms, the conveyances or grants would not conform with Schedule 6A,][1]

he may direct landlords generally, landlords of a particular description or particular landlords not to include covenants or conditions of that kind in such conveyances or grants executed on or after a date specified in the direction.

(2) A direction under this section may be varied or withdrawn by a subsequent direction.

Amendments

1 Inserted by the Leasehold Reform, Housing and Urban Development Act 1993, s 187(1), Sch 21, para 17.

168 Effect of direction under s. 167 on existing covenants and conditions

(1) If a direction under section 167 so provides, the provisions of this section shall apply in relation to a covenant or condition which—

(a) was included in a conveyance or grant executed before the date specified in the direction, and

(b) could not have been so included if the conveyance or grant had been executed on or after that date.

(2) The covenant or condition shall be discharged or (if the direction so provides) modified, as from the specified date, to such extent or in such manner as may be provided by the direction; and the discharge or modification is binding on all persons entitled or capable of becoming entitled to the benefit of the covenant or condition.

(3) The landlord by whom the conveyance or grant was executed shall, within such period as may be specified in the direction—

(a) serve on the person registered as the proprietor of the dwelling-house, and on any person registered as the proprietor of a charge affecting the dwelling-house, a written notice informing him of the discharge or modification, and

(b) on behalf of the person registered as the proprietor of the dwelling-house, apply to the Chief Land Registrar (and pay the appropriate fee) for notice of the discharge or modification to be entered in the register.

(4) …[1]

(5) …[2]

Amendments

1 Repealed by the Land Registration Act 1988, s 2, Schedule.

2 Repealed by the Land Registration Act 2002, s 135, Sch 13.

169 Power to obtain information, etc.

(1) Where it appears to the Secretary of State necessary or expedient for the purpose of determining whether his powers under section 164 or 166 (general power to intervene) or section 167 or 168 (power to give directions as to covenants and conditions) are exercisable, or for or in connection with the exercise of those powers, he may by notice in writing to a landlord require it—

(a) at such time and at such place as may be specified in the notice, to produce any document, or

(b) within such period as may be so specified or such longer period as the Secretary of State may allow, to furnish a copy of any document or supply any information.

(2) Any officer of the landlord designated in the notice for that purpose or having custody or control of the document or in a position to give that information shall, without instructions from the landlord, take all reasonable steps to ensure that the notice is complied with.

(3) In this section references to a landlord include—

(a) a landlord by whom a conveyance or grant was executed in pursuance of this Part ...[1]

(b) ...[1]

Amendments

1 Repealed by the Leasehold Reform, Housing and Urban Development Act 1993, s 187(2), Sch 22.

170 Power to give assistance in connection with legal proceedings.

(1) This section applies to—

(a) proceedings under this Part or to determine a question arising under or in connection with this Part, and

(b) proceedings to determine a question arising under or in connection with a conveyance or grant executed in pursuance of this Part,

other than proceedings to determine a question as to the value of a dwelling-house (or part of a dwelling-house).

(2) A party or prospective party to proceedings or prospective proceedings to which this section applies, who—

(a) has claimed to exercise or has exercised the right to buy or the [right to acquire on rent to mortgage terms][1], or

(b) is a successor in title of a person who has exercised either of those rights,

may apply to the Secretary of State for assistance under this section.

(3) The Secretary of State may grant the application if he thinks fit to do so on the ground—

(a) that the case raises a question of principle, or

(b) that it is unreasonable having regard to the complexity of the case, or to any other matter, to expect the applicant to deal with it without such assistance,

or by reason of any other special consideration.

(4) Assistance by the Secretary of State under this section may include—

(a) giving advice.

(b) procuring or attempting to procure the settlement of the matter in dispute,

(c) arranging for the giving of advice or assistance by a solicitor or counsel,

(d) arranging for representation by a solicitor or counsel, including such assistance as is usually given by a solicitor or counsel in the steps preliminary or incidental to any proceedings, or in arriving at or giving effect to a compromise to avoid or bring to an end any proceedings, and

(e) any other form of assistance which the Secretary of State may consider appropriate;

but paragraph (d) does not affect the law and practice regulating the descriptions of persons who may appear in, conduct, defend and address the court in any proceedings.

(5) In so far as expenses are incurred by the Secretary of State in providing the applicant with assistance under this section, the recovery of those expenses (as taxed or assessed in such manner as may be prescribed by rules of court) shall constitute a first charge for the benefit of the Secretary of State—

(a) on any costs which (whether by virtue of a judgment or order of a court or an agreement or otherwise) are payable to the applicant by any other person in respect of the matter in connection with which the assistance was given, and

(b) so far as relates to any costs, on his rights under any compromise or settlement arrived at in connection with that matter to avoid or bring to an end any proceedings;

but subject to any charge [imposed by [section 25 of the Legal Aid, Sentencing and Punishment of Offenders Act 2012][2] and any provision in, or made under, Part I of that Act for the payment of any sum to the [Lord Chancellor][2]][3].

(6) References in this section to a solicitor include the Treasury Solicitor.

Amendments

1 Substituted by the Leasehold Reform, Housing and Urban Development Act 1993, s 187(1), Sch 21, para 18.

2 Substituted by the Legal Aid, Sentencing and Punishment of Offenders Act 2012, s 39(1), Sch 5, para 33.

3 Substituted by the Access to Justice Act 1999, s 24, Sch 4, para 37.

Power to extend right to buy, etc.

171 Power to extend right to buy, etc.

(1) The Secretary of State may by order provide that, where there are in a dwelling-house let on a secure tenancy one or more interest to which this

section applies, this Part and Part IV (secure tenancies) have effect with such modifications as are specified in the order.

(2) This section applies to an interest held by—

a local authority,

a new town corporation,

[a housing action trust][1]

an urban development corporation,

[a Mayoral development corporation,][2]

...[3]

The [[Regulator of Social Housing][4] or Scottish Homes][5], [a non-profit registered provider of social housing][6] or

a [registered social landlord][7],

which is immediately superior to the interest of the landlord or to another interest to which this section applies.

(3) An order under this section—

(a) may make different provision with respect to different cases or descriptions of case;

(b) may contain such consequential, supplementary or transitional provisions as appear to the Secretary of State to be necessary or expedient; and

(c) shall be made by statutory instrument which shall be subject to annulment in pursuance of a resolution of either House of Parliament.

Amendments

1 Inserted by the Housing Act 1988, s 83(1), (5)

2 Inserted by the Localism Act 2011, s 222, Sch 22, paras 9, 13

3 Repealed by the Government of Wales Act 1998, s 152, Sch 18, Pt IV.

4 Substituted by the Housing and Regeneration Act 2008 (Consequential Provisions) Order 2010, SI 2010/866, art 5, Sch 2, paras 15, 27(a).

5 Substituted by the Government of Wales Act 1998, s 140, Sch 16, paras 4, 13.

6 Inserted by the Housing and Regeneration Act 2008 (Consequential Provisions) Order 2010, SI 2010/866, art 5, Sch 2, paras 15, 27(b).

7 Substituted by the Housing Act 1996 (Consequential Provisions) Order 1996, SI 1996/2325, art 5(1), Sch 2, para 14(1), (15)

[Preservation of right to buy on disposal to private sector landlord

171A Cases in which right to buy is preserved.

(1) The provisions of this Part continue to apply where a person ceases to be a secure tenant of a dwelling-house by reason of the disposal by the landlord

of an interest in the dwelling-house [in England][1] to a person who is not an authority or body within section 80 (the landlord condition for secure tenancies).

(2) In the following provisions of this Part—

(a) references to the preservation of the right to buy and to a person having the preserved right to buy are to the continued application of the provisions of this Part by virtue of this section and to a person in relation to whom those provisions so apply;

(b) 'qualifying disposal' means a disposal in relation to which this section applies, and

(c) 'former secure tenant' and the 'former landlord' are the persons mentioned in subsection (1).

(3) This section does not apply—

(a) where the former landlord was a person against whom the right to buy could not be exercised by virtue of paragraph 1, 2 or 3 of Schedule 5 (charities and certain housing associations), or

(b) in such other cases as may be excepted from the operation of this section by order of the Secretary of State.

(4) Orders under subsection (3)(b)—

(a) may relate to particular disposals and may make different provision with respect to different cases or descriptions of case, including different provision for different areas, and

(b) shall be made by statutory instrument which shall be subject to annulment in pursuance of a resolution of either House of Parliament.][2]

Amendments

1 Inserted by the Abolition of the Right to Buy and Associated Rights (Wales) Act 2018 (Consequential Amendments and Savings Provisions) Regulations 2019, SI 2019/110, reg 3(l).

2 Inserted by the Housing and Planning Act 1986, s 8(1)

[171B Extent of preserved right: qualifying persons and dwelling-houses.

(1) A person to whom this section applies has the preserved right to buy [a relevant dwelling-house in England][1] so long as he occupies the relevant dwelling-house as his only or principal home, subject to the following provisions of this Part.

[(1A) A person to whom this section applies ceases to have the preserved right to buy if the tenancy of a relevant dwelling-house becomes a demoted tenancy by virtue of a demotion order under section 6A of the Housing Act 1988.][2]

(2) References in this Part to a 'qualifying person' and 'qualifying dwelling-house', in relation to the preserved right to buy, are to a person who has that right and to a dwelling-house in relation to which a person has that right.

(3) The following are the persons to whom this section applies—

(a) the former secure tenant, or in the case of a joint tenancy, each of them;

(b) a qualifying successor as defined in subsection (4); and

(c) a person to whom a tenancy of a dwelling-house is granted jointly with a person who has the preserved right to buy in relation to that dwelling-house.

(4) The following are qualifying successors for this purpose—

[(a) where the former secure tenancy was not a joint tenancy and, immediately before his death, the former secure tenant was tenant under an assured tenancy of a dwelling-house in relation to which he had the preserved right to buy, a member of the former secure tenant's family who acquired that assured tenancy under the will or intestacy of the former secure tenant [or in whom that assured tenancy vested under section 17 of the Housing Act 1988 (statutory succession to assured tenancy)][3];

(aa) where the former secure tenancy was not a joint tenancy, a member of the former secure tenant's family to whom the former secure tenant assigned his assured tenancy of a dwelling-house in relation to which, immediately before the assignment, he had the preserved right to buy;][4]

(b) a person who becomes the tenant of a dwelling-house in pursuance of—

(i) a property adjustment order undersection 23A or 24 of the Matrimonial Causes Act 1973, or

(ii) an order under Schedule 1 to the Matrimonial Homes Act 1983 [or Schedule 7 to the Family Law Act 1996][5] transferring the tenancy, [or

(iii) a property adjustment order under section 17(1) of the Matrimonial and Family Proceedings Act 1984 (property adjustment orders after overseas divorce, &c.), or

(iv) an order under paragraph 1 of Schedule 1 to the Children Act 1989 (orders for financial relief against parents),][6] [or

(v) an order under Part 2 of Schedule 5, or a property adjustment order under paragraph 9(2) or (3) of Schedule 7, to the Civil Partnership Act 2004 (property adjustment orders in connection with civil partnership proceedings or after overseas dissolution of civil partnership, etc.),][7]

in place of a person who had the preserved right to buy in relation to that dwelling-house.

(5) The relevant dwelling-house is in the first instance—

(a) in relation to a person within paragraph (a) subsection (3), the dwelling-house which was the subject of the qualifying disposal;

(b) in relation to a person within paragraph (b) of that subsection, the dwelling-house of which he became the statutory tenant or tenant as mentioned in [subsection (4)][8];

(c) in relation to a person within paragraph (c) of subsection (3), the dwelling-house of which he became a joint tenant as mentioned in that paragraph.

(6) If a person having the preserved right to buy becomes the tenant of another dwelling-house [in England][1] in place of the relevant dwelling-house (whether the new dwelling-house is entirely different or partly or substantially the same as the previous dwelling-house) and the landlord is the same person as the landlord of the previous dwelling-house or, where that landlord was a company, is a connected company, the new dwelling-house becomes the relevant dwelling-house for the purposes of the preserved right to buy.

For this purpose 'connected company' means a subsidiary or holding company within the meaning of [section 1159 of the Companies Act 2006][9].

(7) …[10]][11]

Amendments

1 Inserted by the Abolition of the Right to Buy and Associated Rights (Wales) Act 2018 (Consequential Amendments and Savings Provisions) Regulations 2019, SI 2019/110, reg 3(m).

2 Inserted by the Anti-social Behaviour Act 2003, s 14(5), Sch 1, para 2(1), (3).

3 Inserted by the Housing Act 1996, s 222, Sch 18, para 26(1)(a).

4 Substituted by the Housing Act 1988, s 127(1).

5 Inserted by the Family Law Act 1996, s 66(1), Sch 8, para 56.

6 Inserted by the Housing Act 1996, s 222, Sch 18, para 16.

7 Inserted by the Civil Partnership Act 2004, s 81, Sch 8, para 31.

8 Substituted by the Housing Act 1996, s 222, Sch 18, para 26(1)(b).

9 Substituted by the Companies Act 2006 (Consequential Amendments, Transitional Provisions and Savings) Order 2009, SI 2009/1941, art 2(1), Sch 1, para 62(1), (5).

10 Repealed by the Abolition of the Right to Buy and Associated Rights (Wales) Act 2018, s 6(2)(a).

11 Inserted by the Housing and Planning Act 1986, s 8(1).

[171C Modifications of this Part in relation to preserved right.

(1) Where the right to buy is preserved, the provisions of this Part have effect subject to such exceptions, adaptations and other modifications as may be prescribed by regulations made by the Secretary of State.

(2) The regulations may in particular provide—

(a) that paragraphs [1, 3 and][1] 5 to 11 of Schedule 5 (certain exceptions to the right to buy) do not apply;

(b) ...[2]

(c) that the provisions of this Part relating to the [right to acquire on rent to mortgage terms][3] do not apply; and

(d) that the landlord is not required to but may include a covenant for the repayment of discount, provided its terms are no more onerous than those of the covenant provided for in section 155.

(3) The prescribed exceptions, adaptations and other modifications shall take the form of textual amendments of the provisions of this Part as they apply in cases where the right to buy is preserved; and the first regulations, and any subsequent consolidating regulations, shall set out the provisions of this Part as they so apply.

(4) The regulations—

(a) may make different provision for different cases or descriptions of case, including different provision for different areas,

(b) may contain such incidental, supplementary and transitional provisions as the Secretary of State considers appropriate, and

(c) shall be made by statutory instrument which shall be subject to annulment in pursuance of a resolution of either House of Parliament.

[(5) The disapplication by the regulations of paragraph 1 of Schedule 5 shall not be taken to authorise any action on the part of a charity which would conflict with the trusts of the charity.][1]][4]

Amendments

1 Inserted by the Housing Act 1988, s 127(2), (3).

2 Repealed by the Leasehold Reform, Housing and Urban Development Act 1993, s 187(2), Sch 22.

3 Substituted by the Leasehold Reform, Housing and Urban Development Act 1993, s 187(1), Sch 21, para 19.

4 Inserted by the Housing and Planning Act 1986, s 8(1).

[171D Subsequent dealings: disposal of landlord's interest in qualifying dwelling-house.

(1) The disposal by the landlord of an interest in the qualifying dwelling-house, whether his whole interest or a lesser interest, does not affect the preserved right to buy, unless—

(a) as a result of the disposal an authority or body within section 80(1) (the landlord condition for secure tenancies) becomes the landlord of the qualifying person or persons, or

(b) paragraph 6 of Schedule 9A applies (effect of failure to register entry protecting preserved right to buy),

in which case the right to buy ceases to be preserved.

(2) The disposal by the landlord of a qualifying dwelling-house of less than his whole interest as landlord of the dwelling-house, or in part of it, requires the consent of the [Secretary of State][1], unless the disposal is to the qualifying person or persons.

[(2ZA) Subsection (2) does not apply to a disposal of land by a private registered provider of social housing [or by a registered social landlord][2].][3]

[(2A) …[4]][5]

(3) Consent may be given in relation to a particular disposal or generally in relation to disposals of a particular description and may, in either case, be given subject to conditions.

(4) A disposal made without the consent required by subsection (2) is void, except in a case where, by reason of a failure to make the entries on the land register or land charges register required by Schedule 9A, the preserved right to buy does not bind the person to whom the disposal is made.][6]

Amendments

1 Substituted by the Abolition of the Right to Buy and Associated Rights (Wales) Act 2018 (Consequential Amendments and Savings Provisions) Regulations 2019, SI 2019/110, reg 3(n)(i).

2 Inserted by the Regulation of Registered Social Landlords (Wales) Act 2018, s 13(1).

3 Inserted by the Housing and Planning Act 2016, s 92, Sch 4, para 1(1), (2).

4 Repealed by the Abolition of the Right to Buy and Associated Rights (Wales) Act 2018 (Consequential Amendments and Savings Provisions) Regulations 2019, SI 2019/110, reg 3(n)(ii).

5 Inserted by the Housing and Regeneration Act 2008, s 191(1)(b).

6 Inserted by the Housing and Planning Act 1986, s 8(1).

[171E Subsequent dealings: termination of landlord's interest in qualifying dwelling-house.

(1) On the termination of the landlord's interest in the qualifying dwelling-house—

(a) on the occurrence of an event determining his estate or interest, or by re-entry on a breach of condition or forfeiture, or

(b) where the interest is a leasehold interest, by notice given by him or a superior landlord, on the expiry or surrender of the term, or otherwise (subject to subsection (2)),

the right to buy ceases to be preserved.

(2) The termination of the landlord's interest by merger on his acquiring a superior interest, or on the acquisition by another person of the landlord's interest together with a superior interest, does not affect the preserved right to buy, unless—

(a) as a result of the acquisition an authority or body within section 80(1) (the landlord condition for secure tenancies) becomes the landlord of the qualifying person or persons, or

(b) paragraph 6 of Schedule 9A applies (effect of failure to register entry protecting preserved right to buy),

in which case the right to buy ceases to be preserved.

(3) Where the termination of the landlord's interest as mentioned in subsection (1) is caused by the act or omission of the landlord, a qualifying person who is thereby deprived of the preserved right to buy is entitled to be compensated by him.][1]

Amendments

1 Inserted by the Housing and Planning Act 1986, s 8(1)

[171F Subsequent dealings: transfer of qualifying person to alternative accommodation.

The court shall not order a qualifying person to give up possession of the qualifying dwelling-house in pursuance of section 98(1)(a) of the Rent Act 1977 [or on Ground 9 in Schedule 2 to the Housing Act 1988][1] (suitable alternative accommodation) unless the court is satisfied—

(a) that the preserved right to buy will, by virtue of section 171B(6) (accommodation with same landlord or connected company), continue to be exercisable in relation to the dwelling-house offered by way of alternative accommodation and that the interest of the landlord in the new dwelling-house will be—

(i) where the new dwelling-house is a house, not less than the interest of the landlord in the existing dwelling-house, or

(ii) where the new dwelling-house is a flat, not less than the interest of the landlord in the existing dwelling-house or a term of years of which 80 years or more remain unexpired, whichever is the less; or

(b) that the landlord of the new dwelling-house will be an authority or body within section 80(1) (the landlord condition for secure tenancies).][2]

Amendments

1 Inserted by the Housing Act 1988, s 140(1), Sch 17, para 42.

2 Inserted by the Housing and Planning Act 1986, s 8(1).

[171G Land registration and related matters.

Schedule 9A has effect with respect to registration of title and related matters arising in connection with the preservation of the right to buy.][1]

Amendments

1 Inserted by the Housing and Planning Act 1986, s 8(1).

[171H Disposal after notice claiming to exercise right to buy, etc.

(1) Where notice has been given in respect of a dwelling-house claiming to exercise the right to buy ...[1] and before the completion of the exercise of that right the dwelling-house is the subject of—

(a) a qualifying disposal, or

(b) a disposal to which section 171D(1)(a) or 171E(2)(a) applies (disposal to authority or body satisfying landlord condition for secure tenancies),

all parties shall, subject to subsection (2), be in the same position as if the disponee had become the landlord before the notice was given and had been given that notice and any further notice given by the tenant to the landlord and had taken all steps which the landlord had taken.

(2) If the circumstances after the disposal differ in any material respect, as for example where—

(a) the interest of the disponee in the dwelling-house after the disposal differs from that of the disponor before the disposal, or

(b) ...[1]

(c) any of the provisions of Schedule 5 (exceptionsto the right to buy) becomes or ceases to be applicable,

all those concerned shall, as soon as practicable after the disposal, take all such steps (whether by way of amending or withdrawing and re-serving any notice or extending any period or otherwise) as may be requisite for the purpose of securing that all parties are, as nearly as may be, in the same position as they would have been if those circumstances had obtained before the disposal.][2]

Amendments

1 Repealed by the Leasehold Reform, Housing and Urban Development Act 1993, s 187(2), Sch 22.

2 Inserted by the Housing and Planning Act 1986, s 8(1).

Modifications of Leasehold Reform Act 1967 in relation to leases granted under this Part

172 Exclusion of leases where landlord is housing association and freeholder is a charity.

(1) Part I of the Leasehold Reform Act 1967 (enfranchisement and extension of long leaseholds) does not apply where, in the case of a tenancy or sub-

tenancy to which this section applies, the landlord is a housing association and the freehold is owned by a body of persons or trust established for charitable purposes only.

(2) This section applies to a tenancy created by the grant of a lease in pursuance of this Part of a dwelling-house which is a house.

(3) Where Part I of the 1967 Act applies as if there had been a single tenancy granted for a term beginning at the same time as the term under a tenancy falling within subsection (2) and expiring at the same time as the term under a later tenancy, this section also applies to that later tenancy.

(4) This section applies to any sub-tenancy directly or indirectly derived out of a tenancy falling within subsection (2) or (3).

173 ...[1]

Amendments

1 Repealed by the Statute Law (Repeals) Act 1998, s 1(1), Sch 1, Pt X, Group 5.

174 Leases granted under this Part to be treated as long leases at a low rent.

For the purposes of Part I of the Leasehold Reform Act 1967 (enfranchisement and extension of long leaseholds)—

(a) a tenancy created by the grant of a lease in pursuance of this part of a dwelling-house which is a house shall be treated as being a long tenancy notwithstanding that it is granted for a term of 21 years or less, ...[1]

(b) ...[1]

Amendments

1 Repealed by the Statute Law (Repeals) Act 1998, s 1(1), Sch 1, Pt X, Group 5.

175 Determination of price payable

(1) Where, in the case of a tenancy or sub-tenancy to which this section applies, the tenant exercises his right to acquire the freehold under Part I of the Leasehold Reform Act 1967, the price payable for the dwelling-house shall be determined in accordance with section 9(1A) of that Act notwithstanding that [the circumstances specified in that section do not apply][1].

(2) This section applies to a tenancy created by the grant of a lease in pursuance of this Part of a dwelling-house which is a house.

(3) Where Part I of the 1967 Act applies as if there had been a single tenancy granted for a term beginning at the same time as the term under a tenancy falling within subsection (2) and expiring at the same time as the term under a later tenancy, this section also applies to that later tenancy.

(4) This section applies to any sub-tenancy directly or indirectly derived out of a tenancy falling within subsection (2) or (3).

(5) This section also applies to a tenancy granted in substitution for a tenancy or sub-tenancy falling within subsections (2) to (4) in pursuance of Part I of the 1967 Act.

Amendments

1 Substituted by the References to Rating (Housing) Regulations 1990, SI 1990/434, reg 2, Schedule, para 20.

Supplementary provisions

176 Notices

(1) The Secretary of State may by regulations prescribe the form of any notice under this Part and the particulars to be contained in the notice.

(2) Where the form of, and the particulars to be contained in, a notice under this Part are so prescribed, a tenant who proposes to claim, or has claimed, to exercise the right to buy may request the landlord to supply him with a form for use in giving such notice; and the landlord shall do so within seven days of the request.

(3) A notice under this Part may be served by sending it by post.

(4) Where the landlord is a housing association, a notice to be served by the tenant on the landlord under this Part may be served by leaving it at, or sending it to, the principal office of the association or the office of the association with which the tenant usually deals.

(5) Regulations under this section—

(a) may make different provision with respect to different cases or descriptions of case, including different provision for different areas, and

(b) shall be made by statutory instrument.

177 Errors and omissions in notices

(1) A notice served by a tenant under this Part is not invalidated by an error in, or omission from, the particulars which are required by regulations under section 176 to be contained in the notice.

(2) Where as a result of such an error or omission—

(a) the landlord has mistakenly admitted or denied the right to buy or the [right to acquire on rent to mortgage terms][1] in a notice under section 124 or 146, or

(b) the landlord …[2] has formed a mistaken opinion as to any matter required to be stated in a notice by any of the provisions mentioned in sub-section (3) and has stated that opinion in the notice, the parties shall, as soon as practicable after they become aware of the mistake, take all such steps (whether by way of amending, withdrawing or re-serving any notice or extending any period or otherwise) as may be requisite for the propose of securing that all parties are, as nearly as may be, in the same position as they would have been if the mistake had not been made.

(3) The provisions referred to in subsection (2)(b) are—

section 125 (notice of purchase price, etc.),

...[2]

[section 146 (landlord's notice admitting or denying right to acquire on rent to mortgage terms).][1]

...[2]

(4) Subsection (2) does not apply where the tenant has exercised the right to which the notice relates before the parties become aware of the mistake.

Amendments

1 Substituted by the Leasehold Reform, Housing and Urban Development Act 1993, s 187(1), Sch 21, para 20.

2 Repealed by the Leasehold Reform, Housing and Urban Development Act 1993, s 187(2), Sch 22.

[178 Costs

An agreement between the landlord and a tenant claiming to exercise—

(a) the right to buy,

(b) the right to acquire on rent to mortgage terms, or

(c) any such right as is mentioned in paragraph 2(1) or 6(1) of Schedule 6A (redemption of landlord's share: right to make final or interim payment),

is void in so far as it purports to oblige the tenant to bear any part of the costs incurred by the landlord in connection with the tenant's exercise of that right.][1]

Amendments

1 Substituted by the Leasehold Reform, Housing and Urban Development Act 1993, s 187(1), Sch 21, para 21.

179 Provisions restricting right to buy, etc. of no effect.

(1) A provision of a lease held by the landlord or a superior landlord, or of an agreement (whenever made), is void in so far as it purports to prohibit or restrict—

(a) the grant of a lease in pursuance of the right to buy or the [right to acquire on rent to mortgage terms][1], or

(b) the subsequent disposal (whether by way of assignment, sub-lease or otherwise) of a lease so granted

or to authorise a forfeiture, or impose on the landlord or superior landlord a penalty or disability, in the event of such a grant or disposal.

(2) Where a dwelling-house let on a secure tenancy is land held—

(a) for the purposes of section 164 of the Public Health Act 1875 (pleasure grounds),or

(b) in accordance with section 10 of the Open Spaces Act 1906 (duty of local authority to maintain open spaces and burial grounds),

then, for the purposes of this Part, the dwelling-house shall be deemed to be freed from any trust arising solely by virtue of its being land held in trust for enjoyment by the public in accordance with section 164 or, as the case may be, section 10.

Amendments

1 Substituted by the Leasehold Reform, Housing and Urban Development Act 1993, s 187(1) Sch 21, para 22.

180 Statutory declarations.

A landlord, …[1] or the Secretary of State may, if the landlord, …[1] or Secretary of State thinks fit, accept a statutory declaration made for the purposes of this Part as sufficient evidence of the matters declared in it.

Amendments

1 Repealed by the Leasehold Reform, Housing and Urban Development Act 1993, s 187(2), Sch 22.

181 Jurisdiction of county court.

(1) [The county court][1] has jurisdiction—

(a) to entertain any proceedings brought under this Part, and

(b) to determine any question arising under this Part or under [a conveyance or grant executed in pursuance of the right to acquire on rent to mortgage terms][2];

but subject to sections 128[, 128B][3][, 155C and 158][4] …[5] (which provide for matters of valuation to be determined by the district valuer).

(2) The jurisdiction conferred by this section includes jurisdiction to entertain proceedings on any such question as is mentioned in subsection (1)(b) notwithstanding that no other relief is sought than a declaration.

(3) If a person takes proceedings in the High Court which, by virtue of this section, he could have taken in the county court, he is not entitled to recover any costs.

(4) ...[6]

(5) ...[6]

Amendments

1 Substituted by the Crime and Courts Act 2013, s 17(5), Sch 9, para 52.

2 Substituted by the Leasehold Reform, Housing and Urban Development Act 1993, s 187(1), Sch 21, para 23.

3 Inserted by the Housing and Regeneration Act 2008, s 306(1), (11).

4 Substituted by the Housing Act 2004, s 186(2).

5 Repealed by the Leasehold Reform, Housing and Urban Development Act 1993, s 187(2), Sch 22.

6 Repealed by the Constitutional Reform Act 2005, ss 15, 146, Sch 4, para 182, Sch 18, Pt 2.

182 Power to repeal or amend local Acts.

(1) The Secretary of State may by order repeal or amend a provision of a local Act passed before 8th August 1980 where it appears to him that the provision is inconsistent with a provision of this Part relating to the right to buy ...[1].

(2) Before making an order under this section the Secretary of State shall consult any local housing authority appearing to him to be concerned.

(3) An order made under this section may contain such transitional, incidental or supplementary provisions as the Secretary of State considers appropriate.

(4) An order under this section—

(a) may make different provision with respect to different cases or descriptions of case, including different provision for different areas, and

(b) shall be made by statutory instrument which shall be subject to annulment in pursuance of a resolution of either House of Parliament.

Amendments

1 Repealed by the Leasehold Reform, Housing and Urban Development Act 1993, s 187(2), Sch 22.

183 Meaning of 'house', 'flat' and 'dwelling-house'.

(1) The following provisions apply to the interpretation of 'house', 'flat' and 'dwelling-house' when used in this Part.

(2) A dwelling-house is a house if, and only if, it (or so much of its as does not consist of land included by virtue of section 184) is a structure reasonably so called; so that—

(a) where a building is divided horizontally, the flats or other units into which it is divided are not houses;

(b) where a building is divided vertically, the units into which it is divided may be houses;

(c) where a building is not structurally detached, it is not a house if a material part of it lies above or below the remainder of the structure.

(3) A dwelling-house which is not a house is a flat.

184 Land let with or used for purposes of dwelling-house.

(1) For the purpose of this Part land let together with a dwelling-house shall be treated as part of the dwelling-house, unless the land is agricultural land (within the meaning set out in section 26(3)(a) of the General Rate Act 1967) exceeding two acres.

(2) There shall be treated as included in a dwelling-house any land which is not within subsection (1) but is or has been used for the purpose of the dwelling-house if—

(a) the tenant, by a written notice served on the landlord at any time before he exercises the right to buy or the [right to acquire on rent to mortgage terms][1], requires the land to be included in the dwelling-house, and

(b) it is reasonable in all the circumstances for the land to be so included.

(3) A notice under subsection (2) may be withdrawn by a written notice served on the landlord at any time before the tenant exercises the right to buy or the [right to acquire on rent to mortgage terms][1].

(4) Where a notice under subsection (2) is served or withdrawn after the service of the notice under section 125 (landlord's notice of purchase price, etc.), the parties shall, as soon as practicable after the service or withdrawal, take all such steps (whether by way of amending, withdrawing or re-serving any notice or extending any period or otherwise) as may be requisite for the purpose of securing that all parties are, as nearly as may be, in the same position as they would have been in if the notice under subsection (2) had been served or withdrawn before the service of the notice under section 125.

Amendments

1 Substituted by the Leasehold Reform, Housing and Urban Development Act 1993, s 187(1), Sch 21, para 24.

185 Meaning of 'secure tenancy' and 'secure tenant'.

(1) References in this Part to a secure tenancy or a secure tenant in relation to a time before 26th August 1984 are to a tenancy which would have been a secure tenancy if Chapter II of Part I of the Housing Act 1980 and Part I of the Housing and Building Control Act 1984 had then been in force or to a person who would then have been a secure tenant.

(2) For the purpose of determining whether a person would have been a secure tenant and his tenancy a secure tenancy—

(a) a predecessor of a local authority shall be deemed to have been such an authority, and

(b) a housing association shall be deemed to have been registered if it is or was [a [private registered provider of social housing or][1] registered social landlord][2] at any later time.

Amendments

1 Inserted by the Housing and Regeneration Act 2008 (Consequential Provisions) Order 2010, SI 2010/866, art 5, Sch 2, paras 15, 28.

2 Substituted by the Housing Act 1996 (Consequential Provisions) Order 1996, SI 1996/2325, art 5(1), Sch 2, para 14(1), (16).

186 Members of a person's family.

(1) A person is a member of another's family within the meaning of this Part if—

(a) he is the spouse [or civil partner][1] of that person, or he and that person live together [as if they were a married couple or][2] [civil partners][1], or

(b) he is that person's parent, grandparent, child, grandchild, brother, sister, uncle, aunt, nephew or niece.

(2) For the purposes of subsection (1)(b)—

(a) a relationship by marriage [or civil partnership][1] shall be treated as a relationship by blood,

(b) a relationship of the half-blood shall be treated as a relationship of the whole blood,

(c) the stepchild of a person shall be treated as his child, and

(d) an illegitimate child shall be treated as the legitimate child of his mother and reputed father.

Amendments

1 Inserted by the Civil Partnership Act 2004, s 81, Sch 8, para 27.

2 Substituted by the Civil Partnership (Opposite-sex Couples) Regulations 2019, SI 2019/1458, reg 41(1), Sch 3, para 10(1), (4).

187 Minor definitions.

In this Part—

'improvement' means[, in relation to a dwelling house,][1] any alteration in, or addition to, [the dwelling-house][2] and includes—

(a) any addition to, or alteration in, landlord's fixtures and fittings and any addition or alteration connected with the provision of services to [the dwelling-house][2],

(b) the erection of a wireless or television aerial, and

(c) the carrying out of external decoration;

[and shall be similarly construed in relation to any other building or land;][1]

['improvement contribution' means an amount payable by a tenant of a flat in respect of improvements to the flat, the building in which it is situated or any other building or land, other than works carried out in discharge of any such obligations as are referred to in paragraph 16A(1) of Schedule 6 (obligations to repair, reinstate, etc.);][1]

'long tenancy' means—

(a) a long tenancy within the meaning of part IV,

(b) a tenancy falling within paragraph 1 of Schedule 1 to the Tenants' Rights, Etc. (Scotland) Act 1980, or

(c) a tenancy falling within paragraph 1 of Schedule 2 to the Housing (Northern Ireland) Order 1983;

and 'long lease' shall be construed accordingly;

...[3].

Amendments

1 Inserted by the Housing and Planning Act 1986, s 24(2), Sch 5, para 30(1), (2)(a), (c), (3).

2 Substituted by the Housing and Planning Act 1986, s 24(2), Sch 5, para 30(1), (2)(b).

3 Repealed by the Leasehold Reform, Housing and Urban Development Act 1993, s 187(2), Sch 22.

188 Index of defined expressions: Part V

The following Table shows provisions defining or otherwise explaining expressions used in this Part (other than provisions defining or explaining an expression used in the same section or paragraph):—

...[1]	...[1]
Bank	section 622
building society	section 622
cemetery	section 622
Charity	section 662
compulsory disposal	section 161
co-operative housing association	section 5(2)
...[2]	...[2]
[disposal and instrument effecting disposal (in Schedule 9A)][3]	[paragraph 10 of Schedule][3]

[district valuer][4]	[section 622][4]
dwelling-house	sections 183 and 184
...[1]	...[1]
exempted disposal	section 160
family (member of)	section 186
[final payment][4]	[paragraph 1 of Schedule 6A][4]
Flat	section 183
[former landlord and former secure tenant (in relation to a qualifying disposal)][3]	[section 171A(2)(c)][3]
friendly society	section 622
...[1]	...[1]
House	section 183
housing association	section 5(1)
housing trust	section 6
Improvement	section 187
[improvement contribution][3]	[section 187][3]
Incumbrances	paragraph 7 of Schedule 6
[initial payment and interim payment][4]	[section 143B and paragraph 6 of Schedule 6A][4]
...[1]	...[1]
insurance company	section 622
[landlord's share][4]	[section 148 and paragraph 7 of Schedule 6A][4]
Lease	section 621
local authority	section 4(e)
local housing authority	section 1, 2(2)
long tenancy (and long lease)	section 187
[minimum initial payment and maximum initial payment][4]	[section 143B][4]
new town corporation	section 4(b)
...[1]	...[1]
[prescribed][4]	[section 614][4]
[preserved right to buy][3]	[section 171A(2)(a)][3]
public sector tenancy (and public sector tenant)	paragraphs 6 to 10 of Schedule 4
purchase price	section 126
[qualifying disposal (in relation to the preserved right to buy)][3]	[section 171A(2)(b)][3]
[qualifying dwelling-house and qualifying person (in relation to the preserved right to buy)][3]	[section 171B(1)][3]
[reference period (for purposes of s. 125A or 125B)][3]	[section 125C][3]

[registered social landlord][5]	[section 5(4) and (5)][5]
regular armed forces of the Crown	section 622
[the Relevant Authority][6]	[section 6A][6]
relevant disposal	section 159 (and see section 452(3))
relevant time	section 122(2)
. . .[1]	. . .[1]
[right to acquire on rent to mortgage terms][4]	[section 143][4]
right to buy	section 118(1)
. . .[1]	. . .[1]
. . .[1]	. . .[1]
secure tenancy and secure tenant	sections 79 and 185
[service charge][3]	[section 621A][3]
tenant's incumbrance	paragraph 7 of Schedule 6
. . .[1]	. . .[1]
trustee savings bank	section 622
urban development corporation	section 4(d)

Amendments

1 Repealed by the Leasehold Reform, Housing and Urban Development Act 1993, s 187(2), Sch 22.

2 Repealed by the Government of Wales Act 1998, ss 140, 152, Sch 16, paras 4, 14(a), Sch 18, Pt VI.

3 Inserted by the Housing and Planning Act 1986, s 24(2), Sch 5, para 31.

4 Inserted by the Leasehold Reform, Housing and Urban Development Act 1993, s 187(1), Sch 21, para 25.

5 Substituted by the Housing Act 1996 (Consequential Provisions) Order 1996, SI 1996/2325, art 5(1), Sch 2, para 14(1), (17)

6 Inserted by the Government of Wales Act 1998, s 140, Sch 16, paras 4, 14(b).

SCHEDULE 2
GROUNDS FOR POSSESSION OF DWELLING-HOUSES LET UNDER SECURE TENANCIES

Section 84.

Part I
Grounds on which Court may Order Possession if it Considers it Reasonable

Ground 1

Rent lawfully due from the tenant has not been paid or an obligation of the tenancy has been broken or not performed.

Ground 5

The tenant is the person, or one of the persons, to whom the tenancy was granted and the landlord was induced to grant the tenancy by a false statement made knowingly or recklessly [by—

(a) the tenant, or

(b) a person acting at the tenant's instigation][1].

Amendments

1 Substituted by the Housing Act 1996, s 146.

Housing Act 1988

PART I
RENTED ACCOMMODATION

Chapter I
Assured Tenancies

Meaning of assured tenancy etc.

1 Assured tenancies.

(1) A tenancy under which a dwelling-house [in England][1] is let as a separate dwelling is for the purposes of this Act an assured tenancy if and so long as—

(a) the tenant or, as the case may be, each of the joint tenants is an individual; and

(b) the tenant or, as the case may be, at least one of the joint tenants occupies the dwelling-house as his only or principal home; and

(c) the tenancy is not one which, by virtue of subsection (2) or subsection (6) below, cannot be an assured tenancy.

[(1A) Subsection (1) has effect subject to section 15A (loss of assured tenancy status).][2]

(2) Subject to subsection (3) below, if and so long as a tenancy falls within any paragraph in Part I of Schedule 1 to this Act, it cannot be an assured tenancy; and in that Schedule—

(a) 'tenancy' means a tenancy under which a dwelling-house is let as a separate dwelling;

(b) Part II has effect for determining the rateable value of a dwelling-house for the purposes of Part I; and

(c) Part III has effect for supplementing paragraph 10 in Part I.

[(2A) The Secretary of State may by order replace any amount referred to in paragraphs 2 and 3A of Schedule 1 to this Act by such amount as is specified in the order; and such an order shall be made by statutory instrument which shall be subject to annulment in pursuance of a resolution of either House of Parliament.][3]

(3) Except as provided in Chapter V below, at the commencement of this Act, a tenancy—

(a) under which a dwelling-house was then let as a separate dwelling, and

(b) which immediately before that commencement was an assured tenancy for the purposes of sections 56 to 58 of the Housing Act 1980 (tenancies granted by approved bodies), shall become an assured tenancy for the purposes of this Act.

(4) In relation to an assured tenancy falling within subsection (3) above—

(a) Part I of Schedule 1 to this Act shall have effect, subject to subsection (5) below, as if it consisted only of paragraphs 11 and 12; and

(b) sections 56 to 58 of the Housing Act 1980 (and Schedule 5 to that Act) shall not apply after the commencement of this Act.

(5) In any case where—

(a) immediately before the commencement of this Act the landlord under a tenancy is a fully mutual housing association, and

(b) at the commencement of this Act the tenancy becomes an assured tenancy by virtue of subsection (3) above,

then, so long as that association remains the landlord under that tenancy *(and under any statutory periodic tenancy which arises on the coming to an end of that tenancy)*[4], paragraph 12 of Schedule 1 to this Act shall have effect in relation to that tenancy with the omission of sub-paragraph (1)(h).

(6) …[5]

(7) …[5]

Amendments

1 Inserted by the Renting Homes (Wales) Act 2016 (Consequential Amendments) Regulations 2022, SI 2022/1166, reg 16(1), (2).

2 Inserted by the Prevention of Social Housing Fraud Act 2013, s 10, Schedule, para 4.

3 Inserted by the References to Rating (Housing) Regulations 1990, SI 1990/434, reg 2, Schedule, para 27.

4 Words in italics repealed by the Renters' Rights Act 2025, s 29, Sch 2, paras 20, 21, from 1 May 2026 for the purposes of assured tenancies that are not social housing assured tenancies.

5 Repealed by the Housing Act 1996, s 227, Sch 19, Pt VIII.

[1A Application of Chapters 1, 2 and 3 of this Part to dwelling in Wales

(1) As a result of section 239 of the Renting Homes (Wales) Act 2016 (anaw 1), no tenancy or licence (whenever made) of a dwelling-house that is in Wales can be an assured tenancy or an assured agricultural occupancy.

(2) Accordingly, subject to subsection (3), nothing in sections 1 to 25 of this Act applies to a dwelling-house in Wales.

(3) The provisions of this Act which are referred to in Schedule 10 to the Local Government and Housing Act 1989 (c. 42) continue to apply, for the purposes of that Schedule, to a dwelling-house in Wales which is subject to a long tenancy[, without the amendments made by the Renters' Rights Act 2025][1].

(4) For the purposes of subsection (3), 'long tenancy' has the meaning given by paragraph 8 of Schedule 2 to the Renting Homes (Wales) Act 2016.][2]

Amendments

1 Inserted by the Renters' Rights Act 2025, s 29, Sch 2, paras 20, 22, from 1 May 2026 for the purposes of assured tenancies that are not social housing assured tenancies.

2 Inserted by the Renting Homes (Wales) Act 2016 (Consequential Amendments) Regulations 2022, SI 2022/1166, reg 16(1), (3).

[4A Assured tenancies to be periodic with rent period not exceeding a month

(1) Terms of an assured tenancy are of no effect so far as they provide—

(a) for a tenancy to be a fixed term tenancy, or

(b) for periods of the tenancy to be different from the periods for which rent is payable ('rent periods').

(2) Where terms of an assured tenancy are of no effect by virtue of subsection (1)(a) or (b), the tenancy has effect as a periodic tenancy under which the periods of the tenancy are the same as the rent periods.

(3) Terms of an assured tenancy which provide for the rent periods are of no effect unless each rent period is—

(a) a period of 28 days or shorter, or

(b) a monthly rent period.

(4) Those terms may provide for different rent periods at different times during the assured tenancy (but each rent period must be permitted by subsection (3)).

(5) Where terms of an assured tenancy are of no effect by virtue of subsection (3), the tenancy has effect as if it provided—

(a) for successive rent periods of one month beginning with the first day of the tenancy, and

(b) for the rent for each such rent period—

(i) to be the amount calculated in accordance with the formula in subsection (6), and

(ii) to be due on the first day of the period.

(6) The formula is—

$(R / D) \times 30.42$

where—

R is the rent that would have been due for the first rent period of the tenancy under the terms that are of no effect by virtue of subsection (3);

D is the number of whole days in that period.

(7) Except as provided by subsections (1) and (3), nothing in this section limits any right of the landlord and the tenant to vary a term of a tenancy by agreement.

(8) For the purposes of this section, terms of an assured tenancy provide for 'monthly' rent periods if they provide for rent to be payable for successive periods of one month, disregarding any provision for the first period to be a different period not exceeding 30 days.][1]

Amendment

1 Inserted by the Renters' Rights Act 2025, s 1, from 1 May 2026 for the purposes of assured tenancies that are not social housing assured tenancies.

[4B Assured tenancy: prohibition of rent in advance (except initial rent)

(1) Terms of an assured tenancy which provide for when rent is due are of no effect so far as they provide for rent to be due in advance.

(2) But subsection (1) does not apply—

(a) to a tenancy entered into before the commencement date (which has the same meaning as in section 146(3) of the Renters' Rights Act 2025),

(b) to an excepted tenancy, or

(c) to terms of any other assured tenancy so far as they provide for initial rent to be due during the permitted pre-tenancy period.

(3) Where terms of an assured tenancy providing for when the rent for a rent period is due are of no effect by virtue of this section, the tenancy has effect as if it provided for the rent for that rent period to be due on the substitute rent day for that rent period.

(4) In a case where the terms of the tenancy (after taking account of section 4A) are such that—

(a) one or more of the periods of the tenancy will be compliant rent periods, and

(b) the compliant rent periods have a regular pattern,

the regular rent day which falls during a rent period is the 'substitute rent day' for the rent period.

(5) In any other case, the first day of a rent period is the 'substitute rent day' for the rent period.

(6) The compliant rent periods of a tenancy 'have a regular pattern' if those periods meet the following two conditions—

(a) all of the compliant rent periods will be the same length (and, for this purpose, all periods of one month are the same length);

(b) the rent for all of the compliant periods will be due—

(i) on the same day during each of the periods (such as the same day of the week in a weekly period or the same date in the month in a monthly period), or

(ii) on the same description of day during each of the periods (such as the last day, or first weekday, of a period);

and that day, or day of that description, is the 'regular rent day'.

(7) The condition in subsection (6)(a) is met even if the first period of the tenancy is of a different length from all the other compliant periods; and, in such a case, the condition in subsection (6)(b) is met even if the rent for the first period of the tenancy is due on a different day, or description of day, from all the other compliant periods.

(8) For provision enabling a holding deposit to be used to pay initial rent due during the permitted pre-tenancy period, see Schedule 2 to the Tenant Fees Act 2019.

(9) The Secretary of State may, by regulations, amend this section for the purpose of making provision about the descriptions of rent due in advance to which subsection (1) does not apply.

(10) Regulations under subsection (9)—

(a) may make different provision for different purposes;

(b) are to be made by statutory instrument.

(11) A statutory instrument containing regulations under subsection (9) may not be made unless a draft of the instrument has been laid before and approved by a resolution of each House of Parliament.

(12) In this paragraph—

'compliant rent period': a rent period is a compliant rent period if the rent for the period is due during the period — and, in determining this, the effect of this section on when rent is due must be disregarded;

'due in advance', in relation to rent, means due before the rent period for which it is payable;

'excepted tenancy' means—

(a) an assured tenancy of social housing (within the meaning of Part 2 of the Housing and Regeneration Act 2008) if the landlord is a private registered provider of social housing;

(b) an assured tenancy granted pursuant to Part 7 of the Housing Act 1996 (homelessness);

'initial rent' means rent that is payable for—

(a) the first rent period, or

(b) any later rent period which ends during the initial 28 day period;

and here 'initial 28 day period' means the period of 28 days beginning with the first day of the first rent period;

'permitted pre-tenancy period' means the period that—

(a) begins when the tenancy is entered into, and

(b) ends with the day before the first day of the tenancy;

'regular rent day' has the meaning given in subsection (6)(b);

'rent period' means a period for which rent is payable under the assured tenancy;

'substitute rent day' means the day determined in accordance with subsection (4) or (5).][1]

Amendment

1 Inserted by the Renters' Rights Act 2025, s 8, from 1 May 2026 for the purposes of assured tenancies that are not social housing assured tenancies.

Security of tenure

5 Security of tenure.

[(1) An assured tenancy cannot be brought to an end by the landlord except by—

(a) obtaining—

(i) an order of the court for possession of the dwelling-house under section 7 *or 21*[1], and

(ii) the execution of the order,

(b) *obtaining an order of the court under section 6A (demotion order),*[1] …[2]

(c) *in the case of a fixed term tenancy which contains power for the landlord to determine the tenancy in certain circumstances, by the exercise of that power*[1][, or

(d) in the case of an assured tenancy—

(i) which is a residential tenancy agreement within the meaning of Chapter 1 of Part 3 of the Immigration Act 2014, and

(ii) in relation to which the condition in section 33D(2) of that Act is met,

giving a notice in accordance with that section,][3]

and, accordingly, the service by the landlord of a notice to quit is of no effect in relation to *a periodic* [an][4] assured tenancy.

(1A) Where an order of the court for possession of the dwelling-house is obtained, the tenancy ends when the order is executed.][5]

(2) If an assured tenancy which is a fixed term tenancy comes to an end otherwise than by virtue of—

(a) an order of the court [of the kind mentioned in subsection (1)(a) or (b) or any other order of the court][6], …[2]

(b) a surrender or other action on the part of the tenant[, or

(c) the giving of a notice under section 33D of the Immigration Act 2014,][3]

then, subject to section 7 and Chapter II below, the tenant shall be entitled to remain in possession of the dwelling-house let under that tenancy and, subject to subsection (4) below, his right to possession shall depend upon a periodic tenancy arising by virtue of this section.

(3) The periodic tenancy referred to in subsection (2) above is one—

(a) taking effect in possession immediately on the coming to an end of the fixed term tenancy;

(b) deemed to have been granted by the person who was the landlord under the fixed term tenancy immediately before it came to an end to the person who was then the tenant under that tenancy;

(c) under which the premises which are let are the same dwelling-house as was let under the fixed term tenancy;

(d) under which the periods of the tenancy are the same as those for which rent was last payable under the fixed term tenancy; and

(e) under which, subject to the following provisions of this Part of this Act, the other terms are the same as those of the fixed term tenancy immediately before it came to an end, except that any term which makes provision for determination by the landlord or the tenant shall not have effect while the tenancy remains an assured tenancy.

(4) The periodic tenancy referred to in subsection (2) above shall not arise if, on the coming to an end of the fixed term tenancy, the tenant is entitled, by virtue of the grant of another tenancy, to possession of the same or substantially the same dwelling-house as was let to him under the fixed term tenancy.

(5) If, on or before the date on which a tenancy is entered into or is deemed to have been granted as mentioned in subsection (3)(b) above, the person who is to be the tenant under that tenancy—

(a) enters into an obligation to do any act which (apart from this subsection) will cause the tenancy to come to an end at a time when it is an assured tenancy, or

(b) executes, signs or gives any surrender, notice to quit or other document which (apart from this subsection) has the effect of bringing the tenancy to an end at a time when it is an assured tenancy,

the obligation referred to in paragraph (a) above shall not be enforceable or, as the case may be, the surrender, notice to quit or other document referred to in paragraph (b) above shall be of no effect.

[(5A) Nothing in subsection (5) affects any right of pre-emption—

(a) which is exercisable by the landlord under a tenancy in circumstances where the tenant indicates his intention to dispose of the whole of his interest under the tenancy, and

(b) in pursuance of which the landlord would be required to pay, in respect of the acquisition of that interest, an amount representing its market value.

'Dispose' means dispose by assignment or surrender, and 'acquisition' has a corresponding meaning.][7]

(6) If, by virtue of any provision of this Part of this Act, Part I of Schedule 1 to this Act has effect in relation to a fixed term tenancy as if it consisted only of paragraphs 11 and 12, that Part shall have the like effect in relation to any periodic tenancy which arises by virtue of this section on the coming to an end of the fixed term tenancy.

(7) Any reference in this Part of this Act to a statutory periodic tenancy is a reference to a periodic tenancy arising by virtue of this section.[1]

Amendments

1 Words in italics repealed by the Renters' Rights Act 2025, s 29, Sch 2, paras 20, 23(a)(i), (ii), (b), from 1 May 2026 for the purposes of assured tenancies that are not social housing assured tenancies.

2 Repealed by the Immigration Act 2016, s 40(6).

3 Inserted by the Immigration Act 2016, s 40(6).

4 Word in square brackets substituted for words in italics by the Renters' Rights Act 2025, s 29, Sch 2, paras 20, 23(a)(iii), from 1 May 2026 for the purposes of assured tenancies that are not social housing assured tenancies.

5 Substituted by the Housing and Regeneration Act 2008, s 299, Sch 11, paras 5, 6(1), (2).

6 Inserted by the Housing and Regeneration Act 2008, s 299, Sch 11, paras 5, 6(1), (3).

7 Inserted by the Housing Act 2004, s 222(1), (2).

7 Orders for possession.

(1) The court shall not make an order for possession of a dwelling-house let on an assured tenancy except on one or more of the grounds set out in Schedule 2 to this Act; but nothing in this Part of this Act relates to proceedings for possession of such a dwelling-house which are brought by a mortgagee, within the meaning of the Law of Property Act 1925, who has lent money on the security of the assured tenancy.

(2) The following provisions of this section have effect, subject to section 8 below, in relation to proceedings for the recovery of possession of a dwelling-house let on an assured tenancy.

(3) If the court is satisfied that any of the grounds in Part I of Schedule 2 to this Act is established then, subject to [*subsections (5A) and (6)* [the following

provisions of this section][1]][2] [and section 10A][3] below [(and to any available defence based on the tenant's Convention rights, within the meaning of the Human Rights Act 1998)][4], the court shall make an order for possession.

(4) If the court is satisfied that any of the grounds in Part II of Schedule 2 to this Act is established, then, *subject to [subsections (5A) and (6)]*[2] *below,*[5] the court may make an order for possession if it considers it reasonable to do so.

(5) Part III of Schedule 2 to this Act shall have effect for supplementing Ground 9 in that Schedule *and Part IV of that Schedule shall have effect in relation to notices given as mentioned in Grounds 1 to 5 of that Schedule*[5].

[(5ZA) The court may not make an order for possession of a dwelling-house on any of Grounds 1 to 5H or Ground 6A where—

(a) a smallholding was previously let to the tenant under a tenancy to which the Agricultural Holdings Act 1986 applies ('the agricultural tenancy'),

(b) the agricultural tenancy came to an end as a result of the operation of a notice to quit given in case A in Part 1 of Schedule 3 to that Act ('case A'),

(c) the assured tenancy was granted immediately after the agricultural tenancy came to an end, and

(d) the dwelling-house is let under the assured tenancy—

(i) by the person who was the landlord under the agricultural tenancy ('the former agricultural landlord'), or

(ii) by another person pursuant to a contract or other agreement entered into with the former agricultural landlord under which—

(A) the dwelling-house is to be let as suitable alternative accommodation for the purposes of paragraph (b) of case A, and

(B) this subsection is to apply.

(5ZB) The court may not make an order for possession of a dwelling-house let on an assured tenancy on any of Grounds 1 to 5H or Ground 6A where, on the basis of the proposed let of the dwelling-house on that tenancy, the dwelling-house was deemed to be suitable alternative accommodation under paragraph 1(c) of Part 4 of Schedule 2 to the Housing Act 1985 for the purposes of section 84(2)(b) and (c) of that Act.][6]

[(5A) The court shall not make an order for possession of a dwellinghouse let on an assured periodic tenancy arising under Schedule 10 to the Local Government and Housing Act 1989 on any of the following grounds, that is to say,—

(a) Grounds 1, *2[, 5* [to 5H, 6A, 6B][1][, 7A and 7B][7]][8] in Part I of Schedule 2 to this Act;

(b) *Ground 16 in Part II of that Schedule;*[5] and

(c) if the assured periodic tenancy arose on the termination of a former 1954 Act tenancy, within the meaning of the said Schedule 10, Ground 6 in Part I of Schedule 2 to this Act.][9]

[(5B) The court may not make an order for possession of a dwelling-house let on an assured tenancy granted in accordance with section 554(3)(c) (before its repeal) or (ca) of the Housing Act 1985 on any of Grounds 1 to 5H or Ground 6A.

(5C) In relation to the making of an order for possession of a dwelling-house let on an assured periodic tenancy arising under Schedule 10 to the Local Government and Housing Act 1989, Ground 6 is to apply as if—

(a) in paragraph (b), the words ', but only in a case where section 7(5ZA) applies in relation to the tenancy' were omitted;

(b) in the general redevelopment conditions, paragraph (f) was omitted;

(c) in the landlord's acquisition condition, in paragraph (a), the reference to the grant of the tenancy is a reference to the grant of the long residential tenancy which existed immediately before the assured periodic tenancy arose.

(5D) If the only grounds for possession which the court is satisfied are established are either or both of Grounds 7A and 14 in Schedule 2, the court may not make an order for possession to take effect within—

(a) the period of 14 days beginning with the date of service of the notice under section 8; or

(b) where the court has exercised the power conferred by section 8(1)(b), the period of 14 days beginning—

(i) if a purported notice of possession (within the meaning given by section 16M) was served on the tenant and the court considers it just and equitable, with the date on which the notice was served;

(ii) otherwise, with the date on which the proceedings for possession began.

(5E) In subsection (5C), a reference to a 'long residential tenancy' is a reference to a tenancy to which Schedule 10 to the Local Government and Housing Act 1989 applies.][6]

(6) The court shall not make an order for possession of a dwelling-house to take effect at a time when it is let on an assured fixed term tenancy unless—

(a) the ground for possession is Ground 2[, Ground 7A][4][, Ground 7B][3] or Ground 8 in Part I of Schedule 2 to this Act or any of the grounds in Part II of that Schedule, other than Ground 9 or Ground 16; and

(b) the terms of the tenancy make provision for it to be brought to an end on the ground in question (whether that provision takes the form of a provision for re-entry, for forfeiture, for determination by notice or otherwise).

[(6A) In the case of a dwelling-house in England, subsection (6)(a) has effect as if it also referred to Ground 7 in Part 1 of Schedule 2 to this Act.][10]

[(6B) The requirement in subsection (6)(b) that would otherwise apply to an order for possession of a dwelling-house let on an assured fixed term tenancy does not apply where the ground for possession is Ground 7B in Part 1 of Schedule 2 to this Act.][3]

(7) Subject to the preceding provisions of this section, the court may make an order for possession of a dwelling-house on grounds relating to a fixed term tenancy which has come to an end; and where an order is made in such circumstances, any statutory periodic tenancy which has arisen on the ending of the fixed term tenancy shall end (without any notice and regardless of the period) [in accordance with section 5(1A)][11].[5]

Amendments

1 Words in square brackets substituted for words in italics by the Renters' Rights Act 2025, s 3(2)(a), (e)(i), from 1 May 2026 for the purposes of assured tenancies that are not social housing assured tenancies.

2 Substituted by the Local Government and Housing Act 1989, s 194(1), Sch 11, para 101(1), (2).

3 Inserted by the Immigration Act 2016, s 41(1), (3)(a), (c), (d).

4 Inserted by the Anti-social Behaviour, Crime and Policing Act 2014, s 181(1), Sch 11, para 18(1), (2), (4).

5 Words in italics repealed by the Renters' Rights Act 2025, s 3(2)(b), (c), (e)(ii), (g), from 1 May 2026 for the purposes of assured tenancies that are not social housing assured tenancies.

6 Inserted by the Renters' Rights Act 2025, s 3(2)(d), (f), from 1 May 2026 for the purposes of assured tenancies that are not social housing assured tenancies.

7 Substituted by the Immigration Act 2016, s 41(1), (3)(b).

8 Substituted by the Anti-social Behaviour, Crime and Policing Act 2014, s 181(1), Sch 11, para 18(1), (3).

9 Inserted by the Local Government and Housing Act 1989, s 194(1), Sch 11, para 101(3).

10 Inserted by the Localism Act 2011, s 162(4).

11 Substituted by the Housing and Regeneration Act 2008, s 299, Sch 11, paras 5, 7.

8 Notice of proceedings for possession.

(1) The court shall not entertain proceedings for possession of a dwelling-house let on an assured tenancy unless—

(a) the landlord or, in the case of joint landlords, at least one of them has served on the tenant a notice in accordance with this section and the proceedings are begun within the time limits stated in the notice in accordance with [subsections (3) to *(4B)* [(4AA)][1]][2] below; or

(b) the court considers it just and equitable to dispense with the requirement of such a notice.

(2) The court shall not make an order for possession on any of the grounds in Schedule 2 to this Act unless that ground and particulars of it are specified in

the notice under this section; but the grounds specified in such a notice may be altered or added to with the leave of the court.

(3) A notice under this section is one in the prescribed form informing the tenant that—

(a) the landlord intends to begin proceedings for possession of the dwelling-house on one or more of the grounds specified in the notice; and

(b) those proceedings will not begin earlier than a date specified in the notice [in accordance with [subsections *(3A)* [(4)][1]][3] *to (4B)* [to (4AA)][1] below][2]; and

(c) those proceedings will not begin later than twelve months from the date of service of the notice.

[(3A) If a notice under this section specifies in accordance with subsection (3) (a) Ground 7A in Schedule 2 to this Act (whether with or without other grounds), the date specified in the notice as mentioned in subsection (3)(b) is not to be earlier than—

(a) in the case of a periodic tenancy,

(b) in the case of a fixed term tenancy, one month after the date on which the notice was served.[4]][5]

[(4) If a notice under this section specifies in accordance with subsection (3) (a) above *Ground 14* [either or both of Grounds 7A and 14][1] in Schedule 2 to this Act [(whether [with or][6] without other grounds *or with any ground other than Ground 7A*[4])][3], the date specified in the notice as mentioned in subsection (3)(b) above shall not be earlier than the date of the service of the notice.

(4A) If a notice under this section specifies in accordance with subsection (3) (a) above, any of Grounds 1, 2, 5 to 7, 9 and 16 in Schedule 2 to this Act (whether without other grounds or with any ground other than Ground [7A or][5] 14), the date specified in the notice as mentioned in subsection (3)(b) above shall not be earlier than—

(a) two months from the date of service of the notice; and

(b) if the tenancy is a periodic tenancy, the earliest date on which, apart from section 5(1) above, the tenancy could be brought to an end by a notice to quit given by the landlord on the same date as the date of service of the notice under this section.

(4B) In any other case, the date specified in the notice as mentioned in subsection (3)(b) above shall not be earlier than the expiry of the period of two weeks from the date of the service of the notice.

[(4AA) If a notice under this section does not specify Ground 7A or 14 in Schedule 2, the date specified in the notice as mentioned in subsection (3)(b) must not be before the end of the longest period shown in the following table for any ground specified in the notice.

Ground specified in notice	*Period*
1, 1A, 1B, 2, 2ZA, 2ZB, 2ZC, 2ZD, 4A, 6, 6A, 6B	four months beginning with the date of service of the notice
5, 5A, 5B, 5C, 5D, 5H, 7, 9	two months beginning with the date of service of the notice
5E, 5F, 5G, 8, 10, 11, 18	four weeks beginning with the date of service of the notice
4, 7B, 12, 13, 14ZA, 14A, 15, 17	two weeks beginning with the date of service of the notice][1]

[(4C) A notice under this section that specifies in accordance with subsection (3)(a) Ground 7A in Schedule 2 to this Act (whether with or without other grounds) must be served on the tenant within the time period specified in subsection (4D), (4E) or (4F).

(4D) Where the landlord proposes to rely on condition 1, 3 or 5 in Ground 7A, the notice must be served on the tenant within—

(a) the period of 12 months beginning with the day of the conviction, or

(b) if there is an appeal against the conviction, the period of 12 months beginning with the day on which the appeal is finally determined or abandoned.

(4E) Where the landlord proposes to rely on condition 2 in Ground 7A, the notice must be served on the tenant within—

(a) the period of 12 months beginning with the day on which the court has made the finding, or

(b) if there is an appeal against the finding, the period of 12 months beginning with the day on which the appeal is finally determined, abandoned or withdrawn.

(4F) Where the landlord proposes to rely on condition 4 in Ground 7A, the notice must be served on the tenant within—

(a) the period of 3 months beginning with the day on which the closure order was made, or

(b) if there is an appeal against the making of the order, the period of 3 months beginning with the day on which the appeal is finally determined, abandoned or withdrawn.][5]

(5) The court may not exercise the power conferred by subsection (1)(b) above if the landlord seeks to recover possession on Ground [7A[, 7B][7] or][5] 8 in Schedule 2 to this Act.

[(5A) A notice given by an intermediate landlord under Ground 2ZA is to be treated, when the superior tenancy ends, as a notice given by the person who became the landlord by virtue of section 18 under Ground 2ZC.

(5B) A notice given by an intermediate landlord under Ground 2ZB is to be treated, when the superior tenancy ends, as a notice given by the person who became the landlord by virtue of section 18 under Ground 2ZD.][6]

(6) Where a notice under this section—

(a) is served at a time when the dwelling-house is let on a fixed term tenancy, or

(b) is served after a fixed term tenancy has come to an end but relates (in whole or in part) to events occurring during that tenancy,

the notice shall have effect notwithstanding that the tenant becomes or has become tenant under a statutory periodic tenancy arising on the coming to an end of the fixed term tenancy.[4]

[(7) Regulations made under section 45(1) by virtue of subsection (3) may—

(a) provide for the form to be published by the Secretary of State;

(b) provide that the form to be used is the version that has effect at the time the requirement applies.][8]

Amendments

1 Words in square brackets substituted for words in italics by the Renters' Rights Act 2025, s 3(3)(a), (b), (d)(i), (e), from 1 May 2026 for the purposes of assured tenancies that are not social housing assured tenancies.

2 Substituted by the Housing Act 1996, s 151.

3 Substituted by the Anti-social Behaviour, Crime and Policing Act 2014, s 97(2)(a), (c).

4 Words in italics repealed by the Renters' Rights Act 2025, s 3(3)(c), (d)(iii), (g), from 1 May 2026 for the purposes of assured tenancies that are not social housing assured tenancies.

5 Inserted by the Anti-social Behaviour, Crime and Policing Act 2014, s 97(2)(b), (d)–(f).

6 Inserted by the Renters' Rights Act 2025, s 3(3)(d)(ii), (f), from 1 May 2026 for the purposes of assured tenancies that are not social housing assured tenancies.

7 Inserted by the Immigration Act 2016, s 41(1), (4).

8 Inserted by the Renters' Rights Act 2025, s 5, from 1 May 2026 for the purposes of assured tenancies that are not social housing assured tenancies.

[8ZA Disapplication of conditions where notice dispensed with

(1) This section applies where the court exercises the power conferred by section 8(1)(b) in proceedings relating to Ground 4A, 5G or 6 in Schedule 2.

(2) The court may, if it considers it just and equitable to do so—

(a) where the proceedings relate to Ground 4A, disapply paragraph (d) of the ground;

(b) where the proceedings relate to Ground 5G, disapply paragraph (b) of the ground;

(c) where the proceedings relate to Ground 6, disapply paragraph (aa)(ii)(B) of the ground.

(3) References in this section to grounds in Schedule 2 are to those grounds read in accordance with paragraph 12(2) of that Schedule.][1]

Amendments

1 Inserted by the Renters' Rights Act 2025, s 3(4), from 1 May 2026 for the purposes of assured tenancies that are not social housing assured tenancies.

9 Extended discretion of court in possession claims.

(1) Subject to subsection (6) below, the court may adjourn for such period or periods as it thinks fit proceedings for possession of a dwelling-house let on an assured tenancy.

(2) On the making of an order for possession of a dwelling-house let on an assured tenancy or at any time before the execution of such an order, the court, subject to subsection (6) below, may—

(a) stay or suspend execution of the order, or

(b) postpone the date of possession,

for such period or periods as the court thinks just.

(3) On any such adjournment as is referred to in subsection (1) above or on any such stay, suspension or postponement as is referred to in subsection (2) above, the court, unless it considers that to do so would cause exceptional hardship to the tenant or would otherwise be unreasonable, shall impose conditions with regard to payment by the tenant of arrears of rent (if any) and rent …[1] and may impose such other conditions as it thinks fit.

(4) If any such conditions as are referred to in subsection (3) above are complied with, the court may, if it thinks fit, discharge or rescind any such order as is referred to in subsection (2) above.

(5) …[1]

[(5A) …[1]][2]

(6) This section does not apply if the court is satisfied that the landlord is entitled to possession of the dwelling-house—

(a) on any of the grounds in Part I of Schedule 2 to this Act; *or*

(b) by virtue of subsection (1) or subsection (4) of section 21 below[3].

Amendments

1 Repealed by the Housing and Regeneration Act 2008, ss 299, 321(1), Sch 11, para 8(1), (2), (4), Sch 16.

2 Inserted by the Family Law Act 1996, s 66(1), Sch 8, para 59(1), (3)

3 Words in italics repealed by the Renters' Rights Act 2025, s 29, Sch 2, paras 20, 25, from 1 May 2026 for the purposes of assured tenancies that are not social housing assured tenancies.

12 Compensation for misrepresentation or concealment.

Where a landlord obtains an order for possession of a dwelling-house let on an assured tenancy on one or more of the grounds in Schedule 2 to this Act and it is subsequently made to appear to the court that the order was obtained by misrepresentation or concealment of material facts, the court may order the landlord to pay to the former tenant such sum as appears sufficient as compensation for damage or loss sustained by that tenant as a result of the order.

Rent and other terms

15 Limited prohibition on assignment etc. without consent.

(1) Subject to subsection (3) below, it shall be an implied term of every assured tenancy which is a periodic tenancy that, except with the consent of the landlord, the tenant shall not—

(a) assign the tenancy (in whole or in part); or

(b) sub-let or part with possession of the whole or any part of the dwelling-house let on the tenancy.

(2) Section 19 of the Landlord and Tenant Act 1927 (consents to assign not to be unreasonably withheld etc.) shall not apply to a term which is implied into an assured tenancy by subsection (1) above.

(3) In the case of a periodic tenancy which is not *a statutory periodic tenancy*[1] [*or*[1] an assured periodic tenancy arising under Schedule 10 to the Local Government and Housing Act 1989][2] subsection (1) above does not apply if—

(a) there is a provision (whether contained in the tenancy or not) under which the tenant is prohibited (whether absolutely or conditionally) from assigning or sub-letting or parting with possession or is permitted (whether absolutely or conditionally) to assign, sub-let or part with possession; or

(b) a premium is required to be paid on the grant or renewal of the tenancy.

(4) In subsection (3)(b) above 'premium' includes—

(a) any fine or other like sum;

(b) any other pecuniary consideration in addition to rent; and

(c) any sum paid by way of deposit, other than one which does not exceed one-sixth of the annual rent payable under the tenancy immediately after the grant or renewal in question.

Amendments

1 Words in italics repealed by the Renters' Rights Act 2025, s 29, Sch 2, paras 20, 27, from 1 May 2026 for the purposes of assured tenancies that are not social housing assured tenancies.

2 Inserted by the Local Government and Housing Act 1989, s 194(1), Sch 11, para 102.

[15A Loss of assured tenancy status

(1) Subsection (2) applies if, in breach of an express or implied term of the tenancy, a tenant of a dwelling-house let under an assured tenancy to which this section applies—

(a) parts with possession of the dwelling-house, or

(b) sub-lets the whole of the dwelling-house (or sub-lets first part of it and then the remainder).

(2) The tenancy ceases to be an assured tenancy and cannot subsequently become an assured tenancy.

(3) This section applies to an assured tenancy—

(a) under which the landlord is a private registered provider of social housing or a registered social landlord, and

(b) which is not a shared ownership lease.

(4) In this section 'registered social landlord' has the same meaning as in Part 1 of the Housing Act 1996.

(5) In this section 'shared ownership lease' means a lease of a dwelling-house—

(a) granted on payment of a premium calculated by reference to a percentage of the value of the dwelling-house or of the cost of providing it, or

(b) under which the lessee (or the lessee's personal representatives) will or may be entitled to a sum calculated by reference, directly or indirectly, to the value of the dwelling-house.][1]

Amendments

1 Inserted by the Prevention of Social Housing Fraud Act 2013, s 6.

Miscellaneous

17 Succession to [assured tenancy][1].

(1) [Subject to subsection (1D),][2] in any case where—

(a) the sole tenant under an assured *periodic*[3] tenancy dies, and

(b) immediately before the death, the tenant's spouse [or civil partner][4] was occupying the dwelling-house as his or her only or principal home, …[5]

(c) …[5]

then, on the death, the tenancy vests by virtue of this section in the spouse [or civil partner][4] (and, accordingly, does not devolve under the tenant's will or intestacy).

[(1A) Subject to subsection (1D), in any case where—

(a) there is an assured *periodic*[3] tenancy of a dwelling-house in England under which—

(i) the landlord is a private registered provider of social housing, and

(ii) the tenant is a sole tenant,

(b) the tenant under the tenancy dies,

(c) immediately before the death, the dwelling-house was not occupied by a spouse or civil partner of the tenant as his or her only or principal home,

(d) an express term of the tenancy makes provision for a person other than such a spouse or civil partner of the tenant to succeed to the tenancy, and

(e) there is a person whose succession is in accordance with that term,

then, on the death, the tenancy vests by virtue of this section in that person (and, accordingly, does not devolve under the tenant's will or intestacy).

(1B) Subject to subsection (1D), in any case where—

(a) there is an assured tenancy of a dwelling-house in England for a fixed term of not less than two years under which—

(i) the landlord is a private registered provider of social housing, and

(ii) the tenant is a sole tenant,

(b) the tenant under the tenancy dies, and

(c) immediately before the death, the tenant's spouse or civil partner was occupying the dwelling-house as his or her only or principal home,

then, on the death, the tenancy vests by virtue of this section in the spouse or civil partner (and, accordingly, does not devolve under the tenant's will or intestacy).[3]

(1C) Subject to subsection (1D), in any case where—

(a) there is an assured tenancy of a dwelling-house in England for a fixed term of not less than two years under which—

(i) the landlord is a private registered provider of social housing, and

(ii) the tenant is a sole tenant,

(b) the tenant under the tenancy dies,

(c) immediately before the death, the dwelling-house was not occupied by a spouse or civil partner of the tenant as his or her only or principal home,

(d) an express term of the tenancy makes provision for a person other than such a spouse or civil partner of the tenant to succeed to the tenancy, and

(e) there is a person whose succession is in accordance with that term,

then, on the death, the tenancy vests by virtue of this section in that person (and accordingly does not devolve under the tenant's will or intestacy).[3]

(1D) Subsection (1), *(1A), (1B) or (1C)* [or (1A)][6] does not apply if the tenant was himself a successor as defined in subsection (2) or subsection (3).

(1E) In such a case, on the death, the tenancy vests by virtue of this section in a person ('P') (and, accordingly, does not devolve under the tenant's will or intestacy) if, and only if—

(a) (in a case within subsection (1)) the tenancy is of a dwelling-house in England under which the landlord is a private registered provider of social housing,

(b) an express term of the tenancy makes provision for a person to succeed a successor to the tenancy, and

(c) P's succession is in accordance with that term.][2]

(2) For the purposes of this section, a tenant is a successor in relation to a tenancy if—

(a) the tenancy became vested in him either by virtue of this section or under the will or intestacy of a previous tenant; or

(b) at some time before the tenant's death the tenancy was a joint tenancy held by himself and one or more other persons and, prior to his death, he became the sole tenant by survivorship; or

(c) he became entitled to the tenancy as mentioned in section 39(5) below.

(3) For the purposes of this section, a tenant is also a successor in relation to a tenancy (in this subsection referred to as 'the new tenancy') which was granted to him (alone or jointly with others) if—

(a) at some time before the grant of the new tenancy, he was, by virtue of subsection (2) above, a successor in relation to an earlier tenancy of the same or substantially the same dwelling-house as is let under the new tenancy; and

(b) at all times since he became such a successor he has been a tenant (alone or jointly with others) of the dwelling-house which is let under the new tenancy or of a dwelling-house which is substantially the same as that dwelling-house.

[(4) For the purposes of this section, a person who was living with the tenant as if they were a married couple or civil partners is to be treated as the tenant's spouse or civil partner.][7]

(5) If, on the death of the tenant, there is, by virtue of subsection (4) above, more than one person who fulfils the condition in subsection (1)(b) [*or (1B) (c)*[3]][2] above, such one of them as may be decided by agreement or, in default of agreement, by the county court [shall for the purposes of this section be [treated as the tenant's spouse][8] [or civil partner][7].][9]

[(6) If, on the death of the tenant, there is more than one person in whom the tenancy would otherwise vest by virtue of subsection (1A), *(1C)*[3] or (1E), the tenancy vests in such one of them as may be agreed between them or, in default of agreement, as is determined by the county court.

(7) This section does not apply to a fixed term assured tenancy that is a lease of a dwelling-house—

(a) granted on payment of a premium calculated by reference to a percentage of the value of the dwelling-house or of the cost of providing it, or

(b) under which the lessee (or the lessee's personal representatives) will or may be entitled to a sum calculated by reference, directly or indirectly, to the value of the dwelling-house.[3]][2]

Amendments

1 Substituted by the Localism Act 2011, s 161(1), (2).

2 Inserted by the Localism Act 2011, s 161(1), (3)(a), (4)–(6).

3 Words in italics repealed by the Renters' Rights Act 2025, s 29, Sch 2, paras 20, 28(a)-(d), (f)-(h), from 1 May 2026 for the purposes of assured tenancies that are not social housing assured tenancies.

4 Inserted by the Civil Partnership Act 2004, s 81, Sch 8, para 41(1), (2).

5 Repealed by the Localism Act 2011, s 161(1), (3)(b), 237, Sch 25, Pt 23.

6 Words in square brackets substituted for words in italics by the Renters' Rights Act 2025, s 29, Sch 2, paras 20, 28(e), from 1 May 2026 for the purposes of assured tenancies that are not social housing assured tenancies.

7 Substituted by the Civil Partnership (Opposite-sex Couples) Regulations 2019, SI 2019/1458, reg 41, Sch 3, para 12(2).

8 Substituted by the Marriage (Same Sex Couples) Act 2013 (Consequential and Contrary Provisions and Scotland) Order 2014, SI 2014/560, art 2, Sch 1, para 20.

9 Substituted by the Civil Partnership Act 2004, s 81, Sch 8, para 41(1), (4).

SCHEDULE 2
GROUNDS FOR POSSESSION OF DWELLING-HOUSES LET ON ASSURED TENANCIES

Section 7.

Part II
Grounds on which Court may Order Possession

Ground 12

Any obligation of the tenancy (other than one related to the payment of rent) has been broken or not performed.

[Ground 17

The tenant is the person, or one of the persons, to whom the tenancy was granted and the landlord was induced to grant the tenancy by a false statement made knowingly or recklessly by—

(a) the tenant, or

(b) a person acting at the tenant's instigation.][1]

Amendments

1 Inserted by the Housing Act 1996, s 102.

Fraud Act 2006

Fraud

1 Fraud

(1) A person is guilty of fraud if he is in breach of any of the sections listed in subsection (2) (which provide for different ways of committing the offence).

(2) The sections are—

(a) section 2 (fraud by false representation),

(b) section 3 (fraud by failing to disclose information), and

(c) section 4 (fraud by abuse of position).

(3) A person who is guilty of fraud is liable—

(a) on summary conviction, to imprisonment for a term not exceeding [the general limit in a magistrates' court][1] or to a fine not exceeding the statutory maximum (or to both);

(b) on conviction on indictment, to imprisonment for a term not exceeding 10 years or to a fine (or to both).

(4) Subsection (3)(a) applies in relation to Northern Ireland as if the reference to 12 months were a reference to 6 months.

Amendments

1 Substituted by the Judicial Review and Courts Act 2022 (Magistrates' Court Sentencing Powers) Regulations 2023, SI 2023/149, reg 2(1), Schedule, Pt 1.

2 Fraud by false representation

(1) A person is in breach of this section if he—

(a) dishonestly makes a false representation, and

(b) intends, by making the representation—

(i) to make a gain for himself or another, or

(ii) to cause loss to another or to expose another to a risk of loss.

(2) A representation is false if—

(a) it is untrue or misleading, and

(b) the person making it knows that it is, or might be, untrue or misleading.

(3) 'Representation' means any representation as to fact or law, including a representation as to the state of mind of—

(a) the person making the representation, or

(b) any other person.

(4) A representation may be express or implied.

(5) For the purposes of this section a representation may be regarded as made if it (or anything implying it) is submitted in any form to any system or device designed to receive, convey or respond to communications (with or without human intervention).

3 Fraud by failing to disclose information

A person is in breach of this section if he—

(a) dishonestly fails to disclose to another person information which he is under a legal duty to disclose, and

(b) intends, by failing to disclose the information—

(i) to make a gain for himself or another, or

(ii) to cause loss to another or to expose another to a risk of loss.

4 Fraud by abuse of position

(1) A person is in breach of this section if he—

(a) occupies a position in which he is expected to safeguard, or not to act against, the financial interests of another person,

(b) dishonestly abuses that position, and

(c) intends, by means of the abuse of that position—

(i) to make a gain for himself or another, or

(ii) to cause loss to another or to expose another to a risk of loss.

(2) A person may be regarded as having abused his position even though his conduct consisted of an omission rather than an act.

5 'Gain' and 'loss'

(1) The references to gain and loss in sections 2 to 4 are to be read in accordance with this section.

(2) 'Gain' and 'loss'—

(a) extend only to gain or loss in money or other property;

(b) include any such gain or loss whether temporary or permanent;

and 'property' means any property whether real or personal (including things in action and other intangible property).

(3) 'Gain' includes a gain by keeping what one has, as well as a gain by getting what one does not have.

(4) 'Loss' includes a loss by not getting what one might get, as well as a loss by parting with what one has.

6 Possession etc. of articles for use in frauds

(1) A person is guilty of an offence if he has in his possession or under his control any article for use in the course of or in connection with any fraud.

(2) A person guilty of an offence under this section is liable—

(a) on summary conviction, to imprisonment for a term not exceeding [the general limit in a magistrates' court][1] or to a fine not exceeding the statutory maximum (or to both);

(b) on conviction on indictment, to imprisonment for a term not exceeding 5 years or to a fine (or to both).

(3) Subsection (2)(a) applies in relation to Northern Ireland as if the reference to 12 months were a reference to 6 months.

Amendments

1 Substituted by the Judicial Review and Courts Act 2022 (Magistrates' Court Sentencing Powers) Regulations 2023, SI 2023/149, reg 2(1), Schedule, Pt 1.

7 Making or supplying articles for use in frauds

(1) A person is guilty of an offence if he makes, adapts, supplies or offers to supply any article—

(a) knowing that it is designed or adapted for use in the course of or in connection with fraud, or

(b) intending it to be used to commit, or assist in the commission of, fraud.

(2) A person guilty of an offence under this section is liable—

(a) on summary conviction, to imprisonment for a term not exceeding [the general limit in a magistrates' court][1] or to a fine not exceeding the statutory maximum (or to both);

(b) on conviction on indictment, to imprisonment for a term not exceeding 10 years or to a fine (or to both).

(3) Subsection (2)(a) applies in relation to Northern Ireland as if the reference to 12 months were a reference to 6 months.

Amendments

1 Substituted by the Judicial Review and Courts Act 2022 (Magistrates' Court Sentencing Powers) Regulations 2023, SI 2023/149, reg 2(1), Schedule, Pt 1.

8 'Article'

(1) For the purposes of—

(a) sections 6 and 7, and

(b) the provisions listed in subsection (2), so far as they relate to articles for use in the course of or in connection with fraud, 'article' includes any program or data held in electronic form.

(2) The provisions are—

(a) section 1(7)(b) of the Police and Criminal Evidence Act 1984 (c. 60),

(b) section 2(8)(b) of the Armed Forces Act 2001 (c. 19), and

(c) Article 3(7)(b) of the Police and Criminal Evidence (Northern Ireland) Order 1989 (S.I. 1989/1341 (N.I. 12));

(meaning of 'prohibited articles' for the purposes of stop and search powers).

9 Participating in fraudulent business carried on by sole trader etc.

(1) A person is guilty of an offence if he is knowingly a party to the carrying on of a business to which this section applies.

(2) This section applies to a business which is carried on—

(a) by a person who is outside the reach of [section 993 of the Companies Act 2006][1] (offence of fraudulent trading) , and

(b) with intent to defraud creditors of any person or for any other fraudulent purpose.

(3) The following are within the reach of [that section][1]—

(a) a company [(as defined in section 1(1) of the Companies Act 2006)][2];

(b) a person to whom that section applies (with or without adaptations or modifications) as if the person were a company;

(c) a person exempted from the application of that section.

(4) …[3]

(5) 'Fraudulent purpose' has the same meaning as in [that section][1].

(6) A person guilty of an offence under this section is liable—

(a) on summary conviction, to imprisonment for a term not exceeding [the general limit in a magistrates' court][4] or to a fine not exceeding the statutory maximum (or to both);

(b) on conviction on indictment, to imprisonment for a term not exceeding 10 years or to a fine (or to both).

(7) Subsection (6)(a) applies in relation to Northern Ireland as if the reference to 12 months were a reference to 6 months.

Amendments

1 Substituted by the Companies Act 2006 (Commencement No. 3, Consequential Amendments, Transitional Provisions and Savings) Order 2007, SI 2007/2194, art 10(1), Sch 4, para 111(1), (2), (3)(a), (5).

2 Substituted by the Companies Act 2006 (Consequential Amendments, Transitional Provisions and Savings) Order 2009, SI 2009/1941, art 2(1), Sch 1, para 257.

3 Repealed by the Companies Act 2006 (Commencement No. 3, Consequential Amendments, Transitional Provisions and Savings) Order 2007, SI 2007/2194, art 10(1), (3), Sch 4, para 111(1), (4), Sch 5.

4 Substituted by the Judicial Review and Courts Act 2022 (Magistrates' Court Sentencing Powers) Regulations 2023, SI 2023/149, reg 2(1), Schedule, Pt 1.

Prevention of Social Housing Fraud Act 2013

1 Unlawful sub-letting: secure tenancies

(1) A tenant of a dwelling-house [in England][1] let under a secure tenancy commits an offence if—

(a) in breach of an express or implied term of the tenancy, the tenant sub-lets or parts with possession of—

(i) the whole of the dwelling-house, or

(ii) part of the dwelling-house without the landlord's written consent,

(b) the tenant ceases to occupy the dwelling-house as the tenant's only or principal home, and

(c) the tenant knows that the conduct described in paragraph (a) is a breach of a term of the tenancy.

(2) A tenant of a dwelling-house let under a secure tenancy commits an offence if—

(a) dishonestly and in breach of an express or implied term of the tenancy, the tenant sub-lets or parts with possession of—

(i) the whole of the dwelling-house, or

(ii) part of the dwelling-house without the landlord's written consent, and

(b) the tenant ceases to occupy the dwelling-house as the tenant's only or principal home.

(3) The offence under subsection (1) is not committed where the tenant takes the action described in paragraphs (a) and (b) of that subsection because of violence or threats of violence by a person residing in, or in the locality of, the dwelling-house—

(a) towards the tenant, or

(b) towards a member of the family of the tenant who was residing with the tenant immediately before the tenant ceased to occupy the dwelling-house.

(4) The offence under subsection (1) is not committed if a person ('P') who occupies the dwelling-house as a result of the conduct described in subsection (1)(a) is—

(a) a person entitled to apply to the court for an order giving P a right to occupy the dwelling-house or to have the tenancy transferred to P, or

(b) a person in respect of whom an application may be made to have the tenancy transferred to P or to another person to be held for P's benefit.

(5) A person convicted of an offence under subsection (1) is liable on summary conviction to a fine not exceeding level 5 on the standard scale.

(6) A person convicted of an offence under subsection (2) is liable—

(a) on summary conviction, to imprisonment for a term not exceeding 6 months or a fine not exceeding the statutory maximum (or both);

(b) on conviction on indictment, to imprisonment for a term not exceeding 2 years or a fine (or both).

Amendment

1 Inserted by the Renting Homes (Wales) Act 2016 (Consequential Amendments) Regulations 2022, SI 2022/1166, reg 33(1), (2).

2 Unlawful sub-letting: assured tenancies [and secure contracts][1]

(1) A tenant of a dwelling-house let under an assured tenancy [or a secure contract][1] to which this section applies commits an offence if—

(a) in breach of an express or implied term of the tenancy, the tenant sub-lets or parts with possession of the whole or part of the dwelling-house,

(b) the tenant ceases to occupy the dwelling-house as the tenant's only or principal home, and

(c) the tenant knows that the conduct described in paragraph (a) is a breach of a term of the tenancy.

(2) A tenant of a dwelling-house let under an assured tenancy [or a secure contract][1] to which this section applies commits an offence if—

(a) dishonestly and in breach of an express or implied term of the tenancy, the tenant sub-lets or parts with possession of the whole or part of the dwelling-house, and

(b) the tenant ceases to occupy the dwelling-house as the tenant's only or principal home.

(3) This section applies to an assured tenancy [or a secure contract][1]—

(a) under which the landlord is a private registered provider of social housing[,][2] a registered social landlord [or in relation to Wales a community landlord][1], and

(b) which is not a shared ownership lease.

(4) The offence under subsection (1) is not committed where the tenant takes the action described in paragraphs (a) and (b) of that subsection because of violence or threats of violence by a person residing in, or in the locality of, the dwelling-house—

(a) towards the tenant, or

(b) towards a member of the family of the tenant who was residing with the tenant immediately before the tenant ceased to occupy the dwelling-house.

(5) The offence under subsection (1) is not committed if a person ('P') who occupies the dwelling-house as a result of the conduct described in subsection (1)(a) is—

(a) a person entitled to apply to the court for an order giving P a right to occupy the dwelling-house or to have the tenancy transferred to P, or

(b) a person in respect of whom an application may be made to have the tenancy transferred to P or to another person to be held for P's benefit.

(6) A person convicted of an offence under subsection (1) is liable on summary conviction to a fine not exceeding level 5 on the standard scale.

(7) A person convicted of an offence under subsection (2) is liable—

(a) on summary conviction, to imprisonment for a term not exceeding 6 months or a fine not exceeding the statutory maximum (or both);

(b) on conviction on indictment, to imprisonment for a term not exceeding 2 years or a fine (or both).

Amendments

1 Inserted by the Renting Homes (Wales) Act 2016 (Consequential Amendments) Regulations 2022, SI 2022/1166, reg 33(1), (3)(a)-(c), (d)(i), (ii)(bb).

2 Substituted by the Renting Homes (Wales) Act 2016 (Consequential Amendments) Regulations 2022, SI 2022/1166, reg 33(1), (3)(d)(i)(aa).

3 Prosecution of offences

(1) Proceedings for an offence under section 1(1) or 2(1) may be brought within the period of 6 months beginning with the date on which evidence sufficient in the opinion of the prosecutor to warrant the proceedings came to the prosecutor's knowledge.

(2) But no such proceedings may be brought more than three years—

(a) after the commission of the offence, or

(b) in the case of continuous contravention, after the last date on which the offence was committed.

(3) A certificate signed by the prosecutor and stating the date on which such evidence came to the prosecutor's knowledge is conclusive evidence of that fact; and a certificate to that effect and purporting to be so signed is to be treated as being so signed unless the contrary is proved.

(4) Subsections (1) to (3) also apply in relation to an associated offence which is a summary offence (to the extent that they would not otherwise apply to that offence).

(5) A local authority may prosecute an offence under section 1 or 2 in relation to a dwelling-house—

(a) whether or not the dwelling-house is or was let under a tenancy under which the local authority is or was the landlord, and

(b) whether or not the dwelling-house is located in the local authority's area.

(6) Subsection (5) also applies in relation to an associated offence (to the extent that it would not otherwise apply to that offence).

4 Unlawful profit orders: criminal proceedings

(1) This section applies if a person ('the offender') is convicted of—

(a) an offence under section 1 or 2, or

(b) an associated offence in relation to an offence under section 1 or 2.

(2) The court by or before which the offender is convicted—

(a) must, on application or otherwise, decide whether to make an unlawful profit order, and

(b) may, if it considers it appropriate to do so, make such an order, instead of or in addition to dealing with the offender in any other way.

(3) An 'unlawful profit order' is an order requiring the offender to pay the landlord an amount representing the profit made by the offender as a result of the conduct constituting the offence.

(4) If the court decides not to make an unlawful profit order, it must give reasons for that decision on passing sentence on the offender.

(5) The amount payable under an unlawful profit order must be such amount as the court considers appropriate, having regard to any evidence and to any representations that are made by or on behalf of the offender or the prosecutor, but subject to subsections (6) and (7).

(6) The maximum amount payable under an unlawful profit order is calculated as follows—

Step 1 Determine the total amount the offender received as a result of the conduct constituting the offence (or the best estimate of that amount).

Step 2 Deduct from the amount determined under step 1 the total amount, if any, paid by the offender as rent to the landlord (including service charges) over the period during which the offence was committed.

(7) Where an unlawful profit order has been made against the offender under section 5, an order under this section may only provide for the landlord to recover an amount equal to the aggregate of the following—

(a) any amount by which the amount of the offender's profit found under this section exceeds the amount payable under the order made under section 5, and

(b) a sum equal to any portion of the amount payable under the order made under section 5 that the landlord fails to recover,

and the landlord may not enforce the order under this section, so far as it relates to a sum mentioned in paragraph (b), without the leave of the court.

(8) Subsection (9) applies where the court considers—

(a) that, as well as being appropriate to make an unlawful profit order, it would be appropriate to impose a fine, and

(b) that the offender has insufficient means to pay both—

(i) an appropriate sum under an unlawful profit order, and

(ii) an appropriate sum under a fine.

(9) The court must give preference to making an unlawful profit order (though it may impose a fine as well).

(10) If the amount required to be paid by a person under an unlawful profit order is not paid when it is required to be paid, that person must pay interest on the amount for the period for which it remains unpaid.

(11) The rate of interest is the same rate as that for the time being specified in section 17 of the Judgments Act 1838 (interest on civil judgment debts).

(12) [Sections 141 to 143 of the Sentencing Code][1] (supplementary provisions about compensation orders) apply to unlawful profit orders as if—

(a) references to a compensation order were to an unlawful profit order (subject to paragraph (d)),

(b) references to the compensation to be paid under a compensation order were to the amount to be paid under an unlawful profit order,

[(c) section 143(3)(a) and (b) were omitted, and

(d) the reference in section 143(5)(b)(ii) to an unlawful profit order under section 4 were to a compensation order under Chapter 2 of Part 7 of the Sentencing Code.][1]

(13) In this section 'the landlord' means the landlord under the tenancy in respect of which the offence was committed.

Amendments

1 Substituted by the Sentencing Act 2020, s 410, Sch 24, para 290.

5 Unlawful profit orders: civil proceedings

(1) The court may, on the application of the landlord of a dwelling-house let under a secure or an assured tenancy [or a secure contract][1], make an unlawful profit order if—

(a) in the case of a secure tenancy, the conditions in subsection (3) are met, and

(b) in the case of an assured tenancy [or a secure contract][1], the conditions in subsection (4) are met.

(2) An 'unlawful profit order' is an order requiring the tenant against whom it is made to pay the landlord an amount representing the profit made by the tenant from the conduct described in subsection (3)(a) or (4)(c).

(3) The conditions in the case of a secure tenancy are that a tenant under the tenancy—

(a) in breach of an express or implied term of the tenancy, has sub-let or parted with possession of—

(i) the whole of the dwelling-house, or

(ii) part of the dwelling-house without the landlord's written consent,

(b) has ceased to occupy the dwelling-house as the tenant's only or principal home, and

(c) has received money as a result of the conduct described in paragraph (a).

(4) The conditions in the case of an assured tenancy [or a secure contract][1] are that—

(a) the landlord is a private registered provider of social housing[,][2] a registered social landlord [or in relation to Wales a community landlord][1],

(b) the tenancy is not a shared ownership lease,

(c) in breach of an express or implied term of the tenancy, a tenant under the tenancy has sub-let or parted with possession of the whole or part of the dwelling-house,

(d) the tenant has ceased to occupy the dwelling-house as the tenant's only or principal home, and

(e) the tenant has received money as a result of the conduct described in paragraph (c).

(5) The amount payable under an unlawful profit order must be such amount as the court considers appropriate, having regard to any evidence and to any representations that are made by or on behalf of the landlord or the tenant, but subject to subsections (6) and (7).

(6) The maximum amount payable under an unlawful profit order is calculated as follows—

Step 1 Determine the total amount the tenant received as a result of the conduct described in subsection (3)(a) or (4)(c) (or the best estimate of that amount).

Step 2 Deduct from the amount determined under step 1 the total amount, if any, paid by the tenant as rent to the landlord (including service charges) over the period during which the conduct described in subsection (3)(a) or (4)(c) took place.

(7) Where an unlawful profit order has been made against the tenant under section 4, an order under this section may only provide for the landlord to recover an amount equal to the aggregate of the following—

(a) any amount by which the amount of the tenant's profit found under this section exceeds the amount payable under the order made under section 4, and

(b) a sum equal to any portion of the amount payable under the order made under section 4 that the landlord fails to recover,

and the landlord may not enforce the order under this section, so far as it relates to a sum mentioned in paragraph (b), without the leave of the court.

(8) For the purposes of this section 'the court' means the High Court or the county court.

(9) Section 110(3) of the Housing Act 1985 (by which the claimant in proceedings relating to a secure tenancy may not recover the claimant's costs if the proceedings are taken in the High Court) does not apply to proceedings under this section.

Amendments

1 Inserted by the Renting Homes (Wales) Act 2016 (Consequential Amendments) Regulations 2022, SI 2022/1166, reg 33(1), (4)(a), (b)(i), (ii)(bb).

2 Substituted by the Renting Homes (Wales) Act 2016 (Consequential Amendments) Regulations 2022, SI 2022/1166, reg 33(1), (4)(b)(ii)(aa).

7 Regulations about powers to require information

(1) The appropriate authority may by regulations provide for the exercise, for prescribed housing fraud investigation purposes, of powers to require the provision of information.

(2) The appropriate authority may by regulations—

(a) make provision about the persons by whom powers conferred by regulations under this section may be exercised;

(b) in particular, make provision for the authorisation by local authorities of persons to exercise those powers.

(3) The provision that may be made by regulations under this section includes, in particular, provision equivalent to—

(a) provision made by a relevant enactment, or

(b) provision that is capable of being made under a relevant enactment,

with such modifications as the appropriate authority thinks fit.

(4) For the purposes of subsection (3), each of the following enactments is a 'relevant enactment'—

(a) section 109B of the Social Security Administration Act 1992 (powers to require information);

(b) section 110A of that Act (authorisations by local authorities to exercise powers of investigation);

(c) section 121DA(2) and (3) of that Act (interpretation of Part 6 of that Act).

(5) After the repeal of section 110A of the Social Security Administration Act 1992 by Part 1 of Schedule 14 to the Welfare Reform Act 2012, the reference to that section in subsection (4) is to that section as it had effect immediately before it was repealed.

(6) A person exercising powers conferred by regulations under this section must have regard to guidance issued or approved by the appropriate authority.

(7) In this section 'housing fraud investigation purposes' means purposes relating to the prevention, detection or securing of evidence for a conviction of—

(a) an offence under this Act;

(b) an offence under the Fraud Act 2006 relating to the unlawful sub-letting or parting with possession of the whole or part of a dwelling-house let by a local authority, a private registered provider of social housing or a registered social landlord,

(c) an offence under the Fraud Act 2006 relating to an application for an allocation of housing accommodation under Part 6 of the Housing Act 1996,

(d) an offence under the Fraud Act 2006 relating to an application for accommodation, or for assistance in obtaining accommodation, under Part 7 of the Housing Act 1996,

(e) an offence under the Fraud Act 2006 relating to—

(i) a claim to exercise the right to buy under Part 5 of the Housing Act 1985,

(ii) a claim to exercise the right to acquire under section 16 of the Housing Act 1996 [before the repeal of that section by the Abolition of the Right to Buy and Associated Rights (Wales) Act 2017 came into force][1], or

(iii) a claim to exercise the right to acquire under section 180 of the Housing and Regeneration Act 2008, or

(f) an associated offence in relation to an offence mentioned in any of paragraphs (a) to (e).

(8) In this section 'prescribed' means prescribed by regulations under this section.

Amendments

1 Inserted by the Abolition of the Right to Buy and Associated Rights (Wales) Act 2018, s 6(3), Sch 1, para 8.

8 Regulations about related offence

(1) The appropriate authority may by regulations provide for the creation of an offence that may be committed by a person by refusing or failing to provide

any information or document when required to do so by or under regulations under section 7.

(2) Regulations under this section—

(a) must provide for an offence under the regulations to be triable only summarily;

(b) may not provide for such an offence to be punishable with a fine exceeding level 3 on the standard scale.

(3) Regulations under this section—

(a) may provide, in a case where a person is convicted of an offence under the regulations and the act or omission constituting the offence continues after the conviction, for the person to be guilty of a further offence and liable on summary conviction to a daily fine;

(b) may not provide for the daily fine to exceed £40.

(4) The appropriate authority may by regulations make provision—

(a) about defences to an offence under regulations under this section;

(b) about the commission by a body corporate of such an offence;

(c) about the conduct of proceedings for such an offence;

(d) about the time limits for bringing such proceedings;

(e) about the determination of issues arising in such proceedings;

(f) about other matters of procedure and evidence in relation to such an offence.

9 Regulations: supplementary

(1) In sections 7 and 8 'the appropriate authority' means—

(a) the Secretary of State, in relation to England, and

(b) the Welsh Ministers, in relation to Wales.

(2) Regulations under section 7 or 8—

(a) are to be made by statutory instrument,

(b) may make different provision for different cases or circumstances, and

(c) may contain incidental, supplementary, consequential, transitional, transitory or saving provision.

(3) A statutory instrument containing regulations made by the Secretary of State under section 7 or 8 may not be made unless a draft of the instrument has been laid before and approved by a resolution of each House of Parliament.

(4) A statutory instrument containing regulations made by the Welsh Ministers under section 7 or 8 may not be made unless a draft of the instrument has

been laid before and approved by a resolution of the National Assembly for Wales.

10 Consequential amendments

The Schedule (consequential amendments) has effect.

11 Interpretation

(1) In this Act—

(a) 'secure tenancy' has the meaning given by section 79 of the Housing Act 1985, …[1]

(b) 'assured tenancy' has the same meaning as in Part 1 of the Housing Act 1988[, and][2]

[(c) 'secure contract' has the same meaning as in section 8 of the Renting Homes (Wales) Act 2016 (anaw 1).][3]

(2) In the application of this Act in relation to a secure tenancy, the following expressions have the same meaning as in the Housing Act 1985—

'dwelling-house' (see section 112 of that Act);

'landlord' (see section 621 of that Act);

'tenancy' (see section 621 of that Act);

'tenant' (see section 621 of that Act).

(3) In the application of this Act in relation to an assured tenancy, the following expressions have the same meaning as in the Housing Act 1988—

'dwelling-house' (see section 45(1) of that Act);

'landlord' (see section 45(1) and (3) of that Act);

'tenancy' (see section 45(1) of that Act);

'tenant' (see section 45(1) and (3) of that Act).

[(3A) In the application of this Act in relation to a secure contract, the following expressions have the same meaning as in the Renting Homes (Wales) Act 2016 (anaw 1)—

(a) 'community landlord' (see section 9 of that Act);

(b) 'secure contract' (see section 8 of that Act).][3]

(4) References in this Act to a member of the tenant's family (in relation to a secure or an assured tenancy [or a secure contract][3]) are to be construed in accordance with section 113 of the Housing Act 1985.

[(4A) References in this Act to a member of the tenant's family (in relation to a secure contract) are to be construed in accordance with section 250 of the Renting Homes (Wales) Act 2016.][3]

(5) In this Act 'shared ownership lease' means a lease of a dwelling-house—

(a) granted on payment of a premium calculated by reference to a percentage of the value of the dwelling-house or of the cost of providing it, or

(b) under which the lessee (or the lessee's personal representatives) will or may be entitled to a sum calculated by reference, directly or indirectly, to the value of the dwelling-house.

(6) References in this Act to the landlord under a secure or an assured tenancy [or a secure contract][3] include—

(a) in a case where the tenancy has ended, a person who was the landlord under the tenancy, and

(b) in a case where the tenancy has ceased to be a secure or an assured tenancy [or a secure contract][3], the person who was the landlord under the tenancy when it was a secure or an assured tenancy [or a secure contract][3].

(7) References in this Act to the tenant under a secure or an assured tenancy [or a secure contract][3] include—

(a) in a case where the tenancy has ended, a person who was the tenant under the tenancy, and

(b) in a case where the tenancy has ceased to be a secure or an assured tenancy [or a secure contract][3], a person who was the tenant under the tenancy when it was a secure or an assured tenancy [or a secure contract][3].

(8) In this Act 'local authority' means a county council, a county borough council, a district council, a London borough council, the Common Council of the City of London or the Council of the Isles of Scilly.

(9) In this Act 'registered social landlord' has the same meaning as in Part 1 of the Housing Act 1996.

(10) In this Act 'associated offence', in relation to an offence, means—

(a) an offence of aiding, abetting, counselling or procuring the commission of that offence,

(b) an offence of attempting or conspiring to commit that offence, or

(c) an offence under Part 2 of the Serious Crime Act 2007 (encouraging or assisting crime) in relation to that offence.

Amendments

1 Repealed by the Renting Homes (Wales) Act 2016 (Consequential Amendments) Regulations 2022, SI 2022/1166, reg 33(1), (5)(a)(i).

2 Substituted by the Renting Homes (Wales) Act 2016 (Consequential Amendments) Regulations 2022, SI 2022/1166, reg 33(1), (5)(a)(ii).

3 Inserted by the Renting Homes (Wales) Act 2016 (Consequential Amendments) Regulations 2022, SI 2022/1166, reg 33(1), (5)(a)(iii), (b)-(f).

12 Extent, commencement and short title

(1) This Act extends to England and Wales only, subject to subsection (2).

(2) An amendment of an Act made by this Act has the same extent as the provision to which it relates.

(3) The provisions of this Act, apart from this section, come into force—

(a) in relation to England, on such day as the Secretary of State may by order appoint;

(b) in relation to Wales, on such day as the Welsh Ministers may by order appoint.

(4) An order under subsection (3) is to be made by statutory instrument.

(5) An order under subsection (3) may—

(a) appoint different days for different purposes, and

(b) make transitional, transitory or saving provision.

(6) This Act may be cited as the Prevention of Social Housing Fraud Act 2013.

Renters' Rights Act 2025

PART 1
TENANCY REFORM

Chapter 1
Assured tenancies

End of certain kinds of assured tenancy

1 Assured tenancies to be periodic with rent period not exceeding a month

In the 1988 Act, before section 5 insert—

'4A Assured tenancies to be periodic with rent period not exceeding a month

(1) Terms of an assured tenancy are of no effect so far as they provide—

(a) for a tenancy to be a fixed term tenancy, or

(b) for periods of the tenancy to be different from the periods for which rent is payable ('rent periods').

(2) Where terms of an assured tenancy are of no effect by virtue of subsection (1)(a) or (b), the tenancy has effect as a periodic tenancy under which the periods of the tenancy are the same as the rent periods.

(3) Terms of an assured tenancy which provide for the rent periods are of no effect unless each rent period is—

(a) a period of 28 days or shorter, or

(b) a monthly rent period.

(4) Those terms may provide for different rent periods at different times during the assured tenancy (but each rent period must be permitted by subsection (3)).

(5) Where terms of an assured tenancy are of no effect by virtue of subsection (3), the tenancy has effect as if it provided—

(a) for successive rent periods of one month beginning with the first day of the tenancy, and

(b) for the rent for each such rent period—

(i) to be the amount calculated in accordance with the formula in subsection (6), and

(ii) to be due on the first day of the period.

(6) The formula is—

$(R / D) \times 30.42$

where—

R is the rent that would have been due for the first rent period of the tenancy under the terms that are of no effect by virtue of subsection (3);

D is the number of whole days in that period.

(7) Except as provided by subsections (1) and (3), nothing in this section limits any right of the landlord and the tenant to vary a term of a tenancy by agreement.

(8) For the purposes of this section, terms of an assured tenancy provide for 'monthly' rent periods if they provide for rent to be payable for successive periods of one month, disregarding any provision for the first period to be a different period not exceeding 30 days.

2 Abolition of assured shorthold tenancies

In the 1988 Act—

(a) omit section 6A (demotion to assured shorthold tenancy because of anti-social behaviour);

(b) omit Chapter 2 of Part 1 (assured shorthold tenancies).

Grounds for possession

3 Changes to grounds for possession

(1) Schedule 1 contains amendments of Schedule 2 to the 1988 Act (grounds for possession of dwelling-houses let on assured tenancies).

(2) In section 7 of the 1988 Act (orders for possession)—

(a) in subsection (3), for 'subsections (5A) and (6)' substitute 'the following provisions of this section';

(b) in subsection (4) omit ', subject to subsections (5A) and (6) below,';

(c) in subsection (5) omit the words from 'and Part IV' to the end';

(d) after subsection (5) insert—

'(5ZA) The court may not make an order for possession of a dwelling-house on any of Grounds 1 to 5H or Ground 6A where—

(a) a smallholding was previously let to the tenant under a tenancy to which the Agricultural Holdings Act 1986 applies ('the agricultural tenancy'),

(b) the agricultural tenancy came to an end as a result of the operation of a notice to quit given in case A in Part 1 of Schedule 3 to that Act ('case A'),

(c) the assured tenancy was granted immediately after the agricultural tenancy came to an end, and

(d) the dwelling-house is let under the assured tenancy—

(i) by the person who was the landlord under the agricultural tenancy ('the former agricultural landlord'), or

(ii) by another person pursuant to a contract or other agreement entered into with the former agricultural landlord under which—

(A) the dwelling-house is to be let as suitable alternative accommodation for the purposes of paragraph (b) of case A, and

(B) this subsection is to apply.

(5ZB) The court may not make an order for possession of a dwelling-house let on an assured tenancy on any of Grounds 1 to 5H or Ground 6A where, on the basis of the proposed let of the dwelling-house on that tenancy, the dwelling-house was deemed to be suitable alternative accommodation under paragraph 1(c) of Part 4 of Schedule 2 to the Housing Act 1985 for the purposes of section 84(2)(b) and (c) of that Act.';

(e) in subsection (5A)—

(i) in paragraph (a), for ', 2, 5' substitute 'to 5H, 6A, 6B'

(ii) omit paragraph (b) (but not the 'and' at the end).

(f) after subsection (5A) insert—

'(5B) The court may not make an order for possession of a dwelling-house let on an assured tenancy granted in accordance with section 554(3)(c) (before its repeal) or (ca) of the Housing Act 1985 on any of Grounds 1 to 5H or Ground 6A.

(5C) In relation to the making of an order for possession of a dwelling-house let on an assured periodic tenancy arising under Schedule 10 to the Local Government and Housing Act 1989, Ground 6 is to apply as if—

(a) in paragraph (b), the words ', but only in a case where section 7(5ZA) applies in relation to the tenancy' were omitted;

(b) in the general redevelopment conditions, paragraph (f) was omitted;

(c) in the landlord's acquisition condition, in paragraph (a), the reference to the grant of the tenancy is a reference to the grant of the long residential tenancy which existed immediately before the assured periodic tenancy arose.

(5D) If the only grounds for possession which the court is satisfied are established are either or both of Grounds 7A and 14 in Schedule 2, the court may not make an order for possession to take effect within—

(a) the period of 14 days beginning with the date of service of the notice under section 8; or

(b) where the court has exercised the power conferred by section 8(1)(b), the period of 14 days beginning—

(i) if a purported notice of possession (within the meaning given by section 16M) was served on the tenant and the court considers it just and equitable, with the date on which the notice was served;

(ii) otherwise, with the date on which the proceedings for possession began.

(5E) In subsection (5C), a reference to a 'long residential tenancy' is a reference to a tenancy to which Schedule 10 to the Local Government and Housing Act 1989 applies.'

(g) omit subsections (6), (6A), (6B) and (7).

(3) In section 8 of the 1988 Act (notice of proceedings for possession)—

(a) in subsection (1)(a) for '(4B)' substitute '(4AA)';

(b) in subsection (3)(b) for '(3A) to (4B)' substitute '(4) to (4AA)';

(c) omit subsection (3A);

(d) in subsection (4)—

(i) for 'Ground 14' substitute 'either or both of Grounds 7A and 14';

(ii) after 'whether' insert 'with or';

(iii) omit 'or with any ground other than Ground 7A';

(e) for subsections (4A) and (4B) substitute—

'(4AA) If a notice under this section does not specify Ground 7A or 14 in Schedule 2, the date specified in the notice as mentioned in subsection (3)(b) must not be before the end of the longest period shown in the following table for any ground specified in the notice.

Ground specified in notice	*Period*
1, 1A, 1B, 2, 2ZA, 2ZB, 2ZC, 2ZD, 4A, 6, 6A, 6B	four months beginning with the date of service of the notice
5, 5A, 5B, 5C, 5D, 5H, 7, 9	two months beginning with the date of service of the notice
5E, 5F, 5G, 8, 10, 11, 18	four weeks beginning with the date of service of the notice
4, 7B, 12, 13, 14ZA, 14A, 15, 17	two weeks beginning with the date of service of the notice';

(f) after subsection (5) insert—

'(5A) A notice given by an intermediate landlord under Ground 2ZA is to be treated, when the superior tenancy ends, as a notice given by the person who became the landlord by virtue of section 18 under Ground 2ZC.

(5B) A notice given by an intermediate landlord under Ground 2ZB is to be treated, when the superior tenancy ends, as a notice given by the person who became the landlord by virtue of section 18 under Ground 2ZD.';

(g) omit subsection (6).

(4) After section 8 of the 1988 Act insert—

'8ZA Disapplication of conditions where notice dispensed with

(1) This section applies where the court exercises the power conferred by section 8(1)(b) in proceedings relating to Ground 4A, 5G or 6 in Schedule 2.

(2) The court may, if it considers it just and equitable to do so—

(a) where the proceedings relate to Ground 4A, disapply paragraph (d) of the ground;

(b) where the proceedings relate to Ground 5G, disapply paragraph (b) of the ground;

(c) where the proceedings relate to Ground 6, disapply paragraph (aa)(ii)(B) of the ground.

(3) References in this section to grounds in Schedule 2 are to those grounds read in accordance with paragraph 12(2) of that Schedule.'

(5) After section 11 of the 1988 Act insert—

'11A Possession on ground 6B: compensation of tenant

(1) This section applies where a court makes an order for possession of a dwelling-house let on an assured tenancy on Ground 6B in Schedule 2 to this Act (whether or not the order is also made on any other ground).

(2) The court may order the landlord to pay to the tenant such sum as appears sufficient as compensation for damage or loss sustained by that tenant as a result of the order for possession.

(3) In deciding whether to make an order under this section, and what compensation to order, the court must (in particular) take into account the circumstances which led to Ground 6B being available as a ground for making an order for possession (including any conduct by the tenant which caused or contributed to Ground 6B being available).'

5 Form of notice of proceedings for possession

In section 8 of the 1988 Act, after subsection (6) insert—

'(7) Regulations made under section 45(1) by virtue of subsection (3) may—

(a) provide for the form to be published by the Secretary of State;

(b) provide that the form to be used is the version that has effect at the time the requirement applies.'

Chapter 2
Tenancies that cannot be assured tenancies

31 Long tenancies and financial services products

(1) In Part 1 of Schedule 1 to the 1988 Act (tenancies which cannot be assured tenancies), after paragraph 3C insert—

'Fixed term tenancies of more than 21 years

3D A fixed term tenancy of a term certain of more than 21 years from the date of the grant of the tenancy.

Fixed term tenancies of 7 to 21 years granted before the Renters' Rights Act 2025

3E

(1) A tenancy of a term certain of—

(a) 21 years or less, but

(b) more than 7 years,

from the date of the grant of the tenancy.

(2) This paragraph applies only to tenancies entered into—

(a) before the day on which the Renters' Rights Act 2025 was passed,

(b) during the period of two months beginning with that day, or

(c) after the end of that period under a contract entered into before the end of that period.

Regulated home purchase plans

3F

(1) A tenancy which, when it is granted, forms part of a regulated home purchase plan.

(2) In this paragraph 'regulated home purchase plan' has the same meaning that it has from time to time in regulation 63F(3)(a) of the Financial Services and Markets Act 2000 (Regulated Activities) Order 2001 (S.I. 2001/544).

(3) The Secretary of State may, by regulations, amend this paragraph in consequence of an order made under section 22 of the Financial Services and Markets Act 2000.

(4) Regulations under this paragraph—

(a) may make different provision for different purposes;

(b) are to be made by statutory instrument.

(5) A statutory instrument containing regulations under this paragraph may not be made unless a draft of the instrument has been laid before and approved by a resolution of each House of Parliament.'

(2) In section 133 of the 1988 Act (consent required for certain subsequent disposals), in subsection (11)(f), for '4' substitute '3D'.

(3) In the Landlord and Tenant Act 1985—

(a) in section 9B (leases to which section 9A of that Act applies), in subsection (1)(b)—

(i) after 'subsection (1A)' insert ', (1AA)';

(ii) for the words from 'leases' to 'more' substitute 'certain leases to which section 11 applies';

(b) in section 13 (leases to which section 11 of that Act applies: general rule)—

(i) after subsection (1) insert—

'(1AZA) But that is subject to subsections (1ZA) to (1ZC).';

(ii) in subsection (1ZA), for 'But in' substitute 'In';

(iii) after subsection (1ZB) insert—

'(1ZC) Section 11 does not apply to a lease of a dwelling-house in England which—

(a) was an assured tenancy immediately before the commencement date (which has the meaning given by section 146(3) of the Renters' Rights Act 2025), and

(b) was granted—

(i) for a term of seven years or more, and

(ii) by a person other than a private registered provider of social housing.';

(iv) in subsection (1A) omit paragraph (b) and the word 'or' preceding it;

(v) after subsection (1A) insert—

'(1AA) Section 11 also applies to a lease of a dwelling-house in England granted on or after the day on which section 166 of the Localism Act 2011 came into force which is a tenancy for a fixed term of more than seven years that—

(a) would be an assured tenancy if it were not for a term of more than seven years,

(b) is not a shared ownership lease, and

(c) is granted by a private registered provider of social housing.';

(vi) in subsection (1B), for 'In subsection (1A)' substitute 'In this section'.

(4) In paragraph 1 of Schedule 10 to the Local Government and Housing Act 1989 (security of tenure on ending of long residential tenancies), in sub-paragraph (1)(a) after 'low rent' insert 'and were not for a term of more than seven years'.

(5) Where, immediately before the day on which this section comes into force, proceedings for an order for possession under section 8 of the 1988 Act in reliance on a valid notice given under that section of that Act have been commenced in relation to a tenancy and have not been concluded, or have not been commenced but have not become time-barred—

(a) the tenancy remains an assured tenancy, and the notice remains valid, until any time when such proceedings in reliance on the notice become time-barred or are concluded, and

(b) until that time the amendments made by subsections (1) and (4) do not apply in relation to the tenancy.

(6) For the purposes of subsection (5), proceedings are 'time-barred' after the time limit mentioned in section 8(3)(c) of the 1988 Act.

APPENDIX B

Secondary Legislation

References

Notices to Quit etc. (Prescribed Information) Regulations 1988, SI 1988/2201
regs 1–3, Sch

UK General Data Protection Regulation 2016
arts 1–11A

Full-Text Provisions

PREVENTION OF SOCIAL HOUSING FRAUD (POWER TO REQUIRE INFORMATION) (ENGLAND) REGULATIONS 2014, SI 2014/899

1 Citation, commencement and application

(1) These Regulations may be cited as the Prevention of Social Housing Fraud (Power to Require Information) (England) Regulations 2014 and come into force on the third day after the day on which they are made.

(2) These Regulations apply in relation to England only.

2 Interpretation

(1) In these Regulations—

'authorised officer' means a person acting in accordance with any authorisation for the purposes of these Regulations which is for the time being in force in relation to that person.

(2) For the purposes of these Regulations—

(a) references to a document include references to anything in which information is recorded in electronic or any other form;

(b) the requirement that notice be given by an authorised officer in writing shall be taken to be satisfied in any case where the contents of the notice—

(i) are transmitted to the recipient of the notice by electronic means; and

(ii) are received by that person in a form that is legible and capable of being recorded for future reference.

3 Authorisations by local authorities

(1) Subject to paragraphs (2) and (3), a local authority may grant an authorisation to an individual to exercise the powers conferred on an authorised officer under regulation 4.

(2) A local authority may only grant authorisation to an individual if that person is—

(a) an individual employed by that authority;

(b) an individual employed by another local authority or joint committee that carries out functions relating to housing fraud investigation purposes on behalf of that authority.

(3) An authorisation granted to an individual for the purposes of these Regulations—

(a) must be in writing and provided to that individual as evidence of that individual's entitlement to exercise powers conferred by these Regulations;

(b) may contain provision as to the period for which the authorisation is to have effect; and,

(c) may restrict the powers exercisable by virtue of the authorisation so as to prohibit their exercise except for particular purposes or in particular circumstances.

(4) An authorisation may be withdrawn at any time in writing by the local authority that granted it.

(5) The written authorisation or withdrawal of an authorisation by any local authority must be issued under the hand of either—

(a) the officer designated under section 4 of the Local Government and Housing Act 1989 as the head of the authority's paid service; or

(b) the officer who is the authority's chief finance officer (within the meaning of section 5 of that Act).

(6) A local authority may grant an authorisation for housing fraud investigation purposes in relation to offences in the area of another local authority, as well as in relation to offences in the area of the authority granting the authorisation.

4 Power to require information

(1) An authorised officer may exercise the powers conferred by this regulation for any of the housing fraud investigation purposes (but not for any other purpose).

(2) An authorised officer who has reasonable grounds for suspecting that a person—

(a) is a person falling within paragraph (3) below, and

(b) has or may have possession of or access to any information about any matter that is relevant to housing fraud investigation purposes,

may, by written notice, require that person to provide all such information described in the notice of which that person has possession, or to which that person has access, and which it is reasonable for the authorised officer to require for the purpose so mentioned.

(3) The persons who fall within this paragraph are—

(a) any bank;

(b) any person carrying on a business the whole or a significant part of which consists in the provision of credit (whether secured or unsecured) to members of the public;

(c) any water undertaker or sewerage undertaker;

(d) any person who—

(i) is the holder of a licence under section 7 of the Gas Act 1986 to convey gas through pipes; or,

(ii) is the holder of a licence under section 7A of that Act to supply gas through pipes;

(e) any person who (within the meaning of the Electricity Act 1989) distributes or supplies electricity;

(f) ...[1]

(g) any servant or agent of any person mentioned in sub-paragraphs (a) to [(e)][2].

(4) Subject to the following provisions of this regulation, the powers conferred by this regulation on an authorised officer to require information from any person by virtue of that person falling within paragraph (3) shall be exercisable for the purpose only of obtaining information relating to a particular person identified (by name or description) by the officer.

(5) An authorised officer shall not, in exercise of those powers, require any information from any person by virtue of that person falling within paragraph (3) unless it appears to that officer that there are reasonable grounds for believing that the person to whom it relates is—

(a) a person who has committed, is committing or intends to commit an offence listed in section 7(7) of the Prevention of Social Housing Fraud Act 2013; or

(b) a person who is a member of the family of a person falling within sub-paragraph (a).

(6) ...[1]

(7) ...[1]

(8) The obligation of a person to provide information in accordance with a notice under this regulation shall be discharged only by the provision of that information, at such reasonable time and in such form as may be specified in the notice, to the authorised officer who—

(a) is identified by or in accordance with the terms of the notice; or

(b) has been identified, since the giving of the notice, by a further written notice given by the authorised officer who imposed the original requirement or another authorised officer.

(9) The power of an authorised officer under this regulation to require the provision of information shall include a power to require the production and delivery up and (if necessary) creation of any such documents containing the information as may be specified or described in the notice imposing the requirement, or the creation of copies of or extracts from any such documents.

(10) No person shall be required under this regulation to provide—

(a) any information that tends to incriminate either that person or, in the case of a person who is married or is a civil partner, that person's spouse or civil partner; or

(b) any information in respect of which a claim to legal professional privilege would be successful in any proceedings;

and for the purposes of this paragraph it is immaterial whether the information is in documentary form or not.

[(10A) Nothing in this regulation is to be read as enabling a person to secure the disclosure by a telecommunications operator or postal operator of communications data without the consent of the operator.][3]

(11) In this regulation—

'bank' means—

(a) a person who has permission under Part 4A of the Financial Services and Markets Act 2000 to accept deposits;

(b) …[4] or

(c) a person who does not require permission under that Act to accept deposits in the course of that person's business in the United Kingdom;

['communications data' has the same meaning as in the Investigatory Powers Act 2016 (see sections 261 and 262 of that Act);][3]

'credit' includes a cash loan or any form of financial accommodation, including the cashing of a cheque;

'family' is to be construed in accordance with section 113 of the Housing Act 1985;

['postal operator' has the same meaning as in the Investigatory Powers Act 2016 (see section 262 of that Act);][3]

['telecommunications operator' has the same meaning as in the Investigatory Powers Act 2016 (see section 261 of that Act).][1]

(12) The definition of 'bank' in paragraph (11) must be read in accordance with—

(a) section 22 of the Financial Services and Marketing Act 2000;

(b) any relevant order under that section; and

(c) Schedule 2 to that Act.

Amendments

1 Repealed by the Investigatory Powers Act 2016, s 12(1), Sch 2, para 11(a), (c), (e)(iii).

2 Substituted by the Investigatory Powers Act 2016, s 12(1), Sch 2, para 11(b).

3 Inserted by the Investigatory Powers Act 2016, s 12(1), Sch 2, para 11(d), (e)(i), (ii).

4 Repealed by the EEA Passport Rights (Amendment, etc., and Transitional Provisions) (EU Exit) Regulations 2018, SI 2018/1149, reg 1(3), Schedule, para 80.

5 Delay, obstruction etc of an authorised officer

(1) If a person (P) —

(a) intentionally delays or obstructs an authorised officer in the exercise of any power under regulation 4; or

(b) refuses or fails, without reasonable excuse, to provide any information or to provide any document when required to do so under regulation 4,

P shall be guilty of an offence and liable on summary conviction to a fine not exceeding level 3 on the standard scale.

(2) Where P is convicted of an offence under paragraph (1)(b) and the refusal or failure is continued by P after P's conviction, P shall be guilty of a further offence and liable on summary conviction to a fine not exceeding £40 for each day on which it is continued.

6 Liability of directors etc.

(1) Where an offence under regulation 5 which has been committed by a body corporate is proved to have been committed with the consent or connivance of, or to be attributable to any neglect on the part of, a director, manager, secretary or other similar officer of the body corporate, or any person who was purporting to act in any such capacity, that person, as well as the body corporate, shall be guilty of that offence and be liable to be proceeded against accordingly.

(2) Where the affairs of a body corporate are managed by its members, paragraph (1) applies in relation to the acts and defaults of a member in connection with that member's functions of management as if that member were a director of the body corporate.

7 Legal proceedings

(1) Proceedings for an offence under regulation 5 may be brought within the period of 6 months beginning with the date on which evidence sufficient in the opinion of the prosecutor to warrant the proceedings came to the prosecutor's knowledge.

(2) But no such proceedings may be brought more than three years —

(a) after the commission of the offence, or

(b) in the case of a continuous contravention, after the last date on which the offence was committed.

(3) A certificate signed by the prosecutor and stating the date on which such evidence came to the prosecutor's knowledge is conclusive evidence of that fact; and a certificate to that effect and purporting to be signed is to be treated as being so signed unless the contrary is proved.

APPENDIX C

Civil Procedure Rules

Civil Procedure Rules 1998, SI 1998/3132

PART 3
THE COURT'S CASE [AND COSTS][1] MANAGEMENT POWERS

[Section I
Case Management][1]

The court's general powers of management

3.1

(1) The list of powers in this rule is in addition to any powers given to the court by any other rule or practice direction or by any other enactment or any powers it may otherwise have.

(2) Except where these Rules provide otherwise, the court may—

(a) extend or shorten the time for compliance with any rule, practice direction or court order (even if an application for extension is made after the time for compliance has expired);

(b) adjourn or bring forward a hearing;

[[(c)][2] require that any proceedings in the High Court be heard by a Divisional Court of the High Court;][3]

[(d)][2] require a party or a party's legal representative to attend the court;

[(e)][2] hold a hearing and receive evidence by telephone or by using any other method of direct oral communication;

[(f)][2] direct that part of any proceedings (such as a counterclaim) be dealt with as separate proceedings;

[(g)][2] stay[(GL)] the whole or part of any proceedings or judgment either generally or until a specified date or event;

[(h)][2] consolidate proceedings;

[(i)][2] try two or more claims on the same occasion;

[(j)][2] direct a separate trial of any issue;

[(k)][2] decide the order in which issues are to be tried;

[(l)][2] exclude an issue from consideration;

[(m)][2] dismiss or give judgment on a claim after a decision on a preliminary issue;

[[(n)][2] order any party to file and [exchange a costs budget][4];][5]

[(o) order the parties to engage in alternative dispute resolution; and][6]

[(p)][2] take any other step or make any other order for the purpose of managing the case and furthering the overriding objective[, including hearing an Early Neutral Evaluation with the aim of helping the parties settle the case][7].

(3) When the court makes an order, it may—

(a) make it subject to conditions, including a condition to pay a sum of money into court; and

(b) specify the consequence of failure to comply with the order or a condition.

[(3A) Where the court has made a direction in accordance with paragraph [(2)(c)][8] the proceedings shall be heard by a Divisional Court of the High Court and not by a single judge.][3]

(4) Where the court gives directions it [will][9] take into account whether or not a party has complied with [the Practice Direction (Pre-Action Conduct) and][10] any relevant pre-action protocol[(GL)].

(5) The court may order a party to pay a sum of money into court if that party has, without good reason, failed to comply with a rule, practice direction or a relevant pre-action protocol.

(6) When exercising its power under paragraph (5) the court must have regard to—

(a) the amount in dispute; and

(b) the costs which the parties have incurred or which they may incur.

[(6A) Where a party pays money into court following an order under paragraph (3) or (5), the money shall be security for any sum payable by that party to any other party in the proceedings ...[11].

...[11]][12]

(7) A power of the court under these Rules to make an order includes a power to vary or revoke the order.

[(8) The court may contact the parties from time to time in order to monitor compliance with directions. The parties must respond promptly to any such enquiries from the court.][1]

Amendments

1 Inserted by the Civil Procedure (Amendment) Rules 2013, SI 2013/262, r 5(a), (c), (d).

2 Renumbered by the Civil Procedure (Amendment No. 3) Rules 2024, SI 2024/839, rr 2, 5(1)(a)(i), (ii), (iv).

3 Inserted by the Civil Procedure (Amendment No. 2) Rules 2017, SI 2017/889, rr 2, 3.

4 Substituted by the Civil Procedure (Amendment No. 7) Rules 2013, SI 2013/1974, r 4(a).

5 Inserted by the Civil Procedure (Amendment No. 3) Rules 2005, SI 2005/2292, rr 2, 3.

6 Inserted by the Civil Procedure (Amendment No. 3) Rules 2024, SI 2024/839, rr 2, 5(1)(a)(iii).

7 Inserted by the Civil Procedure (Amendment No. 4) Rules 2015, SI 2015/1569, rr 2, 4.

8 Substituted by the Civil Procedure (Amendment No. 3) Rules 2024, SI 2024/839, rr 2, 5(1)(b).

9 Substituted by the Civil Procedure (Amendment No. 3) Rules 2008, SI 2008/3327, r 3(a).

10 Inserted by the Civil Procedure (Amendment No. 3) Rules 2008, SI 2008/3327, r 3(b).

11 Repealed by the Civil Procedure (Amendment No. 3) Rules 2006, SI 2006/3435, r 3.

12 Inserted by the Civil Procedure (Amendment) Rules 1999, SI 1999/1008, r 4.

Case management – unrepresented parties

3.1A

(1) This rule applies in any proceedings where at least one party is unrepresented.

(2) When the court is exercising any powers of case management, it must have regard to the fact that at least one party is unrepresented.

(3) Both the parties and the court must, when drafting case management directions in the multi-track[, intermediate track][1] and fast track, take as their starting point any relevant standard directions which can be found online at www.justice.gov.uk/courts/procedure-rules/civil and adapt them as appropriate to the circumstances of the case.

(4) The court must adopt such procedure at any hearing as it considers appropriate to further the overriding objective.

(5) At any hearing where the court is taking evidence this may include—

(a) ascertaining from an unrepresented party the matters about which the witness may be able to give evidence or on which the witness ought to be cross-examined; and

(b) putting, or causing to be put, to the witness such questions as may appear to the court to be proper.][2]

Amendments

1 Inserted by the Civil Procedure (Amendment No. 2) Rules 2023, SI 2023/572, rr 3, 5(1).

2 Inserted by the Civil Procedure (Amendment No. 4) Rules 2015, SI 2015/1569, rr 2, 5.

Court officer's power to refer to a judge

3.2

Where a step is to be taken by a court officer—

(a) the court officer may consult a judge before taking that step;

(b) the step may be taken by a judge instead of the court officer.

Court's power to make order of its own initiative

3.3

(1) Except where a rule or some other enactment provides otherwise, the court may exercise its powers on an application or of its own initiative.

(Part 23 sets out the procedure for making an application)

(2) Where the court proposes to make an order of its own initiative—

(a) it may give any person likely to be affected by the order an opportunity to make representations; and

(b) where it does so it must specify the time by and the manner in which the representations must be made.

(3) Where the court proposes—

(a) to make an order of its own initiative; and

(b) to hold a hearing to decide whether to make the order,

it must give each party likely to be affected by the order at least 3 days' notice of the hearing.

(4) The court may make an order of its own initiative without hearing the parties or giving them an opportunity to make representations.

(5) Where the court has made an order under paragraph (4)—

(a) a party affected by the order may apply to have it set aside(GL), varied or stayed(GL); and

(b) the order must contain a statement of the right to make such an application.

(6) An application under paragraph (5)(a) must be made—

(a) within such period as may be specified by the court; or

(b) if the court does not specify a period, not more than 7 days after the date on which the order was served on the party making the application.

[(7) An application under paragraph (5)(a) shall be considered at an oral hearing unless the court decides and states in an order that the application is totally without merit.

(8) If the court decides under paragraph (7) that the application is totally without merit, an application under paragraph (5)(a) may be made for reconsideration without an oral hearing.][1]

[[(9)][2] If the court of its own initiative strikes out a statement of case or dismisses an application [(including an application for permission to appeal or for permission to apply for judicial review)][3], and it considers that the claim or application is totally without merit—

(a) the court's order must record that fact; and

(b) the court must at the same time consider whether it is appropriate to make a civil restraint order.][4]

Amendments

1 Inserted by the Civil Procedure (Amendment No. 3) Rules 2023, SI 2023/788, rr 2, 3(2)(a).

2 Renumbered by the Civil Procedure (Amendment No. 3) Rules 2023, SI 2023/788, rr 2, 3(2)(b).

3 Inserted by the Civil Procedure (Amendment No. 3) Rules 2005, SI 2005/2292, rr 2, 4.

4 Inserted by the Civil Procedure (Amendment No. 2) Rules 2004, SI 2004/2072, r 4.

Power to strike out a statement of case

3.4

(1) In this rule and rule 3.5, reference to a statement of case includes reference to part of a statement of case.

(2) The court may strike out[(GL)] a statement of case if it appears to the court—

(a) that the statement of case discloses no reasonable grounds for bringing or defending the claim;

(b) that the statement of case is an abuse of the court's process or is otherwise likely to obstruct the just disposal of the proceedings; …[1]

(c) that there has been a failure to comply with a rule, practice direction or court order[; or][2]

[(d) that, in the case of a claimant's statement of case—

(i) the claim is strategic litigation against public participation, being a SLAPP claim within the meaning of section 195 of the Economic Crime and Corporate Transparency Act 2023; and

(ii) the claimant has failed to show that it is more likely than not the claim would succeed at trial.

(Rules 20.2 and 20.3 provide that counterclaims and other additional claims are treated as claims and that references to a claimant include a party bringing an additional claim.)][3]

(3) When the court strikes out a statement of case it may make any consequential order it considers appropriate.

(4) Where—

(a) the court has struck out a claimant's statement of case;

(b) the claimant has been ordered to pay costs to the defendant; and

(c) before the claimant pays those costs, [the claimant][4] starts another claim against the same defendant, arising out of facts which are the same or substantially the same as those relating to the claim in which the statement of case was struck out,

the court may, on the application of the defendant, stay[(GL)] that other claim until the costs of the first claim have been paid.

(5) Paragraph (2) does not limit any other power of the court to strike out[(GL)] a statement of case.

[(6) If the court strikes out a claimant's statement of case and it considers that the claim is totally without merit—

(a) the court's order must record that fact; and

(b) the court must at the same time consider whether it is appropriate to make a civil restraint order.][5]

[(7) If a defendant applies to strike out all or part of the claim form or particulars of claim, that defendant need not file a defence before the hearing.][6]

Amendments

1 Repealed by the Civil Procedure (Amendment) Rules 2025, SI 2025/106, rr 3, 4(a).

2 Substituted by the Civil Procedure (Amendment) Rules 2025, SI 2025/106, rr 3, 4(b).

3 Inserted by the Civil Procedure (Amendment) Rules 2025, SI 2025/106, rr 3, 4(c).

4 Substituted by the Civil Procedure (Amendment) Rules 2014, SI 2014/407, r 6(a).

5 Inserted by the Civil Procedure (Amendment No. 2) Rules 2004, SI 2004/2072, r 5.

6 Inserted by the Civil Procedure (Amendment No. 2) Rules 2022, SI 2022/783, rr 2, 4(1).

Judgment without trial after striking out

3.5

(1) This rule applies where—

(a) the court makes an order which includes a term that the statement of case of a party shall be struck out if the party does not comply with the order; and

(b) the party against whom the order was made does not comply with it.

(2) A party may obtain judgment with costs by filing a request for judgment if—

(a) the order referred to in paragraph (1)(a) relates to the whole of a statement of case; and

(b) where the party wishing to obtain judgment is the claimant, the claim is for—

(i) a specified amount of money;

(ii) an amount of money to be decided by the court;

(iii) delivery of goods where the claim form gives the defendant the alternative of paying their value; or

(iv) any combination of these remedies.

[(3) Where judgment is obtained under this rule in a case to which paragraph (2)(b)(iii) applies, it will be judgment requiring the defendant to deliver the goods, or (if [the defendant][1] does not do so) pay the value of the goods as decided by the court (less any payments made).][2]

[(4)][3] The request must state that the right to enter judgment has arisen because the court's order has not been complied with.

[(5)][3] A party must make an application in accordance with Part 23 if [they wish][1] to obtain judgment under this rule in a case to which paragraph (2) does not apply.

Amendments

1 Substituted by the Civil Procedure (Amendment) Rules 2014, SI 2014/407, r 6(c).

2 Inserted by the Civil Procedure (Amendment) Rules 2000, SI 2000/221, r 3(c).

3 Renumbered by the Civil Procedure (Amendment) Rules 2000, SI 2000/221, r 3(a), (b).

[[Judgment without trial after striking out a claim in the [Civil National Business Centre]1

3.5A

(1) If a claimant files a request for judgment in the [Civil National Business Centre] in accordance with rule 3.5, in a claim which includes an amount of money to be decided by the court, the claim will be sent to the preferred hearing centre.

(2) If a claim is sent to a preferred hearing centre pursuant to paragraph (1), any further correspondence should be sent to, and any further requests should be made at, the hearing centre to which the claim was sent.][2]][3]

Amendments

1 Substituted by the Civil Procedure (Amendment No. 3) Rules 2023, SI 2023/788, rr 2, 3(3).

2 Substituted by the Civil Procedure (Amendment) Rules 2014, SI 2014/407, r 6(d).

3 Inserted by the Civil Procedure (Amendment No.4) Rules 2011, SI 2011/3103, r 4(b).

Setting aside judgment entered after striking out

3.6

(1) A party against whom the court has entered judgment under rule 3.5 may apply to the court to set the judgment aside.

(2) An application under paragraph (1) must be made not more than 14 days after the judgment has been served on the party making the application.

(3) If the right to enter judgment had not arisen at the time when judgment was entered, the court must set aside[(GL)] the judgment.

(4) If the application to set aside[(GL)] is made for any other reason, rule 3.9 (relief from sanctions) shall apply.

[3.6A

If—

(a) a party against whom judgment has been entered under rule 3.5 applies to set the judgment aside;

(b) the claim is for a specified sum;

(c) the claim was started in the [Civil National Business Centre][1]; and

(d) the claim has not been sent to a County Court hearing centre,

the claim will be sent to—

(i) if the defendant is an individual, the defendant's home court; and

(ii) if the defendant is not an individual, the preferred hearing centre.][2]

Amendments

1 Substituted by the Civil Procedure (Amendment No. 3) Rules 2023, SI 2023/788, rr 2, 3(4).

2 Inserted by the Civil Procedure (Amendment) Rules 2014, SI 2014/407, r 6(e).

Sanctions for non-payment of certain fees [by the claimant][1]

3.7

[(1) [Except where rule 3.7A1 applies, this rule applies to fees payable by the claimant where—][2]

(a) …[3]

(b) …[3]

(c) …[3] …[4]

(d) the court has made an order giving permission to proceed with a claim for judicial review[; or][5]

[(e) the fee payable for a hearing specified by the [Civil Proceedings Fees Order 2008 (Fees Order 2008)][2] is not paid.][6]

…[3]

(Rule 54.12 provides for the service of the order giving permission to proceed with a claim for judicial review)

(2) The court will serve a notice on the claimant requiring payment of the fee specified in the [Fees Order 2008][2] if, at the time the fee is due, the claimant has not paid it or made an application for [full or part][5] remission.][7]

(3) The notice will specify the date by which the claimant must pay the fee.

(4) If the claimant does not—

(a) pay the fee; or

(b) make an application for [full or part][5] remission of the fee,

by the date specified in the notice—

(i) [the claim will automatically be struck out without further order of the court][8]; and

(ii) the claimant [will][9] be liable for the costs which the defendant has incurred unless the court orders otherwise.

(Rule [44.9][10] provides for the basis of assessment where a right to costs arises under this rule [and contains provisions about when a costs order is deemed to have been made and applying for an order under section 194(3) of the Legal Services Act 2007][11])

[(5) Where an application for—

(a) full or part remission of a fee is refused, the court will serve notice on the claimant requiring payment of the full fee by the date specified in the notice; or

(b) part remission of a fee is granted, the court will serve notice on the claimant requiring payment of the balance of the fee by the date specified in the notice.][5]

(6) If the claimant does not pay the fee by the date specified in the notice—

(a) [the claim will automatically be struck out without further order of the court][8]; and

(b) the claimant [will][9] be liable for the costs which the defendant has incurred unless the court orders otherwise.

[(7) If—

(a) a claimant applies to have the claim reinstated; and

(b) the court grants relief,

the relief [will][9] be conditional on the claimant either paying the fee or filing evidence of [full or part][5] remission of the fee within the period specified in paragraph (8).

(8) The period referred to in paragraph (7) is—

(a) if the order granting relief is made at a hearing at which a claimant is present or represented, 2 days from the date of the order;

(b) in any other case, 7 days from the date of service of the order on the claimant.][12]

Amendments

1 Inserted by the Civil Procedure (Amendment) Rules 2017, SI 2017/95, rr 4, 5(2).

2 Substituted by the Civil Procedure (Amendment) Rules 2017, SI 2017/95, rr 4, 5(3)(a), (c), (4).

3 Repealed by the Civil Procedure (Amendment) Rules 2017, SI 2017/95, rr 4, 5(3)(b), (d).

4 Repealed by the Civil Procedure (Amendment No. 2) Rules 2007, SI 2007/3543, r 3(a).

5 Substituted by the Civil Procedure (Amendment No. 2) Rules 2007, SI 2007/3543, r 3(b), (d)-(g).

6 Inserted by the Civil Procedure (Amendment No. 2) Rules 2007, SI 2007/3543, r 3(c).

7 Substituted by the Civil Procedure (Amendment No. 4) Rules 2000, SI 2000/2092, r 4.

8 Substituted by the Civil Procedure (Amendment No. 3) Rules 2005, SI 2005/2292, rr 2, 5.

9 Substituted by the Civil Procedure (Amendment) Rules 2008, SI 2008/2178, r 4(a), (c), (d).

10 Substituted by the Civil Procedure (Amendment No. 7) Rules 2013, SI 2013/1974, r 4(b).

11 Inserted by the Civil Procedure (Amendment) Rules 2008, SI 2008/2178, r 4(b).

12 Substituted by the Civil Procedure (Amendment No. 2) Rules 2003, SI 2003/1242, r 4.

[Sanctions for non-payment of the trial fee by the claimant

3.7A1

(1) In this rule and in rule 3.7AA—

(a) 'Fees Order 2008' means the Civil Proceedings Fees Order 2008;

(b) 'fee notice' means a notice of—

(i) the amount of a trial fee;

(ii) the trial fee payment date; and

(iii) the consequences of non-payment of the trial fee;

(c) 'trial date' means the date of the trial in relation to which the trial fee is payable, and if the trial in relation to which the trial fee is payable is scheduled to commence during the course of a specified period, 'trial date' means the date of the Monday of the first week of that specified period;

(d) 'trial fee' means fee 2.1 set out in the Table in Schedule 1 to the Fees Order 2008 and payable for the trial of a case on the multi-track[, intermediate track][1], fast track or small claims track;

(e) 'trial fee payment date' means the date by which the trial fee must be paid, calculated in accordance with the Fees Order 2008;

(f) 'revised trial fee payment date' means, if an application for fee remission is denied in whole or part, the revised date by which the fee or part of it is to be paid, calculated in accordance with the Fees Order 2008.

(2) This rule applies in relation to trial fees where that fee is to be paid by the claimant and the court notifies the parties in writing of the trial date.

(3) When the court notifies the parties in writing of the trial date, the court must also send a fee notice to the claimant.

(4) The fee notice may be contained in the same document as the notice of trial date, or may be a separate document.

(5) Where an application for full or part remission of a trial fee is refused, when the court sends written notice to the claimant of the refusal, the court must also notify the claimant in writing—

(a) that the claimant is required to pay the full trial fee by the revised trial fee payment date; and

(b) of the consequences of non-payment of the trial fee.

(6) Where part remission of a fee is granted, when the court sends written notice to the claimant of the part remission, the court must also notify the claimant in writing—

(a) that the claimant is required to pay the balance of the trial fee by the revised trial fee payment date; and

(b) of the consequences of non-payment of the balance of the trial fee.

(7) If—

(a) the claimant has had notice in accordance with this rule to pay the trial fee;

(b) the claimant has not applied to have the trial fee remitted in whole or part; and

(c) the trial fee has not been paid on or before the trial fee payment date,

the claim will automatically be struck out without further order of the court, and unless the court orders otherwise, the claimant will be liable for the [defendant's costs in accordance with rule 44.9(1)][2].

(8) If—

(a) the claimant has had notice in accordance with this rule to pay the trial fee;

(b) the claimant has applied to have the trial fee remitted in whole or part;

(c) remission is refused or only part remission of the trial fee is granted;

(d) following the decision on remission, the claimant has had notice in accordance with this rule to pay the full trial fee or balance of it; and

(e) the full trial fee or balance of it (as appropriate) has not been paid on or before the revised trial fee payment date,

the claim will automatically be struck out without further order of the court, and, unless the court orders otherwise, the claimant will be liable for the [defendant's costs in accordance with rule 44.9(1)][2].

(Rule 44.9 provides for the basis of assessment where a right to costs arises under this rule and contains provisions about when a costs order is deemed to have been made and applying for an order under section 194(3) of the Legal Services Act 2007.)

(9) If—

(a) a claimant applies to have the claim reinstated; and

(b) the court grants relief,

the relief must be conditional on the claimant either paying the trial fee or filing evidence of full or part remission of that fee within the period specified in paragraph (10).

(10) The period referred to in paragraph (9) is—

(a) if the order granting relief is made at a hearing at which the claimant is present or represented, 2 days from the date of the order;

(b) in any other case, 7 days from the date of service of the order on the claimant.

(11) If a fee is not paid for a claim where there is also a counterclaim, the counterclaim will still stand.][3]

Amendments

1 Inserted by the Civil Procedure (Amendment No. 2) Rules 2023, SI 2023/572, rr 3, 5(2).

2 Substituted by the Civil Procedure (Amendment No. 3) Rules 2024, SI 2024/839, rr 2, 5(2).

3 Inserted by the Civil Procedure (Amendment) Rules 2017, SI 2017/95, rr 4, 5(5).

[Sanctions for non-payment of certain fees by the defendant][1]

[3.7A

[(1) [Except where rule 3.7AA applies, this rule applies to fees payable by the defendant where—][2]

(a) a defendant files a counterclaim without—

(i) payment of the fee specified by the [Civil Proceedings Fees Order 2008 (Fees Order 2008)][2]; or

(ii) making an application for full or part remission of the fee; or

(b) the proceedings continue on the counterclaim alone and—

(i) …[3]

(ii) …[3]

(iii) …[3]

(iv) the fee payable for a hearing specified by the [Fees Order 2008][2] is not paid.][4]

(2) The court will serve a notice on the defendant requiring payment of the fee specified in the [Fees Order 2008][2] if, at the time the fee is due, the defendant has not paid it or made an application for [full or part][4] remission.

(3) The notice will specify the date by which the defendant must pay the fee.

(4) If the defendant does not—

(a) pay the fee; or

(b) make an application for [full or part][4] remission of the fee,

by the date specified in the notice, the counterclaim will automatically be struck out without further order of the court.

[(5) Where an application for—

(a) full or part remission of a fee is refused, the court will serve notice on the defendant requiring payment of the full fee by the date specified in the notice; or

(b) part remission of a fee is granted, the court will serve notice on the defendant requiring payment of the balance of the fee by the date specified in the notice.][4]

(6) If the defendant does not pay the fee by the date specified in the notice, the counterclaim will automatically be struck out without further order of the court.

(7) If—

(a) the defendant applies to have the counterclaim reinstated; and

(b) the court grants relief,

the relief will be conditional on the defendant either paying the fee or filing evidence of [full or part][4] remission of the fee within the period specified in paragraph (8).

(8) The period referred to in paragraph (7) is—

(a) if the order granting relief is made at a hearing at which the defendant is present or represented, 2 days from the date of the order;

(b) in any other case, 7 days from the date of service of the order on the defendant.][5]

Amendments

1 Inserted by the Civil Procedure (Amendment) Rules 2017, SI 2017/95, rr 4, 5(6).

2 Substituted by the Civil Procedure (Amendment) Rules 2017, SI 2017/95, rr 4, 5(7)(a). (b), (c)(ii), (8).

3 Repealed by the Civil Procedure (Amendment) Rules 2017, SI 2017/95, rr 4, 5(7)(c)(i).

4 Substituted by the Civil Procedure (Amendment No. 2) Rules 2007, SI 2007/3543, r 4.

5 Inserted by the Civil Procedure (Amendment No. 3) Rules 2005, SI 2005/2292, rr 2, 6.

[Sanctions for non-payment of the trial fee by the defendant, where proceedings continue on the counterclaim alone

3.7AA

(1) This rule applies in relation to trial fees where that fee is to be paid by the defendant and the court notifies the defendant in writing of the trial date.

(Definitions contained in rule 3.7A1(1) apply to this rule also.)

(2) When the court notifies the parties in writing of the trial date, the court must also send a fee notice to the defendant.

(3) The fee notice may be contained in the same document as the notice of trial date, or may be a separate document.

(4) Where an application for full or part remission of a trial fee is refused, when the court sends written notice to the defendant of the refusal, the court must also notify the defendant in writing—

(a) that the defendant is required to pay the full trial fee by the revised trial fee payment date; and

(b) of the consequences of non-payment of the trial fee.

(5) Where part remission of a fee is granted, when the court sends written notice to the defendant of the part remission, the court must also notify the defendant in writing—

(a) that the defendant is required to pay the balance of the trial fee by the revised trial fee payment date; and

(b) of the consequences of non-payment of the balance.

(6) If—

(a) the defendant has had notice in accordance with this rule to pay the trial fee;

(b) the defendant has not applied to have the trial fee remitted in whole or part; and

(c) the trial fee has not been paid on or before the trial fee payment date,

the counterclaim will automatically be struck out without further order of the court.

(7) If—

(a) the defendant has had notice in accordance with this rule to pay the trial fee;

(b) the defendant has applied to have the trial fee remitted in whole or part;

(c) remission is refused or only part remission of the trial fee is granted;

(d) following the decision on remission, the defendant has had notice in accordance with this rule to pay the full trial fee or balance of it; and

(e) the full trial fee or balance of it (as appropriate) has not been paid on or before the revised trial fee payment date,

the counterclaim will automatically be struck out without further order of the court.

(8) If—

(a) a defendant applies to have the counterclaim reinstated; and

(b) the court grants relief,

the relief will be conditional on the defendant either paying the trial fee or filing evidence of full or part remission of the fee within the period specified in paragraph (9).

(9) The period referred to in paragraph (8) is—

(a) if the order granting relief is made at a hearing at which the defendant is present or represented, 2 days from the date of the order;

(b) in any other case, 7 days from the date of service of the order on the defendant.][1]

Amendments

1 Inserted by the Civil Procedure (Amendment) Rules 2017, SI 2017/95, rr 4, 5(9).

[Sanctions for dishonouring cheque

3.7B

(1) This rule applies where any fee is paid by cheque and that cheque is subsequently dishonoured.

(2) The court will serve a notice on the paying party requiring payment of the fee which will specify the date by which the fee must be paid.

(3) If the fee is not paid by the date specified in the notice—

(a) where the fee is payable by the claimant, the claim will automatically be struck out without further order of the court;

(b) where the fee is payable by the defendant, the defence will automatically be struck out without further order of the court,

and the paying party shall be liable for the costs which any other party has incurred unless the court orders otherwise.

(Rule [44.9][1] provides for the basis of assessment where a right to costs arises under this rule)

(4) If—

(a) the paying party applies to have the claim or defence reinstated; and

(b) the court grants relief,

the relief shall be conditional on that party paying the fee within the period specified in paragraph (5).

(5) The period referred to in paragraph (4) is—

(a) if the order granting relief is made at a hearing at which the paying party is present or represented, 2 days from the date of the order;

(b) in any other case, 7 days from the date of service of the order on the paying party.

(6) For the purposes of this rule, 'claimant' includes a [claimant in a counterclaim or other additional claim][2] and 'claim form' includes a [counterclaim or other additional claim][2].][3]

Amendments

3 Inserted by the Civil Procedure (Amendment No. 3) Rules 2005, SI 2005/2292, rr 2, 7.

1 Substituted by the Civil Procedure (Amendment No. 7) Rules 2013, SI 2013/1974, r 4(c).

2 Substituted by the Civil Procedure (Amendment) Rules 2023, SI 2023/105, rr 2, 4(1).

Sanctions have effect unless defaulting party obtains relief

3.8

(1) Where a party has failed to comply with a rule, practice direction or court order, any sanction for failure to comply imposed by the rule, practice direction or court order has effect unless the party in default applies for and obtains relief from the sanction.

(Rule 3.9 sets out the circumstances which the court [will][1] consider on an application to grant relief from a sanction)

(2) Where the sanction is the payment of costs, the party in default may only obtain relief by appealing against the order for costs.

(3) Where a rule, practice direction or court order—

(a) requires a party to do something within a specified time, and

(b) specifies the consequence of failure to comply,

the time for doing the act in question may not be extended by agreement between the parties [except as provided in paragraph (4)][2].

[(4) In the circumstances referred to in paragraph (3) and unless the court orders otherwise, the time for doing the act in question may be extended by prior written agreement of the parties for up to a maximum of 28 days, provided always that any such extension does not put at risk any hearing date.][2]

Amendments

1 Substituted by the Civil Procedure (Amendment) Rules 2013, SI 2013/262, r 5(f).

2 Inserted by the Civil Procedure (Amendment No. 5) Rules 2014, SI 2014/1233, r 3.

Relief from sanctions

3.9

[(1) On an application for relief from any sanction imposed for a failure to comply with any rule, practice direction or court order, the court will consider all the circumstances of the case, so as to enable it to deal justly with the application, including the need—

(a) for litigation to be conducted efficiently and at proportionate cost; and

(b) to enforce compliance with rules, practice directions and orders.][1]

(2) An application for relief must be supported by evidence.

Amendments

1 Substituted by the Civil Procedure (Amendment) Rules 2013, SI 2013/262, r 5(g).

General power of the court to rectify matters where there has been an error of procedure

3.10

Where there has been an error of procedure such as a failure to comply with a rule or practice direction—

(a) the error does not invalidate any step taken in the proceedings unless the court so orders; and

(b) the court may make an order to remedy the error.

[Orders restraining civil proceedings] 1

3.11

[(1) A 'civil proceedings order' and an 'all proceedings order' under section 42(1A) of the Senior Courts Act 1981 shall include provision for applying to begin, continue or make any application in any civil proceedings.][2]

[(2)][3] A practice direction may set out—

(a) the circumstances in which the court has the power to make a civil restraint order against a party to proceedings;

(b) the procedure where a party applies for a civil restraint order against another party; and

(c) the consequences of the court making a civil restraint order.

Amendments

1 Substituted by the Civil Procedure (Amendment No. 2) Rules 2022, SI 2022/783, rr 2, 4(3)(a).

2 Inserted by the Civil Procedure (Amendment No. 2) Rules 2022, SI 2022/783, rr 2, 4(3)(b).

3 Renumbered by the Civil Procedure (Amendment No. 2) Rules 2022, SI 2022/783, rr 2, (3)(c).

[Section II
Costs Management

Application of this Section and the purpose of costs management

3.12

[(1) This Section and Practice Direction [3D][1] apply to all Part 7 multi-track cases, except—

(a) where the claim is commenced on or after 22nd April 2014 and the amount of money claimed as stated on the claim form is £10 million or more; or

(b) where the claim is commenced on or after 22nd April 2014 and is for a monetary claim which is not quantified or not fully quantified or is for a non-monetary claim and in any such case the claim form contains a statement that the claim is valued at £10 million or more; or

[(c) where in proceedings commenced on or after 6th April 2016 a claim is made by or on behalf of a person under the age of 18 (a child) (and on a child reaching majority this exception will continue to apply unless the court otherwise orders); or

(d) where the proceeding are the subject of fixed costs or scale costs; or

(e) the court otherwise orders.][2]

(1A) This Section and Practice Direction [3D][1] will apply to any other proceedings (including applications) where the court so orders.][3]

(2) The purpose of costs management is that the court should manage both the steps to be taken and the costs to be incurred by the parties to any proceedings [(or variation costs as provided in rule 3.15A)][4] so as to further the overriding objective.][5]

Amendments

1 Substituted by the Civil Procedure (Amendment No. 2) Rules 2022, SI 2022/783, rr 2, 4(4).

2 Substituted by the Civil Procedure (Amendment) Rules 2016, SI 2016/234, r 5.

3 Substituted by the Civil Procedure (Amendment No. 4) Rules 2014, SI 2014/867, r 4(a)

4 Inserted by the Civil Procedure (Amendment No. 3) Rules 2020, SI 2020/747, rr 3, 4(1).

5 Inserted by the Civil Procedure (Amendment) Rules 2013, SI 2013/262, r 5(h).

[Filing and exchanging budgets [and budget discussion reports]1

[3.13

(1) Unless the court otherwise orders, all parties except litigants in person must file and exchange budgets—

(a) where the stated value of the claim on the claim form is less than £50,000, with their directions questionnaires; or

(b) in any other case, not later than 21 days before the first case management conference.

(2) In the event that a party files and exchanges a budget under paragraph (1), all other parties, not being litigants in person, must file an agreed budget

discussion report no later than 7 days before the first case management conference.

[(3) The court—

(a) may, on its own initiative or on application, order the parties to file and exchange costs budgets in a case where the parties are not otherwise required by this Section to do so;

(b) shall (other than in an exceptional case) make an order to file and exchange costs budgets if all parties consent to an application for such an order.

(4) The court may, in a substantial case, direct that budgets are to be limited in the first instance to part only of the proceedings and extended later to cover the whole proceedings.

(5) Every budget must be dated and verified by a statement of truth signed by a senior legal representative of the party.

(6) Even though a litigant in person is not required to prepare a budget, each other party (other than a litigant in person) must provide the litigant in person with a copy of that party's budget.][2]][3]][4]

Amendments

1 Inserted by the Civil Procedure (Amendment) Rules 2016, SI 2016/234, r 6(a).

2 Inserted by the Civil Procedure (Amendment No. 3) Rules 2020, SI 2020/747, rr 3, 4(2).

3 Substituted by the Civil Procedure (Amendment) Rules 2016, SI 2016/234, r 6(b).

4 Inserted by the Civil Procedure (Amendment) Rules 2013, SI 2013/262, r 5(h).

[Failure to file a budget

3.14

Unless the court otherwise orders, any party which fails to file a budget despite being required to do so will be treated as having filed a budget comprising only the applicable court fees.][1]

Amendments

1 Inserted by the Civil Procedure (Amendment) Rules 2013, SI 2013/262, r 5(h).

[Costs management orders

3.15

(1) In addition to exercising its other powers, the court may manage the costs to be incurred [(the budgeted costs)][1] by any party in any proceedings.

(2) The court may at any time make a 'costs management order'. [Where costs budgets have been filed and exchanged the court will make a costs management order unless it is satisfied that the litigation can be conducted justly and at proportionate cost in accordance with the overriding objective without such an order being made. By a costs management order the court will—][2]

(a) record the extent to which the [budgeted costs][3] are agreed between the parties;

(b) in respect of [the budgeted costs][3] which are not agreed, record the court's approval after making appropriate revisions[;

(c) record the extent (if any) to which incurred costs are agreed].

(3) If a costs management order has been made, the court will thereafter control the parties' budgets in respect of recoverable costs.

[(4) Whether or not the court makes a costs management order, it may record on the face of any case management order any comments it has about the incurred costs which are to be taken into account in any subsequent assessment proceedings.][1]

[(5) Save in exceptional circumstances—

(a) the recoverable costs of initially completing Precedent H (the form to be used for a costs budget) shall not exceed the higher of—

(i) £1,000; or

(ii) 1% of the total of the incurred costs (as agreed or allowed on assessment) and the budgeted costs (agreed or approved); and

(b) all other recoverable costs of the budgeting and costs management process shall not exceed 2% of the total of the incurred costs (as agreed or allowed on assessment) and the budgeted (agreed or approved) costs.

(Precedent H is annexed to Practice Direction [3D][4].)

(6) The court may set a timetable or give other directions for future reviews of budgets.

(7) After a party's budgeted costs have been approved or agreed, the party must re-file and re-serve the budget—

(a) in the form approved or agreed with re-cast figures; and

(b) annexed to the order approving the budgeted costs or recording the parties' agreement.

(8) A costs management order concerns the totals allowed for each phase of the budget, and while the underlying detail in the budget for each phase used by the party to calculate the totals claimed is provided for reference purposes to assist the court in fixing a budget, it is not the role of the court in the costs management hearing to fix or approve the hourly rates claimed in the budget.][5]][6]

Amendments

1 Inserted by the Civil Procedure (Amendment) Rules 2017, SI 2017/95, rr 4, 5(10)(a), (b)(iii), (c).

2 Substituted by the Civil Procedure (Amendment No. 4) Rules 2014, SI 2014/867, r 5.

3 Substituted by the Civil Procedure (Amendment) Rules 2017, SI 2017/95, rr 4, 5(10)(b)(i), (ii).

4 Substituted by the Civil Procedure (Amendment No. 2) Rules 2022, SI 2022/783, rr 2, 4(5).

5 Inserted by the Civil Procedure (Amendment No. 3) Rules 2020, SI 2020/747, rr 3, 4(3).

6 Inserted by the Civil Procedure (Amendment) Rules 2013, SI 2013/262, r 5(h).

[Revision and variation of costs budgets on account of significant developments ('variation costs')

3.15A

(1) A party ('the revising party') must revise its budgeted costs upwards or downwards if significant developments in the litigation warrant such revisions.

(2) Any budgets revised in accordance with paragraph (1) must be submitted promptly by the revising party to the other parties for agreement, and subsequently to the court, in accordance with paragraphs (3) to (5).

(3) The revising party must—

(a) serve particulars of the variation proposed on every other party, using the form prescribed by Practice Direction [3D][1];

(b) confine the particulars to the additional costs occasioned by the significant development; and

(c) certify, in the form prescribed by [Practice Direction 3D][2], that the additional costs are not included in any previous budgeted costs or variation.

(4) The revising party must submit the particulars of variation promptly to the court, together with the last approved or agreed budget, and with an explanation of the points of difference if they have not been agreed.

(5) The court may approve, vary or disallow the proposed variations, having regard to any significant developments which have occurred since the date when the previous budget was approved or agreed, or may list a further costs management hearing.

(6) Where the court makes an order for variation, it may vary the budget for costs related to that variation which have been incurred prior to the order for variation but after the costs management order.][3]

Amendments

1 Substituted by the Civil Procedure (Amendment No. 2) Rules 2022, SI 2022/783, rr 2, 4(6).

2 Substituted by the Civil Procedure (Amendment) Rules 2023, SI 2023/105, rr 2, 4(2).

3 Inserted by the Civil Procedure (Amendment No. 3) Rules 2020, SI 2020/747, rr 3, 4(4).

[Costs management conferences

3.16

(1) Any hearing which is convened solely for the purpose of costs management (for example, to approve a revised budget) is referred to as a 'costs management conference'.

(2) Where practicable, costs management conferences should be conducted by telephone or in writing.][1]

Amendment

1 Inserted by the Civil Procedure (Amendment) Rules 2013, SI 2013/262, r 5(h).

[Court to have regard to budgets and to take account of costs

3.17

(1) When making any case management decision, the court will have regard to any available budgets of the parties and will take into account the costs involved in each procedural step.

(2) Paragraph (1) applies whether or not the court has made a costs management order.

[(3) Subject to rule 3.15A, the court—

(a) may not approve costs incurred [to and including][1] the date of any costs management hearing; but

(b) may record its comments on those costs and take those costs into account when considering the reasonableness and proportionality of all budgeted costs.

(4) If an interim application is made but is not included in a budget, the court may, if it considers it reasonable not to have included the application in the budget, treat the costs of such interim application as additional to the approved budgets.][2]][3]

Amendments

1 Substituted by the Civil Procedure (Amendment) Rules 2021, SI 2021/117, rr 4, 5.

2 Inserted by the Civil Procedure (Amendment No. 3) Rules 2020, SI 2020/747, rr 3, 4(5).

3 Inserted by the Civil Procedure (Amendment) Rules 2013, SI 2013/262, r 5(h).

[Assessing costs on the standard basis where a costs management order has been made

3.18

In any case where a costs management order has been made, when assessing costs on the standard basis, the court will—

(a) have regard to the receiving party's last approved or agreed [budgeted costs][1] for each phase of the proceedings; …[2]

(b) not depart from such approved or agreed [budgeted costs][1] unless satisfied that there is good reason to do so[; and

(c) take into account any comments made pursuant to rule 3.15(4) or [3.17(3)][3] and recorded on the face of the order][4]

(Attention is drawn to [rules 44.3(2)(a) and 44.3(5)][5], which concern proportionality of costs.)][6]

Amendments

1 Substituted by the Civil Procedure (Amendment) Rules 2017, SI 2017/95, rr 4, 5(11)(a)(i), (b).

2 Repealed by the Civil Procedure (Amendment) Rules 2017, SI 2017/95, rr 4, 5(11)(a)(ii).

3 Substituted by the Civil Procedure (Amendment No. 3) Rules 2020, SI 2020/747, rr 3, 4(6).

4 Inserted by the Civil Procedure (Amendment) Rules 2017, SI 2017/95, rr 4, 5(11)(c).

5 Substituted by the Civil Procedure (Amendment) Rules 2016, SI 2016/234, r 7.

6 Inserted by the Civil Procedure (Amendment) Rules 2013, SI 2013/262, r 5(h).

[Section III
Costs Capping

Costs capping orders – General

3.19

[(1) For the purposes of this Section—

(a) 'costs capping order' means an order limiting the amount of future costs (including disbursements) which a party may recover pursuant to an order for costs subsequently made; and

(b) 'future costs' means costs incurred in respect of work done after the date of the costs capping order but excluding the amount of any additional liability.

(2) This Section does not apply to judicial review costs capping orders under Part 4 of the Criminal Justice and Courts Act 2015 or to protective costs orders.

(Rules 46.16 to 46.19 make provision for judicial review costs capping orders under Part 4 of the Criminal Justice and Courts Act 2015.)][1]

(3) …[2]

(4) A costs capping order may be in respect of—

(a) the whole litigation; or

(b) any issues which are ordered to be tried separately.

(5) The court may at any stage of proceedings make a costs capping order against all or any of the parties, if—

(a) it is in the interests of justice to do so;

(b) there is a substantial risk that without such an order costs will be disproportionately incurred; and

(c) it is not satisfied that the risk in subparagraph (b) can be adequately controlled by–

(i) case management directions or orders made under this Part; and

(ii) detailed assessment of costs.

(6) In considering whether to exercise its discretion under this rule, the court will consider all the circumstances of the case, including—

(a) whether there is a substantial imbalance between the financial position of the parties;

(b) whether the costs of determining the amount of the cap are likely to be proportionate to the overall costs of the litigation;

(c) the stage which the proceedings have reached; and

(d) the costs which have been incurred to date and the future costs.

(7) A costs capping order, once made, will limit the costs recoverable by the party subject to the order unless a party successfully applies to vary the order. No such variation will be made unless—

(a) there has been a material and substantial change of circumstances since the date when the order was made; or

(b) there is some other compelling reason why a variation should be made.][3]

Amendments

1 Substituted by the Civil Procedure (Amendment No. 2) Rules 2016, SI 2016/707, r 4(a).

2 Repealed by the Civil Procedure (Amendment No. 2) Rules 2016, SI 2016/707, r 4(b).

3 Inserted by the Civil Procedure (Amendment) Rules 2013, SI 2013/262, r 5(h).

[Application for a costs capping order

3.20

(1) An application for a costs capping order must be made on notice in accordance with Part 23.

(2) The application notice must –

(a) set out –

(i) whether the costs capping order is in respect of the whole of the litigation or a particular issue which is ordered to be tried separately; and

(ii) why a costs capping order should be made; and

(b) be accompanied by a budget setting out –

(i) the costs (and disbursements) incurred by the applicant to date; and

(ii) the costs (and disbursements) which the applicant is likely to incur in the future conduct of the proceedings.

(3) The court may give directions for the determination of the application and such directions may –

(a) direct any party to the proceedings –

(i) to file a schedule of costs in the form set out in paragraph 3 of Practice Direction [3E][1] – Costs capping;

(ii) to file written submissions on all or any part of the issues arising;

(b) fix the date and time estimate of the hearing of the application;

(c) indicate whether the judge hearing the application will sit with an assessor at the hearing of the application; and

(d) include any further directions as the court sees fit.][2]

Amendments

1 Substituted by the Civil Procedure (Amendment No. 2) Rules 2022, SI 2022/783, rr 2, 4(7).

2 Inserted by the Civil Procedure (Amendment) Rules 2013, SI 2013/262, r 5(h).

[Application to vary a costs capping order

3.21

An application to vary a costs capping order must be made by application notice pursuant to Part 23.][1]

Amendment

1 Inserted by the Civil Procedure (Amendment) Rules 2013, SI 2013/262, r 5(h).

PRACTICE DIRECTION 3A – STRIKING OUT A STATEMENT OF CASE

This Practice Direction supplements CPR Rule 3.4

Introductory

1.1 This practice direction sets out the procedure a party should follow if they wish to make an application for an order under rule 3.4(2)(a) (where a statement of case discloses no reasonable grounds for bringing or defending a claim); or under rule 3.4(2)(b) (where a statement of case is an abuse of the court's process or otherwise likely to obstruct the just disposal of the proceedings).

1.2 The following are examples of cases where the court may conclude that particulars of claim (whether contained in a claim form or filed separately) fall within rule 3.4(2)(a):

(1) those which set out no facts indicating what the claim is about, for example 'Money owed £5000',

(2) those which are incoherent and make no sense,

(3) those which contain a coherent set of facts but those facts, even if true, do not disclose any legally recognisable claim against the defendant.

1.3 A claim may fall within rule 3.4(2)(b) where it is vexatious, scurrilous or obviously ill-founded.

1.4 A defence may fall within rule 3.4(2)(a) where:

(1) it consists of a bare denial or otherwise sets out no coherent statement of facts, or

(2) the facts it sets out, while coherent, would not amount in law to a defence to the claim even if true.

1.5 A party may believe they can show without a trial that an opponent's case has no real prospect of success on the facts, or that the case is bound to succeed or fail, as the case may be, because of a point of law (including the interpretation of a document). In such a case the party concerned may make an application under rule 3.4 or apply for summary judgment under Part 24 (or both) as they think appropriate.

1.6 Where a rule, practice direction or order states 'shall be struck out or dismissed' or 'will be struck out or dismissed' this means that the striking out or dismissal will be automatic and that no further order of the court is required.

Claims which appear to fall within rule 3.4(2)(a) or (b)

2.1 If a court officer is asked to issue a claim form which they believe may fall within rule 3.4(2)(a) or (b) they should issue it, but may then consult a judge (under rule 3.2) before returning the claim form to the claimant or taking any other step to serve the defendant. The judge may on their own initiative make an immediate order designed to ensure that the claim is disposed of or proceeds in a way that accords with the rules.

2.2 The judge may allow the claimant a hearing before deciding whether to make such an order.

2.3 Orders the judge may make include:

(1) an order that the claim be stayed until further order,

(2) an order that the claim form be retained by the court and not served until the stay is lifted,

(3) an order that no application by the claimant to lift the stay be heard unless they file such further documents (for example a witness statement or an amended claim form or particulars of claim) as may be specified in the order.

2.4 Where the judge makes any such order or, subsequently, an order lifting the stay they may give directions about the service on the defendant of the order and any other documents on the court file.

2.5 The fact that a judge allows a claim referred to them by a court officer to proceed does not prejudice the right of any party to apply for any order against the claimant.

Defences which appear to fall within rule 3.4(2)(a) or (b)

3.1 A court officer may similarly consult a judge about any document filed which purports to be a defence and which he believes may fall within rule 3.4(2)(a) or (b).

3.2 If the judge decides that the document falls within rule 3.4(2)(a) or (b) they may on their own initiative make an order striking it out. Where they do so they may extend the time for the defendant to file a proper defence.

3.3 The judge may allow the defendant a hearing before deciding whether to make such an order.

3.4 Alternatively the judge may make an order under rule 18.1 requiring the defendant within a stated time to clarify his defence or to give additional information about it. The order may provide that the defence will be struck out if the defendant does not comply.

3.5 The fact that a judge does not strike out a defence on their own initiative does not prejudice the right of the claimant to apply for any order against the defendant.

General provisions

4.1 The court may exercise its powers under rule 3.4(2)(a) or (b) on application or on its own initiative at any time.

4.2 Where a judge at a hearing strikes out all or part of a party's statement of case they may enter such judgment for the other party as that party appears entitled to.

Applications for orders under rule 3.4(2)

5.1 Attention is drawn to Part 23 (General Rules about Applications) and to Practice Direction 23A. The practice direction requires all applications to be made as soon as possible and before allocation if possible.

5.2 While many applications under rule 3.4(2) can be made without evidence in support, the applicant should consider whether facts need to be proved and, if so, whether evidence in support should be filed and served.

Applications for summary judgment

6.1 Applications for summary judgment may be made under Part 24. Attention is drawn to that Part.

PRACTICE DIRECTION 3B – SANCTIONS FOR NON-PAYMENT OF FEES

This Practice Direction supplements CPR rules 3.7, 3.7A1 and 3.7AA

1 If a claim is struck out under rule 3.7, the court will send notice that it has been struck out to the defendant. If a claim or counterclaim is struck out under rule 3.7A1 or 3.7AA, the court will send notice that it has been struck out to both the claimant and the defendant.

2 In relation to the notice sent out under rule 3.7 or 3.7A1, the notice will also explain the effect of rule 25.10. This provides that any interim injunction will cease to have effect 14 days after the date the claim is struck out under rule 3.7. Paragraph (3) provides that if the claimant applies to reinstate the claim before the interim injunction ceases to have effect, the injunction will continue until the hearing of the application unless the court orders otherwise. If the claimant makes such an application, the defendant will be given notice in the ordinary way under rule 23.4.

PRACTICE DIRECTION 3C – CIVIL RESTRAINT ORDERS

This practice direction supplements CPR rule 3.11

Introduction

1 This practice direction applies where the court is considering whether to make –

(a) a limited civil restraint order;

(b) an extended civil restraint order; or

(c) a general civil restraint order,

against a party who has issued claims or made applications which are totally without merit.

Rules 3.3(9), 3.4(6) and 23.12 provide that where a statement of case or application is struck out or dismissed and is totally without merit, the court order must specify that fact and the court must consider whether to make a civil restraint order. Rule 52.20(6) makes similar provision where the appeal court refuses an application for permission to appeal, strikes out an appellant's notice or dismisses an appeal.

Limited civil restraint orders

2.1 A limited civil restraint order may be made by a judge of any court where a party has made 2 or more applications which are totally without merit.

2.2 Where the court makes a limited civil restraint order, the party against whom the order is made –

(1) will be restrained from making any further applications in the proceedings in which the order is made without first obtaining the permission of a judge identified in the order;

(2) may apply for amendment or discharge of the order provided he has first obtained the permission of a judge identified in the order; and

(3) may apply for permission to appeal the order and if permission is granted, may appeal the order.

2.3 Where a party who is subject to a limited civil restraint order –

(1) makes a further application in the proceedings in which the order is made without first obtaining the permission of a judge identified in the order, such application will automatically be dismissed –

(a) without the judge having to make any further order; and

(b) without the need for the other party to respond to it;

(2) repeatedly makes applications for permission pursuant to that order which are totally without merit, the court may direct that if the party makes any further application for permission which is totally without merit, the decision to dismiss the application will be final and there will be no right of appeal, unless the judge who refused permission grants permission to appeal.

2.4 A party who is subject to a limited civil restraint order may not make an application for permission under paragraphs 2.2(1) or 2.2(2) without first serving notice of the application on the other party in accordance with paragraph 2.5.

2.5 A notice under paragraph 2.4 must –

(1) set out the nature and grounds of the application; and

(2) provide the other party with at least 7 days within which to respond.

2.6 An application for permission under paragraphs 2.2(1) or 2.2(2) –

(1) must be made in writing;

(2) must include the other party's written response, if any, to the notice served under paragraph 2.4; and

(3) will be determined without a hearing.

2.7 An order under paragraph 2.3(2) may only be made by –

(1) a Court of Appeal judge;

(2) a High Court judge or Master; or

(3) a Designated Civil Judge or their appointed deputy.

2.8 Where a party makes an application for permission under paragraphs 2.2(1) or 2.2(2) and permission is refused, any application for permission to appeal –

(1) must be made in writing; and

(2) will be determined without a hearing.

2.9 A limited civil restraint order –

(1) is limited to the particular proceedings in which it is made;

(2) will remain in effect for the duration of the proceedings in which it is made, unless the court otherwise orders; and

(3) must identify the judge or judges to whom an application for permission under paragraphs 2.2(1), 2.2(2) or 2.8 should be made.

Extended civil restraint orders

3.1 An extended civil restraint order may be made by –

(1) a judge of the Court of Appeal;

(2) a judge of the High Court; or

(3) a Designated Civil Judge or their appointed deputy in the County Court, where a party has persistently issued claims or made applications which are totally without merit.

3.2 Unless the court otherwise orders, where the court makes an extended civil restraint order, the party against whom the order is made –

(1) will be restrained from issuing claims or making applications in –

(a) any court if the order has been made by a judge of the Court of Appeal;

(b) the High Court or the County Court if the order has been made by a judge of the High Court; or

(c) the County Court if the order has been made by a designated civil judge or their appointed deputy, concerning any matter involving or relating to or touching upon or leading to the proceedings in which the order is made without first obtaining the permission of a judge identified in the order;

(2) may apply for amendment or discharge of the order provided he has first obtained the permission of a judge identified in the order; and

(3) may apply for permission to appeal the order and if permission is granted, may appeal the order.

3.3 Where a party who is subject to an extended civil restraint order –

(1) issues a claim or makes an application in a court identified in the order concerning any matter involving or relating to or touching upon or leading to the proceedings in which the order is made without first obtaining the permission of a judge identified in the order, the claim or application will automatically be struck out or dismissed –

(a) without the judge having to make any further order; and

(b) without the need for the other party to respond to it;

(2) repeatedly makes applications for permission pursuant to that order which are totally without merit, the court may direct that if the party makes any further application for permission which is totally without merit, the decision to dismiss the application will be final and there will be no right of appeal, unless the judge who refused permission grants permission to appeal.

3.4 A party who is subject to an extended civil restraint order may not make an application for permission under paragraphs 3.2(1) or 3.2(2) without first serving notice of the application on the other party in accordance with paragraph 3.5.

3.5 A notice under paragraph 3.4 must –

(1) set out the nature and grounds of the application; and

(2) provide the other party with at least 7 days within which to respond.

3.6 An application for permission under paragraphs 3.2(1) or 3.2(2) –

(1) must be made in writing;

(2) must include the other party's written response, if any, to the notice served under paragraph 3.4; and

(3) will be determined without a hearing.

3.7 An order under paragraph 3.3(2) may only be made by –

(1) a Court of Appeal judge;

(2) a High Court judge; or

(3) a Designated Civil Judge or their appointed deputy.

3.8 Where a party makes an application for permission under paragraphs 3.2(1) or 3.2(2) and permission is refused, any application for permission to appeal –

(1) must be made in writing; and

(2) will be determined without a hearing.

3.9 An extended civil restraint order –

(1) will be made for a specified period not exceeding 3 years;

(2) must identify the courts in which the party against whom the order is made is restrained from issuing claims or making applications; and

(3) must identify the judge or judges to whom an application for permission under paragraphs 3.2(1), 3.2(2) or 3.8 should be made.

3.10 The court may extend the duration of an extended civil restraint order, if it considers it appropriate to do so, but it must not be extended for a period greater than 3 years on any given occasion.

3.11 If they consider that it would be appropriate to make an extended civil restraint order –

(1) a Master or a District Judge in a district registry of the High Court must transfer the proceedings to a High Court judge; and

(2) a Circuit Judge or a District Judge in the County Court must transfer the proceedings to the Designated Civil Judge.

General civil restraint orders

4.1 A general civil restraint order may be made by –

(1) a judge of the Court of Appeal;

(2) a judge of the High Court; or

(3) a Designated Civil Judge or their appointed deputy in the County Court,

where the party against whom the order is made persists in issuing claims or making applications which are totally without merit, in circumstances where an extended civil restraint order would not be sufficient or appropriate.

4.2 Unless the court otherwise orders, where the court makes a general civil restraint order, the party against whom the order is made –

(1) will be restrained from issuing any claim or making any application in –

(a) any court if the order has been made by a judge of the Court of Appeal;

(b) the High Court or the County Court if the order has been made by a judge of the High Court; or

(c) the County Court identified in the order if the order has been made by a Designated Civil Judge or their appointed deputy, without first obtaining the permission of a judge identified in the order;

(2) may apply for amendment or discharge of the order provided he has first obtained the permission of a judge identified in the order; and

(3) may apply for permission to appeal the order and if permission is granted, may appeal the order.

4.3 Where a party who is subject to a general civil restraint order –

(1) issues a claim or makes an application in a court identified in the order without first obtaining the permission of a judge identified in the order, the claim or application will automatically be struck out or dismissed –

(a) without the judge having to make any further order; and

(b) without the need for the other party to respond to it;

(2) repeatedly makes applications for permission pursuant to that order which are totally without merit, the court may direct that if the party makes any further application for permission which is totally without merit, the decision to dismiss that application will be final and there will be no right of appeal, unless the judge who refused permission grants permission to appeal.

4.4 A party who is subject to a general civil restraint order may not make an application for permission under paragraphs 4.2(1) or 4.2(2) without first serving notice of the application on the other party in accordance with paragraph 4.5.

4.5 A notice under paragraph 4.4 must –

(1) set out the nature and grounds of the application; and

(2) provide the other party with at least 7 days within which to respond.

4.6 An application for permission under paragraphs 4.2(1) or 4.2(2) –

(1) must be made in writing;

(2) must include the other party's written response, if any, to the notice served under paragraph 4.4; and

(3) will be determined without a hearing.

4.7 An order under paragraph 4.3(2) may only be made by –

(1) a Court of Appeal judge;

(2) a High Court judge; or

(3) a Designated Civil Judge or their appointed deputy.

4.8 Where a party makes an application for permission under paragraphs 4.2(1) or 4.2(2) and permission is refused, any application for permission to appeal –

(1) must be made in writing; and

(2) will be determined without a hearing.

4.9 A general civil restraint order –

(1) will be made for a specified period not exceeding 3 years;

(2) must identify the courts in which the party against whom the order is made is restrained from issuing claims or making applications; and

(3) must identify the judge or judges to whom an application for permission under paragraphs 4.2(1), 4.2(2) or 4.8 should be made.

4.10 The court may extend the duration of a general civil restraint order, if it considers it appropriate to do so, but it must not be extended for a period greater than 3 years on any given occasion.

4.11 If they consider that it would be appropriate to make a general civil restraint order –

(1) a Master or a District Judge in a district registry of the High Court must transfer the proceedings to a High Court judge; and

(2) a Circuit Judge or a District Judge in the County Court must transfer the proceedings to the Designated Civil Judge.

General

5.1 The other party or parties to the proceedings may apply for any civil restraint order.

5.2 An application under paragraph 5.1 must be made using the Part 23 procedure unless the court otherwise directs and the application must specify which type of civil restraint order is sought.

5.3 Examples of a limited civil restraint order, an extended civil restraint order and a general civil restraint order are annexed to this practice direction. These examples may be modified as appropriate in any particular case.

PART 18
FURTHER INFORMATION

Obtaining further information

18.1

(1) The court may at any time order a party to—

(a) clarify any matter which is in dispute in the proceedings; or

(b) give additional information in relation to any such matter,

whether or not the matter is contained or referred to in a statement of case.

(2) Paragraph (1) is subject to any rule of law to the contrary.

(3) Where the court makes an order under paragraph (1), the party against whom it is made must—

(a) file [their][1] response; and

(b) serve it on the other parties,

within the time specified by the court.

(Part 22 requires a [statement of case, including a][2] response to be verified by a statement of truth)

[(Part 53 (defamation) restricts requirements for providing further information about sources of information in defamation claims)][3]

Amendments

1 Substituted by the Civil Procedure (Amendment No. 3) Rules 2023, SI 2023/788, rr 2, 9(a).

2 Inserted by the Civil Procedure (Amendment No. 3) Rules 2023, SI 2023/788, rr 2, 9(b).

3 Inserted by the Civil Procedure (Amendment) Rules 2000, SI 2000/221, r 8.

Restriction on the use of further information

18.2

The court may direct that information provided by a party to another party (whether given voluntarily or following an order made under rule 18.1) must not be used for any purpose except for that of the proceedings in which it is given.

PRACTICE DIRECTION 18 – FURTHER INFORMATION

This Practice Direction supplements CPR Part 18

Attention is also drawn to Part 22 (Statements of Truth).

Preliminary Request for further information or clarification

1.1 Before making an application to the court for an order under Part 18, the party seeking clarification or information (the first party) should first serve on the party from whom it is sought (the second party) a written request for that clarification or information (a Request) stating a date by which the response to the Request should be served. The date must allow the second party a reasonable time to respond.

1.2 A Request should be concise and strictly confined to matters which are reasonably necessary and proportionate to enable the first party to prepare his own case or to understand the case he has to meet.

1.3 Requests must be made as far as possible in a single comprehensive document and not piecemeal.

1.4 A Request may be made by letter if the text of the Request is brief and the reply is likely to be brief; otherwise the Request should be made in a separate document.

1.5 If a Request is made in a letter, the letter should, in order to distinguish it from any other that might routinely be written in the course of a case,

(1) state that it contains a Request made under Part 18, and

(2) deal with no matters other than the Request.

1.6

(1) A Request (whether made by letter or in a separate document) must –

(a) be headed with the name of the court and the title and number of the claim,

(b) in its heading state that it is a Request made under Part 18, identify the first party and the second party and state the date on which it is made,

(c) set out in a separate numbered paragraph each request for information or clarification,

(d) where a Request relates to a document, identify that document and (if relevant) the paragraph or words to which it relates,

(e) state the date by which the first party expects a response to the Request.

(2)

(a) A Request which is not in the form of a letter may, if convenient, be prepared in such a way that the response may be given on the same document.

(b) To do this the numbered paragraphs of the Request should appear on the left hand half of each sheet so that the paragraphs of the response may then appear on the right.

(c) Where a Request is prepared in this form an extra copy should be served for the use of the second party.

1.7 Subject to the provisions of rule 6.23(5) and (6) and paragraphs 4.1 to 4.3 of Practice Direction 6A, a request should be served by e-mail if reasonably practicable.

Responding to a Request

2.1 A response to a Request must be in writing, dated and signed by the second party or his legal representative.

2.2

(1) Where the Request is made in a letter the second party may give his response in a letter or in a formal reply.

(2) Such a letter should identify itself as a response to the Request and deal with no other matters than the response.

2.3

(1) Unless the Request is in the format described in paragraph 1.6(2) and the second party uses the document supplied for the purpose, a response must:

(a) be headed with the name of the court and the title and number of the claim,

(b) in its heading identify itself as a response to that Request,

(c) repeat the text of each separate paragraph of the Request and set out under each paragraph the response to it,

(d) refer to and have attached to it a copy of any document not already in the possession of the first party which forms part of the response.

(2) A second or supplementary response to a Request must identify itself as such in its heading.

2.4 The second party must when he serves his response on the first party serve on every other party and file with the court a copy of the Request and of his response.

Statements of Truth

3 Attention is drawn to Part 22 and to the definition of a statement of case in Part 2 of the rules; a response should be verified by a statement of truth.

General matters

4.1

(1) If the second party objects to complying with the Request or part of it or is unable to do so at all or within the time stated in the Request he must inform the first party promptly and in any event within that time.

(2) He may do so in a letter or in a separate document (a formal response), but in either case he must give reasons and, where relevant, give a date by which he expects to be able to comply.

4.2

(1) There is no need for a second party to apply to the court if he objects to a Request or is unable to comply with it at all or within the stated time. He need only comply with paragraph 4.1(1) above.

(2) Where a second party considers that a Request can only be complied with at disproportionate expense and objects to comply for that reason he should say so in his reply and explain briefly why he has taken that view.

Applications for Orders under Part 18

5.1 Attention is drawn to Part 23 (Applications) and to Practice Direction 23A.

5.2 An application notice for an order under Part 18 should set out or have attached to it the text of the order sought and in particular should specify the matter or matters in respect of which the clarification or information is sought.

5.3

(1) If a Request under paragraph 1 for the information or clarification has not been made, the application notice should, in addition, explain why not.

(2) If a Request for clarification or information has been made, the application notice or the evidence in support should describe the response, if any.

5.4 Both the first party and the second party should consider whether evidence in support of or in opposition to the application is required.

5.5

(1) Where the second party has made no response to a Request served on him, the first party need not serve the application notice on the second party, and the court may deal with the application without a hearing.

(2) Sub-paragraph (1) above only applies if at least 14 days have passed since the Request was served and the time stated in it for a response has expired.

5.6 Unless paragraph 5.5 applies the application notice must be served on the second party and on all other parties to the claim.

5.7 An order made under Part 18 must be served on all parties to the claim.

5.8 Costs:

(1) Attention is drawn to the Practice Directions 44 to 48 on costs and, in particular, Subsections 8 and 9 of Practice Direction 44, which relate to the court's power to make a summary assessment of costs.

(2) Attention is also drawn to rule 44.10(1) which provides that the general rule is that if an order does not mention costs no party is entitled to costs relating to that order.

PART 31
DISCLOSURE AND INSPECTION OF DOCUMENTS

Scope of this Part

31.1

(1) This Part sets out rules about the disclosure and inspection of documents.

(2) This Part applies to all claims except a claim on the small claims track.

Meaning of disclosure

31.2

A party discloses a document by stating that the document exists or has existed.

Right of inspection of a disclosed document

31.3

(1) A party to whom a document has been disclosed has a right to inspect that document except where—

(a) the document is no longer in the control of the party who disclosed it;

(b) the party disclosing the document has a right or a duty to withhold inspection of it; [or][1]

(c) paragraph (2) applies ; …[2]

(d) …[2].

(Rule 31.8 sets out when a document is in the control of a party)

(Rule 31.19 sets out the procedure for claiming a right or duty to withhold inspection)

…[2]

(2) Where a party considers that it would be disproportionate to the issues in the case to permit inspection of documents within a category or class of document disclosed under rule 31.6(b)—

(a) he is not required to permit inspection of documents within that category or class; but

(b) he must state in his disclosure statement that inspection of those documents will not be permitted on the grounds that to do so would be disproportionate.

(Rule 31.6 provides for standard disclosure)

(Rule 31.10 makes provision for a disclosure statement)

(Rule 31.12 provides for a party to apply for an order for specific inspection of documents)

Amendments

1 Inserted by the Civil Procedure Rules 1998 (Amendment) (EU Exit) Regulations 2019, SI 2019/521, regs 2, 10(1), (2)(a)(i).

2 Repealed by the Civil Procedure Rules 1998 (Amendment) (EU Exit) Regulations 2019, SI 2019/521, regs 2, 10(1), (2)(a)(ii), (iii), (b).

Meaning of document

31.4

In this Part—

'document' means anything in which information of any description is recorded; and

'copy', in relation to a document, means anything onto which information recorded in the document has been copied, by whatever means and whether directly or indirectly.

Disclosure ...1

31.5

(1) ...[2]

(2) Unless the court otherwise orders, paragraphs (3) to (8) apply to all [intermediate and][3] multi-track claims, other than those which include a claim for personal injuries.

(3) Not less than 14 days before the first case management conference[, if any,][2] each party must file and serve a report verified by a statement of truth, which—

(a) describes briefly what documents exist or may exist that are or may be relevant to the matters in issue in the case;

(b) describes where and with whom those documents are or may be located;

(c) in the case of electronic documents, describes how those documents are stored;

(d) estimates the broad range of costs that could be involved in giving standard disclosure in the case, including the costs of searching for and disclosing any electronically stored documents; and

(e) states which of the directions under paragraphs (7) or (8) are to be sought.

(4) In cases where the Electronic Documents Questionnaire has been exchanged, the Questionnaire should be filed with the report required by paragraph (3).

(5) Not less than seven days before the first case management conference, and on any other occasion as the court may direct, the parties must, at a meeting or by telephone, discuss and seek to agree a proposal in relation to disclosure that meets the overriding objective.

(6) If—

(a) the parties agree proposals for the scope of disclosure; and

(b) the court considers that the proposals are appropriate in all the circumstances,

the court may approve them without a hearing and give directions in the terms proposed.

(7) At the first or any subsequent case management conference, the court will decide, having regard to the overriding objective and the need to limit disclosure to that which is necessary to deal with the case justly, which of the following orders to make in relation to disclosure—

(a) an order dispensing with disclosure;

(b) an order that a party disclose the documents on which it relies, and at the same time request any specific disclosure it requires from any other party;

(c) an order that directs, where practicable, the disclosure to be given by each party on an issue by issue basis;

(d) an order that each party disclose any documents which it is reasonable to suppose may contain information which enables that party to advance its own case or to damage that of any other party, or which leads to an enquiry which has either of those consequences;

(e) an order that a party give standard disclosure;

(f) any other order in relation to disclosure that the court considers appropriate.

(8) The court may at any point give directions as to how disclosure is to be given, and in particular—

(a) what searches are to be undertaken, of where, for what, in respect of which time periods and by whom and the extent of any search for electronically stored documents;

(b) whether lists of documents are required;

(c) how and when the disclosure statement is to be given;

(d) in what format documents are to be disclosed (and whether any identification is required);

(e) what is required in relation to documents that once existed but no longer exist; and

(f) whether disclosure shall take place in stages.

(9) To the extent that the documents to be disclosed are electronic, the provisions of Practice Direction 31B – Disclosure of Electronic Documents will apply in addition to paragraphs (3) to (8).

(The court may make an order requiring standard disclosure under rule 28.3 which deals with directions in relation to cases on the fast track and under rule 29.2 which deals with case management in relation to cases on the multi-track)

Amendments

1 Repealed by the Civil Procedure (Amendment No. 7) Rules 2013, SI 2013/1974, r 13.

2 Repealed by the Civil Procedure (Amendment) Rules 2024, SI 2024/106, rr 2, 8(a).

3 Inserted by the Civil Procedure (Amendment) Rules 2024, SI 2024/106, rr 2, 8(b), (c).

Standard disclosure—what documents are to be disclosed

31.6

Standard disclosure requires a party to disclose only—

(a) the documents on which he relies; and

(b) the documents which—

(i) adversely affect his own case;

(ii) adversely affect another party's case; or

(iii) support another party's case; and

(c) the documents which he is required to disclose by a relevant practice direction.

Duty of search

31.7

(1) When giving standard disclosure, a party is required to make a reasonable search for documents falling within rule 31.6(b) or (c).

(2) The factors relevant in deciding the reasonableness of a search include the following—

(a) the number of documents involved;

(b) the nature and complexity of the proceedings;

(c) the ease and expense of retrieval of any particular document; and

(d) the significance of any document which is likely to be located during the search.

(3) Where a party has not searched for a category or class of document on the grounds that to do so would be unreasonable, he must state this in his disclosure statement and identify the category or class of document.

(Rule 31.10 makes provision for a disclosure statement)

Duty of disclosure limited to documents which are or have been in party's control

31.8

(1) A party's duty to disclose documents is limited to documents which are or have been in his control.

(2) For this purpose a party has or has had a document in his control if—

(a) it is or was in his physical possession;

(b) he has or has had a right to possession of it; or

(c) he has or has had a right to inspect or take copies of it.

Disclosure of copies

31.9

(1) A party need not disclose more than one copy of a document.

(2) A copy of a document that contains a modification, obliteration or other marking or feature—

(a) on which a party intends to rely; or

(b) which adversely affects his own case or another party's case or supports another party's case;

shall be treated as a separate document.

(Rule 31.4 sets out the meaning of a copy of a document)

Procedure for standard disclosure

31.10

(1) The procedure for standard disclosure is as follows.

(2) Each party must make and serve on every other party, a list of documents in the relevant practice form.

(3) The list must identify the documents in a convenient order and manner and as concisely as possible.

(4) The list must indicate—

(a) those documents in respect of which the party claims a right or duty to withhold inspection; and

(b)

(i) those documents which are no longer in the party's control; and

(ii) what has happened to those documents.

(Rule 31.19 (3) and (4) require a statement in the list of documents relating to any documents inspection of which a person claims he has a right or duty to withhold)

(5) The list must include a disclosure statement.

(6) A disclosure statement is a statement made by the party disclosing the documents—

(a) setting out the extent of the search that has been made to locate documents which he is required to disclose;

(b) certifying that he understands the duty to disclose documents; and

(c) certifying that to the best of his knowledge he has carried out that duty.

(7) Where the party making the disclosure statement is a company, firm, association or other organisation, the statement must also—

(a) identify the person making the statement; and

(b) explain why he is considered an appropriate person to make the statement.

(8) The parties may agree in writing—

(a) to disclose documents without making a list; and

(b) to disclose documents without the disclosing party making a disclosure statement.

(9) A disclosure statement may be made by a person who is not a party where this is permitted by a relevant practice direction.

Duty of disclosure continues during proceedings

31.11

(1) Any duty of disclosure continues until the proceedings are concluded.

(2) If documents to which that duty extends come to a party's notice at any time during the proceedings, he must immediately notify every other party.

Specific disclosure or inspection

31.12

(1) The court may make an order for specific disclosure or specific inspection.

(2) An order for specific disclosure is an order that a party must do one or more of the following things—

(a) disclose documents or classes of documents specified in the order;

(b) carry out a search to the extent stated in the order;

(c) disclose any documents located as a result of that search.

(3) An order for specific inspection is an order that a party permit inspection of a document referred to in rule 31.3(2).

(Rule 31.3(2) allows a party to state in his disclosure statement that he will not permit inspection of a document on the grounds that it would be disproportionate to do so)

...[1]

Amendments

1 Repealed by the Civil Procedure Rules 1998 (Amendment) (EU Exit) Regulations 2019, SI 2019/521, regs 2, 10(1), (3).

[Ordering a party to request another person to disclose a document

31.12A

The court may order a party to request any person to produce for disclosure and inspection any document which may support the case or adversely affect the case of any party to the proceedings.][1]

Amendments

1 Inserted by the Civil Procedure (Amendment) Rules 2026, SI 2026/97, rr 2, 4(2)

Disclosure in stages

31.13

The parties may agree in writing, or the court may direct, that disclosure or inspection or both shall take place in stages.

Documents referred to in statements of case etc.

31.14

[(1)][1] A party may inspect a document mentioned in—

(a) a statement of case;

(b) a witness statement;

(c) a witness summary; [or][2]

(d) an affidavit[(GL)][.][3]

(e) ...[4]

(Rule 35.10(4) makes provision in relation to instructions referred to in an expert's report)

[(2) Subject to rule 35.10(4), a party may apply for an order for inspection of any document mentioned in an expert's report which has not already been disclosed in the proceedings.][2]

Amendments

1 Renumbered by the Civil Procedure (Amendment No. 5) Rules 2001, SI 2001/4015, r 20(a).

2 Inserted by the Civil Procedure (Amendment No. 5) Rules 2001, SI 2001/4015, r 20(b), (e).

3 Substituted by the Civil Procedure (Amendment No. 5) Rules 2001, SI 2001/4015, r 20(c).

4 Repealed by the Civil Procedure (Amendment No. 5) Rules 2001, SI 2001/4015, r 20(d).

Inspection and copying of documents

31.15

Where a party has a right to inspect a document—

(a) that party must give the party who disclosed the document written notice of his wish to inspect it;

(b) the party who disclosed the document must permit inspection not more than 7 days after the date on which he received the notice; and

(c) that party may request a copy of the document and, if he also undertakes to pay reasonable copying costs, the party who disclosed the document must supply him with a copy not more than 7 days after the date on which he received the request.

(Rule 31.3 and 31.14 deal with the right of a party to inspect a document)

Disclosure before proceedings start

31.16

(1) This rule applies where an application is made to the court under any Act for disclosure before proceedings have started.

(2) The application must be supported by evidence.

(3) The court may make an order under this rule only where—

(a) the respondent is likely to be a party to subsequent proceedings;

(b) the applicant is also likely to be a party to those proceedings;

(c) if proceedings had started, the respondent's duty by way of standard disclosure, set out in rule 31.6, would extend to the documents or classes of documents of which the applicant seeks disclosure; and

(d) disclosure before proceedings have started is desirable in order to—

(i) dispose fairly of the anticipated proceedings;

(ii) assist the dispute to be resolved without proceedings; or

(iii) save costs.

(4) An order under this rule must—

(a) specify the documents or the classes of documents which the respondent must disclose; and

(b) require him, when making disclosure, to specify any of those documents—

(i) which are no longer in his control; or

(ii) in respect of which he claims a right or duty to withhold inspection.

(5) Such an order may—

(a) require the respondent to indicate what has happened to any documents which are no longer in his control; and

(b) specify the time and place for disclosure and inspection.

...[1]

Amendments

1 Repealed by the Civil Procedure Rules 1998 (Amendment) (EU Exit) Regulations 2019, SI 2019/521, regs 2, 10(1), (4).

Orders for disclosure against a person not a party

31.17

(1) This rule applies where an application is made to the court under any Act for disclosure by a person who is not a party to the proceedings.

(2) The application must be supported by evidence.

(3) The court may make an order under this rule only where—

(a) the documents of which disclosure is sought are likely to support the case of the applicant or adversely affect the case of one of the other parties to the proceedings; and

(b) disclosure is necessary in order to dispose fairly of the claim or to save costs.

(4) An order under this rule must—

(a) specify the documents or the classes of documents which the respondent must disclose; and

(b) require the respondent, when making disclosure, to specify any of those documents—

(i) which are no longer in his control; or

(ii) in respect of which he claims a right or duty to withhold inspection.

(5) Such an order may—

(a) require the respondent to indicate what has happened to any documents which are no longer in his control; and

(b) specify the time and place for disclosure and inspection.

. . .[1]

Amendments

1 Repealed by the Civil Procedure Rules 1998 (Amendment) (EU Exit) Regulations 2019, SI 2019/521, regs 2, 10(1), (5).

Rules not to limit other powers of the court to order disclosure

31.18

Rules 31.16 and 31.17 do not limit any other power which the court may have to order—

(a) disclosure before proceedings have started; and

(b) disclosure against a person who is not a party to proceedings.

Claim to withhold inspection or disclosure of a document

31.19

(1) A person may apply, without notice, for an order permitting him to withhold disclosure of a document on the ground that disclosure would damage the public interest.

(2) Unless the court orders otherwise, an order of the court under paragraph (1)—

(a) must not be served on any other person; and

(b) must not be open to inspection by any person.

(3) A person who wishes to claim that he has a right or a duty to withhold inspection of a document, or part of a document, must state in writing—

(a) that he has such a right or duty; and

(b) the grounds on which he claims that right or duty.

(4) The statement referred to in paragraph (3) must be made—

(a) in the list in which the document is disclosed; or

(b) if there is no list, to the person wishing to inspect the document.

(5) A party may apply to the court to decide whether a claim made under paragraph (3) should be upheld.

(6) For the purpose of deciding an application under paragraph (1) (application to withhold disclosure) or paragraph (3) (claim to withhold inspection) the court may—

(a) require the person seeking to withhold disclosure or inspection of a document to produce that document to the court; and

(b) invite any person, whether or not a party, to make representations.

(7) An application under paragraph (1) or paragraph (5) must be supported by evidence.

(8) This Part does not affect any rule of law which permits or requires a document to be withheld from disclosure or inspection on the ground that its disclosure or inspection would damage the public interest.

Restriction on use of a privileged document inspection of which has been inadvertently allowed

31.20

Where a party inadvertently allows a privileged(GL) document to be inspected, the party who has inspected the document may use it or its contents only with the permission of the court.

Consequence of failure to disclose documents or permit inspection

31.21

A party may not rely on any document which he fails to disclose or in respect of which he fails to permit inspection unless the court gives permission.

Subsequent use of disclosed documents [and completed Electronic Documents Questionnaires] I

31.22

(1) A party to whom a document has been disclosed may use the document only for the purpose of the proceedings in which it is disclosed, except where—

(a) the document has been read to or by the court, or referred to, at a hearing which has been held in public;

(b) the court gives permission; or

(c) the party who disclosed the document and the person to whom the document belongs agree.

(2) The court may make an order restricting or prohibiting the use of a document which has been disclosed, even where the document has been read to or by the court, or referred to, at a hearing which has been held in public.

(3) An application for such an order may be made—

(a) by a party; or

(b) by any person to whom the document belongs.

[(4) For the purpose of this rule, an Electronic Documents Questionnaire which has been completed and served by another party pursuant to Practice Direction 31B is to be treated as if it is a document which has been disclosed.][1]

Amendments

1 Inserted by the Civil Procedure (Amendment No. 2) Rules 2010, SI 2010/1953, r 4(b), (c).

[False, disclosure statements

31.23

(1) Proceedings for contempt of court may be brought against a person if he makes, or causes to be made, a false disclosure statement, without an honest belief in its truth.

[[(Part 81 deals with proceedings in relation to contempt of court.)][1]][2]

(2) …[3]][4]

Amendments

1 Substituted by the Civil Procedure (Amendment No. 3) Rules 2020, SI 2020/747, rr 3, 7.

2 Inserted by the Civil Procedure (Amendment No. 2) Rules 2012, SI 2012/2208, r 5(a).

3 Repealed by the Civil Procedure (Amendment No. 2) Rules 2012, SI 2012/2208, r 5(b).

4 Inserted by the Civil Procedure (Amendment) Rules 2000, SI 2000/221, r 16.

PRACTICE DIRECTION 31A – DISCLOSURE AND INSPECTION

This Practice Direction supplements CPR Part 31

General

1.1 In order to give standard disclosure the disclosing party must make a reasonable search for documents falling within the paragraphs of rule 31.6.

1.2 Having made the search the disclosing party must (unless rule 31.10(8) applies) make a list of the documents of whose existence the party is aware that fall within those paragraphs and which are or have been in the party's control (see rule 31.8).

1.3 The obligations imposed by an order for standard disclosure may be dispensed with or limited either by the court or by written agreement between the parties. Any such written agreement should be lodged with the court.

The search

2 The extent of the search which must be made will depend upon the circumstances of the case including, in particular, the factors referred to in rule 31.7(2). The parties should bear in mind the overriding principle of proportionality (see rule 1.1(2)(c)). It may, for example, be reasonable to decide not to search for documents coming into existence before some particular date, or to limit the search to documents in some particular place or places, or to documents falling into particular categories.

Electronic disclosure

2A.1 Rule 31.4 contains a broad definition of a document. This extends to electronic documents, including e-mail and other electronic communications, word processed documents and databases. In addition to documents that are readily accessible from computer systems and other electronic devices and media, the definition covers those documents that are stored on servers and back-up systems and electronic documents that have been 'deleted'. It also extends to additional information stored and associated with electronic documents known as metadata.

2A.2 Practice Direction 31B contains additional provisions in relation to the disclosure of electronic documents in cases that are likely to be allocated to the multi-track.

The list

3.1 The list should be in Form N265.

3.2 In order to comply with rule 31.10(3) it will normally be necessary to list the documents in date order, to number them consecutively and to give each a concise description (e.g. letter, claimant to defendant). Where there is a large number of documents all falling into a particular category the disclosing party may list those documents as a category rather than individually e.g. 50 bank statements relating to account number _ at _ Bank, _20_ to _20_; or, 35 letters passing between _ and _ between _20_ and _20_.

3.3 The obligations imposed by an order for disclosure will continue until the proceedings come to an end. If, after a list of documents has been prepared and served, the existence of further documents to which the order applies comes to the attention of the disclosing party, the party must prepare and serve a supplemental list.

Disclosurestatement

4.1 A list of documents must (unless rule 31.10(8)(b) applies) contain a disclosure statement complying with rule 31.10. The form of disclosure statement is set out in the Annex to this practice direction.

4.2 The disclosure statement should:

(1) expressly state that the disclosing party believes the extent of the search to have been reasonable in all the circumstances, and

(2) in setting out the extent of the search (see rule 31.10(6)) draw attention to any particular limitations on the extent of the search which were adopted for proportionality reasons and give the reasons why the limitations were adopted, e.g. the difficulty or expense that a search not subject to those limitations would have entailed or the marginal relevance of categories of documents omitted from the search.

4.3 Where rule 31.10(7) applies, the details given in the disclosure statement about the person making the statement must include his name and address and the office or position he holds in the disclosing party or the basis upon which he makes the statement on behalf of the party.

4.4 If the disclosing party has a legal representative acting for him, the legal representative must endeavour to ensure that the person making the disclosure statement (whether the disclosing party or, in a case to which rule 31.10(7) applies, some other person) understands the duty of disclosure under Part 31.

4.5 If the disclosing party wishes to claim that he has a right or duty to withhold a document, or part of a document, in his list of documents from inspection (see rule 31.19(3)), he must state in writing:

(1) that he has such a right or duty, and

(2) the grounds on which he claims that right or duty.

4.6 The statement referred to in paragraph 4.5 above should normally be included in the disclosure statement and must indicate the document, or part of a document, to which the claim relates.

4.7 An insurer or the Motor Insurers' Bureau may sign a disclosure statement on behalf of a party where the insurer or the Motor Insurers' Bureau has a financial interest in the result of proceedings brought wholly or partially by or against that party. Rule 31.10(7) and paragraph 4.3 above shall apply to the insurer or the Motor Insurers' Bureau making such a statement.

Specific disclosure

5.1 If a party believes that the disclosure of documents given by a disclosing party is inadequate he may make an application for an order for specific disclosure (see rule 31.12).

5.2 The application notice must specify the order that the applicant intends to ask the court to make and must be supported by evidence (see rule 31.12(2) which describes the orders the court may make).

5.3 The grounds on which the order is sought may be set out in the application notice itself but if not there set out must be set out in the evidence filed in support of the application.

5.4 In deciding whether or not to make an order for specific disclosure the court will take into account all the circumstances of the case and, in particular, the overriding objective described in Part 1. But if the court concludes that the party from whom specific disclosure is sought has failed adequately to comply with the obligations imposed by an order for disclosure (whether by failing to make a sufficient search for documents or otherwise) the court will usually make such order as is necessary to ensure that those obligations are properly complied with.

5.5 An order for specific disclosure may in an appropriate case direct a party to –

(1) carry out a search for any documents which it is reasonable to suppose may contain information which may–

(a) enable the party applying for disclosure either to advance his own case or to damage that of the party giving disclosure; or

(b) lead to a train of enquiry which has either of those consequences; and

(2) disclose any documents found as a result of that search.

Claims to withhold disclosure or inspection of a document

6.1 A claim to withhold inspection of a document, or part of a document, disclosed in a list of documents does not require an application to the court. Where such a claim has been made, a party who wishes to challenge it must apply to the court (see rule 31.19(5)).

6.2 Rule 31.19(1) and (6) provide a procedure enabling a party to apply for an order permitting disclosure of the existence of a document to be withheld.

Inspection of documents mentioned in expert's report (Rule 31.14(2))

7.1 If a party wishes to inspect documents referred to in the expert report of another party, before issuing an application he should request inspection of the documents informally, and inspection should be provided by agreement unless the request is unreasonable.

7.2 Where an expert report refers to a large number or volume of documents and it would be burdensome to copy or collate them, the court will only order inspection of such documents if it is satisfied that it is necessary for the just disposal of the proceedings and the party cannot reasonably obtain the documents from another source.

False disclosure statement

8 Attention is drawn to rule 31.23 which sets out the consequences of making a false disclosure statement without an honest belief in its truth, and to the procedure set out in Part 81— Applications and proceedings in relation to contempt of court..

Annex
Disclosure statement

I, the above named claimant [or defendant] [if party making disclosure is a company, firm or other organisation identify here who the person making the disclosure statement is and why he is the appropriate person to make it] state that I have carried out a reasonable and proportionate search to locate all the documents which I am required to disclose under the order made by the court on day of . I did not search:

(1) for documents predating ....,

(2) for documents located elsewhere than ....,

(3) for documents in categories other than ....

(4) for electronic documents

I carried out a search for electronic documents contained on or created by the following:

[list what was searched and extent of search]

I did not search for the following:

(1) documents created before..........,

(2) documents contained on or created by the Claimant's/Defendant's PCs/portable data storage media/databases/servers/back-up tapes/off-site storage/mobile phones/laptops/notebooks/handheld devices/PDA devices (delete as appropriate),

(3) documents contained on or created by the Claimant's/Defendant's mail files/document files/calendar files/spreadsheet files/graphic and presentation files/web-based applications (delete as appropriate),

(4) documents other than by reference to the following keyword(s)/concepts.......... (delete if your search was not confined to specific keywords or concepts).

I certify that I understand the duty of disclosure and to the best of my knowledge I have carried out that duty. I certify that the list above is a complete list of all documents which are or have been in my control and which I am obliged under the said order to disclose.

PRACTICE DIRECTION 31B – DISCLOSURE OF ELECTRONIC DOCUMENTS

This Practice Direction supplements CPR Part 31

Purpose, scope and interpretation

1 Rule 31.4 contains a broad definition of 'document'. This extends to Electronic Documents.

2 The purpose of this Practice Direction is to encourage and assist the parties to reach agreement in relation to the disclosure of Electronic Documents in a proportionate and cost-effective manner.

3 Unless the court orders otherwise, this Practice Direction only applies to proceedings that are (or are likely to be) allocated to the multi-track.

4 Unless the court orders otherwise, this Practice Direction only applies to proceedings started on or after 1st October 2010. Paragraph 2A.2 to 2A.5 of Practice Direction 31A in force immediately before that date continues to apply to proceedings started before that date.

5 In this Practice Direction –

(1) 'Data Sampling' means the process of checking data by identifying and checking representative individual documents;

(2) 'Disclosure Data' means data relating to disclosed documents, including for example the type of document, the date of the document, the names of the author or sender and the recipient, and the party disclosing the document;

(3) 'Electronic Document' means any document held in electronic form. It includes, for example, email and other electronic communications such as text messages and voicemail, word-processed documents and databases, and documents stored on portable devices such as memory sticks and mobile phones. In addition to documents that are readily accessible from computer systems and other electronic devices and media, it includes documents that are stored on servers and back-up systems and documents that have been deleted. It also includes metadata and other embedded data which is not typically visible on screen or a print out;

(4) 'Electronic Image' means an electronic representation of a paper document;

(5) 'Electronic Documents Questionnaire' means the questionnaire in the Schedule to this Practice Direction;

(6) 'Keyword Search' means a software-aided search for words across the text of an Electronic Document;

(7) 'Metadata' is data about data. In the case of an Electronic Document, metadata is typically embedded information about the document which is not readily accessible once the Native Electronic Document has been converted into an Electronic Image or paper document. It may include

(for example) the date and time of creation or modification of a word-processing file, or the author and the date and time of sending an email. Metadata may be created automatically by a computer system or manually by a user;

(8) 'Native Electronic Document' or 'Native Format' means an Electronic Document stored in the original form in which it was created by a computer software program; and

(9) 'Optical Character Recognition (OCR)' means the computer-facilitated recognition of printed or written text characters in an Electronic Image in which the text-based contents cannot be searched electronically.

General principles

6 When considering disclosure of Electronic Documents, the parties and their legal representatives should bear in mind the following general principles –

(1) Electronic Documents should be managed efficiently in order to minimise the cost incurred;

(2) technology should be used in order to ensure that document management activities are undertaken efficiently and effectively;

(3) disclosure should be given in a manner which gives effect to the overriding objective;

(4) Electronic Documents should generally be made available for inspection in a form which allows the party receiving the documents the same ability to access, search, review and display the documents as the party giving disclosure; and

(5) disclosure of Electronic Documents which are of no relevance to the proceedings may place an excessive burden in time and cost on the party to whom disclosure is given.

Preservation of documents

7 As soon as litigation is contemplated, the parties' legal representatives must notify their clients of the need to preserve disclosable documents. The documents to be preserved include Electronic Documents which would otherwise be deleted in accordance with a document retention policy or otherwise deleted in the ordinary course of business.

Discussions between the parties before the first Case Management Conference in relation to the use of technology and disclosure

8 The parties and their legal representatives must, before the first case management conference, discuss the use of technology in the management

of Electronic Documents and the conduct of proceedings, in particular for the purpose of –

(1) creating lists of documents to be disclosed;

(2) giving disclosure by providing documents and information regarding documents in electronic format; and

(3) presenting documents and other material to the court at the trial.

9 The parties and their legal representatives must also, before the first case management conference, discuss the disclosure of Electronic Documents. In some cases (for example heavy and complex cases) it may be appropriate to begin discussions before proceedings are commenced. The discussions should include (where appropriate) the following matters –

(1) the categories of Electronic Documents within the parties' control, the computer systems, electronic devices and media on which any relevant documents may be held, storage systems and document retention policies;

(2) the scope of the reasonable search for Electronic Documents required by rule 31.7;

(3) the tools and techniques (if any) which should be considered to reduce the burden and cost of disclosure of Electronic Documents, including –

   (a) limiting disclosure of documents or certain categories of documents to particular date ranges, to particular custodians of documents, or to particular types of documents;

   (b) the use of agreed Keyword Searches;

   (c) the use of agreed software tools;

   (d) the methods to be used to identify duplicate documents;

   (e) the use of Data Sampling;

   (f) the methods to be used to identify privileged documents and other non-disclosable documents, to redact documents (where redaction is appropriate), and for dealing with privileged or other documents which have been inadvertently disclosed; and

   (g) the use of a staged approach to the disclosure of Electronic Documents;

(4) the preservation of Electronic Documents, with a view to preventing loss of such documents before the trial;

(5) the exchange of data relating to Electronic Documents in an agreed electronic format using agreed fields;

(6) the formats in which Electronic Documents are to be provided on inspection and the methods to be used;

(7) the basis of charging for or sharing the cost of the provision of Electronic Documents, and whether any arrangements for charging or sharing of

costs are final or are subject to re-allocation in accordance with any order for costs subsequently made; and

(8) whether it would be appropriate to use the services of a neutral electronic repository for storage of Electronic Documents.

The Electronic Documents Questionnaire

10 In some cases the parties may find it helpful to exchange the Electronic Documents Questionnaire in order to provide information to each other in relation to the scope, extent and most suitable format for disclosure of Electronic Documents in the proceedings.

11 The answers to the Electronic Documents Questionnaire must be verified by a statement of truth.

12 Answers to the Electronic Documents Questionnaire will only be available for inspection by non-parties if permission is given under rule 5.4C(2).

13 Rule 31.22 makes provision regulating the use of answers to the Electronic Documents Questionnaire.

Preparation for the first Case Management Conference

14 The documents submitted to the court in advance of the first case management conference should include a summary of the matters on which the parties agree in relation to the disclosure of Electronic Documents and a summary of the matters on which they disagree.

15 If the parties indicate that they have been unable to reach agreement in relation to the disclosure of Electronic Documents and that no agreement is likely, the court will give written directions in relation to disclosure or order a separate hearing in relation to disclosure. When doing so, the court will consider making an order that the parties must complete and exchange all or any part of the Electronic Documents Questionnaire within 14 days or such other period as the court may direct.

16 The person signing the Electronic Documents Questionnaire should attend the first case management conference, and any subsequent hearing at which disclosure is likely to be considered.

Where the parties are unable to reach an appropriate agreement in relation to the disclosure of Electronic Documents

17 If at any time it becomes apparent that the parties are unable to reach agreement in relation to the disclosure of Electronic Documents, the parties should seek directions from the court at the earliest practical date.

18 If the court considers that the parties' agreement in relation to the disclosure of Electronic Documents is inappropriate or insufficient, the court will give directions in relation to disclosure. When doing so, the court will consider

making an order that the parties must complete and exchange all or any part of the Electronic Documents Questionnaire within 14 days or such other period as the court may direct.

19 If a party gives disclosure of Electronic Documents without first discussing with other parties how to plan and manage such disclosure, the court may require that party to carry out further searches for documents or to repeat other steps which that party has already carried out.

The reasonable search

20 The extent of the reasonable search required by rule 31.7 for the purposes of standard disclosure is affected by the existence of Electronic Documents. The extent of the search which must be made will depend on the circumstances of the case including, in particular, the factors referred to in rule 31.7(2). The parties should bear in mind that the overriding objective includes dealing with the case in ways which are proportionate.

21 The factors that may be relevant in deciding the reasonableness of a search for Electronic Documents include (but are not limited to) the following –

(1) the number of documents involved;

(2) the nature and complexity of the proceedings;

(3) the ease and expense of retrieval of any particular document. This includes:

(a) the accessibility of Electronic Documents including e-mail communications on computer systems, servers, back-up systems and other electronic devices or media that may contain such documents taking into account alterations or developments in hardware or software systems used by the disclosing party and/or available to enable access to such documents;

(b) the location of relevant Electronic Documents, data, computer systems, servers, back-up systems and other electronic devices or media that may contain such documents;

(c) the likelihood of locating relevant data;

(d) the cost of recovering any Electronic Documents;

(e) the cost of disclosing and providing inspection of any relevant Electronic Documents; and

(f) the likelihood that Electronic Documents will be materially altered in the course of recovery, disclosure or inspection;

(4) the availability of documents or contents of documents from other sources; and

(5) the significance of any document which is likely to be located during the search.

22 Depending on the circumstances, it may be reasonable to search all of the parties' electronic storage systems, or to search only some part of those systems. For example, it may be reasonable to decide not to search for documents coming into existence before a particular date, or to limit the search to documents in a particular place or places, or to documents falling into particular categories.

23 In some cases a staged approach may be appropriate, with disclosure initially being given of limited categories of documents. Those categories may subsequently be extended or limited depending on the results initially obtained.

24 The primary source of disclosure of Electronic Documents is normally reasonably accessible data. A party requesting under rule 31.12 specific disclosure of Electronic Documents which are not reasonably accessible must demonstrate that the relevance and materiality justify the cost and burden of retrieving and producing it.

Keyword and other automated searches

25 It may be reasonable to search for Electronic Documents by means of Keyword Searches or other automated methods of searching if a full review of each and every document would be unreasonable.

26 However, it will often be insufficient to use simple Keyword Searches or other automated methods of searching alone. The injudicious use of Keyword Searches and other automated search techniques –

(1) may result in failure to find important documents which ought to be disclosed, and/or

(2) may find excessive quantities of irrelevant documents, which if disclosed would place an excessive burden in time and cost on the party to whom disclosure is given.

27 The parties should consider supplementing Keyword Searches and other automated searches with additional techniques such as individually reviewing certain documents or categories of documents (for example important documents generated by key personnel) and taking such other steps as may be required in order to justify the selection to the court.

Disclosure of metadata

28 Where copies of disclosed documents are provided in Native Format in accordance with paragraph 33 below, some metadata will be disclosed with each document. A party requesting disclosure of additional metadata or forensic image copies of disclosed documents (for example in relation to a dispute concerning authenticity) must demonstrate that the relevance and materiality of the requested metadata justify the cost and burden of producing that metadata.

29 Parties using document management or litigation support systems should be alert to the possibility that Metadata or other useful information relating to documents may not be stored with the documents.

Lists of documents

30 If a party is giving disclosure of Electronic Documents, paragraph 3 of Practice Direction 31A is to be read subject to the following –

(1) Form N265 may be amended to accommodate the sub-paragraphs which follow;

(2) a list of documents may by agreement between the parties be an electronic file in .csv (comma-separated values) or other agreed format;

(3) documents may be listed otherwise than in date order where a different order would be more convenient;

(4) save where otherwise agreed or ordered, documents should be listed individually if a party already possesses data relating to the document (for example, type of document and date of creation) which make this possible (so that as far as possible each document may be given a unique reference number);

(5) a party should be consistent in the way in which documents are listed;

(6) consistent column headings should be repeated on each page of the list on which documents are listed, where the software used for preparing the list enables this to be carried out automatically; and

(7) the disclosure list number used in any supplemental list of documents should be unique and should run sequentially from the last number used in the previous list.

Provision of disclosure data in electronic form

31 Where a party provides another party with disclosure data in electronic form, the following provisions will apply unless the parties agree or the court directs otherwise –

(1) Disclosure data should be set out in a single, continuous table or spreadsheet, each separate column containing exclusively one of the following types of disclosure data –

(a) disclosure list number (sequential)

(b) date

(c) document type

(d) author/sender

(e) recipient

(f) disclosure list number of any parent or covering document;

(2) other than for disclosure list numbers, blank entries are permissible and preferred if there is no relevant disclosure data (that is, the field should be left blank rather than state 'Undated');

(3) dates should be set out in the alphanumeric form '01 Jan 2010'; and

(4) Disclosure data should be set out in a consistent manner.

Provision of electronic copies of disclosed documents

32 The parties should co-operate at an early stage about the format in which Electronic Documents are to be provided on inspection. In the case of difficulty or disagreement, the matter should be referred to the court for directions at the earliest practical date, if possible at the first case management conference.

33 Save where otherwise agreed or ordered, electronic copies of disclosed documents should be provided in their Native Format, in a manner which preserves Metadata relating to the date of creation of each document.

34 A party should provide any available searchable OCR versions of Electronic Documents with the original. A party may however choose not to provide OCR versions of documents which have been redacted. If OCR versions are provided, they are provided on an 'as is' basis, with no assurance to the other party that the OCR versions are complete or accurate.

35

(1) Subject to sub-paragraph (2) below, if a party is providing in electronic form copies of disclosed documents and wishes to redact or otherwise make alterations to a document or documents, then –

(a) the party redacting or altering the document must inform the other party in accordance with rule 31.19 that redacted or altered versions are being supplied; and

(b) the party redacting or altering the document must ensure that the original unredacted and unaltered version is preserved, so that it remains available to be inspected if required.

(2) Sub-paragraph (1) above does not apply where the only alteration made to the document is an alteration to the Metadata as a result of the ordinary process of copying and/or accessing the document. Sub-paragraph (1) does apply to the alteration or suppression of Metadata in other situations.

Specialised technology

36 If Electronic Documents are best accessed using technology which is not readily available to the party entitled to disclosure, and that party reasonably requires additional inspection facilities, the party making disclosure shall co-operate in making available to the other party such reasonable additional inspection facilities as may be appropriate in order to afford inspection in accordance with rule 31.3.

Schedule
Electronic Documents Questionnaire

Part 1 – Your disclosure

Extent of a reasonable search

Date range and custodians

1. What date range do you consider that your searches for Electronic Documents should cover ('the date range')?
2. Identify the custodians or creators of your Electronic Documents whose repositories of documents you consider should be searched[1].

Communications

3. Which forms of electronic communication were in use during the date range (so far as is relevant to these proceedings)?

   (a) >

A	*B*	*C*	*D*	*E*
Communication	In use during the date range? (yes/no)	Are you searching for relevant documents in this category? (yes/no)	Where and on what type of software/ equipment/media is this communication stored[2]?	
i) Email[3]				
ii) Other (provide details for each type[4]).				

Electronic Documents

4. Apart from attachments to emails, which forms of Electronic Documents were created or stored by you during the date range?

A	*B*	*C*	*D*	*E*
Document Type	In use during the date range? (yes/no)	Are you searching for relevant documents in this category? (yes/ no)	Where and on what type of software/ equipment/ media are these documents[5]?	(a) Are back-ups or archives of these documents available, and (b) if so, are you searching the back-ups or archives?
i) Word (or equivalent – state which)				
ii) Excel (or equivalent – state which)				

A	*B*	*C*	*D*	*E*
iii) Electronic Images[6]				
iv) Other[7] (state which)				

Databases of Electronic Documents

5. In the following table identify database systems, including document management systems, used by you during the date range and which may contain disclosable Electronic Documents.

A	*B*	*C*	*D*	*E*
Name	Brief description	Nature of data held	Are you disclosing documents held in this database? (yes/no)	Proposals for provision of relevant documents to or access by other parties to this litigation
1.				
2. (etc)				

Method of search

Key words

6. Do you consider that Keyword Searches should be used as part of the process of determining which Electronic Documents you should disclose?

   If yes, provide details of –

   (1) the keywords used or to be used (by reference, if applicable, to individual custodians, creators, repositories, file types and/or date ranges)[8]; and

   (2) the extent to which the Keyword Searches have been or will be supplemented by a review of individual documents.

Other types of automated searches

7. Do you consider that automated searches or automated techniques other than Keyword Searches (for example, concept searches or clustering) should be used as part of the process of determining which Electronic Documents you should disclose? If yes, provide details of –

   (1) the process(es) used or to be used (by reference, if applicable, to individual custodians, creators, repositories, file types and/or date ranges);

   (2) the extent to which the processes have been or will be supplemented by a review of individual documents; and

   (3) how the methodology of automated searches will be made available for consideration by other parties.

8. If the answer to Question 6 or 7 is yes, state whether attachments to (a) emails (b) compressed files (c) embedded files and (d) imaged text will respond to your Keyword Searches or other automated search.

9. Are you using or intending to use computer software for other purposes in relation to disclosure? If so, provide details of the software, processes and methods to be used.

Potential problems with the extent of search and accessibility of Electronic Documents

10. Do any of the sources and/or documents identified in this Electronic Documents Questionnaire raise questions about the reasonableness of the search which ought to be taken into account[9]? If so, give details.

11. Are any documents which may be disclosable encrypted, password-protected or for other reasons difficult to access, or do you have any reason to believe that they may be[10]? If so, state which of the categories identified at Questions 3, 4 and 5 above are affected, and your proposals for making them accessible.

12. Are you aware of any other points in relation to disclosure of your Electronic Documents which require discussion between the parties? If so, give details.

Preservation of Electronic Documents

13. Do you have a document retention policy?

14. Have you given an instruction to preserve Electronic Documents, and if so, when?

Inspection

15. Subject to re-consideration after receiving the responses of other parties to this Electronic Documents Questionnaire, (a) in what format and (b) on what media do you intend to provide to other parties copies of disclosed documents which are or will be available in electronic form?

16. Subject to re-consideration after receiving the responses of other parties to this Electronic Documents Questionnaire, do you intend to provide other parties with Disclosure Data electronically, and if so, (a) in what format and (b) on what media?

17. Insofar as you have available or will have available searchable OCR versions of Electronic Documents, do you intend to provide the searchable OCR version to other parties[11]? If not, why not?

Part 2 – The disclosure of other parties

The extent and content of their search

18. Do you at this stage have any proposals about the date ranges which should be searched by other parties to the proceedings? If so, provide details.

19. Do you at this stage have any proposals about the custodians or creators whose repositories of documents should be searched for disclosable documents by other parties to the proceedings? If so, provide details[12].

20. Do you consider that the other party(ies) should disclose all available metadata[13] attaching to any documents? If yes, provide details of the documents or categories of documents.

Proposals for the method to be adopted for their searches

21. Do you at this stage have any proposals about the Keyword Searches, or other automated searches, which should be applied by other parties to their document sets? If so, provide details.

Inspection

22. Subject to re-consideration after receiving the responses of other parties to this Electronic Documents Questionnaire, (a) in what format and (b) on what media do you wish to receive copies of disclosed documents which are or will be available in electronic form?

23. Subject to re-consideration after receiving the responses of other parties to this Electronic Documents Questionnaire, do you wish to receive Disclosure Data electronically, and if so, (a) in what format and (b) on what media?

Statement of Truth

* [I believe] [The [claimant] [defendant] believes] that the facts stated in the answers to this Electronic Documents Questionnaire are true.

* [I understand] [The [claimant] [defendant] understands] that proceedings for contempt of court may be brought against anyone who makes, or causes to be made, a false statement in a document verified by a statement of truth without an honest belief in its truth.

*I am duly authorised by the [claimant] [defendant] to sign this statement.

Full name______________________________________

Name of legal representative's firm________________

Signed ____

Position or office held (if signing on behalf of firm or company) _____________

Date _________________

* delete as appropriate

WARNING: Unless the court makes some other order, the answers given in this document may only be used for the purposes of the proceedings in which the document is produced unless it has been read to or by the court or referred to at a hearing which has been held in public or the Court gives permission or the party who has completed this questionnaire agrees.

Guidance Notes:

1. Technical expressions are defined in Practice Direction 31B.
2. The questions in the Electronic Documents Questionnaire are not intended to give rise to any implication about how disclosure should or should not be carried out. They are intended only to provide information to other parties and to the court.
3. Further facts and matters may come to parties' attention over the course of the proceedings which affect the answers to the Electronic Documents Questionnaire. Where detailed information is not yet available at the time the Electronic Documents Questionnaire is first answered, parties should give such information as they can, and supplement or amend their answers when further information is available. Answers should be updated by notifying other parties and the court without undue delay, and in any event before each case management conference at which disclosure is likely to be considered.
4. Some of the questions in the Electronic Documents Questionnaire require only a brief answer which may need to be elaborated after Electronic Documents Questionnaires have been exchanged. The purpose of such questions is to assist the parties in identifying the points which may require elaboration in order for meaningful discussions to take place between them.
5. Questions which refer to sources of Electronic Documents that are not considered to be relevant may be answered with a statement to that effect.
6. Questions about 'your' documents and about software, hardware or systems used by 'you' are directed, in the case of solicitors, to the solicitor's lay client's documents or to documents prepared on the lay client's behalf.

Footnotes

1 Include names of all those who may have or have had custody of disclosable documents, including secretaries, personal assistants, former employees and/or former participants. It may be helpful to identify different dates for particular custodians.

2 State the geographical location (if known). Consider (at least) servers, desktop PCs, laptops, notebooks, handheld devices, PDA devices, off-site storage, removable storage media (for example, CD-ROMs, DVDs, USB drives, memory sticks) and databases.

3 Consider all types of e-mail system (for example, Outlook, Lotus Notes, web-based accounts), whether stored on personal computers, portable devices or in web-based accounts (for example, Yahoo, Hotmail, Gmail).

4 For example, instant messaging, voicemail, VOIP (Voice Over Internet Protocol), recorded telephone lines, text messaging, audio files, video files.

5 State the geographical location (if known). Consider (at least) servers, desktops and laptops.

6 For example, .pdf, .tif, .jpg.

7 For example, PowerPoint or equivalent, specialist documents (such as CAD Drawings).

8 Where Keyword Searches are used in order to identify irrelevant documents which are to be excluded from disclosure (for example a confidential name of a client or customer), a general description of the type of search may be given.

9 See Practice Direction 31B, which refers to the following matters which may be relevant: (a) the number of documents involved; (b) the nature and complexity of the proceedings; (c) the ease and expense of retrieval of any particular document; (d) the availability of documents or contents of documents from other sources; and (e) the significance of any document which is likely to be located during the search.

10 For example, back-ups, archives, off-site or outsourced document storage, documents created by former employees, documents stored in other jurisdictions, documents in foreign languages.

11 There is no requirement that you should obtain OCR versions of documents, and this question is directed only to OCR versions which you have available or expect to have available to you. If you do provide OCR versions to another party, they will be provided by you on an 'as is' basis, with no assurance to the other party that the OCR versions are complete or accurate. You may wish to exclude provision of OCR versions of documents which have been redacted.

12 Include names of all those who may have or have had custody of disclosable documents, including secretaries, personal assistants, former employees and/or former participants. It may be helpful to identify different dates for particular custodians.

13 'Metadata' is information about the document or file which is recorded in the computer, such as the date and time of creation or modification of a word-processing file, or the author and the date and time of sending of an e-mail. The question is directed to the more extensive Metadata which may be relevant where for example authenticity is disputed.

PART 32
EVIDENCE

Power of court to control evidence

32.1

(1) The court may control the evidence by giving directions as to—

(a) the issues on which it requires evidence;

(b) the nature of the evidence which it requires to decide those issues; and

(c) the way in which the evidence is to be placed before the court.

(2) The court may use its power under this rule to exclude evidence that would otherwise be admissible.

(3) The court may limit cross-examination(GL).

Evidence of witnesses—general rule

32.2

(1) The general rule is that any fact which needs to be proved by the evidence of witnesses is to be proved—

(a) at trial, by their oral evidence given in public; and

(b) at any other hearing, by their evidence in writing.

(2) This is subject—

(a) to any provision to the contrary contained in these Rules or elsewhere; or

(b) to any order of the court.

[(3) The court may give directions—

(a) identifying or limiting the issues to which factual evidence may be directed;

(b) identifying the witnesses who may be called or whose evidence may be read; or

(c) limiting the length or format of witness statements.][1]

Amendments

1 Inserted by the Civil Procedure (Amendment) Rules 2013, SI 2013/262, r 12.

Evidence by video link or other means

32.3

The court may allow a witness to give evidence through a video link or by other means.

Requirement to serve witness statements for use at trial

32.4

(1) A witness statement is a written statement signed by a person which contains the evidence which that person would be allowed to give orally.

(2) The court will order a party to serve on the other parties any witness statement of the oral evidence which the party serving the statement intends to rely on in relation to any issues of fact to be decided at the trial.

(3) The court may give directions as to—

(a) the order in which witness statements are to be served; and

(b) whether or not the witness statements are to be filed.

Use at trial of witness statements which have been served

32.5

(1) If—

(a) a party has served a witness statement; and

(b) he wishes to rely at trial on the evidence of the witness who made the statement,

he must call the witness to give oral evidence unless the court orders otherwise or he puts the statement in as hearsay evidence.

(Part 33 contains provisions about hearsay evidence)

(2) Where a witness is called to give oral evidence under paragraph (1), his witness statement shall stand as his evidence in chief [(GL)] unless the court orders otherwise.

(3) A witness giving oral evidence at trial may with the permission of the court—

(a) amplify his witness statement; and

(b) give evidence in relation to new matters which have arisen since the witness statement was served on the other parties.

(4) The court will give permission under paragraph (3) only if it considers that there is good reason not to confine the evidence of the witness to the contents of his witness statement.

(5) If a party who has served a witness statement does not—

(a) call the witness to give evidence at trial; or

(b) put the witness statement in as hearsay evidence,

any other party may put the witness statement in as hearsay evidence.

Evidence in proceedings other than at trial

32.6

(1) Subject to paragraph (2), the general rule is that evidence at hearings other than the trial is to be by witness statement unless the court, a practice direction or any other enactment requires otherwise.

(2) At hearings other than the trial, a party may …[1] rely on the matters set out in—

(a) his statement of case; or

(b) his application notice,

if the statement of case or application notice is verified by a statement of truth.

Amendments

1 Repealed by the Civil Procedure (Amendment) Rules 2000, SI 2000/221, r 17.

Order for cross-examination

32.7

(1) Where, at a hearing other than the trial, evidence is given in writing, any party may apply to the court for permission to cross-examine the person giving the evidence.

(2) If the court gives permission under paragraph (1) but the person in question does not attend as required by the order, his evidence may not be used unless the court gives permission.

…[1]

Amendments

1 Repealed by the Civil Procedure Rules 1998 (Amendment) (EU Exit) Regulations 2019, SI 2019/521, regs 2, 11.

Form of witness statement

32.8

A witness statement must comply with the requirements set out in [Practice Direction 32][1].

(Part 22 requires a witness statement to be verified by a statement of truth)

Amendments

1 Substituted by the Civil Procedure (Amendment No. 2) Rules 2009, SI 2009/3390, r 16.

Witness summaries

32.9

(1) A party who—

(a) is required to serve a witness statement for use at trial; but

(b) is unable to obtain one,

may apply, without notice, for permission to serve a witness summary instead.

(2) A witness summary is a summary of—

(a) the evidence, if known, which would otherwise be included in a witness statement; or

(b) if the evidence is not known, the matters about which the party serving the witness summary proposes to question the witness.

(3) Unless the court orders otherwise, a witness summary must include the name and address of the intended witness.

(4) Unless the court orders otherwise, a witness summary must be served within the period in which a witness statement would have had to be served.

(5) Where a party serves a witness summary, so far as practicable rules 32.4 (requirement to serve witness statements for use at trial), 32.5(3) (amplifying witness statements), and 32.8 (form of witness statement) shall apply to the summary.

Consequence of failure to serve witness statement or summary

32.10

If a witness statement or a witness summary for use at trial is not served in respect of an intended witness within the time specified by the court, then the witness may not be called to give oral evidence unless the court gives permission.

Cross-examination on a witness statement

32.11

Where a witness is called to give evidence at trial, he may be cross-examined on his witness statement whether or not the statement or any part of it was referred to during the witness's evidence in chief[(GL)].

Use of witness statements for other purposes

32.12

(1) Except as provided by this rule, a witness statement may be used only for the purpose of the proceedings in which it is served.

(2) Paragraph (1) does not apply if and to the extent that—

(a) the witness gives consent in writing to some other use of it;

(b) the court gives permission for some other use; or

(c) the witness statement has been put in evidence at a hearing held in public.

[(3) This rule applies to affidavits in the same way as it applies to witness statements.][1]

Amendments

1 Inserted by the Civil Procedure (Amendment) Rules 2021, SI 2021/117, rr 4, 8(1).

Availability of witness statements for inspection

32.13

(1) A witness statement which stands as evidence in chief[(GL)] is open to inspection [during the course of the trial unless the court otherwise directs][1].

(2) Any person may ask for a direction that a witness statement is not open to inspection.

(3) The court will not make a direction under paragraph (2) unless it is satisfied that a witness statement should not be open to inspection because of—

(a) the interests of justice;

(b) the public interest;

(c) the nature of any expert medical evidence in the statement;

(d) the nature of any confidential information (including information relating to personal financial matters) in the statement; or

(e) the need to protect the interests of any child or [protected party][2].

(4) The court may exclude from inspection words or passages in the statement.

Amendments

1 Substituted by the Civil Procedure (Amendment) Rules 2001, SI 2001/256, r 12.

2 Substituted by the Civil Procedure (Amendment) Rules 2007, SI 2007/2204, r 10.

[False statements

32.14

Proceedings for contempt of court may be brought against a person who makes or causes to be made a false statement in a document, prepared in anticipation of or during proceedings and verified by a statement of truth, without an honest belief in its truth.

(Part 22 makes provision for statements of truth.)

(Part 81 contains provisions in relation to proceedings for contempt of court.)][1]

Amendments

1 Substituted by the Civil Procedure (Amendment No. 3) Rules 2020, SI 2020/747, rr 3, 8.

Affidavit evidence

32.15

(1) Evidence must be given by affidavit(GL) instead of or in addition to a witness statement if this is required by the court, a provision contained in any other rule, a practice direction or any other enactment.

(2) Nothing in these Rules prevents a witness giving evidence by affidavit(GL) at a hearing other than the trial if he chooses to do so in a case where paragraph (1) does not apply, but the party putting forward the affidavit(GL) may not recover the additional cost of making it from any other party unless the court orders otherwise.

[(Rule 32.12 makes provision about the use of affidavits for purposes other than the proceedings in which they are served.)][1]

Amendments

1 Inserted by the Civil Procedure (Amendment) Rules 2021, SI 2021/117, rr 4, 8(2).

Form of affidavits

32.16

An affidavit(GL) must comply with the requirements set out in [Practice Direction 32][1].

Amendments

1 Substituted by the Civil Procedure (Amendment No. 2) Rules 2009, SI 2009/3390, r 16.

Affidavit made outside the jurisdiction

32.17

A person may make anaffidavit(GL) outside the jurisdiction in accordance with—

(a) this Part; or

(b) the law of the place where he makes the affidavit(GL).

Notice to admit facts

32.18

(1) A party may serve notice on another party requiring him to admit the facts, or the part of the case of the serving party, specified in the notice.

(2) A notice to admit facts must be served no later than 21 days before the trial.

(3) Where the other party makes any admission in response to the notice, the admission may be used against him only—

(a) in the proceedings in which the notice to admit is served; and

(b) by the party who served the notice.

(4) The court may allow a party to amend or withdraw any admission made by him on such terms as it thinks just.

Notice to admit or produce documents

32.19

(1) A party shall be deemed to admit the authenticity of a document disclosed to him under Part 31 (disclosure and inspection of documents) unless he serves notice that he wishes the document to be proved at trial.

(2) A notice to prove a document must be served—

(a) by the latest date for serving witness statements; or

(b) within 7 days of disclosure of the document,

whichever is later.

[Notarial acts and instruments

32.20

A notarial act or instrument may be received in evidence without further proof as duly authenticated in accordance with the requirements of law unless the contrary is proved.][1]

Amendments

1 Inserted by the Civil Procedure (Amendment No. 3) Rules 2005, SI 2005/2292, rr 2, 36.

PRACTICE DIRECTION 32 – EVIDENCE

This Practice Direction supplements CPR Part 32

Evidence in general

1.1 Rule 32.2 sets out how evidence is to be given and facts are to be proved.

1.2 Evidence at a hearing other than the trial should normally be given by witness statement[1] (see paragraph 17 onwards). However a witness may give evidence by affidavit if he wishes to do so[2] (and see paragraph 1.4 below).

1.3 Statements of case (see paragraph 26 onwards) and application notices[3] may also be used as evidence provided that their contents have been verified by a statement of truth[4].

(For information regarding evidence by deposition see Part 34 and Practice Direction 34A.)

1.4 Affidavits must be used as evidence in the following instances:

(1) where sworn evidence is required by an enactment[5], rule, order or practice direction, and

(2) in any application for a search order, a freezing injunction, or an order requiring an occupier to permit another to enter his land.

(By rule 81.4(1), unless and to the extent that the court directs otherwise every contempt application must be supported by written evidence given by affidavit or affirmation.).

1.5 If a party believes that sworn evidence is required by a court in another jurisdiction for any purpose connected with the proceedings, he may apply to the court for a direction that evidence shall be given only by affidavit on any pre-trial applications.

1.6 The court may give a direction under rule 32.15 that evidence shall be given by affidavit instead of or in addition to a witness statement or statement of case:

(1) on its own initiative, or

(2) after any party has applied to the court for such a direction.

1.7 An affidavit, where referred to in the Civil Procedure Rules or a practice direction, also means an affirmation unless the context requires otherwise.

Affidavits

Deponent

2 A deponent is a person who gives evidence by affidavit or affirmation.

Heading

3.1 The affidavit should be headed with the title of the proceedings (see paragraph 4 of Practice Direction 7A and paragraph 5 of Practice Direction 20); where the proceedings are between several parties with the same status it is sufficient to identify the parties as follows:

	Number:
A.B. (and others)	Claimants/Applicants
C.D. (and others)	Defendants/Respondents
	(as appropriate)

3.2 At the top right hand corner of the first page (and on the backsheet) there should be clearly written:

(1) the party on whose behalf it is made,

(2) the initials and surname of the deponent,

(3) the number of the affidavit in relation to that deponent,

(4) the identifying initials and number of each exhibit referred to, and

(5) the date sworn.

Body of affidavit

4.1 The affidavit must, if practicable, be in the deponent's own words, the affidavit should be expressed in the first person and the deponent should:

(1) commence 'I (full name) of (address) state on oath ......',

(2) if giving evidence in his professional, business or other occupational capacity, give the address at which he works in (1) above, the position he holds and the name of his firm or employer,

(3) give his occupation or, if he has none, his description, and

(4) state if he is a party to the proceedings or employed by a party to the proceedings, if it be the case.

4.2 An affidavit must indicate:

(1) which of the statements in it are made from the deponent's own knowledge and which are matters of information or belief, and

(2) the source for any matters of information or belief.

4.3 Where a deponent:

(1) refers to an exhibit or exhibits, he should state 'there is now shown to me marked '...' the (description of exhibit)', and

(2) makes more than one affidavit (to which there are exhibits) in the same proceedings, the numbering of the exhibits should run consecutively throughout and not start again with each affidavit.

Jurat

5.1 The jurat of an affidavit is a statement set out at the end of the document which authenticates the affidavit.

5.2 It must:

(1) be signed by all deponents,

(2) be completed and signed by the person before whom the affidavit was sworn whose name and qualification must be printed beneath his signature,

(3) contain the full address of the person before whom the affidavit was sworn, and

(4) follow immediately on from the text and not be put on a separate page.

Format of affidavits

6.1 An affidavit should:

(1) be produced on durable quality A4 paper with a 3.5cm margin,

(2) be fully legible and should normally be typed on one side of the paper only,

(3) where possible, be bound securely in a manner which would not hamper filing, or otherwise each page should be endorsed with the case number and should bear the initials of the deponent and of the person before whom it was sworn,

(4) have the pages numbered consecutively as a separate document (or as one of several documents contained in a file),

(5) be divided into numbered paragraphs,

(6) have all numbers, including dates, expressed in figures, and

(7) give the reference to any document or documents mentioned either in the margin or in bold text in the body of the affidavit.

6.2 It is usually convenient for an affidavit to follow the chronological sequence of events or matters dealt with; each paragraph of an affidavit should as far as possible be confined to a distinct portion of the subject.

Inability of Deponent to read or sign affidavit

7.1 Where an affidavit is sworn by a person who is unable to read or sign it, the person before whom the affidavit is sworn must certify in the jurat that:

(1) he read the affidavit to the deponent,

(2) the deponent appeared to understand it, and

(3) the deponent signed or made his mark, in his presence.

7.2 If that certificate is not included in the jurat, the affidavit may not be used in evidence unless the court is satisfied that it was read to the deponent and that he appeared to understand it. Two versions of the form of jurat with the certificate are set out at Annex 1 to this practice direction.

Alterations to affidavits

8.1 Any alteration to an affidavit must be initialled by both the deponent and the person before whom the affidavit was sworn.

8.2 An affidavit which contains an alteration that has not been initialled may be filed or used in evidence only with the permission of the court.

Who may administer oaths and take affidavits

9.1 Only the following may administer oaths and take affidavits –

(1) a commissioner for oaths[6];

(2) omitted;

(3) other persons specified by statute[7];

(4) certain officials of the Senior Courts[8];

(5) a circuit judge or district judge[9];

(6) any justice of the peace[10]; and

(7) certain officials of any county court appointed by the judge of that court for the purpose[11].

9.2 An affidavit must be sworn before a person independent of the parties or their representatives.

Filing of affidavits

10.1 If the court directs that an affidavit is to be filed[12], it must be filed in the court or Division, or Office or Registry of the court or Division where the action in which it was or is to be used, is proceeding or will proceed.

10.2 Where an affidavit is in a foreign language:

(1) the party wishing to rely on it –

(a) must have it translated, and

(b) must file the foreign language affidavit with the court, and

(2) the translator must make and file with the court an affidavit verifying the translation and exhibiting both the translation and a copy of the foreign language affidavit.

Exhibits

Manner of exhibiting documents

11.1 A document used in conjunction with an affidavit should be:

(1) produced to and verified by the deponent, and remain separate from the affidavit, and

(2) identified by a declaration of the person before whom the affidavit was sworn.

11.2 The declaration should be headed with the name of the proceedings in the same way as the affidavit.

11.3 The first page of each exhibit should be marked:

(1) as in paragraph 3.2 above, and

(2) with the exhibit mark referred to in the affidavit.

Letters

12.1 Copies of individual letters should be collected together and exhibited in a bundle or bundles. They should be arranged in chronological order with the earliest at the top, and firmly secured.

12.2 When a bundle of correspondence is exhibited, the exhibit should have a front page attached stating that the bundle consists of original letters and copies. They should be arranged and secured as above and numbered consecutively.

Other documents

13.1 Photocopies instead of original documents may be exhibited provided the originals are made available for inspection by the other parties before the hearing and by the judge at the hearing.

13.2 Court documents must not be exhibited (official copies of such documents prove themselves).

13.3 Where an exhibit contains more than one document, a front page should be attached setting out a list of the documents contained in the exhibit; the list should contain the dates of the documents.

Exhibits other than documents

14.1 Items other than documents should be clearly marked with an exhibit number or letter in such a manner that the mark cannot become detached from the exhibit.

14.2 Small items may be placed in a container and the container appropriately marked.

General provisions

15.1 Where an exhibit contains more than one document:

(1) the bundle should not be stapled but should be securely fastened in a way that does not hinder the reading of the documents, and

(2) the pages should be numbered consecutively at bottom centre.

15.2 Every page of an exhibit should be clearly legible; typed copies of illegible documents should be included, paginated with 'a' numbers.

15.3 Where affidavits and exhibits have become numerous, they should be put into separate bundles and the pages numbered consecutively throughout.

15.4 Where on account of their bulk the service of exhibits or copies of exhibits on the other parties would be difficult or impracticable, the directions of the court should be sought as to arrangements for bringing the exhibits to the attention of the other parties and as to their custody pending trial.

Affirmations

16 All provisions in this or any other practice direction relating to affidavits apply to affirmations with the following exceptions:

(1) the deponent should commence 'I (name) of (address) do solemnly and sincerely affirm ......'; and

(2) in the jurat the word 'sworn' is replaced by the word 'affirmed'.

Witness statements

Heading

17.1 The witness statement should be headed with the title of the proceedings (see paragraph 4 of Practice Direction 7A and paragraph 5 of Practice Direction 20); where the proceedings are between several parties with the same status it is sufficient to identify the parties as follows:

	Number:
A.B. (and others)	Claimants/Applicants
C.D. (and others)	Defendants/Respondents
	(as appropriate)

17.2 At the top right hand corner of the first page there should be clearly written:

(1) the party on whose behalf it is made,

(2) the initials and surname of the witness,

(3) the number of the statement in relation to that witness,

(4) the identifying initials and number of each exhibit referred to,

(5) the date the statement was made; and

(6) the date of any translation.

Body of witness statement

18.1 The witness statement must, if practicable, be in the intended witness's own words and must in any event be drafted in their own language, the statement should be expressed in the first person and should also state:

(1) the full name of the witness,

(2) his place of residence or, if he is making the statement in his professional, business or other occupational capacity, the address at which he works, the position he holds and the name of his firm or employer,

(3) his occupation, or if he has none, his description,

(4) the fact that he is a party to the proceedings or is the employee of such a party if it be the case; and

(5) the process by which it has been prepared, for example, face-to-face, over the telephone, and/or through an interpreter.

18.2 A witness statement must indicate:

(1) which of the statements in it are made from the witness's own knowledge and which are matters of information or belief, and

(2) the source for any matters of information or belief.

18.3 An exhibit used in conjunction with a witness statement should be verified and identified by the witness and remain separate from the witness statement.

18.4 Where a witness refers to an exhibit or exhibits, he should state 'I refer to the (description of exhibit) marked'...".

18.5 The provisions of paragraphs 11.3 to 15.4 (exhibits) apply similarly to witness statements as they do to affidavits.

18.6 Where a witness makes more than one witness statement to which there are exhibits, in the same proceedings, the numbering of the exhibits should run consecutively throughout and not start again with each witness statement.

Format of witness statement

19.1 A witness statement should:

(1) be produced on durable quality A4 paper with a 3.5cm margin,

(2) be fully legible and should normally be typed on one side of the paper only,

(3) where possible, be bound securely in a manner which would not hamper filing, or otherwise each page should be endorsed with the case number and should bear the initials of the witness,

(4) have the pages numbered consecutively as a separate statement (or as one of several statements contained in a file),

(5) be divided into numbered paragraphs,

(6) have all numbers, including dates, expressed in figures,

(7) give the reference to any document or documents mentioned either in the margin or in bold text in the body of the statement ; and

(8) be drafted in the witness's own language.

19.2 It is usually convenient for a witness statement to follow the chronological sequence of the events or matters dealt with, each paragraph of a witness statement should as far as possible be confined to a distinct portion of the subject.

Statement of Truth

20.1 A witness statement is the equivalent of the oral evidence which that witness would, if called, give in evidence; it must include a statement by the intended witness in their own language that they believe the facts in it are true[13].

20.2 To verify a witness statement the statement of truth is as follows:

'I believe that the facts stated in this witness statement are true. I understand that proceedings for contempt of court may be brought against anyone who makes, or causes to be made, a false statement in a document verified by a statement of truth without an honest belief in its truth.'

20.3 Attention is drawn to rule 32.14 which sets out the consequences of verifying a witness statement containing a false statement without an honest belief in its truth.

(Rule 22.1(9) sets out the procedure to be followed where the person who should sign a document which is verified by a statement of truth is unable to read or sign the document other than by reason of language alone.)

21 Omitted

Alterations to witness statements

22.1 Any alteration to a witness statement must be initialled by the person making the statement or by the authorised person where appropriate (see paragraph 21).

22.2 A witness statement which contains an alteration that has not been initialled may be used in evidence only with the permission of the court.

Filing of witness statements

23.1 If the court directs that a witness statement is to be filed[14], it must be filed in the court or Division, or Office or Registry of the court or Division where the action in which it was or is to be used, is proceeding or will proceed.

23.2 Where a witness statement is in a foreign language—

(a) the party wishing to rely on it must—

(i) have it translated; and

(ii) file the foreign language witness statement with the court; and

(b) the translator must sign the original statement and must certify that the translation is accurate.

Certificate of court officer

24.1 Where the court has ordered that a witness statement is not to be open to inspection by the public[15] or that words or passages in the statement are not to be open to inspection[16] the court officer will so certify on the statement and make any deletions directed by the court under rule 32.13(4).

Defects in affidavits, witness statements and exhibits

25.1 Where:

(1) an affidavit,

(2) a witness statement, or

(3) an exhibit to either an affidavit or a witness statement,

does not comply with Part 32 or this practice direction in relation to its form, the court may refuse to admit it as evidence and may refuse to allow the costs arising from its preparation.

25.2 Permission to file a defective affidavit or witness statement or to use a defective exhibit may be obtained from a judge[17] in the court where the case is proceeding.

Statements of case

26.1 A statement of case may be used as evidence in an interim application provided it is verified by a statement of truth[18].

26.2 To verify a statement of case the statement of truth should be set out as follows:

'[I believe][the (party on whose behalf the statement of case is being signed) believes] that the facts stated in the statement of case are true'.

26.3 Attention is drawn to rule 32.14 which sets out the consequences of verifying a witness statement containing a false statement without an honest belief in its truth.

(For information regarding statements of truth see Part 22 and Practice Direction 22.)

(Practice Directions 7A and 17 provide further information concerning statements of case.)

Agreed bundles for hearings

27.1 The court may give directions requiring the parties to use their best endeavours to agree a bundle or bundles of documents for use at any hearing.

27.2 All documents contained in bundles which have been agreed for use at a hearing shall be admissible at that hearing as evidence of their contents, unless –

(1) the court orders otherwise; or

(2) a party gives written notice of objection to the admissibility of particular documents.

27.3 Rule 39.5 provides that unless the court orders otherwise, the claimant must file a trial bundle containing documents required by—

(a) a relevant practice direction; and

(b) any court order.

27.4 Rule 39.5 provides that the claimant must file the trial bundle not more than 7 days and not less than 3 days before the start of the trial.

27.4A If the trial is to take place in the Family Division, then Practice Direction 27A supplementing the Family Procedure Rules 2010 shall apply to provide what must happen in relation to the trial bundle in place of paragraphs 27.5 to 27.15 below.

27.5 Unless the court orders otherwise, the trial bundle should include a copy of—

(a) the claim form and all statements of case;

(b) a case summary and/or chronology where appropriate;

(c) requests for further information and responses to the requests;

(d) all witness statements to be relied on as evidence;

(e) any witness summaries;

(f) any notices of intention to rely on hearsay evidence under rule 32.2;

(g) any notices of intention to rely on evidence (such as a plan, photograph etc.) under rule 33.6 which is not—

(i) contained in a witness statement, affidavit or experts' report;

(ii) being given orally at trial; and

(iii) hearsay evidence under rule 33.2;

(h) any medical reports and responses to them;

(i) any experts' reports and responses to them;

(j) any order giving directions as to the conduct of the trial; and

(k) any other necessary documents.

27.6 The originals of the documents contained in the trial bundle, together with copies of any other court orders should be available at the trial.

27.7 The preparation and production of the trial bundle, even where it is delegated to another person, is the responsibility of the legal representative who has conduct of the claim on behalf of the claimant. If the claimant is unrepresented, the court may direct that another party must prepare and produce the trial bundle.

27.8 The trial bundle should be paginated (continuously) throughout, and indexed with a description of each document and the page number. Where the total number of pages is more than 100, numbered dividers should be placed at intervals between groups of documents.

27.9 The bundle should normally be contained in a ring binder or lever arch file. Where more than one bundle is supplied, they should be clearly distinguishable, for example, by different colours or letters. If there are numerous bundles, a core bundle should be prepared containing the core documents essential to the proceedings, with references to the supplementary documents in the other bundles.

27.10 For convenience, experts' reports may be contained in a separate bundle and cross referenced in the main bundle.

27.11 If a document to be included in the trial bundle is illegible, a typed copy should be included in the bundle next to it, suitably cross-referenced.

27.12 The contents of the trial bundle should be agreed where possible. The parties should also agree where possible—

(a) that the documents contained in the bundle are authentic even if not disclosed under Part 31; and

(b) that documents in the bundle may be treated as evidence of the facts stated in them even if a notice under the Civil Evidence Act 1995 has not been served.

Where it is not possible to agree the contents of the bundle, a summary of the points on which the parties are unable to agree should be included.

27.13 The party filing the trial bundle should supply identical bundles to all the parties to the proceedings and for the use of the witnesses.

27.14 Unless the court otherwise directs, contemporaneous documents in the trial bundle relied on by the parties or either of them should be assembled as a single unit in chronological order of creation.

27.15 Unless the court otherwise directs, documents in the trial bundle should be copied double-sided.:

Omitted

28.1

1 Where a party alleges that a statement of truth or a disclosure statement is false the party must refer that allegation to the court dealing with the claim in which the statement of truth or disclosure statement has been made.

2 The court may – a exercise any of its powers under the rules; b initiate steps to consider if there is a contempt of court and, where there is, to punish it; (Practice Direction RSC 52 and CCR 29 makes provision where committal to prison is a possibility if contempt is proved) c direct the party making the allegation to refer the matter to the Attorney General with a request that

the Attorney General consider whether to bring proceedings for contempt of court.

28.2

1 A request to the Attorney General must be made in writing and sent to the Attorney General's Office at 20 Victoria Street, London, SW1H 0NF. The request must be accompanied by a copy of the order directing that the matter be referred to the Attorney General and must – a identify the statement said to be false; b explain – i why it is false; and ii why the maker knew the statement to be false at the time it was made; and c explain why contempt proceedings would be appropriate in the light of the overriding objective in Part 1.

2 The Attorney General prefers a request that comes from the court to one made direct by a party to the claim in which the alleged contempt occurred without prior consideration by the court. A request to the Attorney General is not a way of appealing against, or reviewing the decision of the judge.

28.3 Where a party makes an application to the court for permission to commence proceedings for contempt of court, it must be supported by written evidence of the facts and matters specified in paragraph 28.2(1) and the result of the request to the Attorney General made by the applicant.

28.4 The rules do not change the law of contempt or introduce new categories of contempt. A person applying to commence such proceedings should consider whether the incident complained of does amount to contempt of court and whether such proceedings would further the overriding objective in Part 1 of the Civil Procedure Rules.

Video conferencing

29.1 Guidance on the use of video conferencing in the civil courts is set out at Annex 3 to this practice direction.

A list of the sites which are available for video conferencing can be found on HM Courts and Tribunals Service website.

Annex 1

Certificate to be used where a deponent to an affidavit is unable to read or sign it

Sworn at .... this ...... day of .... Before me, I having first read over the contents of this affidavit to the deponent [if there are exhibits, add 'and explained the nature and effect of the exhibits referred to in it'] who appeared to understand it and approved its content as accurate, and made his mark on the affidavit in my presence.

Or; (after, Before me) the witness to the mark of the deponent having been first sworn that he had read over etc. (as above) and that he saw him make his mark on the affidavit. (Witness must sign).

Certificate to be used where a deponent to an affirmation is unable to read or sign it

Affirmed at .... this ...... day of .... Before me, I having first read over the contents of this affirmation to the deponent [if there are exhibits, add 'and explained the nature and effect of the exhibits referred to in it'] who appeared to understand it and approved its content as accurate, and made his mark on the affirmation in my presence.

Or, (after, Before me) the witness to the mark of the deponent having been first sworn that he had read over etc. (as above) and that he saw him make his mark on the affirmation. (Witness must sign).

Annex 2

Omitted

Annex 3
Video conferencing guidance

This guidance is for the use of video conferencing (VCF) in civil proceedings. It is in part based, with permission, upon the protocol of the Federal Court of Australia. It is intended to provide a guide to all persons involved in the use of VCF, although it does not attempt to cover all the practical questions which might arise.

Video conferencing generally

1. The guidance covers the use of VCF equipment both (a) in a courtroom, whether via equipment which is permanently placed there or via a mobile unit, and (b) in a separate studio or conference room. In either case, the location at which the judge sits is referred to as the 'local site'. The other site or sites to and from which transmission is made are referred to as 'the remote site' and in any particular case any such site may be another courtroom. The guidance applies to cases where VCF is used for the taking of evidence and also to its use for other parts of any legal proceedings (for example, interim applications, case management conferences, pre-trial reviews).
2. VCF may be a convenient way of dealing with any part of proceedings: it can involve considerable savings in time and cost. Its use for the taking of evidence from overseas witnesses will, in particular, be likely to achieve a material saving of costs, and such savings may also be achieved by its use for taking domestic evidence. It is, however, inevitably not as ideal as having the witness physically present in court. Its convenience should not therefore be allowed to dictate its use. A judgment must be made in every case in which

the use of VCF is being considered not only as to whether it will achieve an overall cost saving but as to whether its use will be likely to be beneficial to the efficient, fair and economic disposal of the litigation. In particular, it needs to be recognised that the degree of control a court can exercise over a witness at the remote site is or may be more limited than it can exercise over a witness physically before it.

3. When used for the taking of evidence, the objective should be to make the VCF session as close as possible to the usual practice in a trial court where evidence is taken in open court. To gain the maximum benefit, several differences have to be taken into account. Some matters, which are taken for granted when evidence is taken in the conventional way, take on a different dimension when it is taken by VCF: for example, the administration of the oath, ensuring that the witness understands who is at the local site and what their various roles are, the raising of any objections to the evidence and the use of documents.

4. It should not be presumed that all foreign governments are willing to allow their nationals or others within their jurisdiction to be examined before a court in England or Wales by means of VCF. If there is any doubt about this, enquiries should be directed to the Foreign, Commonwealth and Development Office (Public Facing Services, Taking of Evidence Team) TOE.Enquiries@fcdo.gov.uk with a view to ensuring that the country from which the evidence is to be taken raises no objection to it at diplomatic level. The party who is directed to be responsible for arranging the VCF (see paragraph 8 below) will be required to make all necessary inquiries about this well in advance of the VCF and must be able to inform the court what those inquiries were and of their outcome.

5. Time zone differences need to be considered when a witness abroad is to be examined in England or Wales by VCF. The convenience of the witness, the parties, their representatives and the court must all be taken into account. The cost of the use of a commercial studio is usually greater outside normal business hours.

6. Those involved with VCF need to be aware that, even with the most advanced systems currently available, there are the briefest of delays between the receipt of the picture and that of the accompanying sound. If due allowance is not made for this, there will be a tendency to 'speak over' the witness, whose voice will continue to be heard for a millisecond or so after he or she appears on the screen to have finished speaking.

7. With current technology, picture quality is good, but not as good as a television picture. The quality of the picture is enhanced if those appearing on VCF monitors keep their movements to a minimum.

Preliminary arrangements

8. The court's permission is required for any part of any proceedings to be dealt with by means of VCF. Before seeking a direction, the applicant should notify

the listing officer, diary manager or other appropriate court officer of the intention to seek it, and should enquire as to the availability of court VCF equipment for the day or days of the proposed VCF. The application for a direction should be made to the Master, District Judge or Judge, as may be appropriate. If all parties consent to a direction, permission can be sought by letter, fax or e-mail, although the court may still require an oral hearing. All parties are entitled to be heard on whether or not such a direction should be given and as to its terms. If a witness at a remote site is to give evidence by an interpreter, consideration should be given at this stage as to whether the interpreter should be at the local site or the remote site. If a VCF direction is given, arrangements for the transmission will then need to be made. The court will ordinarily direct that the party seeking permission to use VCF is to be responsible for this. That party is hereafter referred to as 'the VCF arranging party'.

9. Subject to any order to the contrary, all costs of the transmission, including the costs of hiring equipment and technical personnel to operate it, will initially be the responsibility of, and must be met by, the VCF arranging party. All reasonable efforts should be made to keep the transmission to a minimum and so keep the costs down. All such costs will be considered to be part of the costs of the proceedings and the court will determine at such subsequent time as is convenient or appropriate who, as between the parties, should be responsible for them and (if appropriate) in what proportions.

10. The local site will, if practicable, be a courtroom but it may instead be an appropriate studio or conference room. The VCF arranging party must contact the listing officer, diary manager or other appropriate officer of the court which made the VCF direction and make arrangements for the VCF transmission. Details of the remote site, and of the equipment to be used both at the local site (if not being supplied by the court) and the remote site (including the number of ISDN lines and connection speed), together with all necessary contact names and telephone numbers, will have to be provided to the listing officer, diary manager or other court officer. The court will need to be satisfied that any equipment provided by the parties for use at the local site and also that at the remote site is of sufficient quality for a satisfactory transmission. The VCF arranging party must ensure that an appropriate person will be present at the local site to supervise the operation of the VCF throughout the transmission in order to deal with any technical problems. That party must also arrange for a technical assistant to be similarly present at the remote site for like purposes.

11. It is recommended that the judge, practitioners and witness should arrive at their respective VCF sites about 20 minutes prior to the scheduled commencement of the transmission.

12. If the local site is not a courtroom, but a conference room or studio, the judge will need to determine who is to sit where. The VCF arranging party must take care to ensure that the number of microphones is adequate for the speakers and that the panning of the camera for the practitioners' table

encompasses all legal representatives so that the viewer can see everyone seated there.

13. The proceedings, wherever they may take place, form part of a trial to which the public is entitled to have access (unless the court has determined that they should be heard in private). If the local site is to be a studio or conference room, the VCF arranging party must ensure that it provides sufficient accommodation to enable a reasonable number of members of the public to attend.

14. In cases where the local site is a studio or conference room, the VCF arranging party should make arrangements, if practicable, for the royal coat of arms to be placed above the judge's seat.

15. In cases in which the VCF is to be used for the taking of evidence, the VCF arranging party must arrange for recording equipment to be provided by the court which made the VCF direction so that the evidence can be recorded. An associate will normally be present to operate the recording equipment when the local site is a courtroom. The VCF arranging party should take steps to ensure that an associate is present to do likewise when it is a studio or conference room. The equipment should be set up and tested before the VCF transmission. It will often be a valuable safeguard for the VCF arranging party also to arrange for the provision of recording equipment at the remote site. This will provide a useful back-up if there is any reduction in sound quality during the transmission. A direction from the court for the making of such a back-up recording must, however, be obtained first. This is because the proceedings are court proceedings and, save as directed by the court, no other recording of them must be made. The court will direct what is to happen to the back-up recording.

16. Some countries may require that any oath or affirmation to be taken by a witness accord with local custom rather than the usual form of oath or affirmation used in England and Wales. The VCF arranging party must make all appropriate prior inquiries and put in place all arrangements necessary to enable the oath or affirmation to be taken in accordance with any local custom. That party must be in a position to inform the court what those inquiries were, what their outcome was and what arrangements have been made. If the oath or affirmation can be administered in the manner normal in England and Wales, the VCF arranging party must arrange in advance to have the appropriate holy book at the remote site. The associate will normally administer the oath.

17. Consideration will need to be given in advance to the documents to which the witness is likely to be referred. The parties should endeavour to agree on this. It will usually be most convenient for a bundle of the copy documents to be prepared in advance, which the VCF arranging party should then send to the remote site.

18. Additional documents are sometimes quite properly introduced during the course of a witness's evidence. To cater for this, the VCF arranging party should ensure that equipment is available to enable documents to

be transmitted between sites during the course of the VCF transmission. Consideration should be given to whether to use a document camera. If it is decided to use one, arrangements for its use will need to be established in advance. The panel operator will need to know the number and size of documents or objects if their images are to be sent by document camera. In many cases, a simpler and sufficient alternative will be to ensure that there are fax transmission and reception facilities at the participating sites.

The hearing

19. The procedure for conducting the transmission will be determined by the judge. He will determine who is to control the cameras. In cases where the VCF is being used for an application in the course of the proceedings, the judge will ordinarily not enter the local site until both sites are on line. Similarly, at the conclusion of the hearing, he will ordinarily leave the local site while both sites are still on line. The following paragraphs apply primarily to cases where the VCF is being used for the taking of the evidence of a witness at a remote site. In all cases, the judge will need to decide whether court dress is appropriate when using VCF facilities. It might be appropriate when transmitting from courtroom to courtroom. It might not be when a commercial facility is being used.
20. At the beginning of the transmission, the judge will probably wish to introduce himself and the advocates to the witness. He will probably want to know who is at the remote site and will invite the witness to introduce himself and anyone else who is with him. He may wish to give directions as to the seating arrangements at the remote site so that those present are visible at the local site during the taking of the evidence. He will probably wish to explain to the witness the method of taking the oath or of affirming, the manner in which the evidence will be taken, and who will be conducting the examination and cross-examination. He will probably also wish to inform the witness of the matters referred to in paragraphs 6 and 7 above (co-ordination of picture with sound, and picture quality).
21. The examination of the witness at the remote site should follow as closely as possible the practice adopted when a witness is in the courtroom. During examination, cross-examination and re-examination, the witness must be able to see the legal representative asking the question and also any other person (whether another legal representative or the judge) making any statements in regard to the witness's evidence. It will in practice be most convenient if everyone remains seated throughout the transmission.

Footnotes

1 See rule 32.6(1).

2 See rule 32.15(2).

3 See Part 23 for information about making an application.

4 Rule 32.6(2) and see Part 22 for information about the statement of truth.

5 See, e.g., s.3(5)(a) of the Protection from Harassment Act 1997.

6 Commissioner for Oaths Act 1889 and 1891.

7 Sections 12 and 18 of, and Schedules 2 and 4 to, the Legal Services Act 2007.

8 Section 2 of the Commissioners for Oaths Act 1889.

9 Section 58 of the County Courts Act 1984.

10 Section 58 as above.

11 Section 58 as above.

12 Rules 32.1(3) and 32.4(3)(b).

13 See Part 22 for information about the statement of truth.

14 Rule 32.4(3)(b).

15 Rule 32.13(2).

16 Rule 32.13(4).

17 Rule 2.3(1); definition of judge.

18 See rule 32.6(2)(a).

PART 33
MISCELLANEOUS RULES ABOUT EVIDENCE

Introductory

33.1

In this Part—

(a) 'hearsay' means a statement, made otherwise than by a person while giving oral evidence in proceedings, which is tendered as evidence of the matters stated; and

(b) references to hearsay include hearsay of whatever degree.

Notice of intention to rely on hearsay evidence

33.2

(1) Where a party intends to rely on hearsay evidence at trial and either—

(a) that evidence is to be given by a witness giving oral evidence; or

(b) that evidence is contained in a witness statement of a person who is not being called to give oral evidence;

that party complies with section 2(1)(a) of the Civil Evidence Act 1995 by serving a witness statement on the other parties in accordance with the court's order.

(2) Where paragraph (1)(b) applies, the party intending to rely on the hearsay evidence must, when he serves the witness statement—

(a) inform the other parties that the witness is not being called to give oral evidence; and

(b) give the reason why the witness will not be called.

(3) In all other cases where a party intends to rely on hearsay evidence at trial, that party complies with section 2(1)(a) of the Civil Evidence Act 1995 by serving a notice on the other parties which—

(a) identifies the hearsay evidence;

(b) states that the party serving the notice proposes to rely on the hearsay evidence at trial; and

(c) gives the reason why the witness will not be called.

(4) The party proposing to rely on the hearsay evidence must—

(a) serve the notice no later than the latest date for serving witness statements; and

(b) if the hearsay evidence is to be in a document, supply a copy to any party who requests him to do so.

Circumstances in which notice of intention to rely on hearsay evidence is not required

33.3

Section 2(1) of the Civil Evidence Act 1995 (duty to give notice of intention to rely on hearsay evidence) does not apply—

(a) to evidence at hearings other than trials;

[(aa) to an affidavit or witness statement which is to be used at trial but which does not contain hearsay evidence;][1]

(b) to a statement which a party to a probate action wishes to put in evidence and which is alleged to have been made by the person whose estate is the subject of the proceedings; or

(c) where the requirement is excluded by a practice direction.

Amendments

1 Inserted by the Civil Procedure (Amendment) Rules 1999, SI 1999/1008, r 10.

Power to call witness for cross-examination on hearsay evidence

33.4

(1) Where a party—

(a) proposes to rely on hearsay evidence; and

(b) does not propose to call the person who made the original statement to give oral evidence,

the court may, on the application of any other party, permit that party to call the maker of the statement to be cross-examined on the contents of the statement.

(2) An application for permission to cross-examine under this rule must be made not more than 14 days after the day on which a notice of intention to rely on the hearsay evidence was served on the applicant.

Credibility

33.5

(1) Where a party—

(a) proposes to rely on hearsay evidence; but

(b) does not propose to call the person who made the original statement to give oral evidence; and

(c) another party wishes to call evidence to attack the credibility of the person who made the statement,

the party who so wishes must give notice of his intention to the party who proposes to give the hearsay statement in evidence.

(2) A party must give notice under paragraph (1) not more than 14 days after the day on which a hearsay notice relating to the hearsay evidence was served on him.

Use of plans, photographs and models as evidence

33.6

(1) This rule applies to evidence (such as a plan, photograph or model) which is not—

(a) contained in a witness statement, affidavit[(GL)] or expert's report;

(b) to be given orally at trial; or

(c) evidence of which prior notice must be given under rule 33.2.

(2) This rule includes documents which may be received in evidence without further proof under section 9 of the Civil Evidence Act 1995.

(3) Unless the court orders otherwise the evidence shall not be receivable at a trial unless the party intending to put it in evidence has given notice to the other parties in accordance with this rule.

(4) Where the party intends to use the evidence as evidence of any fact then, except where paragraph (6) applies, he must give notice not later than the latest date for serving witness statements.

(5) He must give notice at least 21 days before the hearing at which he proposes to put in the evidence, if—

(a) there are not to be witness statements; or

(b) he intends to put in the evidence solely in order to disprove an allegation made in a witness statement.

(6) Where the evidence forms part of expert evidence, he must give notice when the expert's report is served on the other party.

(7) Where the evidence is being produced to the court for any reason other than as part of factual or expert evidence, he must give notice at least 21 days before the hearing at which he proposes to put in the evidence.

(8) Where a party has given notice that he intends to put in the evidence, he must give every other party an opportunity to inspect it and to agree to its admission without further proof.

Evidence of finding on question of foreign law

33.7

(1) This rule sets out the procedure which must be followed by a party who intends to put in evidence a finding on a question of foreign law by virtue of section 4(2) of the Civil Evidence Act 1972.

(2) He must give any other party notice of his intention.

(3) He must give the notice—

(a) if there are to be witness statements, not later than the latest date for serving them; or

(b) otherwise, not less than 21 days before the hearing at which he proposes to put the finding in evidence.

(4) The notice must—

(a) specify the question on which the finding was made; and

(b) enclose a copy of a document where it is reported or recorded.

Evidence of consent of trustee to act

33.8

A document purporting to contain the written consent of a person to act as trustee and to bear his signature verified by some other person is evidence of such consent.

[Human Rights

33.9

(1) This rule applies where a claim is—

(a) for a remedy under section 7 of the Human Rights Act 1998 in respect of a judicial act which is alleged to have infringed the claimant's Article 5 Convention rights; and

(b) based on a finding by a court or tribunal that the claimant's Convention rights have been infringed.

(2) The court hearing the claim—

(a) may proceed on the basis of the finding of that other court or tribunal that there has been an infringement but it is not required to do so, and

(b) may reach its own conclusion in the light of that finding and of the evidence heard by that other court or tribunal.][1]

Amendments

1 Inserted by the Civil Procedure (Amendment No. 4) Rules 2000, SI 2000/2092, r 15.

PRACTICE DIRECTION 33 – CIVIL EVIDENCE ACT 1995

This Practice Direction supplements CPR Part 33

1 Section 16(3A) of the Civil Evidence Act 1995 (c. 38.) (as amended) provides that transitional provisions for the application of the provisions of the Civil Evidence Act 1995 to proceedings begun before 31 January 1997 may be made by practice direction.

2 Except as provided for by paragraph 3, the provisions of the Civil Evidence Act 1995 apply to claims commenced before 31 January 1997.

3 The provisions of the Civil Evidence Act 1995 do not apply to claims commenced before 31 January 1997 if, before 26 April 1999:

(a) directions were given, or orders were made, as to the evidence to be given at the trial or hearing; or

(b) the trial or hearing had begun.

PART 34
[WITNESSES, DEPOSITIONS AND EVIDENCE FOR FOREIGN COURTS][1]

[I Witnesses and depositions

Scope of this Section

34.1

(1) This Section of this Part provides—

(a) for the circumstances in which a person may be required to attend court to give evidence or produce a document; and

(b) for a party to obtain evidence before a hearing to be used at the hearing.

(2) In this Section, reference to a hearing includes a reference to the trial.][1]

Amendments

1 Substituted by the Civil Procedure (Amendment) Rules 2002, SI 2002/2058, r 12(a), (c).

Witness summonses

34.2

(1) A witness summons is a document issued by the court requiring a witness to—

(a) attend court to give evidence; or

(b) produce documents to the court.

(2) A witness summons must be in the relevant practice form.

(3) There must be a separate witness summons for each witness.

(4) A witness summons may require a witness to produce documents to the court either—

(a) on the date fixed for a hearing; or

(b) on such date as the court may direct.

(5) The only documents that a summons under this rule can require a person to produce before a hearing are documents which that person could be required to produce at the hearing.

Issue of a witness summons

34.3

(1) A witness summons is issued on the date entered on the summons by the court.

(2) A party must obtain permission from the court where he wishes to—

(a) have a summons issued less than 7 days before the date of the trial;

(b) have a summons issued for a witness to attend court to give evidence or to produce documents on any date except the date fixed for the trial; or

(c) have a summons issued for a witness to attend court to give evidence or to produce documents at any hearing except the trial.

(3) A witness summons must be issued by—

(a) the court where the case is proceeding; or

(b) the court where the hearing in question will be held.

(4) The court may set aside(GL) or vary a witness summons issued under this rule.

Witness summons in aid of inferior court or of tribunal

34.4

(1) The court may issue a witness summons in aid of an inferior court or of a tribunal.

(2) The court which issued the witness summons under this rule may set it aside.

(3) In this rule, 'inferior court or tribunal' means any court or tribunal that does not have power to issue a witness summons in relation to proceedings before it.

Time for serving a witness summons

34.5

(1) The general rule is that a witness summons is binding if it is served at least 7 days before the date on which the witness is required to attend before the court or tribunal.

(2) The court may direct that a witness summons shall be binding although it will be served less than 7 days before the date on which the witness is required to attend before the court or tribunal.

(3) A witness summons which is—

(a) served in accordance with this rule; and

(b) requires the witness to attend court to give evidence,

is binding until the conclusion of the hearing at which the attendance of the witness is required.

Who is to serve a witness summons

34.6

(1) A witness summons is to be served by the court unless the party on whose behalf it is issued indicates in writing, when he asks the court to issue the summons, that he wishes to serve it himself.

(2) Where the court is to serve the witness summons, the party on whose behalf it is issued must deposit, in the court office, the money to be paid or offered to the witness under rule 34.7.

Right of witness to travelling expenses and compensation for loss of time

34.7

At the time of service of a witness summons the witness must be offered or paid—

(a) a sum reasonably sufficient to cover his expenses in travelling to and from the court; and

(b) such sum by way of compensation for loss of time as may be specified in [Practice Direction 34A][1].

Amendments

1 Substituted by the Civil Procedure (Amendment No. 2) Rules 2009, SI 2009/3390, r 17.

[Fines imposed under section 55 of the County Courts Act 1984

34.7A

If a person has failed to comply with an order under section 55 of the County Courts Act 1984 but can demonstrate any reason why they should not be (or should not have been) fined for failure to comply with the order, the court may direct that that person give evidence by witness statement, affidavit or otherwise.

(Part 70 contains general rules about fines imposed under the County Courts Act 1984.)][1]

Amendments

1 Inserted by the Civil Procedure (Amendment No. 3) Rules 2020, SI 2020/747, rr 3, 9(2).

Evidence by deposition

34.8

(1) A party may apply for an order for a person to be examined before the hearing takes place.

(2) A person from whom evidence is to be obtained following an order under this rule is referred to as a 'deponent' and the evidence is referred to as a 'deposition'.

(3) An order under this rule shall be for a deponent to be examined on oath before—

(a) a judge;

(b) an examiner of the court; or

(c) such other person as the court appoints.

(Rule 34.15 makes provision for the appointment of examiners of the court)

(4) The order may require the production of any document which the court considers is necessary for the purposes of the examination.

(5) The order must state the date, time and place of the examination.

(6) At the time of service of the order the deponent must be offered or paid—

(a) a sum reasonably sufficient to cover his expenses in travelling to and from the place of examination; and

(b) such sum by way of compensation for loss of time as may be specified in [Practice Direction 34A][1].

(7) Where the court makes an order for a deposition to be taken, it may also order the party who obtained the order to serve a witness statement or witness summary in relation to the evidence to be given by the person to be examined.

(Part 32 contains the general rules about witness statements and witness summaries)

Amendments

1 Substituted by the Civil Procedure (Amendment No. 2) Rules 2009, SI 2009/3390, r 17.

Conduct of examination

34.9

(1) Subject to any directions contained in the order for examination, the examination must be conducted in the same way as if the witness were giving evidence at a trial.

(2) If all the parties are present, the examiner may conduct the examination of a person not named in the order for examination if all the parties and the person to be examined consent.

(3) The examiner may conduct the examination in private if he considers it appropriate to do so.

(4) The examiner must ensure that the evidence given by the witness is recorded in full.

(5) The examiner must send a copy of the deposition—

(a) to the person who obtained the order for the examination of the witness; and

(b) to the court where the case is proceeding.

(6) The party who obtained the order must send each of the other parties a copy of the deposition which he receives from the examiner.

Enforcing attendance of witness

34.10

(1) If a person served with an order to attend before an examiner—

(a) fails to attend; or

(b) refuses to be sworn for the purpose of the examination or to answer any lawful question or produce any document at the examination,

a certificate of his failure or refusal, signed by the examiner, must be filed by the party requiring the deposition.

(2) On the certificate being filed, the party requiring the deposition may apply to the court for an order requiring that person to attend or to be sworn or to answer any question or produce any document, as the case may be.

(3) An application for an order under this rule may be made without notice.

(4) The court may order the person against whom an order is made under this rule to pay any costs resulting from his failure or refusal.

Use of deposition at a hearing

34.11

(1) A deposition ordered under rule 34.8 may be given in evidence at a hearing unless the court orders otherwise.

(2) A party intending to put in evidence a deposition at a hearing must serve notice of his intention to do so on every other party.

(3) He must serve the notice at least 21 days before the day fixed for the hearing.

(4) The court may require a deponent to attend the hearing and give evidence orally.

(5) Where a deposition is given in evidence at trial, it shall be treated as if it were a witness statement for the purposes of rule 32.13 (availability of witness statements for inspection).

Restrictions on subsequent use of deposition taken for the purpose of any hearing except the trial

34.12

(1) Where the court orders a party to be examined about his or any other assets for the purpose of any hearing except the trial, the deposition may be used only for the purpose of the proceedings in which the order was made.

(2) However, it may be used for some other purpose—

(a) by the party who was examined;

(b) if the party who was examined agrees; or

(c) if the court gives permission.

Where a person to be examined is out of the jurisdiction—letter of request

34.13

[(1) This rule applies where a party wishes to take a deposition from a person who is—

(a) out of the jurisdiction; …[1]

(b) …[1]

(1A) The High Court may order the issue of a letter of request to the judicial authorities of the country in which the proposed deponent is.][2]

(2) A letter of request is a request to a judicial authority to take the evidence of that person, or arrange for it to be taken.

(3) The High Court may make an order under this rule in relation to [County Court][3] proceedings [and tribunal proceedings][4].

(4) If the government of [a][5] country …[6] allows a person appointed by the High Court to examine a person in that country, the High Court may make an order appointing a special examiner for that purpose.

(5) A person may be examined under this rule on oath or affirmation or in accordance with any procedure permitted in the country in which the examination is to take place.

(6) If the High Court makes an order for the issue of a letter of request, the party who sought the order must file [with the Foreign Process Section of the Central Office of the High Court in the Royal Courts of Justice][4]—

(a) the following documents and, except where paragraph (7) applies, a translation of them—

(i) a draft letter of request;

(ii) a statement of the issues relevant to the proceedings;

(iii) a list of questions or the subject matter of questions to be put to the person to be examined; and

(b) an undertaking to be responsible for the Secretary of State's expenses.

(7) There is no need to file a translation if—

(a) English is one of the official languages of the country where the examination is to take place; or

(b) a practice direction has specified that country as a country where no translation is necessary.

Amendments

1 Repealed by the Civil Procedure Rules 1998 (Amendment) (EU Exit) Regulations 2019, SI 2019/521, regs 2, 12(1), (3).

2 Substituted by the Civil Procedure (Amendment No. 4) Rules 2003, SI 2003/2113, r 7.

3 Substituted by the Civil Procedure (Amendment) Rules 2014, SI 2014/407, r 4(a)(iii).

4 Inserted by the Civil Procedure (Amendment No. 3) Rules 2023, SI 2023/788, rr 2, 18.

5 Substituted by the Civil Procedure (Amendment) Rules 1999, SI 1999/1008, r 11(a)(i).

6 Repealed by the Civil Procedure (Amendment) Rules 1999, SI 1999/1008, r 11(a)(ii).

[Letter of request – Proceeds of Crime Act 2002

34.13A

(1) This rule applies where a party to existing or contemplated proceedings in—

(a) the High Court; or

(b) a magistrates' court,

under Part 5 of the Proceeds of Crime Act 2002 (civil recovery of the proceeds etc. of unlawful conduct) wishes to take a deposition from a person who is out of the jurisdiction.

(2) The High Court may, on the application of such a party, order the issue of a letter of request to the judicial authorities of the country in which the proposed deponent is.

(3) Paragraphs (4) to (7) of rule 34.13 shall apply irrespective of where the proposed deponent is …[1].][2]

Amendments

1 Repealed by the Civil Procedure Rules 1998 (Amendment) (EU Exit) Regulations 2019, SI 2019/521, regs 2, 12(1), (4).

2 Inserted by the Civil Procedure (Amendment No. 5) Rules 2003, SI 2003/3361, r 6.

Fees and expenses of examiner [of the court][1]

34.14

[(1) An examiner of the court may charge a fee for the examination.][2]

(2) He need not send the deposition to the court unless the fee is paid.

(3) The examiner's fees and expenses must be paid by the party who obtained the order for examination.

(4) If the fees and expenses due to an examiner are not paid within a reasonable time, he may report that fact to the court.

(5) The court may order the party who obtained the order for examination to deposit in the court office a specified sum in respect of the examiner's fees and, where it does so, the examiner will not be asked to act until the sum has been deposited.

(6) An order under this rule does not affect any decision as to the party who is ultimately to bear the costs of the examination.

Amendments

1 Inserted by the Civil Procedure (Amendment) Rules 1999, SI 1999/1008, r 11(b)(i).

2 Substituted by the Civil Procedure (Amendment) Rules 1999, SI 1999/1008, r 11(b)(ii).

Examiners of the court

34.15

(1) The Lord Chancellor shall appoint persons to be examiners of the court.

(2) The persons appointed shall be barristers or solicitor-advocates who have been practising for a period of not less than three years.

(3) The Lord Chancellor may revoke an appointment at any time.

[II Evidence for foreign courts

[Scope and interpretation

34.16

(1) This Section applies to an application for an order under the 1975 Act for evidence to be obtained …[1].

(2) In this Section—

(a) 'the 1975 Act' means the Evidence (Proceedings in Other Jurisdictions) Act 1975[; and][2]

(b) ['the Hague Evidence Convention' means the Hague Convention of 18 March 1970 on the Taking of Evidence Abroad in Civil or Commercial Matters][2].][3]][4]

Amendments

1 Repealed by the Civil Procedure Rules 1998 (Amendment) (EU Exit) Regulations 2019, SI 2019/521, regs 2, 12(1), (5)(a).

2 Inserted by the Civil Procedure (Amendment No. 3) Rules 2020, SI 2020/747, rr 3, 9(3).

3 Substituted by the Civil Procedure (Amendment No. 4) Rules 2003, SI 2003/2113, r 8.

4 Inserted by the Civil Procedure (Amendment) Rules 2002, SI 2002/2058, r 12(b), Sch 2, Pt 2.

[[Application for order

34.17

(1) An application for an order under the 1975 Act for evidence to be obtained must be made to the High Court and may be made without notice.

(2) The application may be made either—

(a) by an application notice under Part 23, which must be—

(i) supported by written evidence; and

(ii) accompanied by the request as a result of which the application is made, and where appropriate, a translation of the request into English; or

(b) where—

(i) the requesting state is a party to the Hague Evidence Convention, by a Letter of Request using the Model Form published by the Permanent Bureau of the Hague Conference on Private International Law (which is annexed to Practice Direction 34A); or

(ii) the requesting state is not a party to the Hague Evidence Convention, by a Letter of Request submitted via the Foreign and Commonwealth Office.][1]][2]

Amendments

1 Substituted by the Civil Procedure (Amendment No. 3) Rules 2020, SI 2020/747, rr 3, 9(4).

2 Inserted by the Civil Procedure (Amendment) Rules 2002, SI 2002/2058, r 12(b), Sch 2, Pt 2.

[Examination

34.18

(1) The court may order an examination to be taken before—

(a) any fit and proper person nominated by the person applying for the order;

(b) an examiner of the court; or

(c) any other person whom the court considers suitable.

(2) Unless the court orders otherwise—

(a) the examination will be taken as provided by rule 34.9; and

(b) rule 34.10 applies.

(3) The court may make an order under rule 34.14 for payment of the fees and expenses of the examination.][1]

Amendments

1 Inserted by the Civil Procedure (Amendment) Rules 2002, SI 2002/2058, r 12(b), Sch 2, Pt 2.

[Dealing with deposition

34.19

(1) The examiner must send the deposition of the witness to the Senior Master unless the court orders otherwise.

(2) The Senior Master will—

(a) give a certificate sealed with the seal of the [Senior Courts][1] for use out of the jurisdiction identifying the following documents—

(i) the request;

(ii) the order of the court for examination; and

(iii) the deposition of the witness; and

(b) send the certificate and the documents referred to in paragraph (a) to—

(i) the Secretary of State; or

(ii) where the request was sent to the Senior Master by another person in accordance with a Civil Procedure Convention, to that other person,

for transmission to the court or tribunal requesting the examination.][2]

Amendments

1 Substituted by the Civil Procedure (Amendment) Rules 2009, SI 2009/2092, r 4.

2 Inserted by the Civil Procedure (Amendment) Rules 2002, SI 2002/2058, r 12(b), Sch 2, Pt 2.

[Claim to privilege

34.20

(1) This rule applies where—

(a) a witness claims to be exempt from giving evidence on the ground specified in section 3(1)(b) of the 1975 Act; and

(b) that claim is not supported or conceded as referred to in section 3(2) of that Act.

(2) The examiner may require the witness to give the evidence which he claims to be exempt from giving.

(3) Where the examiner does not require the witness to give that evidence, the court may order the witness to do so.

(4) An application for an order under paragraph (3) may be made by the person who obtained the order under section 2 of the 1975 Act.

(5) Where such evidence is taken—

(a) it must be contained in a document separate from the remainder of the deposition;

(b) the examiner will send to the Senior Master—

(i) the deposition; and

(ii) a signed statement setting out the claim to be exempt and the ground on which it was made.

(6) On receipt of the statement referred to in paragraph (5)(b)(ii), the Senior Master will—

(a) retain the document containing the part of the witness's evidence to which the claim to be exempt relates; and

(b) send the statement and a request to determine that claim to the foreign court or tribunal together with the documents referred to in rule 34.17.

(7) The Senior Master will—

(a) if the claim to be exempt is rejected by the foreign court or tribunal, send the document referred to in paragraph (5)(a) to that court or tribunal;

(b) if the claim is upheld, send the document to the witness; and

(c) in either case, notify the witness and person who obtained the order under section 2 of the foreign court or tribunal's decision.][1]

Amendments

1 Inserted by the Civil Procedure (Amendment) Rules 2002, SI 2002/2058, r 12(b), Sch 2, Pt 2.

[Order under 1975 Act as applied by Patents Act 1977

34.21

Where an order is made for the examination of witnesses under section 1 of the 1975 Act as applied by section 92 of the Patents Act 1977 the court may permit an officer of the European Patent Office to—

(a) attend the examination and examine the witnesses; or

(b) request the court or the examiner before whom the examination takes place to put specified questions to them.][1]

Amendments

1 Inserted by the Civil Procedure (Amendment) Rules 2002, SI 2002/2058, r 12(b), Sch 2, Pt 2.

PRACTICE DIRECTION 34A – DEPOSITIONS AND COURT ATTENDANCE BY WITNESSES

This Practice Direction supplements CPR Part 34

Witness summonses

Issue of witness summons

1.1 A witness summons may require a witness to:

(1) attend court to give evidence,

(2) produce documents to the court, or

(3) both,

on either a date fixed for the hearing or such date as the court may direct[1].

1.2 Two copies of the witness summons[2] should be filed with the court for sealing, one of which will be retained on the court file.

1.3 A mistake in the name or address of a person named in a witness summons may be corrected if the summons has not been served.

1.4 The corrected summons must be re-sealed by the court and marked 'Amended and Re-Sealed'.

Witness summons issued in aid of an inferior court or tribunal

2.1 A witness summons may be issued in the High Court or the County Court in aid of a court or tribunal which does not have the power to issue a witness summons in relation to the proceedings before it[3].

2.2 A witness summons referred to in paragraph 2.1 may be set aside by the court which issued it[4].

2.3 An application to set aside a witness summons referred to in paragraph 2.1 will be heard:

(1) in the High Court by a Master at the Royal Courts of Justice or by a District Judge in a District Registry, and

(2) in the County Court by a District Judge.

2.4 Unless the court otherwise directs, the applicant must give at least 2 days' notice to the party who issued the witness summons of the application, which will normally be dealt with at a hearing.

Travelling expenses and compensation for loss of time

3.1 When a witness is served with a witness summons they must be offered a sum to cover their travelling expenses to and from the court and compensation for their loss of time[5].

3.2 If the witness summons is to be served by the court, the party issuing the summons must deposit with the court:

(1) a sum sufficient to pay for the witness's expenses in travelling to the court and in returning to their home or place of work, and

(2) a sum in respect of the period during which earnings or benefit are lost, or such lesser sum as it may be proved that the witness will lose as a result of their attendance at court in answer to the witness summons.

3.3 The sum referred to in 3.2(2) is to be based on the sums payable to witnesses attending the Crown Court[6].

3.4 Where the party issuing the witness summons wishes to serve it they must

(1) notify the court in writing that they wish to do so, and

(2) at the time of service offer the witness the sums mentioned in paragraph 3.2 above.

Depositions

To be taken in England and Wales for use as evidence in proceedings in courts in England and Wales

4.1 A party may apply for an order for a person to be examined on oath before:

(1) a judge,

(2) an examiner of the court, or

(3) such other person as the court may appoint[8].

4.2 The party who obtains an order for the examination of a deponent before an examiner of the court must:

(1) apply to the Foreign Process Section at the Royal Courts of Justice for the allocation of an examiner; alternatively engage a person who satisfies the criteria in CPR 34.8 (3) (a) or (c);

(2) when allocated or engaged, provide the examiner with copies of all documents in the proceedings necessary to inform the examiner of the issues; and

(3) pay the deponent a sum to cover their travelling expenses to and from the examination and compensation for their loss of time

4.3 In ensuring that the deponent's evidence is recorded in full, the court or the examiner may permit it to be recorded by audio or video, but the deposition[12] must always be recorded in writing by them or by a competent shorthand writer or stenographer.

4.4 If the deposition is not recorded word for word, it must contain, as nearly as may be, the statement of the deponent; the examiner may record word for word any particular questions and answers which appear to them to have special importance.

4.5 If a deponent objects to answering any question or where any objection is taken to any question, the examiner must:

(1) record in the deposition or a document attached to it –

(a) the question,

(b) the nature of and grounds for the objection, and

(c) any answer given, and

(2) give their opinion as to the validity of the objection and must record it in the deposition or a document attached to it.

The court will decide as to the validity of the objection and any question of costs arising from it.

4.6 Documents and exhibits must:

(1) have an identifying number or letter marked on them by the examiner, and

(2) be preserved by the party or their legal representative[13] who obtained the order for the examination, or as the court or the examiner may direct.

4.7 The examiner may put any question to the deponent as to:

(1) the meaning of any of their answers, or

(2) any matter arising in the course of the examination.

4.8 Where a deponent:

(1) fails to attend the examination, or

(2) refuses to:

(a) be sworn, or

(b) answer any lawful question, or

(c) produce any document,

the examiner will sign a certificate[14] of such failure or refusal and may include in their certificate any comment as to the conduct of the deponent or of any person attending the examination.

4.9 The party who obtained the order for the examination must file the certificate with the court and may apply for an order that the deponent attend for examination or as may be[15]. The application may be made without notice[16].

4.10 The court will make such order on the application as it thinks fit including an order for the deponent to pay any costs resulting from their failure or refusal[17].

4.11 A deponent who wilfully refuses to obey an order made against them under Part 34 may be proceeded against for contempt of court.

4.12 A deposition must:

(1) be signed by the examiner,

(2) have any amendments to it initialled by the examiner and the deponent,

(3) be endorsed by the examiner with –

(a) a statement of the time occupied by thc cxamination, and

(b) a record of any refusal by the deponent to sign the deposition and of their reasons for not doing so, and

(4) be sent by the examiner to the court where the proceedings are taking place for filing on the court file.

4.13 Rule 34.14 deals with the fees and expenses of an examiner.

Depositions to be taken abroad for use as evidence in proceedings before courts in England and Wales

5.1 Where a party wishes to take a deposition from a person outside the jurisdiction, the High Court may order the issue of a letter of request to the judicial authorities of the country in which the proposed deponent is[18].

5.2 An application for an order referred to in paragraph 5.1 should be made by application notice in accordance with Part 23.

5.3 The documents which a party applying for an order for the issue of a letter of request must file with their application notice are set out in rule 34.13(6). They are as follows:

(1) a draft letter of request in the form set out in Annex A to this practice direction,

(2) a statement of the issues relevant to the proceedings,

(3) a list of questions or the subject matter of questions to be put to the proposed deponent,

(4) a translation of the documents in (1), (2) and (3) above, unless the proposed deponent is in a country of which English is an official language, and

(5) an undertaking to be responsible for the expenses of the Secretary of State (see Form PF78: Solicitor's Undertaking as to Expenses (rule 34.13(6)(b)) – GOV.UK (www.gov.uk)

In addition to the documents listed above the party applying for the order must file a draft order.

5.4 The above documents should be filed with the Foreign Process Section of the Royal Courts of Justice.

5.5 The application will be dealt with by the Senior Master of the King's Bench Division of the High Court who will, if appropriate, sign the letter of request.

5.6 Attention is drawn to the provisions of rule 23.10 (application to vary or discharge an order made without notice).

5.7 If parties are in doubt as to whether a translation under paragraph 5.3(4) above is required, they should seek guidance from the Foreign Process Section.

5.8 A special examiner appointed under rule 34.13(4) may be the British Consul or the Consul-General or his deputy in the country where the evidence is to be taken if:

(1) there is in respect of that country a Civil Procedure Convention providing for the taking of evidence in that country for the assistance of proceedings in the High Court or other court in this country, or

(2) with the consent of the Secretary of State.

5.9 The provisions of paragraphs 4.1 to 4.12 above apply to the depositions referred to in this paragraph.

Depositions to be taken in England and Wales for use as evidence in proceedings before courts abroad pursuant to letters of request

6.1 Section II of Part 34 relating to obtaining evidence for foreign courts applies to letters of request and should be read in conjunction with this part of the practice direction.

6.2 The Evidence (Proceedings in Other Jurisdictions) Act 1975 applies to these depositions.

6.3 An application under rule 34.17 must be filed with the Foreign Process Section at the Royal Courts of Justice and include or exhibit—

(1) a statement of the issues relevant to the proceedings;

(2) a list of questions or the subject matter of questions to be put to the proposed deponent;

(3) a translation of the documents in (1) and (2) into English, if necessary; and

(4) where the application is made by an application notice under Part 23 in accordance with rule 34.17(2)(a), a draft order.

6.4 (1) The Senior Master will send to the Treasury Solicitor any request –

(a) forwarded by the Secretary of State with a recommendation that effect should be given to the request without requiring an application to be made; or

(b) received by him in pursuance of a Civil Procedure Convention providing for the taking of evidence of any person in England and Wales to assist a court or tribunal in a foreign country where no person is named in the document as the applicant.

(2) In relation to such a request, the Treasury Solicitor may, with the consent of the Treasury –

(a) apply for an order under the 1975 Act; and

(b) take such other steps as are necessary to give effect to the request.

6.5 The order for the deponent to attend and be examined together with the evidence upon which the order was made must be served on the deponent.

6.6 Attention is drawn to the provisions of rule 23.10 (application to vary or discharge an order made without notice).

6.7 Arrangements for the examination to take place at a specified time and place before an examiner of the court or such other person as the court may appoint shall be made by the applicant for the order and approved by the Senior Master.

6.8 The provisions of paragraph 4.2 to 4.12 apply to the depositions referred to in this paragraph, except that the examiner must send the deposition to the Senior Master.

(For further information about evidence see Part 32 and Practice Direction 32.)

Annex A
Draft Letter of Request (where the Taking of Evidence Regulation does not apply)

To the Competent Judicial Authority of [name of court] in [country]

I [name] Senior Master of the King's Bench Division of the Senior Courts of England and Wales respectfully request the assistance of your court with regard to the following matters.

1

A claim is now pending in the Division of the High Court of Justice in England and Wales entitled as follows [set out full title and claim number] in which [name] of [address] is the claimant and [name] of [address] is the defendant.

2

The names and addresses of the representatives or agents of [set out names and addresses of representatives of the parties].

3

The claim by the claimant is for:-

(a) [set out the nature of the claim]

(b) [the relief sought, and]

(c) [a summary of the facts.]

4

It is necessary for the purposes of justice and for the due determination of the matters in dispute between the parties that you cause the following witnesses, who are resident within your jurisdiction, to be examined. The names and addresses of the witnesses are as follows:

5

The witnesses should be examined on oath or if that is not possible within your laws or is impossible of performance by reason of the internal practice and procedure of your court or by reason of practical difficulties, they should be examined in accordance with whatever procedure your laws provide for in these matters.

6

Either/

The witnesses should be examined in accordance with the list of questions annexed hereto.

Or/

The witnesses should be examined regarding [set out full details of evidence sought]

N.B. Where the witness is required to produce documents, these should be clearly identified.

7

I would ask that you cause me, or the agents of the parties (if appointed), to be informed of the date and place where the examination is to take place.

8

Finally, I request that you will cause the evidence of the said witnesses to be reduced into writing and all documents produced on such examinations to be duly marked for identification and that you will further be pleased to authenticate such examinations by the seal of your court or in such other way as is in accordance with your procedure and return the written evidence and documents produced to me addressed as follows:

Senior Master of the King's Bench Division

Royal Courts of Justice

Strand

London WC2A 2LL

England

Dated

Signed

Senior Master of the King's Bench Division

Footnotes

1 Rule 34.2(4).

2 In practice form N20.

3 Rule 34.4(1).

4 Rule 34.4(2).

5 Rule 34.7.

6 Fixed pursuant to the Prosecution of Offences Act 1985 and the Costs in Criminal Cases General Regulations 1986.

7 Rule 34.6(1).

8 Rule 34.8(3).

9 See rule 34.8(2) for explanation of 'deponent' and 'deposition'.

10 For the appointment of examiners of the court see rule 34.15.

11 Rule 34.8(6).

12 See rule 34.8(2) for explanation of 'deponent' and 'deposition'.

13 For the definition of legal representative see rule 2.3.

14 Rule 34.10.

15 Rule 34.10(2) and (3).

16 Rule 34.10(3).

17 Rule 34.10(4).

18 Rule 34.13(1).

Index

[*All references are to paragraph numbers*]

D